# Join the Recom Inns® Travelers' Club and Save!

The Recommended Country Inns® guides are the preeminent guidebooks to the finest country inns in the United States. Authors personally visit and recommend each establishment described in the guides, and **no fees are solicited or accepted for recommendation in the books.**

Now the Recommended Country Inns® guides offer a special new way for travelers to enjoy extra savings: through the Recommended Country Inns® Travelers' Club. Member benefits include savings such as:

- Discounts on accommodations
- Discounts on food
- Discounts on local attractions

**How to Save:** Read the profile for each inn to see if it offers an incentive to members. For participating establishments, look for information at the end of the inn's profile or in the index at the end of the book. Simply mention that you are a member of the Recommended Country Inns® Travelers' Club when making reservations, and show your membership card when you check in. All offers are subject to availability.

**How to Join:** If you wish to become a member of the Recommended Country Inns® Travelers' Club, simply fill out the attached form and send it by mail to:

Recommended Country Inns® Travelers' Club
c/o The Globe Pequot Press
PO Box 833
Old Saybrook, CT 06475
Or fax to: 860-395-2855

A membership card will be mailed to you upon receipt of the form. Please allow four to six weeks for delivery.

*Sign up today and start saving as a Recommended Country Inns® Travelers' Club member!*

(All offers from participating inns expire May 31, 2001, unless otherwise mentioned.)

# Recommended Country Inns®
# Travelers' Club Membership Form

Name: _____

Address: _____

City _____ , State _____ Zip _____

Phone _____ Fax _____ E-mail _____

Age:   18–35 _____;   36–50 _____;   over 50 _____

Sex:   Male _____   Female _____

Marital Status:   Single _____   Married _____

Annual Household Income:

   under $35,000 _____;   $35,000–$75,0000 _____;   over $75,000 _____

Credit cards:

   Mastercard _____;   Visa _____;   Amex _____;

   Discover _____;   Other _____

Book purchased at: Store Name: _____ ;

City _____ , State _____

## Mail completed form to:
Recommended Country Inns® Travelers' Club
c/o The Globe Pequot Press
PO Box 833
Old Saybrook, CT  06475
Or fax to:  860-395-2855

NE

# EXPERIENCE THE WONDER OF FOXWOODS.

Nestled in the beautiful New England countryside, you'll find the world's favorite casino. Foxwoods Resort Casino, now even more breathtaking than ever.

Inside our magnificent new Grand Pequot Tower, you'll find a world class hotel, with 800 luxurious rooms and suites. With gourmet restaurants, and more table games, slot machines and chances to win.

Our new hotel is the perfect complement to our 312-room AAA rated four diamond Great Cedar Hotel, and our quaint Two Trees Inn, with 280 charming rooms.

Foxwoods is fine dining with 24 fabulous restaurants. And room service is

available 24 hours a day, for your convenience. Foxwoods is five different gaming environ-

ments, with over 5,750 Slot Machines, Blackjack, Craps, Roulette and Baccarat,including a Smoke-Free casino.

Foxwoods is High Stakes Bingo, Keno, a Poker Room and the Ultimate Race Book.

Foxwoods is entertainment. With stars like Aretha Franklin, Engelbert Humperdinck, Paul Anka and Bill Cosby. It's two challenging golf courses. It's Championship Boxing. It's Cinetropolis, with the 1,500-seat Fox Theater. It's a Turbo Ride, Cinedrome, and our Dance Club. With its Hotels, Restaurants, Gaming and Entertainment, it's no wonder that Foxwoods has become the hottest entertainment destination in the country.

**FOXWOODS**
RESORT ● CASINO ®

EXPERIENCE THE WONDER OF THE CONNECTICUT WOODS.
Conveniently located in Mashantucket. Exit 92 off I-95 in southeastern CT.
Call 1-800-PLAY-BIG
Visit our website at www.foxwoods.com
Mashantucket Pequot Tribal Nation

*Special*

SILVER ANNIVERSARY EDITION

*Recommended*

# COUNTRY INNS®

## NEW ENGLAND

Connecticut / Maine / Massachusetts
New Hampshire / Rhode Island / Vermont

*Sixteenth Edition*

by Elizabeth Squier

illustrated by Olive Metcalf

The
Globe
Pequot
Press

OLD SAYBROOK, CONNECTICUT

# Contents

# Dedication

I dedicate this book to me! This is my silver anniversary book. Twenty-five years of inn creeping. The miles I've traveled and the wonderful people I've met have made it all worthwhile. I've worn out three automobiles and me too. Thanks to all the friends I've made in these years. Inns will be here long after I'm gone—I just hope I've helped and made a difference.

# A Few Words about Visiting New England Inns

When I first started writing *Recommended Country Inns: New England* back in 1973, country inns were relatively scarce. Since that time, however, the number of country inns has been rapidly growing as more and more people have tired of the monotony of motels and thruway hotels and have begun searching for the infinitely more warming pleasure of a good country inn.

New England is full of good country inns. Its four seasons are ideal for inn-goers to discover all the joys of the region—the glorious fall foliage colors and crisp, cool days; the brisk days of winter as crowds converge on the multitude of downhill ski slopes or cross-country ski areas; spring with its dogwoods, daffodils, and tulips in bright array wherever you look; and the warm, blue-sky'd days of summer, when the myriad lakes and rivers and the miles of seashore offer plenty of opportunities for excitement or relaxation. I love the way so many old New England houses have been turned into gracious country inns, offering guests the opportunity to thrive on history, interesting architecture, and a unique ambience. When you're a guest in New England, you find a diversity of things to do—visiting a historical site, climbing a mountain, sailing on a lake, biking on a country road past farms and pastures, walking in a national forest, picking apples in an orchard, browsing in antiques shops, and much more. And finally, New England is a small region, so it doesn't take very long to travel from one area to another, offering travelers the opportunity to discover all its joys even on a short vacation.

With the constantly growing number of New England inns, it has become more and more difficult for me to wade through the volumes of mail from new country inns. I have had to be increasingly selective in choosing the best inns in each state. Do not be distressed if an inn you like is not in this guide. Please understand that my definition of a country inn is that it must have lodging as well as good food, and it must have a certain ambience that appeals to me. I prefer that the inns I select serve at least two meals a day and be open most of the year, but I have made exceptions when an inn seems just too special to leave out of this guide.

By my descriptions and comments, I have tried to indicate the type of atmosphere you can expect in an inn, including whether it would be a fun place to bring your children or whether it would be more appropriate to leave the children at home. Do not forget that the very reason you are passing up a motel or a hotel is for the bit of adventure and surprise you will find sitting in a weathered farmhouse, eating country cooking, chatting with a newly discovered friend, and finding new delight in a very old tradition.

So, enjoy! This *Recommended Country Inns—New England* was compiled for you, fellow lovers of New England country inns.

—Elizabeth

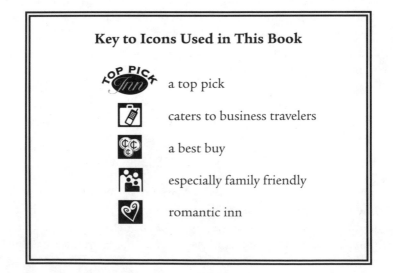

### Key to Icons Used in This Book

TOP PICK *Inn*  a top pick

caters to business travelers

¢¢  a best buy

especially family friendly

romantic inn

# How to Use This Inn Guide

This inn guide contains descriptions of country inns in the six New England states. You'll find them in alphabetical order by state— Connecticut, Maine, Massachusetts, New Hampshire, Rhode Island, and Vermont—and alphabetically by town within each state. Preceding each state listing are a map and a numbered legend of the towns with inns in that state. The map is marked with corresponding numbers to show where the towns are located.

I have personally visited every inn in this book. There is no charge of any kind for an inn to be included in this or any other Globe Pequot country inn guide.

*Indexes:* At the back of the book are various special-category indexes to help you find inns on a lake, inns that serve Sunday brunch, inns that have cross-country skiing on the property, and much more. There is also an alphabetical index of all the inns in the book.

*Rates:* With prices fluctuating so widely in today's economy, I quote an inn's current low and high rates only. This will give you a good, though not exact, indication of the price ranges you can expect. Please realize that rates are subject to change. I have not included the tax rate, service charge, or tipping suggestions for any of the inns. Be sure to inquire about these additional charges when you make your reservations. The following abbreviations are used throughout the book to let you know exactly what, if any, meals are included in the room price.

*Abbreviations:*

EP: European Plan. Room without meals.

EPB: Room with full breakfast. (No abbreviation is used when continental breakfast is included.)

MAP: Modified American Plan. Room with breakfast and dinner.

*Credit cards:* MasterCard and Visa are accepted unless the description says "No credit cards." Many inns also accept additional cards.

*Personal checks:* Inns usually accept personal checks unless the description says "No personal checks."

*Reservations and deposits:* At most of the inns, be prepared to pay a deposit when you make your reservation. Be sure to inquire about refund policies.

*Meals:* Meals included in the cost of the room are indicated with the rates; other meals available at the inn will be in the "Facilities and activities" section of an inn's description. I list some of my favorite foods served at an inn to give you a general idea of the type of meals you can expect, but please realize that menus are likely to change.

*Children:* Many inns are ideal for children, but you know your child best; an inn's description will help you decide if it's a place where your child will be happy. I do not list children's rates, but many inns have them for children who stay in the same room or suite as their parents.

*Pets:* Pets are not permitted at the inns unless otherwise stated in the description. If you need to find a place to leave your pet, call the inn before you go. They may be able to make arrangements for you.

*Wheelchair accessibility:* Some inns have wheelchair accessibility to rooms or dining rooms, and some have at least one room specially equipped for the handicapped. Check the index in the back of the book for inns with rooms for the handicapped. You might also want to call to check for updated information.

*Air conditioning:* The description will indicate if an inn has rooms with air conditioning. Keep in mind that there are areas of New England where air conditioning is totally unnecessary.

*Alcoholic beverages:* Some inns permit their guests to bring their own bottle (BYOB), especially if there is no bar service. If this fact is of interest to you, look in the inn's description for a mention of a bar, liquor license, or BYOB.

*Smoking:* If you see "No smoking inn" in an inn's description, you will know that no smoking is permitted anywhere in the inn. There are other inns that may restrict smoking to certain designated areas indoors. All Vermont inns, for instance, prohibit smoking in their restaurants and common areas in adherence to the state's Clean Indoor Air Act. Call an inn directly to find out about its exact smoking policies.

*Recommended Country Inns® Travelers' Club:* I state the discount, free night's stay, or other value offered by inns welcoming club members. Note that all discounts listed refer to room rates only, not to meals, and that a number of offers are subject to availability.

*Recommended*

# COUNTRY INNS®

## NEW ENGLAND

# Connecticut

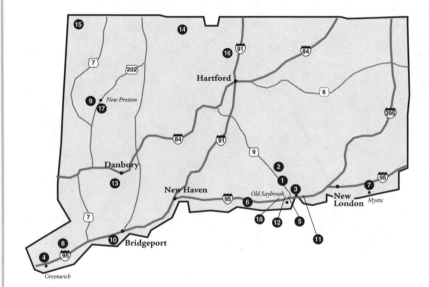

# Connecticut

*Numbers on map refer to towns numbered below.*

*\* A Top Pick Inn*

# The Inn at Chester 🉐 📱
## Chester, Connecticut 06412

**INNKEEPER:** Deborah Lieberman Moore

**ADDRESS/TELEPHONE:** 318 West Main Street; (860) 526–9541 or (800) 949–7829

**WEB SITE:** www.innatchester.com

**ROOMS:** 42, plus 2 suites; all with private bath and air conditioning, some specially equipped for handicapped.

**RATES:** $105 to $185, double occupancy; $215 to $425, suites; continental breakfast.

**OPEN:** All year.

**FACILITIES AND ACTIVITIES:** Lunch, dinner, Sunday brunch. Bar and tavern, elevator, sauna, exercise room, tennis court, conference room, art gallery.

**BUSINESS TRAVEL:** Located 40 minutes from Hartford; 40 minutes from New Haven. All rooms with phone; conference rooms, audiovisual equipment and fax available, corporate rates.

**RECOMMENDED COUNTRY INNS® TRAVELERS' CLUB BENEFIT:** 10 percent discount.

*J*ohn D. Parmelee, the original owner of this inn built from 1776 to 1778, would not know the place today, but he'd probably enjoy it. The old house now serves as a private dining room and has a private suite, and an L-shaped bar now graces the tavern, called Dunks Landing (after the boat landing of the same name in the yesteryear shipbuilding heyday of the town of Chester on the Connecticut River). The tavern serves light dinners and daily specials, plus lunch. Try the spareribs grilled with an Oriental barbecue sauce, chicken wings Cajun-style, or crabcakes and more, while you listen to live music and enjoy your favorite cocktail. The tavern also makes stone pies—a fancy name for pizza. When I was there, there was a chicken one with roasted garlic, mozzarella, basil, and pomodoro sauce—so good.

There is much to do in the inn. Downstairs is the Billiard Room, where you can play billiards, backgammon, or cards. The library is filled with books—a nice place to have nearby. There is an exercise room with weights, stationary bikes, a treadmill, and a Nordic ski machine. Get a massage here

or use the sauna. On the grounds are tennis, bocce, and croquet courts, and bicycles for your riding pleasure.

Each of the inn's rooms is individually appointed with Eldred Wheeler reproductions. The rooms really are lovely and include telephone, television, and air conditioning.

The chef of the inn's Post and Beam restaurant is very talented. Try Mediterranean fish soup, warm duck salad, or entrees like filet of beef, pork loin, lamb stew (so nice to have this on the menu), and lots of other wonderful dishes. The breast of duck sautéed in port wine with peaches, blueberries, and nutty wild rice sounds scrumptious.

This is a lovely inn in a beautiful part of Connecticut. Schedar is the inn cat—do ask about her beginnings. Bacchus means "little dog"—the inn dog is a golden and what a beauty. Well-behaved pets are welcome here.

HOW TO GET THERE: Take exit 6 off Route 9 and turn west on Route 148. Go $3^2/10$ miles to the inn. By private plane, fly to the Chester Airport.

## The Swinging Bridge

Driving into East Haddam on Route 154, you cross the Connecticut River on a metal bridge that pivots to a position parallel to the banks to allow large boats to pass. Some say this is the world's longest swing bridge; it certainly is the longest one in New England. One of just a handful of bridges linking the eastern part of the state to the west, the bridge also links the two sides of East Haddam, the only river town that has land on both sides of the Connecticut. The bridge dates back to 1913. During World War I a militia unit was housed in the opera house at Goodspeed Landing to protect the bridge from sabotage by German submarines.

# The Gelston House 📱
East Haddam, Connecticut 06423

**INNKEEPER:** Bill Murphy

**ADDRESS/TELEPHONE:** Route 82 (mailing address: Box A);
(860) 873–1411; fax (860) 873–9300

**ROOMS:** 3, plus 3 suites; all with private bath, phone, and air
conditioning.

**RATES:** $100 to $125, double occupancy; $225, suites; continental
breakfast.

**OPEN:** All year except Christmas Day.

**FACILITIES AND ACTIVITIES:** Lunch, dinner, Sunday brunch. Terrace
Cafe, bar, lounge, theater, banquet facilities, gift shop.

**BUSINESS TRAVEL:** Located 35 minutes from Hartford. All rooms with
phone, small conference room, computer hookup and fax available, corporate rates.

When you approach the iron swing bridge to cross the Connecticut
River, the first thing you see is the Goodspeed Opera House.
Right next to it is The Gelston House. Let me tell you, it is an
impressive sight. Built in 1853, the inn has seen many changes, not only to
itself but to the surrounding area. In 1853 a room at the inn plus a meal cost
travelers $2.50, which was very expensive at the time.

It was so nice to be able to put this inn back in the book a few
years ago after it was totally redecorated. It's beautiful. The Swan
Room is a suite overlooking the river and the beer garden. The
William Gillette Room has a view
of this lovely village. All
accommodations are
lovely and have queen-
sized beds.

Dining here, watch-
ing the Connecticut
River as it flows by, is
very relaxing. The floor-to-ceiling windows are lovely. Menus change every
thirteen weeks, but I will give you a few ideas of the selections.

Lunch begins with a grilled vegetable minestrone, followed by house-
smoked salmon club sandwich with saffron mayonnaise, five-spice chicken
salad, or linguine with shrimp, chicken, pine nuts, lemon greens, and garlic.

A pre-theater dinner menu is available until 6:30 when the Goodspeed Opera House is open. The prix fixe meal begins with an appetizer (perhaps you'd like tempura fried clams), moves on to three entree choices such as grilled salmon on fennel puree with orange reduction, and finishes with three desserts. Chocolate marquis, anyone?

Another dinner menu is available for those who have more time to savor their food. Chestnut-glazed quail with quinoa pilaf caught my eye, but there are also seafood, sirloin, chicken, and pasta selections. Sunday brunch looks awfully good, too. I'll have to come back another time.

In past summers, the beer garden looking out on the river was very popular. Now it's back, and named The Terrace Cafe. There are a lot of choices—hamburgers and you name it—and beer. There is fun for all, and it is very reasonable.

While you're in East Haddam, you really shouldn't miss seeing a play at the Goodspeed. It's where *Annie* and *Man of La Mancha* began many years ago.

**HOW TO GET THERE:** From I-95 take exit 69 onto Route 9 north, or from I-91 take Route 9 south. Follow Route 9 to exit 7 and follow the signs to the Goodspeed Opera House.

# Griswold Inn 📱
## Essex, Connecticut 06426

**INNKEEPERS:** The Paul Brothers; Sarah Grader, general manager

**ADDRESS/TELEPHONE:** 36 Main Street; (860) 767-1812; fax (860) 767-0481

**E-MAIL:** griswoldinn@snet.net

**WEB SITE:** www.griswoldinn.com

**ROOMS:** 30, including 12 suites; all with private bath and phone, some with fireplace.

**RATES:** $90, double occupancy; $105 to $185, suites; continental breakfast.

**OPEN:** All year except Christmas Eve and Christmas Day.

**FACILITIES AND ACTIVITIES:** Lunch, dinner, Sunday brunch, children's menu, bar.

*E*ssex is a very special town right on the Connecticut River. Although it was settled long before the Revolution, Essex is still a living, breathing, working place, not a re-created museum of a town. The first warship of the Continental Navy, the *Oliver Cromwell*, was built and commissioned here in 1776.

"The Gris," as the inn is fondly called by everyone, is the highlight of anyone's trip to Essex. When you come in from the cold to the welcome of crackling fireplaces, you are doing what others have done before you for more than 200 years.

You can lunch or dine in the cool dimness of the Library or the Gun Room, the latter of which houses a collection of firearms going back to the fifteenth century. This note from a father to a son is in here:

7th month 7th day 1776

*"My dear son Girard,*

*I send you this little gun*

*Do not handle it in fun*

*But with it make ye British run*

*Join ye ranks of ye Washington*

*And when our independence is won*

*We will drink of good old rum"*

—JOHN FRANCIS PUTNAM

Another special spot is the Steamboat Room, where the mural on the far wall floats gently, making you feel that you really are on the river. The inn's collection of Currier & Ives steamboat prints is of museum size and quality.

There is music every night—old-time banjos, sea chanteys, Dixieland jazz, or just good piano, but never rock 'n' roll.

In the bar is a great, old-fashioned popcorn machine. There is popcorn for all. Do ask for some. It's one of many personal touches that make this nice inn such a special place.

The Hunt Breakfast is the renowned Sunday brunch at the inn. This bountiful fare is worth a trip from anywhere. The selection is extensive, with enough good food to satisfy anyone's palate. Dinner just gets better every time I visit. I've enjoyed osso buco and fettucine with two-mushroom sauce.

The chicken stew with dumplings almost got me. The Awful Awful New York strip sirloin steak is awful big and awful good.

The guest rooms are all different, and suites are lovely. The Fenwick Suite, across the street, has a great bath, a small living room, and a bedroom with a king bed, two wing chairs, and a porch. The Hayden House 1801 is next door and has been totally redone—oh, so nicely. It has two suites. There is also a beauty of a suite over the coffee house across the street. The Garden Suite, also located across the street, has a fireplace, a wet bar and refrigerator, and two double beds. Very nice.

HOW TO GET THERE: Take I-95 to exit 69, and follow Route 9 north to exit 3. Turn left at the bottom of the ramp to a traffic light, turn right, and follow this street right through town to the river. The inn is on your right, about 100 yards before you get to the river.

## Marine Art in Essex

In addition to its fine collection of steamboat prints by Currier & Ives and other important New York lithographers, the Griswold Inn houses an outstanding collection of marine oils by Antonio Jacobsen. Sixteen canvases painted around the turn of the twentieth century are displayed in three rooms specially decorated to showcase these works. Marine art aficionados should look in the Essex Room, the Ward Room, and the Library.

Visitors should also explore Essex's Connecticut River Museum (203-767-8269), just steps from the Inn. Located at the foot of Main Street in a restored 1878 dock house, it also houses a notable collection of marine art, including paintings and ships' models, as well as a replica of the 1775 *American Turtle* and many objects and photographs related to river history.

# The Homestead Inn ♥ 📱
## Greenwich, Connecticut 06830

**INNKEEPERS:** Theresa and Thomas Henkelmann

**ADDRESS/TELEPHONE:** Field Point Road; (203) 869–7500

**ROOMS:** 17, plus 6 suites; all with private bath, color TV, clock radio, and phone.

**RATES:** $92, single; $137 to $160, double; $175 to $185, suites; continental breakfast.

**OPEN:** All year.

**FACILITIES AND ACTIVITIES:** Full breakfast, lunch Monday through Friday, dinner seven days a week, Sunday brunch. Bar.

**BUSINESS TRAVEL:** Located 45 minutes from New York City. Phone and desk in room; small conference center; audiovisual equipment, fax, computer available; corporate rates.

**RECOMMENDED COUNTRY INNS® TRAVELERS' CLUB BENEFIT:** 10 percent discount or stay two nights, get third night free, Monday–Thursday.

*T*here are very good reasons why this lovely 1799 inn has been chosen as the best country inn in the country. One of them is that the entire staff makes you feel like royalty. I think we all need this kind of treatment once in a while.

The inn's rooms are beautifully refurbished and redecorated. William Inge wrote *Picnic* while staying at the inn in the 1950s, in Room 26. I stayed

in this one, too. Room 35 has his-and-her desks. Room 32 has delicate stencils on the walls; the stencils were found under six layers of wallpaper dating back to 1860. Room 23 has a queen-sized canopy bed and a marvelous eighteenth-century highboy.

The Inn-Between is the newest building on this lovely property. There are eight glorious rooms out here. The bathrooms are large and have tub, shower, and bidet. All the rooms have porches, and the furnishings are wonderful. The cottage has a lovely suite and two other bedrooms, all very nice and quiet.

The inn's superb contemporary French restaurant, Thomas Henkelmann, is named for its enormously talented chef. The food is more than fabulous—this establishment was just named one of the top twenty-eight restaurants in America by *Esquire* magazine. The dining room itself is elegant in a rustic fashion—hand-hewn chestnut beams, brick walls, fireplaces, skylights, and well-spaced tables with comfortable chairs. A simple bunch of flowers is on each table.

The presentation of the food is so picture perfect, you could almost eat the plate. The ironstone place settings in Wedgwood's Chinese Bird pattern and the beautiful stemware are exquisite. The presentation plates are objets d'art themselves, commissioned from an artist in France.

Besides the extensive menus, there are many specials. One that I had was fresh Dover sole, the best I have ever eaten, sautéed with puree of artichoke. The inn is noted for its fresh fish and splendid, tender veal prepared in many interesting ways. One of the luncheon dishes is escallops of veal, served with fettuccine, basil, and tomatoes. Some of the hors d'oeuvres are ravioli of seasonal mushrooms with a sauce of tomatoes and fines herbes, and sautéed calamari dressed with an aioli sauce. The desserts, needless to say, are spectacular. You must try the warm chocolate soufflé with a liquid chocolate center and housemade vanilla bean ice cream—wow!

Do I like it here! I just wish I lived a bit closer.

HOW TO GET THERE: From New York take I–95 north to exit 3. Turn left at the bottom of the ramp, then left again at the second light onto Horseneck Lane. Turn left at the end of the lane onto Field Point Road. The inn is ¼ mile on the right.

From Boston take I–95 south to exit 3. Turn right at the bottom of the ramp. Turn left at the first light onto Horseneck Lane and proceed as described above.

# Copper Beech Inn ♥ ¢¢

## Ivoryton, Town of Essex, Connecticut 06442

**INNKEEPERS:** Eldon and Sally Senner

**ADDRESS/TELEPHONE:** 46 Main Street; (860) 767–0330 or
(888) 809–2056

**WEB SITE:** www.copperbeechinn.com

**ROOMS:** 4 in inn, 9 in carriage house; all with private bath, carriage
house rooms with whirlpool tub, deck, phone, and TV.

**RATES:** $110 to $180, double occupancy, continental breakfast.

**OPEN:** All year.

**FACILITIES AND ACTIVITIES:** Restaurant closed on Mondays; Tuesdays
in winter; Christmas Eve, Christmas Day, and the first week in January.
Dinner, full license. Victorian-style conservatory.

**RECOMMENDED COUNTRY INNS® TRAVELERS' CLUB BENEFIT:** Stay
two nights, get third night free, when all three days fall Sunday–
Thursday, and none is a holiday.

One of the most beautiful copper beech trees in Connecticut
shades the lawn of this lovely old inn and is the reason for the
inn's name.

The grounds are beautiful. Eldon, who really is a gardener, has done wonders with the property. There is an authentic English garden, many bulbs are
in bloom at different times of the year, and everything is just breathtaking.

Sally is an interior designer, and her expertise really shows in this inn.
There is a lovely parlor on the first floor, with bookcases and a table for playing cards or writing or whatever. Very warm and comfortable.

Accommodations at the Copper Beech are wonderful. There are four
rooms in the inn itself, and they have unbelievable old-fashioned bathrooms.
The towels are soft and fluffy. Nine more guest rooms are in the carriage
house, and each one has a Jacuzzi tub, so delightful after a day of exploring
the lovely towns of Essex, Mystic, and other area attractions. The carriage
house has an elegant country atmosphere. The halls have very nice early
nineteenth-century botanical prints. In fact, there is nineteenth-century art
all over the inn, as well as a wonderful collection of fine Oriental porcelain.
The facilities are not well suited for children under ten years of age.

The four dining rooms have comfortable Chippendale and Queen Anne chairs. The Garden Porch, which is a favorite place for me, features white wicker and nice Audubon prints on the walls. The spacious tables are set far apart for gracious dining. Fresh flowers are everywhere, and the waiters are friendly and courteous.

The hors d'oeuvres menu is a beauty. One is made of layers of delicate puff pastry, with smoked salmon and mousse of smoked salmon, garnished with crème fraîche, diced onions, and capers. Another is a salad of chilled poached lobster and fresh orange with an orange-truf-  fle vinaigrette. The lobster bisque is always spectacular, and there are about eight more appetizers to choose from. Choose from such treats as a salad of chilled, poached lobster, fresh mango and diced red onion, dressed with a mango vinaigrette; fresh cultivated mussels steamed with white wine and served with a lavender-scented butter sauce; or sliced artichoke bottom, spinach, and goat cheese wrapped in a crisp, thin pastry and served with a warm spiced tomato and mushroom cream.

Good fresh fish is used for entrees. The lobster is always easy to eat; no struggling with it here. I had it on my last trip, and on another evening I had one of the veal dishes. The veal was so tender I didn't need to use a knife. Beef Wellington and roast rack of lamb are always winners here, and so are the fresh sweetbreads and a very different grilled breast of free-range chicken—a little French and a little Oriental. Roasted boneless saddle of lamb is a real winner as is the fillet of salmon stuffed with fresh arugula and shiitake mushrooms. The inn has won the AAA four-diamond award—is there any wonder? The food and service are superb.

Desserts are super. I love chocolate and raspberries, so I had some in the form of a cake and mousse and berries. No matter what you order, it is good at the Copper Beech and always exquisitely presented. The menu changes seasonally.

The Victorian conservatory is a wonderful addition to this fine inn. It's so nice for an aperitif before dinner or for coffee and cognac after.

HOW TO GET THERE: The inn is located 1 mile west of Connecticut Route 9, from exit 3 or 4. Follow the signs to Ivoryton. The inn is on Ivoryton's Main Street, on the left side.

# The Inn at Lafayette
## Madison, Connecticut 06443

**INNKEEPER:** Caterina

**ADDRESS/TELEPHONE:** 725 Boston Post Road (mailing address: Box 852); (203) 245–7773 or (800) 660–8984; fax (203) 245–6256

**ROOMS:** 5, all with private bath, TV, and phone.

**RATES:** $100 to $200, double occupancy, continental breakfast.

**OPEN:** All year.

**FACILITIES AND ACTIVITIES:** Lunch, dinner, bar, lounge. Piano music in lounge Thursday, Friday. Nearby: Long Island Sound for swimming, fishing, and boating. Restaurant closed Monday.

**BUSINESS TRAVEL:** Thirty minutes from New Haven. Meeting facilities; secretarial support, copier, fax, audiovisual equipment available.

*T*his inn was built in 1837 as the Madison Methodist Church, complete with local timber and all hand-fitted by local craftsmen. In 1879 the infamous Reverend Hayden was tried for the murder of a young parishioner, but he was acquitted. Rumor has it that his ghost still hangs around the attic. The building was converted into an inn in the 1920s.

The inn's rooms and suites have private marble bathrooms. One has a whirlpool tub. All the accommodations have cable television, two state-of-the-art telephones complete with hands-free "do not disturb" conference and voice box capabilities, computer plug-in, and fax port. Add Egyptian cotton linens, bathrobes, Waterford crystal and Lenox vases, and down-filled comforters—well, I cannot say enough about the rooms. They are truly lovely.

Breakfast—it's a continental one—is served down the hall in the former steeple. This room can also be used for a nice private dinner or small meeting.

The dining rooms of the inn's restaurant, Cafe Allegre, are grand. The Belmont Dining Room serves a light menu. The Forsgate Room has a huge mural, peach-colored walls, and white napery. The Tunxis Room, named for an island off Madison, is light and bright. The Garden Room is a greenhouse with its own entrance; it is used for functions of all kinds in-season.

Now for some of the wonderful food served here. Sunday brunch is a prix fixe menu, offering a choice of four appetizers and entrees like eggs Benedict and Grand Marnier French toast (wow!). The tavern menu is extensive, offering tidbits such as Fire 'Em Up buffalo wings with a secret hot sauce. There are soups, salads, sandwiches, pastas, and daily blackboard specials. For lunch I had cream of mushroom soup and half a roast beef sandwich served with fried onions, tomatoes, and horseradish sauce.

An interesting dinner entree is the pork and spinach meatloaf, but, of course, they have all the usual choices like steak, fish, lamb, veal, and pasta. Save room for the desserts. Oh, I wish I lived closer!

**HOW TO GET THERE:** Take exit 61 off I-95. Turn onto Route 79 going toward Route 1 and Madison center. Go left on Route 1. The inn is on the left.

# Madison Beach Hotel 📱
## Madison, Connecticut 06443

**INNKEEPERS:** Lorraine Casula, manager; Betty and Henry Cooney Sr., Kathleen and Roben Bagdasarian

**ADDRESS/TELEPHONE:** 94 West Wharf Road; (203) 245–1404; fax (203) 245–0410

**ROOMS:** 31, plus 4 suites; all with private bath, air conditioning, cable TV, and phone.

**RATES:** In-season, $105 to $140; suites, $150 to $225; double occupancy; continental breakfast. Off-season, $70 to $90; suites, $125 to $175; double occupancy, continental breakfast; $10 less for single.

**OPEN:** March through December.

**FACILITIES AND ACTIVITIES:** Lunch, dinner. Bar, lounge, private beach on Long Island Sound.

**BUSINESS TRAVEL:** Located 20 minutes from New Haven. Phone in room, conference room with overhead projector, fax available, corporate rates, modems in rooms.

*I*f you are fortunate enough to own a boat, do come to Madison, drop your anchor, and row right in to the Madison Beach Hotel. If you don't own a boat, you don't need to hesitate to come here. The hotel is very easy to reach and should not be missed.

This Victorian beauty dates back to the 1800s. It has had many uses and lots of names, but it has never been better than it is today. The whole inn has been refurbished with an abundance of tender loving care.

Each of its rooms and magnificent suites has its own entrance and balcony overlooking the Long Island Sound and beach. The rooms are large and airy and furnished with antique oak bureaus and wicker and rattan furniture. Soft puffs cover the wicker, so you just sink into comfort. The four suites are absolutely breathtaking; each has its own kitchen, and the views from all of them are just wonderful.

There is a distinct nautical flavor to The Wharf dining room and the lovely Crow's Nest dining room on the upper level. The luncheon menu is extensive. The lobster salad roll is huge, and even I could not quite finish it. Several cold salad plates are offered; these are so nice on a hot day. For dinner they have queen- or king-sized cuts of roast prime rib of beef served with horseradish sauce—such a nice way to serve beef. The Wharf Surf and Turf is excellent. From the sea there is a good choice of entrees, each one sounding more enticing than the next. Among the desserts, black-bottom pie caught my eye and the crème brûlée was excellent; of course, there are more. And on Friday and Saturday nights, there is live music on the upper level.

The staff, starting with Lorraine at the desk to the guys and gals who wait on you, are very nice.

The beach is private, 75 feet of it. The water is clear with no undertow, so the children are safe. There is good fishing off the inn's pier. Or sit on the porch in one of the many wicker rockers and just enjoy where you are.

Do not miss OC, the orange and white inn cat.

**HOW TO GET THERE:** From I-95 turn right onto Route 79 if coming from New York and left if coming from Rhode Island. Go right at the third traffic light onto Route 1. Turn left at the Madison Country Club. The inn is at the end of the road on the water.

# Tidewater Inn ¢¢
## Madison, Connecticut 06443

**INNKEEPERS:** Jean Foy and Rich Evans

**ADDRESS/TELEPHONE:** 949 Boston Post Road; (203) 245-8457; fax (203) 318-0265

**ROOMS:** 9; all with private bath.

**RATES:** $70 to $160, double occupancy, EPB. Business rates available.

**OPEN:** All year.

**FACILITIES AND ACTIVITIES:** Nearby: restaurants, biking, hiking, canoeing, tennis, swimming, fishing.

*T*here are very few inns in this guide that do not serve dinner, but this area and the inn itself should not be ignored. Hammonassett State Park is close by, as are the Madison town beaches. The inn provides beach passes, chairs, and towels for your use. The innkeepers also have menus for nearby restaurants and will help you with reservations.

The inn is a former stagecoach stop that was built in the middle nineteenth century. The accommodations are lovely. There are kings, queens, doubles, and twins. Some are four-posters, and two have canopies. All rooms have telephones, clocks, and televisions. Two of the rooms have fireplaces, and all of the rooms have names. On the second floor is a small refrigerator for guests' use. This is a very nice touch.

The sitting/dining room has a bow window and a nice fireplace, along with a couch and chairs. There are tables for breakfast, and Jean prepares a good one. It always starts with fruit, and then it might be waffles, breakfast breads and muffins, coconut French toast with bacon, blueberry pancakes, sausages, or eggs of some sort. An English garden with benches and tables is a nice spot in the summer for a picnic.

There are very pretty things in the inn and a lot of Oriental pieces. Two small pillows in the Bushnell Room have these quotes on them: "Money is the root of all evil and every woman needs roots," and "Life is short; eat dessert first."

**HOW TO GET THERE:** From the north, take exit 62 off I-95. Go left to the light at Route 1. Turn right and go 1¼ miles to the inn, on your right. From New York take exit 61 off I-95. Take a right at the exit onto Route 79. At the third light go left onto Route 1. The inn is in 1 mile on your left.

## Shopping the Shoreline

If sunbathing isn't your cup of tea, you might want to explore the charming shops of Madison and Clinton. Madison is well known for its independent boutiques, its Front Parlour Tea Room— yum—at the British Shoppe (203-245-4521), its coffeeshops, and its outstanding bookstore, R. J. Julia Booksellers (203-245-3959), recently voted the best independent bookstore in the nation. Located just east of Madison, the town of Clinton is famed for its many antiques shops. Just drive or walk down Route 1 from shop to shop—you'll find plenty of treasures. Also in Clinton is a pre-mium outlet mall of seventy top designers and manufacturers. Called Clinton Crossing (860-664-0700), it has bargains on Ralph Lauren, Liz Claiborne, Tommy Hilfiger, Jones New York, Anne Klein, Waterford/Wedgwood, Le Creuset, Coach, Dooney and Bourke, and many others. I shopped until I was tired.

# The Inn at Mystic
## Mystic, Connecticut 06335

**INNKEEPER:** Jody Dyer

**ADDRESS/TELEPHONE:** Routes 1 and 27; (860) 536–9604; restaurant, (860) 536–8140 or (800) 237–2415; fax (860) 572–1635

**WEB SITE:** www.innatmystic.com

**ROOMS:** 5 in 2 houses; all with private bath.

**RATES:** $165 to $275, double occupancy, EP.

**OPEN:** All year.

**FACILITIES AND ACTIVITIES:** Breakfast, lunch, Sunday brunch, dinner every night except Christmas Eve. Bar, lounge, room service, swimming pool, tennis, canoes, sailboats, walking trails. Nearby: Mystic Seaport Museum, Mystic Marinelife Aquarium, charter boats and tours, miniature golf and driving range; Foxwoods Casino is about a half-hour north in Ledyard.

Every time I think about this beautiful spot, I want to go back there. The views from the inn extend from Mystic Harbor all the way to Fishers Island; they are absolutely breathtaking.

The inn and gatehouse are situated on eight acres of land amid pear, nut, and peach trees and English flower gardens. From the Victorian veranda—furnished, of course, with beautiful old wicker—the view of the natural rock for-

mations and ponds (I watched birds have their baths) and beyond to the harbor is worth a trip from anywhere.

Built in 1904, the inn is elegant. The large living room has walls covered with magnificent pin pine imported from England and contains lovely antiques and comfortable places to sit. The rooms

in both the inn and the gatehouse are beautifully done. Some have a fireplace. My room had a canopy bed, and was it ever comfortable! Each room has an interesting bath with hair dryer and whirlpool soaking tub or Thermacuzzi

# Mystic Attractions

You might never want to leave the Inn at Mystic, but lots of attractions are in this popular tourist area. In the summer months, there's even a shuttle that will pick you up at the inn and take you from place to place to help you avoid the traffic and enjoy the sights.

Mystic Seaport Museum (888-9SEAPORT) is one of the nation's leading maritime museums. See an entire nineteenth-century village recreation, tall ships, and much more. The Mystic Marinelife Aquarium (860-572-5955; www.mysticaquarium.org) is newly expanded and totally redone with lots of new exhibits about the ocean and its creatures. See a 750,000-gallon beluga whale pool, an amazing coral reef display, and much more.

You might also enjoy the Denison Pequotsepos Nature Center (860-536-1216) with 7 miles of hiking and cross-country skiing trails, a trail-side museum, a gift shop and bookstore, and lots of guided walks and talks for visitors of all ages. In nearby Groton, across the Thames River, you can visit the Historic Ship *Nautilus* and the Submarine Force Museum (800-343-0079).

spa. One has a view across the room to the harbor. Now that's a nice way to relax. Look south out the windows and you'll see Mason's Island; on a clear day you can see Long Island and Montauk.

The Flood Tide restaurant has a wonderful executive chef, Bob Tripp, who orchestrates the Tableside Classics prepared or carved at your table. The service here is grand. The baked stuffed two-tail Maine lobster—two claws and two tails—is still here and very good. Whole roast pheasant is served tableside, so is rack of lamb, beef Wellington, and chateaubriand. Jody and I shared the chateaubriand on my last visit and what a treat it was. There are fruits of the sea, veal, chicken, duck, pork, and Vegetarian Fiesta. Then I saw the desserts—chocolate peanut butter mousse torte, chocolate pâté, chocolate mint zabaglione torte . . . Of course, there are other things besides chocolate, but why bother?

The luncheon buffet is lavish, or ask for a picnic basket to take out sightseeing. They have thought of everything to make your stay pleasant. Sunday brunch, as you can imagine, is a bountiful affair.

The lounge is pleasant for lighter fare and is right at the swimming pool. A piano player provides music on a parlor grand piano every night and Sunday brunch. A wedding up here would be ambrosia. The inn combining old-world charm with modern amenities will create the wedding of your dreams.

**HOW TO GET THERE**: Take exit 90 from I-95. Go 2 miles south through Mystic on Route 27 to Route 1. The inn is here. Drive up past the motor inn to the inn at the top of the driveway.

# Roger Sherman Inn
## New Canaan, Connecticut 06840

**INNKEEPERS**: Thomas and Kay Weilenmann; Rudi Granser, general manager

**ADDRESS/TELEPHONE**: 195 Oenoke Ridge; (203) 966-4541

**WEB SITE**: www.RogerShermanInn.com

**ROOMS**: 10; all with private bath, air conditioning, TV, and phone.

**RATES**: $80 to $90, single; $110 to $135, double; continental breakfast.

**OPEN**: All year except Christmas Day.

**FACILITIES AND ACTIVITIES**: Lunch, dinner, Sunday brunch, bar. Nearby: golf, tennis, nature center.

*I*t's so nice to have the Roger Sherman Inn in this guide. Built in the mid-1700s, the inn had fallen into disrepair, but Henry Priegor, once the innkeeper here and now the innkeeper at the Inn at Ridgefield, gutted the old building and wow, what a job he did! Now the inn's new proprietors, Thomas and Kay Weilenmann, have freshened up his improvements and added an eight-room annex called the Carriage House. The inn is within walking distance of New Canaan's town center. This is a wonderful area in Connecticut's esteemed Fairfield County in which to spend a few days.

The rooms are large and nicely furnished with comfortable chairs and couches and good beds. The Carriage House rooms are beautifully finished in a country style with Hitchcock furniture.

The inn has five lovely dining rooms. One is a pretty private one for up to ten people. It's on the main floor along with three other dining rooms and a neat pub and lounge. The porches wrap around the inn, and in warm weather food and cocktails are served here overlooking the lush green lawns.

Downstairs is the wine cellar dining room; it seats up to twenty-six people. There is a notable collection of wines along some of the walls. Wherever you eat, you will find the food sumptuous. There's tableside service seven days a week. The food is French and Mediterranean cuisine and excellent. At lunchtime, you might find fillet of sole, pasta of the day, omelet of your choice, double lamb chop, and fresh curried chicken salad with Major Grey Chutney. Dinner might bring fresh Dover sole, breast of duck with pear, rack of lamb, and much more. For dessert I'm always glad to find an old-favorite, crepe suzette.

Sunday brunch has much to choose from. There are eggs Benedict with smoked salmon, veal, roast loin of pork, pasta of the day, a duck salad with raspberry-vinegar sauce, and good coffees. New Year's Eve is a black-tie affair.

The executive chef, Raymond Péron, is known for his wonderful meals; yes, you can count on him.

**HOW TO GET THERE:** The inn is located on Route 124 North in New Canaan.

# The Birches Inn on Lake Waramaug
## New Preston, Connecticut 06777

**INNKEEPERS:** Karen R. Hamilton and Frederick Favreau (also the chef); Nancy Conant, general manager

**ADDRESS/TELEPHONE:** 233 West Shore Road; (860) 868–1735 or (888) 590–7945; fax (860) 868–1815

**WEB SITE:** www.thebirchesinn.com

**ROOMS:** 8, all private bath, phone, air conditioning, and cable television.

**RATES:** $95 to $300, double occupancy, EPB.

**OPEN:** Inn open all year; dining room closed January and February

**FACILITIES AND ACTIVITIES:** Breakfast all year, dinner Thursday through Monday. Service bar. Bicycles and a canoe are available for guests. Nearby hiking, cross-country ski trails, antiques shops, art galleries, horseback riding, golf, fishing, and numerous points of historic interest.

The Birches Inn has been around for a long time but not like this. Restored in 1995 after being closed for several years, it's a winner today. There are five glorious rooms on the second floor of the inn. All of them have queen- or king-sized beds, two face the lake and have picture windows, two have doors to the deck, and two have small sitting areas. The other three rooms are in the lake house and have private decks. Very nice indeed.

The dining room overlooks the lake. White napery, wood trim, and a touch of jade green in the carpet make the room pretty; the chairs are very comfortable. The breakfast room is next to the dining room and also overlooks the lake and the lovely porch that is used in season. A couple of the appetizers are crispy oysters with red Asian slaw and roasted garlic custard with Balsamic caramel, grilled portobello mushrooms, and baby arugula. Entrees may be grilled Atlantic salmon, penne pasta, pan-seared chicken breast, grilled marinated leg of lamb with Parmesan polenta, sautéed mustard greens, date chutney, and roasted garlic sauce. I love lamb. Their wines are glorious and offer a very good selection.

In the living room there's a fireplace and a player piano with a lot of music rolls, and in the stairwell an artist has painted birch trees. I cannot imagine how she got up there to do this work.

HOW TO GET THERE: From New York take I–84 to Route 7 in Danbury. Follow it north to New Milford. Take a right onto Route 202 to New Preston. Take a left onto Route 45 and a left at the stop sign onto West Shore Road. The inn is 2 ²/₁₀ miles on the left.

# Boulders Inn 🫀
## New Preston, Connecticut 06777

**INNKEEPERS:** Kees and Ulla Adema and Eric

**ADDRESS/TELEPHONE:** Route 45; (860) 868–0541 or (800) 55–BOULD; fax (860) 868–1925

**E-MAIL:** boulders@bouldersinn.com

**WEB SITE:** www.bouldersinn.com

**ROOMS:** 17, including 2 suites and 8 guest houses; all with private bath and fireplace, 5 with Jacuzzi, 1 specially equipped for the handicapped.

**RATES:** $275 to $325, double occupancy, MAP. Higher on weekends in season.

**OPEN:** All year.

**FACILITIES AND ACTIVITIES:** Bar, tennis court, swimming, boating, bicycling, hiking, cross-country skiing.

The stone boulders from which the inn was made jut right into the inn, thus the name Boulders Inn. If you have the energy, take a hike up Pinnacle Mountain behind the inn. From the top of the mountain, you'll be rewarded with a panorama that includes New York State to the west and Massachusetts to the north. Nice to enjoy the woods without having to go very far.

If you're not a hiker, you can partake of the marvelous countryside right from the inn. There is an outside terrace where, in summer, you may enjoy cocktails, dinner, and spectacular sunsets. The spacious living room has large windows, and its comfortable chairs and couches make it a nice place for tea or cocktails. The dining room is octagonal and provides a wonderful view of the lake. Some very good food is served here. There are some different appetizers, like angel hair pasta with prosciutto and aged sheep's milk cheese. On

a recent springtime visit, I had first-crop asparagus salad with truffle oil and Parmesan cheese. And the entrees—oh my! Roasted rack of lamb with black olive mashed potatoes and sun-dried tomato sauce. Salmon and veal. The list goes on and on.

An added reason to go to the inn: It has received the *Wine Spectator's* Award of Excellence and has more than 400 wines on its list.

All the guest accommodations have a view either of the lake or of the woods and are tastefully furnished. There are eight cozy guest houses, all with fireplaces. Five of the guest houses have Jacuzzi tubs, and the furnishings are lovely. Say hello to Mouse, Oscar, and Socksie, the inn cats.

Kees and Ulla have done nice things to the inn. They have interesting paintings, Quimper pottery made in France is on display, and the cut and pierced lampshades were all made by Ulla. As an annual tradition Ulla will be offering classes on her handcrafted lampshades—she does fabulous work.

**HOW TO GET THERE:** From New York take I-84 to Route 7 in Danbury; follow it north to New Milford. Take a right onto Route 202 to New Preston. Take a left onto Route 45, and you will find the inn as you round onto the lake.

# The Hopkins Inn on Lake Waramaug
## New Preston, Connecticut 06777

**INNKEEPERS:** Franz and Beth Schober and Don Toby

**ADDRESS/TELEPHONE:** 22 Hopkins Road; (860) 868-7295

**ROOMS:** 11, plus 2 apartments; 8 with private bath.

**RATES:** $67 to $77, double occupancy, EP.

**OPEN:** All year.

**FACILITIES AND ACTIVITIES:** Breakfast, lunch, dinner (breakfast only meal served January–late March). Bar, lounge, private beach on lake. Nearby: golf, tennis, horseback riding, biking, and hiking.

*S*urrounded by majestic trees on particularly beautiful grounds, this inn overlooks lovely Lake Waramaug. The inn has glorious, unmatched views of the lake.

In season there is dining under the magnificent maple and horse chestnut trees, and dine you will. The inn has a trout pond where you can pick the fish you fancy, and next you have trout meunière; fresher fish would be hard to find.

Franz is the chef, and a few of his specials include lamb curry, veal piccata or milanaise, and boeuf bourguignonne. Those are for lunch. For dinner how about bay scallops in a special garlic sauce, and backhendl with lingonberries? And there is always a special or two. On Sundays, instead of brunch, they have Sunday dinner all day with wonderful lamb and pork roasts. Many Austrian dishes are served here. Strawberries Romanoff, meringue glacé, coupe aux marrons, and homemade cheesecake. Need I say more?

The dining rooms are cheerful. The fireplace has ceramic square tiles across the mantel, and the decorations are wine racks full of wines from all over the world. Naturally, the wine list is quite impressive and pleasantly, fairly priced.

There is a private beach down at the lake for use by inn guests. Bicycling, hiking, horseback riding, golf, and tennis are available nearby.

The rooms are clean, neat, and country inn comfortable. Almost all of the rooms have a view of the lake.

**HOW TO GET THERE:** Take I–84 to Route 202 east to Route 45 in New Preston. Turn left on Route 45 and follow it 2 miles past the lake. Take your first left after the lake. Then take the second right onto Hopkins Road.

---

# Silvermine Tavern
## Norwalk, Connecticut 06850

**INNKEEPER:** Francis C. Whitman Jr.

**ADDRESS/TELEPHONE:** 194 Perry Avenue; (203) 847–4558

**ROOMS:** 10; all with private bath.

**RATES:** $68, single; $99 to $120, double; continental breakfast.

**OPEN:** All year.

**FACILITIES AND ACTIVITIES:** Lunch, dinner, Sunday brunch. Restaurant closed Tuesday. Bar, TV in parlor.

*A*lthough the Colonial crossroads village known as Silvermine has been swallowed up by the surrounding Fairfield County towns of Norwalk, Wilton, and New Canaan, the Silvermine Tavern still lies at the heart of a community of great Old World beauty. It has a remarkable way of sweeping you worlds back in time.

This is one of the most popular dining places in the area, known for delicious New England traditional food. Thursday night is set aside for a fantastic buffet supper featuring steaks, fried chicken, and many salads, all of which you top off with a great array of desserts. Sunday buffet brunch features twenty different dishes. Some of the inn specialties are Oysters Country Gentlemen, scallops Nantucket, mussels steamed in wine, and roast duckling with an apple cider sauce. The food can be savored in one of the six dining rooms or on the riverside deck, which is open from June through September. On the old millpond below, the ducks and swans wait, hoping for some leftovers.

Silvermine Tavern is furnished with old Oriental rugs, antiques, old portraits, and great comfortable chairs and sofas surrounding the six huge fireplaces. The main dining room is decorated with more than 1,000 antiques, primarily old farm tools and household artifacts. Also in

here is an 1887 Regina music box. The drop of a coin will turn a huge disk, and the music will begin. This is a really fun antique. In the front parlor, in front of a cheery fire, you can enjoy sherry and petit fours at the end of your day. This is the life.

The guest rooms are comfortably furnished, many of them with old-fashioned tester beds. One of my favorite rooms has its own deck overlooking the lovely millpond.

If you wish, you can stroll by the waterfall and feed the ducks and swans on the millpond. Across the road from the Tavern you will find the Country Store, run by Frank's wife. It has a back room that is a museum of antique tools and gadgets. It also has a fine collection of Currier & Ives prints. Do take a leisurely drive around the back roads near the inn, too. They are a delight. Also in this area you have the well-known Silvermine Guild of Artists.

**HOW TO GET THERE:** From the Merritt Parkway take exit 40A onto Main Avenue South. Go south to the third traffic light and turn right onto Perry Avenue. Follow it to the second stop sign and turn left. The inn is on the right.

# Bee and Thistle Inn 💟 📱
## Old Lyme, Connecticut 06371

**INNKEEPERS:** Bob and Penny Nelson, Jeff and Lori Nelson

**ADDRESS/TELEPHONE:** 100 Lyme Street; (860) 434–1667 or (860) 622–4946; fax (860) 434–3402

**ROOMS:** 11, plus 1 cottage; all with private bath, all with phone.

**RATES:** $75 to $155, double occupancy; $210, cottage; EP.

**OPEN:** All year except Christmas Eve, Christmas Day, New Year's Day, and first two weeks of January.

**FACILITIES AND ACTIVITIES:** Breakfast. Lunch and dinner every day except Tuesday. Sunday brunch. Afternoon tea, November 1 to May 1. Bar, lounge, library.

**BUSINESS TRAVEL:** Located 20 minutes from New London. All rooms with phone, fax available, meeting space for small groups, corporate rates.

**RECOMMENDED COUNTRY INNS® TRAVELERS' CLUB BENEFIT:** A complimentary bottle of champagne. Guest must mention the offer when making a reservation.

This lovely old inn, built in 1756, sits on five and one-half acres bordering the Lieutenant River in historic Old Lyme, Connecticut. During summer the abundant flower gardens keep the inn filled to overflowing with color.

The guest rooms are all tastefully decorated. Your bed, maybe a fourposter or canopy, is covered with a lovely old quilt or afghan. The bath towels are big and thirsty—how I love them! The cottage is air-conditioned and has a reading room, a bedroom with queen-sized bed, a kitchen, a bath, and a large television room. A deck goes around the outside. There are also a fireplace and a private dock on the river.

There are six fireplaces in the inn. The one in the parlor is most inviting— a nice place for a cocktail or just good conversation. On weekends there is music by A Wrinkle in Time, a wonderful husband-and-wife duo who make magic with their music. There is also a harpist on Saturday nights.

Be sure to say hello to Callebaut (Bo), the Nelsons' large chocolate lab, and to Jack, a real inn dog.

Breakfast in bed is an especially nice feature of the inn. Freshly squeezed orange juice is a refreshing way to start any day. Muffins made fresh each day, buttery crepes folded with strawberry or raspberry preserves, and much more. Lunch is interesting and inventive. Try the wild mushroom lasagne, Maryland-style crabcakes, or the Bee and Thistle shepherd's pie. Sunday brunch is really gourmet. Fresh rainbow trout, chicken hash, three different omelets—I could eat the menu. And, of course, dinners here are magnificent, with candlelit dining rooms, a good selection of appetizers and soups, and entrees such as spiced breast of chicken, pork medallions, shrimp, scallops, veal, and rack of lamb. The list goes on and on. Desserts are wonderful. The menu changes seasonally, each time bringing new delights.

Afternoon tea is served from November 1 to May 1 on Monday, Wednesday, and Thursday from 3:30 to 5:00 P.M. The tea service is beautiful; coffee and aperitifs are also available.

The inn just keeps winning awards. *Connecticut* magazine voted the inn Best Overall Restaurant, Best Dessert, and Most Romantic Place to Dine in Connecticut. Wow! Let me tell you, the inn does deserve it.

This is a fine inn in a most interesting part of New England. You are in the heart of art, antiques, gourmet restaurants, and endless activities. Plan to spend a few days when you come.

HOW TO GET THERE: Traveling north on I–95, take exit 70 immediately on the east side of the Baldwin Bridge. At the bottom of the ramp, turn left. Take the first right at the traffic light, and turn left at the end of the road. The inn is the third house on your left. Traveling south on I–95, take exit 70; turn right at the bottom of the ramp. The inn is the third house on your left.

# Old Lyme Inn

Old Lyme, Connecticut 06371

**INNKEEPER:** Diana Johnson Atwood

**ADDRESS/TELEPHONE:** 85 Lyme Street (mailing address: P.O. Box 787); (860) 434–2600 or (800) 434–5352; fax (860) 434–5352

**ROOMS:** 13; all with private bath, phone, clock radio, and TV.

**RATES:** $99 to $158, double occupancy, continental breakfast.

**OPEN:** All year.

**FACILITIES AND ACTIVITIES:** Lunch, dinner, Sunday brunch. Bar and dining room.

**BUSINESS TRAVEL:** Located 45 minutes from Hartford. Phone in every room. Meeting rooms, fax available, database for computers.

*S*assafras was the inn cat who has a neat lounge named after her. Winslow is the current inn cat, named after the huge Winslow Homer mural in the dining room. In the lounge you'll find television, games, books, and a lovely fireplace for your enjoyment, along with comfortable chairs and couch. The Victorian barroom has a back bar that is more than one

hundred years old and was found by the innkeeper in Philadelphia. There is a beveled mirror over it that most museums would covet. A raw bar is offered in here for light suppers. A very cozy and comfortable room.

The rooms here at the inn are grand. The new wing has eight rooms. The beds are four-posters, and all rooms have telephone, clock radio, and Victorian couch and/or delightful wing chairs. You will find mints on your pillow at night.

There are four separate dining areas, and the food is superb. The menu, of course, changes with the seasons, but I'd like to give you just a few ideas. Several appetizers, soups, and salads are offered. New England crabcake was

# Getting an Impression of Old Lyme and Lyme

At the turn of the twentieth century Miss Florence Griswold of Old Lyme welcomed a group of artists to summer at her pretty yellow mansion on the Lieutenant River. Soon a colony was established there, as now-famed painters like Childe Hassam, William Chadwick, and many others studied the light and shadows of the woods and shoreline. The Lyme Art Colony was responsible for a new style of painting known as American Impressionism. Now Miss Florence's house is a museum devoted to American art and the history of the colony and the region. Open year-round, the Florence Griswold Museum (860-434-5542) is just steps away from both the Bee and Thistle Inn and the Old Lyme Inn.

If you'd prefer to get your own impression of the area, explore the Old Lyme Historic District on foot, then explore Route 156 by bicycle or car. North on this roadway is the beautiful hamlet of Hamburg Cove on the Eight-Mile River. You might even see an artist with an easel painting at the riverside—a frequent sight here. Devil's Hopyard State Park, Selden Neck State Park, and the Nehantic State Forest are all nearby. Ask your innkeepers for tips on visiting these areas.

one; another was imported escargots. I had spinach Waldorf salad with roasted chicken, chopped apples, and walnuts. It was excellent. They also have—get this—Wild American Meatloaf. It's wild boar and buffalo blended into a meatloaf and served with mashed potatoes and mushroom gravy.

Dinner is spectacular. The Old Lyme Inn Pasta is so divine I won't even describe it. You must come and try it. The chef, Stuart London, has been here for a few years. There are nine appetizers, no one better than the others. And soups—well, I had dilled carrot bisque with bay shrimp, and it was quite inventive. Sole and crab imperial is excellent; planked swordfish is different and so pretty; rack of lamb is very good. Of course, there is much more, and there are specials every night. The desserts have been written up in food magazines and have won awards—that's how good they are.

The luncheon menu, too, offers wonderful food. Try the Oriental chicken salad or the grilled pizza. Whatever your selection, do come and sample some of this grand food.

Enjoy your meal along with the music of a jazz guitarist on the weekends. Continental breakfast is served to guests every day except weekends, when a breakfast buffet is offered.

The inn can handle small conferences, weddings, parties, reunions, and such. It would be a lovely place to have a wedding and is easy to find just off I–95. There is much to do and see in this pretty town and area.

Many of the paintings in the Inn represent the Old Lyme School of artists who, at the turn of the twentieth century, resided a few doors down the street at Florence Griswold's home, now the Florence Griswold Museum. In addition there are paintings purchased from current artists featured at the Lyme Art Association shows.

**HOW TO GET THERE:** Traveling north on I–95, take exit 70 immediately on the east side of the Baldwin Bridge. At the bottom of the ramp, turn left. Take the first right at the traffic light, and turn left at the dead end. The inn is on the right. Traveling south on I–95, take exit 70. At the bottom of the ramp, turn right. The inn is on the right.

# Saybrook Point Inn 📱
## Old Saybrook, Connecticut 06475

**INNKEEPER:** Stephen Tagliatela; Peter Scotella, restaurant manager; Lewis Kiesler, general manager

**ADDRESS/TELEPHONE:** 2 Bridge Street; (860) 395–2000 or (800) 243–0212 (outside Connecticut); fax (860) 388–1504

**E-MAIL:** saybrook@snet.net

**WEB SITE:** www.saybrook.com

**ROOMS:** 63, including 6 suites and 1 lighthouse apartment; all with private bath, phone, TV, air conditioning, and refrigerator, 44 with working fireplace. Some smoke-free rooms and suites.

**RATES:** $149 to $295, double occupancy; $295 to $495, suites; EP. Package plans available.

**OPEN:** All year.

**FACILITIES AND ACTIVITIES:** Breakfast, lunch, dinner, Sunday brunch. Smoking in bar only. Banquet and meeting facilities; health club with whirlpool, sauna, and steam; spa; indoor and outdoor pools; marina with 120 slips and floating docks. Nearby: charter boats, theater.

**BUSINESS TRAVEL:** Located 10 minutes from railroad station. All rooms with phones, suites with data ports for computers and fax machines, meeting rooms, secretarial services available.

"Experience the magic at Saybrook Point Inn." These are the inn's words, and they're so true. The panoramic views of the Connecticut River and Long Island Sound are magnificent. From the moment you walk into the lobby, the Italian marble floors, beautiful furniture, and glorious fabrics let you know this is a special inn. Even the carpet is hand-loomed.

All the guest rooms and suites have a water view, and most have a balcony. They are lavishly decorated with eighteenth-century–style furniture, and Italian marble is used in the bathroom with whirlpool bath. Also in the rooms are a miniature wet bar and refrigerator; an unbelievable telephone that turns on lights; double-, queen-, or king-sized bed; and hair dryer. The suites feature VCR and data ports for personal computers and fax machines. Secretarial services are also available, as is an exercise room with life bikes.

This is a full spa, with indoor and outdoor pools, steamroom, sauna, and whirlpool. The licensed staff will pamper you with a therapeutic massage, European facial, manicure, pedicure, even a quality makeup application.

Planning a wedding or business conference? No problem. The inn has banquet facilities for all occasions. The ballroom seats 240 people. Smaller meetings would be ideal in the library, which holds up to sixteen people, or in the executive suites.

Breakfast, lunch, and dinner are served in an exquisite room that overlooks the inn's marina, the river, and Long Island Sound. There was a full moon the evening I dined here. What a beautiful sight to enhance the memorable food!

Appetizers like smoked Norwegian salmon, escargots, smoked pheasant, and beluga caviar are an elegant way to begin your dinner. Pastas are cannelloni, linguine, or wild mushroom. I had one of the best racks of lamb I have ever had. There is always a fresh seafood special. My friend had shrimp Provençale—shrimp sautéed with garlic, shallots, and scallions. A flower may be a garnish on your plate; you can eat it.

Do try to save room for dessert. I had chocolate–chocolate chip cake, which was dark and beautiful and delicious. The service is also superb.

Sunday brunch is a winner. Too much to list, but believe me, you will not go away hungry. I was here for Easter, and the food was glorious.

The inn's fact sheet says, "Situated where the Connecticut River flows into Long Island Sound in the historic town of Old Saybrook." The unmatched views capture the essence of coastal Connecticut.

**HOW TO GET THERE:** From I-95 northbound take exit 67 (southbound, take exit 68) and follow Route 154 and signs to Saybrook Point.

# Stonehenge
Ridgefield, Connecticut 06877

**INNKEEPER:** Douglas Seville

**ADDRESS/TELEPHONE:** P.O. Box 667; (203) 438-6511

**ROOMS:** 14, plus 2 suites; all with private bath, color TV, phone.

**RATES:** $75 to $120, single; $90 to $160, double; $200, suite; continental breakfast. Winter rates available.

**OPEN:** All year except New Year's Day.

**FACILITIES AND ACTIVITIES:** Breakfast, dinner, service bar, lounge. Swimming pool. No dinner on Mondays.

The setting for Stonehenge is serenely beautiful. Outside the inn is a lovely pond, which is bedecked with swans and aflutter with Canada geese and ducks stopping in on their migratory journeys. When I visited here in the spring, the red and yellow tulips were at their best.

In June 1988 the lovely old farmhouse that was the main building of the inn was destroyed in a terrible fire. But now a new Stonehenge has risen. The rooms, all different, are beautiful. No matter whether you're in the guest house or cottage or inn, the accommodations are elegant, color coordinated, and comfortable. The suite has facilities for light cooking. Most of the rooms have a queen- and king-sized bed. All overlook the pond and wooded hillside.

A lovely continental breakfast is brought to you in your room, along with a copy of the morning newspaper. The breakfast consists of freshly squeezed juice, delicious muffin or Danish pastry, and coffee.

The common room has a fireplace flanked by bookcases. The large dining room has picture windows overlooking the pond and terraces. It has always been justifiably famous for its gourmet dinners. The original Stonehenge shrimp in crisp beer batter with a pungent sauce is still here—and glorious. Some of the appetizers are a crepe of wild mushrooms

with Gruyère cheese, and fresh hearts of palm wrapped in prosciutto. There are good salads to choose from, followed by entrees like crisply roasted duckling with wild rice and black currant sauce, or breast of chicken filled with fresh spinach and Gruyère cheese, wrapped in puff pastry and served with a champagne sauce. You could even have roast baby suckling pig (five days' notice for this one). The desserts are stupendous. Do come and try some. Decaffeinated espresso gets my vote.

This is a beautiful place for a wedding or any other special function. The Terrace Room is available for corporate meetings.

HOW TO GET THERE: From the Merritt Parkway take exit 40. Go north on Route 7. The inn's sign is in 13 miles, on the left. From I-84 go south on Route 7. The inn's sign is 4½ miles on the right.

# West Lane Inn and
# The Inn at Ridgefield
Ridgefield, Connecticut 06877

INNKEEPERS: M. M. Mayer and Deborah Prieger; Henry Prieger, owner
of the restaurant

ADDRESS/TELEPHONE: 22 West Lane; (203) 438-7323; Ridgefield,
(203) 438-8282

WEB SITE: www.innbook.com

ROOMS: 18; all with private bath, air conditioning, phone, and TV, some
with fireplace.

RATES: $120, single; $125 to $170, double; EPB.

OPEN: All year.

FACILITIES AND ACTIVITIES: Lunch, dinner, Sunday brunch, bar,
lounge, piano nightly.

RECOMMENDED COUNTRY INNS® TRAVELERS' CLUB BENEFIT: 10 percent discount, Monday–Thursday, subject to availability.

We have a first here: two separate inns next door to each other.
West Lane Inn has the rooms and serves breakfast and a light
menu from the pantry. The Inn at Ridgefield serves delicious
lunch and dinner.

Rich oak paneling and lush carpeting, along with a crackling fire, greet
you as you enter West Lane. The bedrooms are luxurious, with individual cli-
mate control, color television, radio, and telephone. Each room has either
one king- or two queen-sized beds. Some have a working fireplace. These are
really nice on a cold night.

The breakfast room is bright and cheerful, serving freshly squeezed
orange juice. A West Lane breakfast special is yogurt with bananas, honey,
and nuts. Cold cereals in the summer, hot cereals in the winter; Danish,
muffins, or toast; or a poached egg is offered. Everything is done very nicely.
The pantry selections are available from noon until late in the evening. There
are tunafish salad plates, several sandwiches like grilled cheese—even peanut
butter and jelly—and more. There also are desserts.

The ends of the old wooden wine and whiskey crates that line the porch
of The Inn at Ridgefield let you know there are good things inside. Dinner
features hors d'oeuvres like pâté of pistachio and truffles with sauce Cum-
berland, onion soup Calvados gratinée, and vichysoisse. Then entrees such as

frogs legs (they are really good), fresh Dover sole, chateaubriand, and roast rack of spring lamb follow. There are wonderful salads and desserts. Crepes suzettes for two is an old favorite. And believe me, there are more, plus good coffees.

Both inns are just around the corner from the famous Cannon Ball House, which was struck by a British fieldpiece during the Revolution. There are quite a few stores to browse in, as well as antiques stores. The Aldrich and Hammond museums are in town, and you are close to several fine summer theaters. Ridgefield is such a pretty town to visit.

**HOW TO GET THERE:** Coming north from New York on Route 684, or Route 7 from the Merritt Parkway, get off on Route 35 and follow it to Ridgefield. The inns are on Route 35 at the south end of town.

# Old Riverton Inn
## Riverton, Connecticut 06065

**INNKEEPERS:** Pauline and Mark Telford

**ADDRESS/TELEPHONE:** P.O. Box 6; (860) 379–8678 or (800) 378–1796; fax (860) 379–1006

**ROOMS:** 12; all with private bath.

**RATES:** $85 to $175, double occupancy, EPB.

**OPEN:** All year except the first week of January and the first two weeks of March.

**FACILITIES AND ACTIVITIES:** Lunch, dinner every night except Tuesday. Dining room has wheelchair accessibility. Bar.

The Old Riverton Inn was originally opened in 1796 by Jesse Ives. It was on the post road between Hartford and Albany and was known as Ives Tavern. It has passed through many hands since then, and the hands that have it now are very capable.

The Grindstone Terrace was enclosed to make it useful all year. The floor of this room is made of grindstones that, according to century-old records, were quarried in Nova Scotia and sent by ship first to Long Island Sound and then up the Connecticut River to Hartford. From there they were hauled by oxen to Collinsville, where they were used in the making of axes and machetes. A lot of history is here. Once Riverton was known as Hitchcocksville, because the famous Hitchcock furniture factory is here. It is open each day except Sunday until 5:00 P.M.

The Colonial dining room has, of course, Hitchcock chairs and a lovely bow window chock-full of plants. I sat here for luncheon one day and had delicious broiled scrod. The menu offers a lot of choices. Chicken salad plate looked really enticing. Dinner appetizers, such as the homemade soups, also are good. I had the onion soup, and it was delicious. There are several seafood entrees, each one looking better than the last. Other specialties of the inn include boneless breast

of chicken marengo, veal Français, and veal maison. Chef Leo Roy really has a way with food.

A stained-glass window is in the bar. Murals in here were painted by Bobby Walsh, who created murals at the New York World's Fair in the late '30s. As the Telfords say, they "provide hospitality for the hungry, thirsty, and sleepy."

There is a working fireplace in one bedroom. It's a large room with a sitting area and queen-sized bed. A few rooms have a canopy bed. (One room has a "new" old tub that's a pip. Go and see.) Mints placed on the pillows at night is a very special touch I love. A comfortable lounge and library are on this floor, providing you with games, tons of books—and lots of quiet.

**HOW TO GET THERE**: The inn is 3½ miles from Winsted. Take Route 8 or Route 44 to Winsted. Turn east on Route 20, and it is approximately 1½ miles to the inn.

# A Riverton Ramble

Antiques, galleries, the delightfully old-fashioned Riverton General Store, the Hitchcock Museum, the Hitchcock Chair Factory Store, the Village Sweet Shop, and the Catnip Mouse Tea Room are all on the lovely stretch of Route 20 that is Riverton's main street. All are well within walking distance of the inn, and most are open year-round or at least from April through December.

The Hitchcock Museum (860–738–4950) is in the Old Union Church. A visit here reveals the history and handiwork of Lambert Hitchcock, who began producing his notable style of hand-painted American chairs in 1818. You can also visit the factory store (860–379–4826) located in Lambert's original factory building along with Buckingham Galleries.

Down the street are such shops as Antiques and Herbs (860–379–4729), perfect for browsing for treasures. Stop for a treat at the sweet shop or the tea room—boy, are they good.

# Under Mountain Inn
## Salisbury, Connecticut 06068

INNKEEPERS: Marged and Peter Higginson

ADDRESS/TELEPHONE: Route 41; (860) 435–0242; fax (860) 435–2379

ROOMS: 7; all with private bath.

RATES: $170 to $200, double occupancy, MAP.

OPEN: All year.

FACILITIES AND ACTIVITIES: For the public, dinner is available Friday and Saturday. For inn guests, dinner is available every night. Nearby: swimming, canoeing, skiing, fishing, golf.

RECOMMENDED COUNTRY INNS® TRAVELERS' CLUB BENEFIT: Stay two nights, get third night free, Monday–Thursday, subject to availability; October excluded.

Under Mountain Inn was built in the early 1700s. Wood found in the attic was known as "king's wood" because of its special width. It now is the paneling on the front of the bar.

The house is Colonial in style and has been lovingly restored. Each of the seven guest rooms has Posturepedic mattresses. There are doubles, queens, and kings, so take your choice. Marged has a wonderful collection of stuffed animals, and you will find one or two on your bed. What a homey feeling this added touch provides. You will also find sherry and mints in your room for your enjoyment. Beautiful canopies are on most of the beds.

There are three acres of grounds, so in the summer you can wander out under the trees and enjoy their beauty. Shading the inn and terrace is a tree that is rumored to be the oldest thorned locust in Connecticut. Sugar, the inn dog, surely is handsome. Sneakers is the inn cat.

The dining rooms are charming; there are three. Peter is the chef. You can start with Scottish salmon or one of Peter's good soups. Go on to entrees such as roast goose with chestnut stuffing, shepherd's pie, bangers and mash, beef steak and kidney pie . . . I could go on and on. Desserts are homemade and scrumptious. The menu, of course, changes seasonally. In the morning you are served a full English breakfast.

Arabelle's Lounge is small and so comfortable, with a VCR and a wonderful collection of British movies.

There is much to do in this area of Connecticut. The inn has brochures to help you plan your day. You will find canoeing, fishing, swimming, horseback riding, tennis, skiing, and more. There are also many good private schools in this area.

HOW TO GET THERE: Take Route 41 north for 4 miles from Salisbury. The inn is on the left. From New York State take I–684 to Route 22, then Route 44 to Route 41.

# The White Hart
Salisbury, Connecticut 06068

**INNKEEPER:** Juliet Moore

**ADDRESS/TELEPHONE:** Box 545; (800) 832-0041, (860) 435-0030;
fax (860) 435-0040

**ROOMS:** 23, plus 3 suites; all with private bath, cable TV, phone,
and air conditioning, 1 specially equipped for handicapped.

**RATES:** $75 to $125, single; $85 to $170, double; $100 to $195,
suites; EP.

**OPEN:** All year.

**FACILITIES AND ACTIVITIES:** Breakfast, lunch, dinner. Tavern room,
garden room, American Grill restaurant, private function and meeting
rooms. Nearby: swimming, boating, skiing, horseback riding; Tanglewood and Jacob's Pillow.

How nice to have this old beauty back in the book! Looking sharp
and refurbished in a grand style, the inn now boasts an extra wing,
and a sprinkler system has been added. The lobby and common
rooms are beautifully furnished. A small upholstered child-sized wing chair
is a lovely touch in a corner of the lobby. Along with it are a pair of adult-
capacity wing chairs and nice couches, too.

To the left of the lobby is the Hunt Room, used primarily for receptions,
but with a chess table guests can enjoy when the room is not in use.

Accommodations are fine—either two double beds or a queen-sized bed
in each room—and very comfortable. My room on my last visit was the Ford
Room, named for Edsel Ford, the owner of the inn many years ago when his
son went to the Hotchkiss School. He wanted to be assured of a pleasant and
convenient place to stay when he visited his son. It's lovely.

The restaurants include the Garden Room and the Old Tavern. Breakfast,
lunch, and light dinners are served here.

I had my breakfast in the Garden Room. Sunshine and pretty plants
added to the good food—oh my! Fresh-squeezed orange juice, eggs, French
toast, oatmeal, and more. Sunday breakfast, of course, is grand, with almond
poppyseed waffles, eggs White Hart, grilled Idaho trout, and much more.

Lunch has lots of goodies—three-bean chili, the inn's own pizza, Today's Omelet, wilted spinach salad, and on and on. I understand that the Maine crabcakes with sauce rémoulade is so popular, it will never be removed from the menu.

Julie's New American Grill is a wonderful restaurant for fine dining and Sunday brunch. Julie used Italian fabric for the bar stools, chairs, and banquettes, then color-coordinated the walls and drapes. It is lovely. The bartender has been with the Moores for many years. He is a great asset. The food is glorious. Smoked salmon or oysters on the half-shell are not a bad way to start dinner. The pastas are excellent, and I had the black Angus shell steak with shallot mashed potatoes and frizzled leeks. And on my last visit, I had a two-pound baked lobster. Desserts—I do not know where I found the room, but I was glad I did. Go and enjoy.

I think you can tell that I like it here.

Wicker furniture on the porch and afternoon tea served on weekends in the summer—lovely.

**HOW TO GET THERE:** Go north from the Merritt Parkway (Route 15) to Route 7. The inn is on the Green in Salisbury, at the intersection of Routes 44 and 41.

# Simsbury 1820 House
## Simsbury, Connecticut 06070

**INNKEEPER:** Wayne Bursey; Richard Stoppez, general manager

**ADDRESS/TELEPHONE:** 731 Hopmeadow Street; (860) 658–7658 or (800) 879–1820; fax (860) 651–0724

**ROOMS:** 30, plus 3 suites, in 2 buildings; all with private bath, phone, and TV, 2 with wheelchair accessibility.

**RATES:** $135 to $195, double occupancy, continental breakfast.

**OPEN:** All year.

**FACILITIES AND ACTIVITIES:** Dinner, lounge. Nearby: shopping, antiquing.

**BUSINESS TRAVEL:** Located 25 minutes from Hartford. All rooms with phone; conference rooms; fax, computer, and overhead projector available; corporate rates.

uilt in 1820, Simsbury House recently stood vacant for twenty-four years; vandals, time, and weather took their toll. But today, after a lot of hard work, frustration, and expense, it has been beautifully transformed into a fine inn and restaurant.

Relatives of the former owners provided old photographs of the house that were a good reference as it was restored. Two local craftswomen made leaded-glass windows to match the originals. The oak parquet flooring in the inn is the original. The furniture consists of antiques and fine handmade reproductions from England. For example, the four-poster mahogany beds were carved by English cabinetmakers, and they are beauties. Most of them are king-sized and oh, so comfortable.

Twelve hundred rolls of wallpaper and 5,000 yards of fabric were used in restoring the inn and carriage house. The color schemes—blue, green, rose, and burgundy—recur among the rooms. The suites in the carriage house are sumptuous. One has a whirlpool tub. This is the life! All the rooms are different, and each one has an outside terrace.

The inn has a sprinkler system throughout, as well as smoke detectors. There are two rooms for the handicapped.

The dining room, divided into three sections, has an emerald green cotton print, a matching colored linen, and an English wool plaid on the walls. It is a wonderful place to savor the food prepared by the chef, a graduate of the

Culinary Institute of America. Breakfast and dinner are quite an undertaking, but he does it all so well. The menus are grand, with something for everyone. The chef insists on the freshest ingredients and emphasizes light sauces for his seasonal menus of game, seafood, lamb, and veal.

I had an interesting grilled chicken breast salad with a lemon garlic dressing for lunch one day. The soups are unique—pear and scallops bisque was one. (Menus do change, however.)

One dinner appetizer was Maine lobster and grilled black bean crepe. There are good pastas, and entrees like grilled veal loin, salmon, beef, and duck. Desserts include white-chocolate-chunk cheesecake and homemade ice cream. Yum.

**HOW TO GET THERE:** From I–84 take exit 39 onto Route 10 and go to Simsbury. The inn is on the left.

## Skating with the Stars in Simsbury

Not far from the inn, on Simsbury's main Route 10, also known as Hopmeadow Street, the International Ice Skating Center of Connecticut (860-651-4500) draws crowds of skaters and spectators who would like to share the ice with or simply watch in awe such champion figure skaters as Ekaterina Gordeeva, Viktor Petrenko, Oksana Baiul, and Scott Davis. This world-class twin-rink facility is their home base. Visitors can skate, take lessons, and see both figure skating and hockey events and practices. A cafe, a restaurant, and coffeeshop are all here. It's open year-round from 6:00 A.M. to midnight; call for public skating sessions. Rent some skates and have fun.

# The Mayflower Inn
## Washington, Connecticut 06793

**INNKEEPERS:** John Trevenen; Adriana and Robert Mnuchin, owners

**ADDRESS/TELEPHONE:** 118 Woodbury Road (mailing address: P.O. Box 1288); (860) 868–9466; fax (860) 868–1497

**ROOMS:** 18, plus 7 suites; all with private bath, some with balcony, some with fireplace.

**RATES:** $260 to $420, double occupancy; $460 to $670, suites; EP.

**OPEN:** All year.

**FACILITIES AND ACTIVITIES:** Breakfast, lunch, dinner. Bar and lounge, gift shop, spa, heated pool, tennis.

**BUSINESS TRAVEL:** Phones in rooms, conference area. The teahouse is fully equipped for meetings or conferences.

The Mayflower Inn is glorious. The entrance hall is huge and well appointed with antiques, Persian rugs, and many works of art. Much of it has been collected by the Mnuchins over the years during their travels. There is a cherry-paneled library off this, and the other side has a large gameroom full of beautiful things.

The Shop at Mayflower has unusual vintage jewelry, cashmere gloves, sweaters, and silks; it is just grand.

There are rooms in three buildings: the Mayflower, the Standish, and the Speedwell. Facilities are sumptuous, with feather beds and down comforters and pillows. Frette linens grace the beds, which are either queens, kings, or a pair of twins. Some rooms have a balcony, and others have a fireplace. There is also nightly turndown service.

You can dine in one of three dining rooms or, if the weather is nice, outside on the dining terrace that overlooks the grounds and woods. The English pub–style lounge, which has a piano, leads out to the porch, where in summer there is wicker furniture. It is called the "drinking porch."

The teahouse is an executive retreat and a wonderful place for conferences. The spa, with a very strong emphasis on massage, is a plus—I had a massage, and Louise was wonderful. There are special classes down here, too; yoga is one.

Dining here is grand. I had a nice thick veal chop and salad. The inn has special Mayflower mashed potatoes, and boy, are they good! The menu changes not only seasonally but frequently. Foods from the local farms are used. There is not enough room to elaborate on breakfast, or the luncheon specials, or even dinner. But wow, save room for the desserts!

Everyone who works here has a smile, and all are more than willing to make your stay a pleasant one.

Orchids are everywhere, the *New York Times* is brought to your door, and a minibar is in your room. One night was not enough for this inn creeper, so I stayed for two.

**HOW TO GET THERE:** From Hartford, take I-84 west to exit 15, Southbury. Follow Route 6 north through Southbury to Woodbury. It is exactly 5 miles from I-84 to "Canfield Corners" (an 1890s building on your right). Go left here on Route 47 to Washington. It is 8²/₁₀ miles to the inn.

# Water's Edge Inn 📱
## Westbrook, Connecticut 06498

**INNKEEPER:** Sam Arnett, general manager

**ADDRESS/TELEPHONE:** 1535 Boston Post Road; (860) 399-5901 or (800) 222-5901 (outside Connecticut)

**ROOMS:** 22 rooms, 13 suites; all with private bath, cable TV, and phone.

**RATES:** $135 to $275, double occupancy, EP.

**OPEN:** All year.

**FACILITIES AND ACTIVITIES:** Breakfast, lunch, dinner, Sunday brunch. Bar, lounge, room service, entertainment on holidays and special occasions, spa, indoor and outdoor pools, banquet rooms, tennis, private beach on Long Island Sound.

**BUSINESS TRAVEL:** Located 30 minutes from New Haven. All rooms with phone, six conference areas.

*T*here is a song that says, "This one's for me." Well, here it is, and what a gem! Sitting up high, overlooking Long Island Sound, the inn is like a turn-of-the-century resort. With its own sparkling private beach, it offers swimming, plus boating on the inn's fleet of catamarans, sailfish, and paddleboats.

The dining room is decorated in soft shades of peach, rose, and gray. The food is magnificent. The seafood and lobster bisque with crab is excellent. There is a choice of several salads. I had the scrod entree one night and duckling another. Both were very good. I love the way the food is arranged so prettily on the plates.

Sunday brunch is a delight. It is so popular that reservations are a must. Chefs make Belgian waffles to order, as well as omelets with almost anything inside. Roast beef, roast turkey, fish, fruit, and vegetables are also offered. The pastries will really finish you. I know they did my friend Arneta and me. Wow, are they good!

There's an outdoor patio for cocktails and dining in summer, called Le Grille. It is just fabulous, with its view of the Sound. The lounge is warm in feeling and has a nice fireplace, besides. The bar sports comfortable chairs and has the style of a pub.

The rooms and suites are sumptuous. Most of them have a king- or a queen-sized bed. All have comfortable chairs and views of something pretty. Some have a balcony, and there is a wet bar in the suites.

The health club has platform tennis, day and night tennis courts, indoor and outdoor swimming, and sauna. There are banquet and conference rooms for ten to 200 persons. The inn's grounds are very nice for a walk. And there is much to do in this lovely area—marinas, state parks, the lovely town of Essex nearby, and much more.

HOW TO GET THERE: From I–95 take exit 65 at Westbrook. Go south to Route 1, then go east approximately ¼ mile and look for the inn's sign.

# Select List of
# Other Connecticut Inns

## Bishopsgate Inn

7 Norwich Road
P.O. Box 290
East Haddam, CT 06423
(860) 873-1677

*5 rooms, 1 suite with sauna, all rooms with private bath, 4 with fireplace;*
*1818 Colonial within walking distance of Goodspeed Opera House and*
*Connecticut River.*

## Wake Robin Inn

104-106, Sharon Road (Route 41)
Lakeville, CT 06039
(860) 435-2515
Fax (860) 435-2000
Web site: www.wakerobininn.com

*38 rooms in 1896 main inn, all with private bath; 15 rooms in motel.*

## Whaler's Inn

20 East Main Street
Mystic, CT 06355
(860) 536-1506 or (800) 243-2588

*41 rooms, all with private bath; historic inn near Mystic River; children*
*stay free.*

## Randall's Ordinary

Route 2
P.O. Box 243
North Stonington, CT 06359
(860) 599-4540 or (877) 599-4540 (toll free)

*3 rooms in 300-year-old Colonial house, 9 in renovated 1819 barn; suite in silo*
*has fireplace and a winding staircase up to a Jacuzzi. Gourmet open-hearth*
*cooking in restaurant.*

## Three Chimneys Inn

1201 Chapel Street
New Haven, CT 06511
(203) 789-1201 or (800) 443-1554
Fax (203) 776-7363

*10 rooms, all with private bath, 3 with nonfunctional fireplaces; all with air conditioning, TV, phone, dataport for computer; on-site parking; within walking distance of Yale University.*

## The Elms Inn

500 Main Street
Ridgefield, CT 06877
(203) 438-2541 (phone and fax)

*20 rooms, all with private bath, TV, phone; 1760 Colonial on a site of the Battle of Ridgefield in the Revolutionary War.*

## The Inn at Longshore

260 Compo Road South
Westport, CT 06880
(203) 226-3316

*12 rooms, including 3 suites, all with private bath; 1890s seaside inn with extensive outdoor sports facilities and views of Long Island Sound.*

## The Inn at National Hall

2 Post Road West
Westport, CT 06880
(203) 221-1351 or (800) 628-4255
Fax (203) 221-0276

*15 rooms, including 7 suites, all with private bath; 1873 National Historic Register Italianate building overlooking Saugatuck River.*

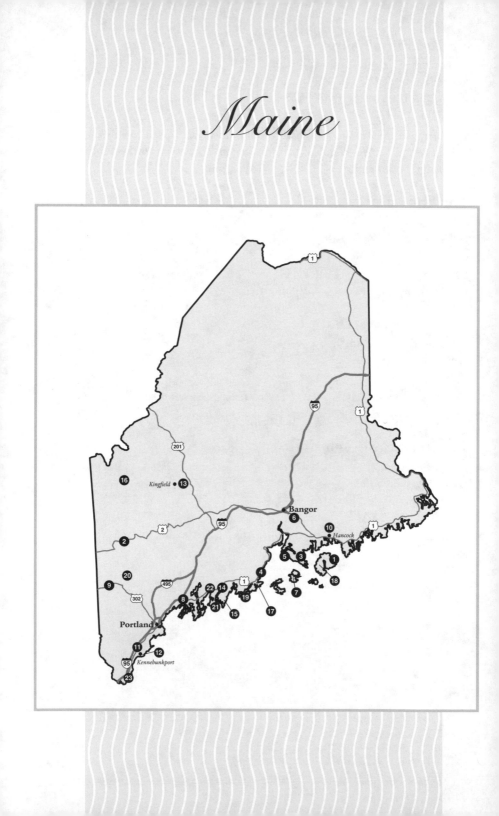

# Maine

*Numbers on map refer to towns numbered below.*

*\* A Top Pick Inn*

# Bar Harbor Hotel–Bluenose Inn
## Bar Harbor, Maine 04609

**INNKEEPERS:** Edward and Judy Hemmingsen

**ADDRESS/TELEPHONE:** 90 Eden Street; (207) 288–3348 or
(800) 445–4077

**WEB SITE:** www.acadia.net/Bluenose

**ROOMS:** 97, all with private bath, 41 with gas fireplace, phone, cable TV,
air conditioning, minifridge

**RATES:** $158 to $288, double occupancy, EP, lower off-season, great
packages.

**OPEN:** May 15 to October 18.

**FACILITIES AND ACTIVITIES:** Breakfast and dinner, bar, lounge, indoor
and outdoor heated pools, fitness center, spa. Nearby: boating, parks,
and beauty.

Why it's taken me so long to get back to Bar Harbor I may never
know, but I'm here now and the place is breathtaking. This inn is
large but made very comfortable by the owners and their staff.

The Mizzentop, built in 1995, has the registration office, a great room
and bar, a function room, fifty-two of the guest rooms, and Raspbeary's gift
shop. A lot of bears and bun-
nies, all handmade, live here.
Judy gave me a small bear to
put in my car. I forgot mine at
home.

Sienna Nordica, another
building, has forty-five rooms,
a glass front elevator and much
comfort. All the rooms have
views of Frenchman Bay.

The third building has the
heated indoor pool, and it's a
beauty, with classic columns and arched windows; the spa and fitness center
are also here. The Rose Garden restaurant is also out here, and it's lovely—

AAA-rated and good food. For starters there are Maine lobster bisque, crab cakes with roasted red pepper coulis and herb oil, shrimp cocktail, grilled ratatouille—these should give you an idea or two. The salads are grand, and entrees may be whole Maine lobster (of course), grilled salmon fillet, or steamed clams, shrimp, scallops, and mussels served over a bed of angel hair pasta with a julienne of vegetables. There's also rack of lamb, veal, beef, and more. Desserts? Well, come on up and see.

The bar's a beauty of handcrafted cherry wood; the great room has a huge wood fireplace. There are fresh flowers everywhere and good couches and comfortable chairs. There are glorious chandeliers everywhere you look.

The property, all of it, has Mobil's four stars. No wonder—it's grand. There are thirty-nine suites, and I was in one on the fourth floor that had a fireplace, two televisions (one for the sitting area, one for the bed area), and a porch overlooking the bay. The standard rooms are beauties, and the suites are fabulous.

Acadia National Park is two minutes away and the dock for the *Bluenose* ferry to and from Nova Scotia is 600 yards away. There's also a high-speed ferry that gets to Nova Scotia in 2½ hours on the *Cat*. I myself prefer the *Bluenose*.

There's also the *Bay Lady*, an 85-foot schooner. Listen to the wind in the rigging while you sail Frenchman Bay. Watch for whales and puffins. I love these birds; I'm doing a needlepoint of some.

This inn is perfect for conferences, weddings, bridal showers, and much more. Dinner meetings in the Rose Garden can seat as many as fifty guests. Can you tell I like it up here?

HOW TO GET THERE: Northbound travelers follow I-95 over the bridge into Maine and continue on I-95 to Exit 45A. Take this exit and follow Route 395 East to Route 1A to Ellsworth. Go straight on Route 3 to Bar Harbor. Pass the *Bluenose* Ferry Terminal. The Bar Harbor Hotel–Bluenose Inn is 600 yards beyond the ferry terminal on the right, across from the College of the Atlantic.

Southbound travelers take I-95 to Exit 45A and follow northbound directions. The Hotel sits high on an elevated site overlooking Frenchman Bay.

# Inn at Canoe Point
## Bar Harbor, Maine 04609

**INNKEEPERS:** Tom and Nancy Cervelli

**ADDRESS/TELEPHONE:** Eden Street, Route 3, Box 216; (207) 288–9511; fax (207) 288–2870

**E-MAIL:** canoe.point@juno.com

**WEB SITE:** www.innatcanoepoint.com

**ROOMS:** 5, all with private bath.

**RATES:** $80 to $245, double occupancy, EPB.

**OPEN:** All year.

**FACILITIES AND ACTIVITIES:** Breakfast is only meal served. Afternoon cheese and crackers. BYOB. Hiking, all winter sports, whale watching, swimming, boating.

When you turn off the highway at the inn's sign, you may think you're driving into the ocean. Take a left turn, however, and there is this fabulous inn right at the edge of the ocean. It was built in 1889 and has not fallen in the sea so far.

It sits on two acres tucked into a quiet cove. You can walk beneath the trees, sit on the rocks, and watch boats sail by. Or, as their brochure says, relax in front of the granite fireplace in the ocean room where you can enjoy the 180-degree view of the sea and mountains beyond. From the surrounding deck you can look out over the ocean while listening to the rolling surf. Breakfast is served on the deck during warm summer mornings.

Accommodations are grand. The Garret Suite takes up the whole third floor, overlooking the water, has a king-sized bed, and separate sitting room. The Master Suite, also overlooking the water, has a queen-sized canopy bed, nice bath, a sitting area with a gas fireplace, and French doors that lead to a shared deck. All of the other rooms have queen-sized beds and much comfort.

The view is of Frenchman Bay and the islands of Bean, Preble, and Bald Rock. Bar Harbor itself is 2 miles away, and the terminal for the ferry to Nova Scotia is 1 mile away. When I passed the entrance on my way to the inn, I was remembering many years ago taking the *Bluenose* from here. Small world department. Acadia National Park is only a quarter-mile away.

Breakfast, the only meal served here, consists of fresh breads or muffins, a fruit course, and one of their daily specialties such as eggs Benedict, blueberry pancakes, lemon French toast, quiche, or omelets. It is served in the ocean room by the fire or on the deck overlooking the sea. Wow, what a place!

HOW TO GET THERE: From Ellsworth, take Route 3 approximately 15 miles toward Bar Harbor. Just beyond the village of Hulls Cove, you'll pass the Acadia National Park entrance to your right. Continue ¼ mile on the left, you'll see the CANOE POINT sign and the drive takes you to the ocean and the Inn at Canoe Point.

# The Bethel Inn and Country Club
Bethel, Maine 04217

INNKEEPERS: Dick Rasor; Bill White, manager

ADDRESS/TELEPHONE: P.O. Box 49; (207) 824–2175 or (800) 367–8884 (in Maine) or (800) 654–0125 (United States and Canada)

E-MAIL: connorsa@nxi.com

WEB SITE: www.bethelinn.com

ROOMS: 137; all with private bath, phone, and cable TV, 56 with fireplace, 2 specially equipped for handicapped.

RATES: $70 to $189, per person, double occupancy, MAP. Package rates available.

OPEN: All year.

FACILITIES AND ACTIVITIES: Lunch, bar, lounge. Golf, tennis, swimming pool, lake house with sailfish and canoes, cross-country skiing, saunas, exercise room, indoor games, supervised activities for children. Own walking-tour guide. Wheelchair access to lobby, conference center, dining room. Nearby: downhill skiing.

The Bethel Inn faces the village common of Bethel, Maine, which is a National Historic District complete with beautifully restored churches, public buildings, and private homes. The rear of the inn overlooks its own 200 acres and eighteen-hole championship golf course.

Guest rooms have private baths and direct-dial telephones. They are well done and very comfortable. A number of rooms have been redecorated with country-print wallpaper, thick carpeting, and fresh paint. The Bingham Suite has a fireplace and a Jacuzzi. I stayed in here last time I was at the inn, and it's glorious.

The huge living room, music room, and library are beautifully furnished for the utter comfort of the guests. The piano, by the way, is a Steinway.

Dining is a pleasure, either in the charming main dining room or on the year-round dining veranda overlooking the golf course. You'll find such entrees as prime rib, roast duck, and lobster and crabmeat casserole on the extensive menu. Just before sunset, look out over the golf course. You'll see literally hundreds of swallows diving into the chimney of the utility building next to the course.

Downstairs is the Mill Brook Tavern. Jim Stoner, a jazz pianist, plays the piano here, on weekends, year-round. Mill Brook cuts through the golf course and was the site of Twitchell's mill, erected in the early 1700s in Sudbury, Canada, which is now Bethel, Maine.

Down here in the bar and lounge is a light supper menu that is nice for the late hiker or skier. In the winter you can have hot cider, hot buttered rum, and glögg. Lunch is nice in the screened-in terrace lounge, but the drinks are

even better. They're called the Kool Krazy Bouncy and Hot drinks. I managed to taste three of them—oh boy!

The lake house, 3 miles away on Lake Songo, features clambakes and barbecues and all water sports.

Skiing is super up here, with Sunday River (I love that name) and Mount Abram right at hand. The inn has special ski packages. Do check them. And as a special special, the inn has more than 25 miles of groomed cross-country trails for your pleasure.

The new recreation center has a heated swimming pool for use all year, saunas, exercise room, lounge, and gameroom. You'll never be at a loss for something to do at The Bethel Inn.

Afternoon teas, punch parties, and lobster bakes are nice to find at an inn.

HOW TO GET THERE: Bethel is located at the intersection of U.S. Route 2 and Maine Routes 5 and 26. From the south take exit 11 off the Maine Turnpike at Gray and follow Route 26 to Bethel. The inn is on the town green.

## *Yankee Ingenuity*

Take a ride on the railroad starting from Bethel's own train station, downtown on Route 26. The St. Lawrence and Atlantic Railroad, which connects Maine to Canada, has offered a one-day excursion ride from morning until evening on the *Yankee Ingenuity*, a 1950s restored dining car. Sit at tables and chairs and look through the etched-glass windows at the scenery outside. See views of the Mahoosuc Mountains, Mount Washington, the flood plains, the ponds, and the paper mills. The trip costs $49 per person and includes a boxed lunch. Call the Massachusetts Bay Railroad Enthusiasts Information Line (617–489–5277) for more details on this and other train excursions.

# The Sudbury Inn
## Bethel, Maine 04217

**INNKEEPERS:** Don Paddock, general manager; Cheri and David (Fuzzy)
Thurston, owners

**ADDRESS/TELEPHONE:** Main Street (mailing address: P.O. Box 369);
(207) 824-2174 or (800) 395-7837; fax (207) 824-2329

**ROOMS:** 16, plus 5 suites in 2 buildings; all with private bath.

**RATES:** $70 to $110, double occupancy, EPB.

**OPEN:** All year.

**FACILITIES AND ACTIVITIES:** Dinner, bar, lounge. Nearby: skiing, ice
skating, canoeing, tennis, golf, hiking.

his inn is located in the very pretty village of Bethel in the mountains of western Maine. The town is home to Gould Academy, one
of Maine's foremost prep schools, which was founded in 1836.
Near the inn are miles of maintained cross-country ski trails, downhill skiing, ice skating, canoeing (flat and white-water), tennis, golfing, and hiking
the Appalachian Trail. The inn provides easy access to the White Mountain
National Forest. The fall foliage around this area is breathtakingly beautiful.

The front of the inn was built in 1873, and the rear was added in the early
1900s. The Thurstons have completely refurbished and renovated the whole
structure.

The main dining room has a huge fireplace and tons of comfort, serving
such appetizers as chilled
garlic shrimp and fettucine
with fresh mussels. Do try
the Crab Gratinée. It is
Maine crabmeat with a
mixture of cream cheese,
garlic, scallions, and herbs,
served piping hot. Wow!

Several soups and sal-
ads, sandwiches and pizza
are offered, and then on to
the main course. Herbed
salmon in pastry, vegetable stir-fry, roast rack of lamb, chateaubriand prepared tableside with a bouquet of fresh vegetables. Oh my, it was nice with a

good red wine! There are several more entrees, all divine. Homemade desserts may be Bavarian apple torte or warmed chocolate walnut pie, followed by espressos and cappuccinos and other after-dinner favorites.

How can I think of breakfast? Well, there's eggs Benedict, not bad for a start to the day. There is also a Bad Boy Breakfast—a loaded omelet with homemade salsa—and, of course, there's more. And I wonder how I gain weight on these trips!

Subs Pub, on the lower level, was created when the old granite-walled basement was dug out and expanded. A lighter menu is served down here, along with six draft beers and more than thirty bottled ones.

The accommodations are clean, neat, and very comfortable. Be sure to take the time to sit in the rockers on the front porch to watch the world go by.

**HOW TO GET THERE:** Take exit 11 off the Maine Turnpike and follow Route 26 to Bethel. The inn is on lower Main Street.

# Blue Hill Inn
## Blue Hill, Maine 04614

**INNKEEPERS:** Don and Mary Hartley

**ADDRESS/TELEPHONE:** Route 177; (207) 374–2844 or (800) 826–7415

**E-MAIL:** bluhilin@downeast.net

**WEB SITE:** www.bluehillinn.com

**ROOMS:** 11; all with private bath, 3 with fireplace, 1 specially equipped for handicapped. No smoking inn.

**RATES:** In-season, $160 to $260, double occupancy, MAP. Special package available. Lower rates in off-season.

**OPEN:** Mid-May through October 31; weekends and Thanksgiving in November.

**FACILITIES AND ACTIVITIES:** Dinner Wednesday through Sunday; breakfast and hors d'oeuvres daily. Wheelchair access to dining room, parlor. Full license. Nearby: cross-country skiing, swimming, boating, concerts.

**RECOMMENDED COUNTRY INNS® TRAVELERS' CLUB BENEFIT:** 10 percent discount, subject to availability. Complimentary bottle of champagne to those celebrating a honeymoon or anniversary.

*B*lue Hill Inn is another no smoking inn. This is really nice. The inn was built in 1830 as the home of Varnum Stevens and has been an inn since 1840. It is located just up the hill from the head of the bay. There are tall beautiful elms all around the property. The garden area is lovely, and during the summer cocktails are so pleasant out here.

There are two common rooms to relax in. You can feel free to curl up in a chair and read—the fireplaces are so nice up here on a cold night. A variety of accommodations is available. All the rooms are comfortable, and all have their own private bath. You'll find some queen- and king-sized beds and some fireplaces in the rooms. The furnishings are nineteenth-century antiques. The inn's facilities are not well suited to children under thirteen.

The inn has a special package available only in June: two nights and meals at the inn and a day of sailing, meals, and overnight on a Pinky schooner. Wow!

There is a 1850 pump melodeon in the inn for you to play. The horse-drawn sleigh rides in this beautiful area are just grand.

Every evening before dinner, guests are invited to the innkeepers' reception, where hors d'oeuvres are served and cocktails are available. The inn guests enjoy meeting one another and making new friends.

Dinner is a five-course affair served by candlelight. (Look for the twenty-candle chandelier.) The first course might be lobster bisque or squash-orange soup or warm quail and wheatberries. The entree could be fresh Maine salmon with honey and fennel, swordfish in citrus marinade, or noisettes of lamb with balsamic vinegar. Fresh fish is special here. All this is followed by a grand dessert—poached pears dipped in chocolate, frozen white-chocolate mousse, white-chocolate gateau with raspberry, among others—and a cup of hot coffee

or tea. The inn has a fine wine list to accompany your meal.

And in the morning your breakfast is a hearty and filling one, with freshly squeezed orange juice, omelets, Maine blueberry pancakes, and more.

There's a new suite with a kitchen, king-sized bedroom and bath, living room with a raised hearth fireplace, cable TV, phone, air conditioning and heat, and a private deck. Make sure you see the tree out here.

**HOW TO GET THERE:** From Belfast follow Route 3 East through Searsport to Bucksport. Bear right after crossing the Bucksport Bridge. After a few miles, turn right onto Route 15 South to Blue Hill. Turn right on Main Street, then bear right again onto Route 177 West. The inn is the first building on your left at the top of the hill.

# The Belmont
## Camden, Maine 04843

**INNKEEPERS:** Gerald Clare and John Mancarella

**ADDRESS/TELEPHONE:** 6 Belmont Avenue; (207) 236–8053 or (800) 238–8053; fax (207) 236–9061

**E-MAIL:** foodeez@midcoast.com

**WEB SITE:** www.midcoast.com/~foodeez/

**ROOMS:** 6; all with private bath.

**RATES:** $260 to $360, double occupancy, EPB. MAP rates are available. Two-night minimum.

**OPEN:** May 1 to December 1.

**FACILITIES AND ACTIVITIES:** Just a 3-minute walk to the downtown and harbor. Dinner mid-May to December 1.

The Belmont is located on a quiet side street in Camden, a busy and beautiful Maine town. It's just a short stroll to the harbor, which is full of sailboats and yummy yachts to drool over.

The inn is well known for its glorious food. There's always a soup of

the day. Get this one—Mexican Hat Dance—pan-sizzled sea scallops, black bean cake, flour tortilla, and Scotch bonnet cream. A nice pâté sampler has pâté des fine herbes and duck liver pâté with apricot. There are two salad choices, followed by such entrees as seafood stew of the day, farm-raised Atlantic salmon, beef Belmont, roast free-range chicken, Wienerschnitzel, and those wonderful garlicky mashed potatoes. Just enough choices to satisfy everyone.

The dining room, with its white napery and good chairs, provides a lovely setting for this superb food. The parlor is restful, with an Oriental rug, reading tables and chairs, and a fireplace. To the right is a neat bar with a fireplace; this leads to the porch, which has wicker furniture.

The accommodations are an elegant mix of traditional and new. One room is all by itself on the third floor.

The innkeepers will tell you how best to explore midcoast Maine, where to go hiking or to find the best water sports, and where to find theater and antiques shops. Their recommendations are right on the mark.

Chester is the orange inn cat.

**HOW TO GET THERE:** The inn is 2 blocks east of Route 1. Turn right at the first busy intersection and go straight. It's on the left on Belmont.

# Blue Harbor House
## Camden, Maine 04843

**INNKEEPERS:** Jody Schmoll and Dennis Hayden

**ADDRESS/TELEPHONE:** 67 Elm Street; (207) 236–3196 or (800) 248–3196; fax (207) 236–6523

**E-MAIL:** balidog@midcoast.com

**ROOMS:** 10, including suites; all with private bath and phone, some with TV, some with air conditioning, suites with kitchen. No smoking inn.

**RATES:** $85 to $135, double occupancy, EPB. Special packages available.

**OPEN:** All year except March.

**FACILITIES AND ACTIVITIES:** Dinner, New Year's package. Nearby: tennis, golf, boating.

Camden, Maine, is called the jewel of the Maine coast with very good reason: It's just beautiful. Blue Harbor House is a restored 1810 New England cape. At one end of the large glass-walled living and dining room are a television, bookcases, and comfortable couches.

The guest rooms have kings, queen, doubles, or twins, some of which are canopied. You're sure to like the quilts on the beds. All the rooms have telephones, and some have their own television. In the front rooms, where there

is noise from Route 1, the innkeepers have installed a white-noise generator and added air conditioning. The carriage house suites have a private entrance, sitting room, kitchen, king-sized bed, television, and whirlpool tub.

Breakfast is a joy and just a bit different. Jody and Dennis have Apple Bakers, and a baked apple never tasted so good. It's filled with vanilla ice cream, of course. You could also start your day with fat-free stuffed French toast. Or blueberry pancakes with blueberry butter—the way to go!

Dinner offerings include lobster stew, Downeast Lobster Bake (served outside on the back patio garden), stuffed rack of lamb, lobster and steamers, tomatoes, and corn on the cob. Follow this with good chocolate chip cookies and vanilla ice cream.

It's just a short walk to the picture-perfect waterfront, with its shops and great boats. Take your car and Dennis will direct you to Route 52; it's a really beautiful drive. Or go to the top of Mount Battie and take a look at Camden Harbor from 900 feet up.

Say hello to the inn cats, Boots and Archie, for me.

HOW TO GET THERE: Coming from the south, take exit 6A from the Maine Turnpike to I-295, which joins I-95 just north of Portland. A few miles north of Freeport, take exit 22 (Coastal Route 1, Brunswick). Continue north on Route 1 through Waldoboro. Six miles past Waldoboro turn left onto Route 90 and follow it for 10 miles until it rejoins Route 1. Turn left onto Route 1 and continue for 2 miles toward Camden. Blue Harbor House is on your left as you come into town.

# Camden Harbour Inn
Camden, Maine 04843

**INNKEEPERS:** Sal Vella and Patti Babij; Julie Ralston, assistant innkeeper

**ADDRESS/TELEPHONE:** 83 Bay View Street; (207) 236–4200 or (800) 236–4266 (out of state only); fax (207) 236–7063

**E-MAIL:** 73204.1222@compuserve.com

**ROOMS:** 22; all with private bath, 8 with fireplace, 8 with balcony or deck.

**RATES:** $175 to $225, peak season (June 7 to mid-October); $95 to $125, off-season; double occupancy, EPB.

**OPEN:** All year.

**FACILITIES AND ACTIVITIES:** Dinner served daily May to October, rest of year extended weekends.  Wheelchair access to dining room. Bar, TV in lounge. Meetings, conferences, and special events. Nearby: golf, skiing, sailing, hiking.

Camden Harbour is one of the best-known ports in Maine, and it's one of the prettiest, too. In the late nineteenth century, when Camden was bustling with cargo and fishing schooners, the inn was built to accommodate passengers who traveled from Boston to Bangor by steamship. Today, boats of yesteryear, both sail and power, as well as modern-day beautiful yachts, moor here by the rolling mountains that come right down to the rocky shores. The inn sits up high above all this and provides a panoramic view all around. The porch is terrific, and guests enjoy it from early morning coffee to evening nightcaps.

All the guest rooms are different in character. They are furnished with period antiques, Victorian pieces, and wicker. Many overlook the harbor and bay and have outside decks. Another is a suite with a foyer, a wet bar, a sitting room adjacent to a large deck, and a comfortably furnished bedroom with a working fireplace. One room has a large sitting area and a brick patio that overlooks the outer harbor. Other rooms have a fireplace, and some have a private outside entrance with reserved parking. The inn is equipped with sprinklers and heat and smoke detectors.

If dinner with a view is to your liking, the full-service restaurant probably has a table for you. The inn's logo is the tail of a whale, and the restaurant's name is Cetacea, which in Latin means "a family of whales." The menu is simple, yet done with a nice flair. Appetizers range from chowder to fresh

## Mount Battie and the Camden Hills State Park

A 25-mile hiking trail system and a 1⁶/10-mile auto road in Camden's Mount Battie State Park (207–236–3109) have helped to open this beautiful area to the thousands of visitors who come here yearly to see the glorious views of Penobscot Bay. A stone mountain tower at the peak marks the location of the former Summit House, built as a hotel in 1887 by Camden resident Columbus Bushwell. Such notables as Theodore Roosevelt and poet Edna St. Vincent Millay climbed to the top of the mountain on an old carriage road that is now a part of the trail system. Visitors today can hike that same footpath year-round or drive up on the auto road from May 1 through November 1. Hikers agree that the view is worth every step.

In addition to Mount Battie, the 6,500-acre park includes Mount Megunticook. The highest point on the Camden Hills as well as one of the highest elevations on the whole Eastern Seaboard, Megunticook is also a popular destination for hikers and picnickers. A small admission fee is charged at the park entrance on Route 1.

Maine crabcakes and good salads. Entrees inlude fresh Maine salmon, sauté of Maine lobster meat, prime rib, duck, loin of pork, and, of course, steamed lobster. A new one on me is old-fashioned salmon pie. And don't forget to save room for the pastry chef's sinful creations.

There are walking tours, bicycle trips, and nature walks in and around Camden. There is hardly a spot in this whole lovely Maine town that is not worth a visit.

This is a wonderful town to muddle about in for days. I was here for two wonderful days and I had such a nice time—wonderful innkeepers and help.

**HOW TO GET THERE:** From Route 1, which runs through the center of town, turn up Bay View Street to number 83.

---

# The Castine Inn
## Castine, Maine 04421

**INNKEEPERS:** Tom and Amy Gutow

**ADDRESS/TELEPHONE:** P.O. Box 41; (207) 326–4365; fax (207) 326–4570

**E-MAIL:** relax@castineinn.com

**WEB SITE:** www.castineinn.com

**ROOMS:** 19; all with private bath.

**RATES:** $60 to $125, double occupancy, EPB.

**OPEN:** May 1 to mid-December.

**FACILITIES AND ACTIVITIES:** Full breakfast daily, dinner daily in season, dinner in off-season on Friday and Saturday only. Pub, sauna. Nearby: harbor.

Castine is a beautiful town, and the Inn is a lovely focal point on a hill overlooking the harbor. You can almost see the water. The porches have chairs for watching and resting. The inn was built in 1898, and guests are as warmly received now as in the past when they came by boat. Some still do.

There are a lot of gardens, and they are a pleasure to see. You enter a large front hall and a parlor with a wood-burning fireplace that is routinely lit in the evening to ward off the chill of coastal Maine. There are books and games in here.

The dining room, from which you can glimpse the water, has a hand-painted mural, done by a former innkeeper. It is of Castine and covers four walls. The food served here is very good. Some appetizers may be Penobscot Bay crab meat cake with a mustard sauce, celery root soup, or a good salad. Entrees may be haddock, salmon, loins of lamb, and chicken. Desserts, well, crème brûlée, ice cream, and more. There are good wines. Breakfast ideas? How about pancakes with blueberries, eggs, and cereals. The pub is cozy.

Guest rooms are cheerful; many have harbor views. The nice wide halls have a full sprinkler system.

Castine itself is just beautiful. The Maine Maritime Academy is the town's only "industry." The International Guild of Miniatures Artisans is also located here. The harbor is dotted with sailing ships, yachts, and windjammers. Penobscot Bay is lovely.

**HOW TO GET THERE:** Take I–95 to Augusta and Route 3 east to the coast. Connect with Route 1 at Belfast, and follow Route 1 north to Bucksport. In 2 miles turn right onto Route 175. Follow it to Route 166, which takes you into Castine.

# The Pentagöet Inn
## Castine, Maine 04421

**INNKEEPERS:** Virginia and Lindsey Miller

**ADDRESS/TELEPHONE:** P.O. Box 4; (207) 326–8616 or (800) 845–1701; fax (207) 326–9382

**WEB SITE:** Pentagoet@Hypernet.com

**ROOMS:** 15, plus 1 suite; all with private bath, suite with fireplace. No smoking inn.

**RATES:** $100 to $130, double occupancy, EPB.

**OPEN:** Mid-May through mid-October.

**FACILITIES AND ACTIVITIES:** Breakfast only meal served. Full-service bar, afternoon tea, and high tea. Nearby: fishing, sailing, golf.

The Pentagöet is a lovely inn located on the unspoiled coast of beautiful Penobscot Bay. Built in 1894, this Victorian inn offers the traveler warmth and a very friendly atmosphere.

Part of the inn is Ten Perkins Street, the building next door, which is more than 200 years old. The suite is here. I stayed in it, and it's a gem. It has a working fireplace, and wood is supplied so that you can light yourself a fire some cold evening.

All the rest of the rooms in both buildings are lovely, too. Some have little alcoves with views of the town and harbor. Some are small and have odd shapes, but this goes well with a country inn. Seven rooms have a queen-sized bed.

There is a library to the right as you come in the door of the main inn. Lots of books, a piano, stereo music, and very restful couches give this room the perfect atmosphere. The sitting room, to the left, has a wood-burning stove and a beautiful picture window. The wraparound porch is a delight. Good food is served in the dining room. Breakfast when I was here included Maine strawberries, which arrived early in the morning, freshly picked at a local farm. Homemade granola, sourdough blueberry pancakes, homemade jellies, red flannel hash, breakfast steaks, eggs Pentagöet, and lots more add up to a good breakfast. All baking is done right here. The inn has piped-in chamber music that's very soothing.

The Maine Maritime Academy is located here, and its training ship, *State of Maine*, is docked at the town wharf. The local professional theater group, Cold Comfort Productions, performs four nights a week.

The innkeepers and Gus, the inn cat, will really make your stay here a pleasant one. There is also Tara, a very nice German shepherd.

**HOW TO GET THERE:** Take I–95 to Augusta; take Route 3 East to coast. Connect with Route 1 at Belfast, and follow Route 1 north to Bucksport. Two miles beyond turn right onto Route 175. Take Route 175 to Route 166, which takes you into Castine.

# The Lucerne Inn
## Dedham, Maine 04429

**INNKEEPERS:** Mya-Lisa King; Bion Foster and Arthur Howard, owners

**ADDRESS/TELEPHONE:** Route 1A; (207) 843–5123 or (800) 325–5123; fax (207) 843–6138

**ROOMS:** 21, plus 4 suites; all with private bath, phone, TV, fireplace, and whirlpool tub.

**RATES:** $109 to $139, high-season; $59 to $99, off-season; double occupancy, continental breakfast. Call for midseason rates and packages including brunch.

**OPEN:** All year.

**FACILITIES AND ACTIVITIES:** Sunday brunch, dinner, full license, bar. Meeting room for up to 90 people, pool, golf.

The regal mountains around The Lucerne Inn make such a beautiful picture that you feel as if you're in Switzerland. The views at sunset are outstanding. Sitting on ten acres overlooking Phillips Lake, the inn started as a farmhouse and stable. It became an inn in 1814.

The location is grand. It's just forty-five minutes from Acadia National Park and Bar Harbor, ninety minutes from Camden, and twenty minutes from Ellsworth and Bangor, where you'll find theaters and shopping.

But why leave? Besides the lake, the inn also has an outdoor swimming pool, and a golf course is right here.

This is quite an inn. There are still reminders of its long history in the guest and common rooms, in the form of "distinguished" antiques. The rooms have everything you could want—fireplaces, telephones, televisions, private baths, heated towel bars, whirlpool tubs, wonderful views, comfortable beds, and nice furniture.

The dining room has a pleasant view of the lake to accompany the delightful food. A few of the appetizers are crab-stuffed mushrooms with lobster sauce, smoked seafood sampler, baked onion soup, and a soup du jour. One of the entrees that's a real beauty is vegetable primavera—assorted vegetables simmered in cream and tossed with pasta. Lobster is prepared in a few different ways, salmon comes broiled, and the rack of lamb is stunning.

Dessert anyone? Come on up to see what they have.

**HOW TO GET THERE:** The inn is on Route 1A between Bangor and Ellsworth. Take I–95 to exit 45A, just south of Bangor. Take I–395 to Route 1A East. In about 10 minutes you will see the inn on your right.

# The Pilgrim's Inn
Deer Isle, Maine 04627

**INNKEEPERS:** Jean and Dud Hendrick

**ADDRESS/TELEPHONE:** Main Street; (207) 348-6615; fax (207) 348-7769

**ROOMS:** 13, plus 1 cottage; 9 with private bath.

**RATES:** $175, private bath; $150 to $215, shared bath; double occupancy, MAP. Ginny's House $205 MAP, $135 EP, double occupancy

**OPEN:** Mid-May through mid-October.

**FACILITIES AND ACTIVITIES:** Bar, lounge. Wheelchair access to dining room. Nearby: Bicycles, sailboats for charter, swimming. Golf or tennis at the island country club as their guest.

**RECOMMENDED COUNTRY INNS® TRAVELERS' CLUB BENEFIT:** 10 percent discount.

In 1793 Ignatius Haskell built this lovely house, following the specifications of his wife, who demanded the luxuries of city living on their country estate. He had his own sawmill nearby and built the house out of northern pine. Today you are welcomed to this rambling inn by the glowing hearths of its many fireplaces.

The beds are very comfortable. All the rooms are different and have a view of the pond or Northwest Harbor. The third floor has marvelous views and a great room. Actually, there are five rooms on the third floor, but one is huge.

The inn has all the right touches, such as tons of books, a huge fireplace, and soft, well-worn wood floors and walls in the common rooms and taproom. There is a small service bar; here the honor system is in effect. If it's before the 6:00 P.M. cocktail hour, you know to leave your tab on the bar.

Crisp linen and flowers are on the tables of the candlelit dining room, which once was a barn. It just glows. Dinner may be poached salmon or tenderloin of beef, done many ways. There is a different special every night of the week. Soups are interesting—billi-bi, cream of celery, and more—accompanied by a different bread each night. All the baking is done right here.

A full breakfast is served. It is a sumptuous buffet, with baskets of muffins, homemade granola, meats and cheeses, melons, and fruit. You are also offered eggs.

Isle au Haut is accessible by mail ferry from the inn—a visit there makes an excellent day trip.

Ginny's house has two very private separate units. Each one has a living room with cable TV, gas stove, kitchenette and dining area, queen-sized bedroom and bath, and a deck with a view.

HOW TO GET THERE: From Route 1 turn right after Bucksport onto Route 15, which goes directly to Deer Isle. In the village turn right on Main Street. The inn is on your left.

# Harraseeket Inn 🎗 📱

Freeport, Maine 04032

**INNKEEPERS:** Nancy and Paul Gray

**ADDRESS/TELEPHONE:** 162 Main Street; (207) 865–9377 or (800) 342–6423

**ROOMS:** 84, all with private bath, TV, phone, and wheelchair accessibility, some with Jacuzzi, fireplace, wood stove, or wet bar, 4 specially equipped for handicapped.

**RATES:** $95 to $235, double occupancy, EPB. Special packages available.

**OPEN:** All year.

**FACILITIES AND ACTIVITIES:** Lunch, high tea, dinner. Elevator, wheelchair access to dining room. Tavern, full liquor license, function rooms. No smoking in the dining room. Nearby: shopping, nature walks, fishing, boating, skiing.

**BUSINESS TRAVEL:** Conference rooms. All rooms with phone, some with modem for personal computers.

*T*he inn is named for the Harraseeket River, which runs through the town and into Casco Bay. It was built in 1850 and is Greek Revival in style. Everything about it is elegant, which is not a surprise, as its sister inn is the very elegant Inn at Mystic in Mystic, Connecticut.

Freeport has long been known for L. L. Bean and a ton of other famous outlet stores, all of which are just a short walk from the inn—oh my! If shopping is not your thing, however, nearby are Casco Bay and South Freeport Harbor, where you can rent a boat and go sailing or fishing. Nature lovers will be in heaven at the Audubon Sanctuary and Wolf Neck Woods State Park.

The rooms and suites are grand. There are canopied beds, antiques, telephones, cable television, and even modems for personal computers. Twenty-four rooms have a Jacuzzi, two have a steam bath, sixteen have a fireplace, and one has a wood stove. Whatever you're looking for, it's all here. You can even arrange a meeting or business conference at the inn, as there are function rooms that overlook the terrace.

Your day begins with a superlative breakfast buffet. Early birds can have coffee at 6:00 A.M. It's nice to find inns that serve lunch. I had crepes, and my

friend had the chicken stir-fry. The lunch menu is extensive, and you can even ask for a basket of lunch to take along if you're headed out for the afternoon. The dinner menu is even more extensive. There are appetizers, soups, salads, and lots of entrees. Like The Inn at Mystic, Harraseeket Inn offers "Tableside Classics" that are prepared and carved at your table. You can have a whole chicken, roast rack of baby lamb, chateaubriand, and various fruits of the sea. They even have two-tailed lobster, honest. The maple-syrup-braised loin of pork is just one of the feasts from the land. Desserts—well, by now you can imagine. Each one is better than the last. The chocolate fondue is an orgy. The Broad Arrow Tavern has its own lighter menu of burgers, pastas, lobster salad, sandwiches, and even a bucket of steamed clams. I could go on and on. The inn also has a grand room-service menu.

This whole inn is just splendid. The innkeepers are native to Maine, and though this is a large inn, it has not lost its charm.

There's an indoor pool kept at a toasty eighty-five degrees. In the living room, where tea is served, is a player piano, seated at which is the largest stuffed polar bear I've ever seen. There's a lovely fireplace in here, too.

If you leave the inn, you'll find so much to do. Besides going shopping, you could explore Wolf Neck Woods State Park, Mast Landing Sanctuary, or the coastline.

HOW TO GET THERE: Take I–95 north to exit 20 to Freeport. The inn is on Main Street.

# Mast Landing Sanctuary

The Maine Audubon Society maintains this 150-acre preserve with field, forest, and tidal marsh habitats. This area was once logged for its tall pines that were used to make masts for the ships of the British Navy, thus the name. The sanctuary is open year-round from dawn to dusk. Self-guided trails take visitors past old apple orchards and millstreams, through woods and meadows. A 1-mile loop trail is a nice walk for brief visits. Enjoy the picnic area if you can stay a while. No fee is charged for parking. The Sanctuary is on Upper Mast Landing Road, off Bow Street.

# The Oxford House Inn
## Fryeburg, Maine 04037

INNKEEPERS: John and Phyllis Morris

ADDRESS/TELEPHONE: Route 302; (207) 935–3442; fax (207) 935–7046

WEB SITE: www.mountwashingtonvalley.com/oxfordhouse

ROOMS: 5; all with private bath.

RATES: $75 to $125, double occupancy, EPB.

OPEN: All year.

FACILITIES AND ACTIVITIES: Dinner. Lounge with a full license. Nearby: canoeing, swimming, fishing, antiquing, hiking.

John and Phyllis have a lot of innkeeping experience and know just how to make an inn inviting and comfortable. There's one thing for sure: They have put together a marvelous brochure. It says that this is the way The Oxford House might have appeared back in 1923, looking through the windows of a spanking new Jordan motorcar.

The rooms are charming and very restful. All of them are named after the names of rooms on the original blueprints. Perhaps you'll sleep in the Sewing Room. The tub in one bathroom is the largest I've ever seen. Care for a swim?

At dinnertime you'll delight as I did in the outstanding and creative dishes offered on the menu. For example, turkey Waldorf is an entree you'll not find many places. It is medallions of turkey breast sautéed with apples and walnuts, then splashed with applejack and cream. Pork, pears, and port is another entree, done in a rich port and ginger sauce. How about veal Oxford? Very nice indeed. Three innovative steaks are also offered. House pâté of the day might be how you'd like to begin your meal. I think it's nice to find variations in pâtés. Or maybe Maine crab chowder will catch your eye. It's good and different. Needless to say, the desserts are all homemade.

On those cold Maine nights, the tavern is very inviting. It has a television, books, and a wood stove.

In warm weather the screened porch is used for dining. I really like porches, and this one is a beauty. You can sit here and look out at the beautiful surrounding mountains or the lovely gardens. Peace and quiet are at hand.

**HOW TO GET THERE:** The inn is on Route 302 in Fryeburg, 8 miles east of North Conway.

# The Domaine
## Hancock, Maine 04640

**INNKEEPER:** Nicole L. Purslow

**ADDRESS/TELEPHONE:** Box 496, Route 1; (207) 422–3395 or 422–3916; (800) 554–8498; fax (207) 422–2316

**ROOMS:** 7; all with private bath.

**RATES:** $200, double occupancy, MAP.

**OPEN:** May to end of October.

**FACILITIES AND ACTIVITIES:** Bar, lounge. Badminton, walking trails. Nearby: boating, swimming, fishing, hiking, Acadia National Park.

*H*ow nice to find an *auberge Provençale* this far up in Maine. On the first floor are the bar and lounge, and a grouping of wicker furniture is around the wood stove. Nicole has one of the wine coolers and servers that are so handy, and someday I'm going to have a small one like it in my home. The French Provincial dining room has crisp linens, gleaming copper, and fresh flowers.

Now for the best part, and that is the food. Nicole, a graduate of the Cordon Bleu school of cooking in Paris, runs one of the finest French restaurants in the East. It was started in 1946 by her mother, who died in 1976. Over the years the inn has received accolades from many publications. The most important accolade of all comes from the many returning guests.

Nicole's exquisite entrees and appetizers change with the seasons. Pâté de foie maison and *saumon fumé d'Ecosse* are just two of the appetizers. Move on to coquilles St. Jacques Provençale, veal à la crème, or steak bordelaise. There is no way I can say enough about her food. It is divine.

The full breakfast can be had in the dining room, at your own table in your room, or on the decks overlooking the pines and gardens. The inn's honey from its own hives or homemade jams go on croissants, muffins, or scones. They come with French cafe au lait or pots of tea, making you feel you are in a true European auberge. In the huge fireplace in the dining room are a rotisserie and a grill Nicole had made in France. On cool evenings she cooks here. Very nice touch!

Nicole is now shipping her own pâté ($30.00 a pound plus $7.25 second-day air shipping—it's worth every cent).

Each room has its own character. All are named for herbs. They all have a library and several have a private porch. This is a real treat.

There are many things to do in this area, including roaming about on the inn's one hundred acres, and Nicole will be glad to help you plan your day.

**HOW TO GET THERE:** The inn is about 9 miles above Ellsworth on Route 1.

# The Kennebunk Inn
Kennebunk, Maine 04043

**INNKEEPERS:** John and Kristen Martin

**ADDRESS/TELEPHONE:** 45 Main Street; (207) 985–3351

**ROOMS:** 26, plus 4 suites; all with private bath and air conditioning; some with TV and/or phone.

**RATES:** Off-season, $60 to $120; in-season, $100 to $160; double occupancy, EP. MAP is available.

**OPEN:** All year except Christmas Day.

**FACILITIES AND ACTIVITIES:** Lunch and dinner every day. Wheelchair access to dining room. Bar, lounge. Nearby: fishing, swimming, boating.

*T*he inn is located right smack on Route 1 in the heart of town, convenient to everything. Even the beaches are very close at hand. The accommodations are very nice. The beds are comfortable, and all the rooms are air-conditioned. There are telephones in some rooms, a plus for busy people. Some rooms even have a television.

The upstairs foyer is a nice place to gather. There are couches and chairs, puzzles, games, books, and a television.

The dining room is very comfortable. Appetizers may be spicy crabcakes over a Thai-style sweet and sour cucumber relish, red pepper and Gorganzola polenta with a wild mushroom ragout, or tortellini. Entrees may be crusted salmon, grilled pork loin, fresh trout, herb-roasted duck, loin of lamb, steak, or scallops. Quite a menu and good desserts.

**HOW TO GET THERE:** Take exit 3 from I–95 (the Maine Turnpike) to Kennebunk. Follow Main Street to the inn at number 45.

# The Captain Fairfield Inn
## Kennebunkport, Maine 04046

**INNKEEPERS:** Bonnie and Dennis Tallagnon

**ADDRESS/TELEPHONE:** Corner of Pleasant and Green Streets (mailing address: P.O. Box 1308); (207) 967–4454 or (800) 322–1928

**E-MAIL:** chefdennis@int-usa-net

**WEB SITE:** www.inntraveler.com/captainfairfield

**ROOMS:** 9; all with private bath, some with fireplace, some with air conditioning.

**RATES:** $89 to $225, double occupancy; EPB and afternoon refreshments, beach passes, and towels.

**OPEN:** All year.

**FACILITIES AND ACTIVITIES:** Guest refrigerator, off-street parking. Nearby: ocean, shopping, restaurants, fishing, art galleries.

These innkeepers—Bonnie and Dennis Tallagnon—once owned the Red Clover Inn in Mendon, Vermont. It's so nice to have them back in this book.

This inn—an 1813 Federal mansion—was given as a wedding present to James Fairfield and his bride from his father-in-law. They knew how to do things right in those days! Today the inn is listed on the National Register of Historic Places. The gardens are striking, and so are the towering trees. There are numerous other lovely captains' houses in the neighborhood, and you are within walking distance of town, the water, shops, and restaurants.

There's an inviting living room with a fireplace and tons of comfort. The library, an all-purpose room, has a television, VCR and movies, and books and games. The guest rooms are furnished with antiques and period furniture, including four-poster and canopy beds. All rooms have private bathrooms, and some have fireplaces. All the amenities are there—firm mattresses, down comforters, generous towels, special soaps, nightlights, and garden flowers.

Breakfast, which is the only meal served here, is generous. Dennis is the chef, and he bakes all his own breads and pastries. All sorts of crepes are offered, plus berries and yogurt and sour cream, a fresh fruit compote, pancakes, omelets, Maine blueberry pancakes, fresh-squeezed juices, and gourmet coffees and teas.

This area offers many things to do—whale watching, coastline excursions, fishing, golf, shopping, art galleries, and beautiful sandy beaches. Go and enjoy. Duncan, a lovely shelty, is the inn dog.

HOW TO GET THERE: Take exit 3 off I-95. Turn left onto Route 35 South, and follow it through Kennebunk to the intersection with Route 9. Go left onto Route 9, over the river and into Dock Square. Turn right onto Ocean Avenue. In 5 blocks go left just past the village green onto the one-way street. The inn is in 1 block on your right.

## Christmas Prelude

Kennebunkport and its neighbors are delightful places to be at Christmastime. A ten-day holiday festival called Christmas Prelude (207-967-0857) is launched in the Kennebunks on the first weekend in December. If you are not in the spirit when you arrive, you will soon be caught up in the magic. A Christmas tree in Kennebunkport's historic Dock Square is decorated with the buoys of local lobstermen, and a community caroling event is held on the first Friday evening. Shopkeepers offer holiday refreshments, Santa arrives by lobsterboat, and the restaurants prepare special Prelude menus. Sleigh rides or hayrides carry revelers through the streets, pageants and concerts are offered at a variety of locations, and twinkling lights are draped on doorways, trees, and shop windows. Before the last two weeks of the Christmas rush begin, Kennebunk reminds visitors of the true meaning of the holiday. Its Walk through Bethlehem is a candlelight procession of 500 carolers led by the Three Wise Men. Do come—it's grand.

# The Captain Jefferds Inn
Kennebunkport, Maine 04046

**INNKEEPERS:** Pat, Dick, and Jane Bartholomew

**ADDRESS/TELEPHONE:** (207) 967–2311 or (800) 839–6844; fax (207) 967–0721

**WEB SITE:** www.captainjefferdsinn.com

**ROOMS:** 12, 4 suites, all with private bath.

**RATES:** $105 to $240, double occupancy, EPB.

**OPEN:** All year except mid-December until a few days after Christmas.

**FACILITIES AND ACTIVITIES:** Full breakfast. BYOB. Nearby: boating, whale watching, and much more.

The Inn was built in 1804. There is a widows' walk on top, built so that the wife of Captain Jefferds could watch for her husband's ship to return from sea. There's a ton of history here.

This beauty has a lot going for it. The rooms are named for favorite places of the owners. The Italian suite has a king-sized bed and an indoor water garden—not many of these around. The Monticello room is in the oldest part of the inn and features Indian shutters and a working fireplace. They are all very lovely.

Breakfast is full and in fall and winter is served by candlelight in front of a warm fire, or in summer on the many terraces overlooking the gardens. Continental breakfast baskets served in-room are also available. Some of the breakfast goodies are pumpkin hazelnut soup, raspberry coffee cake, blueberry yogurt pancakes with lemon sauce, apple

crisp with vanilla ice cream, pumpkin walnut muffins, and eggs Florentine with cheddar cheese sauce.

Hot mulled cider and home-baked sweets are served in the garden room every afternoon, and upon your return from whatever, the inn's golden retriever, Kate, will greet you. There are a few inn cats, my loves.

Much to do here: fishing and sailing, whale watching, hiking, antiquing, canoeing and rafting, biking, horseback riding, beaches, museums, and cross-country skiing. Just ask, and these innkeepers have the answers.

**HOW TO GET THERE:** Take exit 3 from I–95 to Highway 35 South. Follow the signs through Kennebunk to Kennebunkport. Take a left at Route 9 and cross the bridge. Turn right at the monument in dock square to Ocean Avenue. Go 5 short blocks, then turn left on the one-way street just past the green. Take another left at the first corner; look for the inn's white fence on the left.

# Captain Lord Mansion  ♥ 📱
## Kennebunkport, Maine 04046

**INNKEEPERS:** Beverly Davis and Rick Lichfield

**ADDRESS/TELEPHONE:** Ocean Avenue (mailing address: P.O. Box 800); (207) 967–3141; fax (207) 967–3172

**WEB SITE:** www.captainlord.com

**E-MAIL:** captain@biddeford.com

**ROOMS:** 19, plus 1 suite; all with private bath and phone, 18 with working fireplace and whisper-quiet air conditioning.

**RATES:** $149 to $349, double occupancy, EPB.

**OPEN:** All year.

**FACILITIES AND ACTIVITIES:** Breakfast only full meal served. Afternoon tea. BYOB. Gift shop. Nearby: Perkins Cove and Rachel Carson Wildlife Refuge.

**BUSINESS TRAVEL:** Conference room. All rooms with phone.

*T*his is a truly grand inn. The mansion was built in 1812 and has had such good care that the front bedroom still has the wallpaper that dates from that year. Another room has wallpaper that dates back to 1880. Some of the original Lord furniture is in the house. For example, the handsome dining-room table with carved feet and chairs belonged to

Nathaniel Lord's grandson, Charles Clark, and is dated 1880. Throughout the inn are portraits of past owners in the Lord family.

A three-story suspended elliptical staircase, a hand-pulled fireplace that works, a gold vault, and double Indian shutters are but a few of the wonderful things to be found in the inn. There are fireplaces, Oriental rugs, old pine wide-board floors, and claw-footed tables. It's almost a comfortable museum and thus is not well suited to children under twelve. Rick knows the history of the house and loves to tell it.

Twenty of the guest rooms in the inn have working fireplaces. Most of the rooms have padded, deep window seats, a great place to relax and daydream. One of the beds is a four-poster 12 feet high. Rugs and wallpaper, thanks to Beverly's eye for decoration, are well coordinated, thirsty towels are abundant, and extra blankets and pillows help make your stay better than pleasant.

There's a grand suite with a huge bathroom, a double Jacuzzi, and a canopy king-sized bed. There are heated tile floors in some bathrooms. This truly is a grand inn.

Breakfast is the only meal served in the inn, but what a meal! It is served family style. Two long tables in the kitchen are set with Wedgwood blue. There are two stoves in here side by side, a new one and a coal one about a hundred years old. The breakfast bell is a hundred-year-old music box. You'll start your day with good baked food like rhubarb nut bread, French breakfast puffs, pineapple nut upside-down muffins, oat and jam muffins, or strawberry bread. The recipes are available in the lovely gift shop, so now I can bake some of these yummies at home. In addition you'll have eggs, cereal, and fruit—all this, plus an exquisite mansion, good staff, and great innkeepers.

Want more? Gourmet coffees, Swiss water decaf, chocolate cappuccino, or how about Snickerdoodle? Have fun.

This is a bring-your-own-bottle inn, and from the scenic cupola on its top to the parlors on the first floor, you will find many great places to enjoy a drink.

The inn has just received *Mobil Travel Guide*'s four stars.

HOW TO GET THERE: From I-95 take exit 3 off the Maine Turnpike to Kennebunk. Turn left on Route 35 and drive through Kennebunk to Kennebunkport. Turn left at the traffic light at the Sunoco station. Go over draw-bridge and take first right onto Ocean Avenue. Go ³/₁₀ mile and turn left at the mansion. Park behind the building and take the brick walkway to guest entrance.

# The Inn at Harbor Head
## Kennebunkport, Maine 04046

**INNKEEPERS:** Eve and Dick Roesler

**ADDRESS/TELEPHONE:** 41 Pier Road; (207) 967–5564; fax (207) 967–1294

**ROOMS:** 2, plus 2 suites, all with private bath and air conditioning.

**RATES:** $130 to $295, double occupancy, EPB.

**OPEN:** All year except last two weeks in November and last two weeks in December and the month of January.

**FACILITIES AND ACTIVITIES:** Breakfast only meal served, high tea. BYOB.

This inn is a beauty. It sits in a lush area on Cape Porpoise Harbor. There's a dock on the property. The gardens alone are worth the trip. The views of this quaint fishing village are terrific.

The breakfasts are a grand affair. Here's a sample of the menu, just to tease your palate: fresh-squeezed orange juice, herbs and scrambled eggs, sage sausage, fresh fruit, pecan French toast, bacon, wild mushroom tart, asparagus with hollandaise, honey waffles with whipped cream and raspberries, ham, mushroom strata, quiches, and crepes. There's always fruit, and it's served very differently.

Accommodations are neat. The Summer Room has a king-sized wicker bed, gas fireplace, and a deck with a view. The bathroom has a Jacuzzi. There are robes in the rooms. The Harbor Room is a suite with a king-sized canopy bed, a fireplace, couches, hand-painted walls and ceiling, and a small deck overlooking the harbor. The ocean room has a king-sized mahogany head-board, and the garden room has a queen-sized bed and a porch.

The sitting room features couches and a wing-back chair. The dining room has a table for eight. There are inn birds—love birds, of course. A library has a brass Japanese fountain and a picture window with a view, very nice indeed.

A wonderful restaurant, called Seascapes, is run by former innkeepers of the Kennebunk Inn and can be found down the street a bit from this inn. The menu is great, and so is the spot. What a grand water view, grand people, and delicious food.

**HOW TO GET THERE:** Get off the Maine Turnpike at Exit 3 (Kennebunk) and follow Route 35/9A to Kennebunkport. Take a left at the intersection of Routes 9 and 35. Cross the bridge and follow Route 9 east through Dock Square to the stop sign. Take a right on Maine Street and a left on School Street. Continue on Route 9 about 1.5 miles past a school and through some woods to the village of Cape Porpoise. Just after Bradbury's Market, leave Route 9 (don't make the sharp left) and go straight ahead, entering Pier Road. Pass the Wayfarer Restaurant, and go around the head of the cove. From there, the Inn at Harbor Head is ²⁄₁₀ mile on the right—watch for the sign. If you miss it, don't worry—the road ends in ¼ mile, and you'll find it on the way back.

# The Kennebunkport Inn
## Kennebunkport, Maine 04046

**INNKEEPERS:** Rick and Martha Griffin

**ADDRESS/TELEPHONE:** One Dock Square (mailing address: P.O. Box 111); (207) 967–2621 or (800) 248–2621

**ROOMS:** 34; all with private bath, TV, air conditioning, and phone.

**RATES:** $84.50 to $275, double occupancy, EP.

**OPEN:** All year.

**FACILITIES AND ACTIVITIES:** Breakfast and dinner served daily May through October. Bar, lounge, pool. Nearby: beaches, boating, fishing, tennis, golf, shopping.

**RECOMMENDED COUNTRY INNS® TRAVELERS' CLUB BENEFIT:** 10 percent discount, Monday–Sunday.

*T*he Kennebunkport Inn was built in the late 1890s by Burleigh S. Thompson, a wealthy coffee and tea merchant. It was magnificent then, and it still is. It was turned into an inn in 1926, various changes were made, and today it is noted for its charm, warmth, and grace.

Born to shop? Well, you are right in the heart of all the fine shops of Kennebunkport—antiques, arts and crafts, clothing, and lots more. One year I ordered some cut lampshades from one of the shops, and they arrived at my home in fine shape. The town also offers fine beaches, tennis, fishing, boating, golf, theaters, and much more. The inn has a nice swimming pool.

The inn is elegant, a true nineteenth-century mansion. The River House, built in the 1930s as an annex to the inn, is a lovely place to be, but then so are all of the rooms in the inn. Every room has a color television and lots of comfort, and the inn rooms are air-conditioned. Coming back to your room after shopping or sightseeing in busy Kennebunkport is a joy.

The piano bar—lounge is open daily in the summer and Friday and Saturday in the spring and fall. It has a neat fireplace, a friendly bartender, and a pub menu. The piano is played every night from June till the end of October.

There's a lovely terrace alongside of the inn, and lunch is served out here in the summertime. Dinner is elegantly served by candlelight in two dining rooms, on tables covered with pink and white napery. It is a meal you will truly enjoy. Ask Rick to recommend some wine to complement your dinner. He is a connoisseur of fine wines and has developed an excellent wine list. The breakfast buffet has lots of goodies—melon, cereal, muffins, and more.

Martha and Rick are very good innkeepers. They work at it, and it shows. On my last visit I met the Griffin girls, Alexis and Lydia, a pair of charmers. They are almost all grown up and soon out on their own.

HOW TO GET THERE: Take exit 3 from the Maine Turnpike. Turn left on Route 35 and go south to Kennebunkport. At the traffic light at the junction of Route 9, turn left, go over the bridge, and the inn is ahead on the left.

# Old Fort Inn
Kennebunkport, Maine 04046

INNKEEPERS: David and Sheila Aldrich

ADDRESS/TELEPHONE: P.O. Box M; (207) 967–5353 or (800) 828–3678; fax (207) 967–4547

ROOMS: 16; all with private bath, TV, phone, and wet bar, 4 with Jacuzzi, 2 with gas fireplaces.

RATES: $135 to $285, double occupancy, continental breakfast buffet.

OPEN: Mid-April to mid-December.

FACILITIES AND ACTIVITIES: Breakfast only meal served. BYOB. Swimming pool, tennis, antiques shop, bikes for rent. Nearby: ocean.

When you enter the Old Fort Inn, you are in an excellent antiques shop. Next you are in a huge living room that overlooks the swimming pool. (The pool has a solar cover that enables the inn to stretch its swimming season a bit. I know it works because I have one on my pool.) This is a lovely, comfortable living room with a fireplace, a super spot to curl up and read a book.

The rooms are charming. The beds are lovely canopy or four-poster ones with good, comfortable mattresses. The towels are color coordinated, which I always love. There is a nice library in the foyer. One of the suites has a sitting room, two bedrooms, and two bathrooms. There is a television in each room, and four rooms have Jacuzzis. All have telephones.

The breakfast buffet is superb. You can pick and choose from all types of teas and juices, fresh fruit, baked breads, croissants, and sticky buns, which are fantastic. This is a French country breakfast.

The inn provides a laundry. Until you have been on the road a week or so, you do not know how convenient such a facility is. The inn also provides a place to shower and change if you are checking out and still want to swim in the pool or the ocean; the latter is only 1 block away.

The Carriage House has very interesting shadow boxes displaying nineteenth-century clothing. The living room over here is so comfortable and quiet. On the other hand, in the main house's living room you must meet Walter, who "plays" the piano. The inn was awarded four diamonds from AAA.

HOW TO GET THERE: Take I–95 to exit 3. Turn left on Route 35 for 5½ miles. Go left at the Route 9 intersection, into Dock Square; take first right along Ocean Avenue for 9/10 mile. Take a left in front of the Colony Hotel, then go right at the T junction; follow signs for 3/10 mile to the inn.

# The Tides Inn by the Sea
## Kennebunkport, Maine 04046

**INNKEEPERS:** Marie Henrikson and Kristin Blomberg

**ADDRESS/TELEPHONE:** 252 Goose Rocks Beach; (207) 967–3757

**ROOMS:** 22, plus 3 suites; 21 with private bath.

**RATES:** $95 to $225, double occupancy, EP. Family rooms, $225, EP.

**OPEN:** Mid-May to Columbus Day weekend.

**FACILITIES AND ACTIVITIES:** Breakfast, dinner, bar, full license. Nearby: ocean, fishing, boating, harbor cruises.

*L*ocation, location, location. This inn certainly is in a beautiful one. A Victorian inn on the white sands of Goose Rocks Beach, it looks over the sea. Since its beginning at the turn of the century, it has hosted Teddy Roosevelt and Sir Arthur Conan Doyle, the creator of Sherlock Holmes.

The inn's brochure says it well: "Wake to the plaintive cries of seagulls; stroll miles of sandy beaches, and search for shells; doze to the sounds of the surf. You won't find televisions or telephones in the rooms (there is one in the front parlor) and you won't find rooms that look like any other."

The rooms for the most part are small; so what? In this area, who wants to stay inside? Almost all have a view of the Atlantic Ocean. The inn also has very spacious apartments next door.

The inn is a short ride from Kennebunkport, where there are sailboat charters, harbor cruises, fishing, tennis, and more. Timber Island, just off shore, is for exploring. You can see harbor seals basking on the rocks at Goose Rocks. Do bring your camera.

When you enter the inn, the reception desk is on the left and on the right is a really lived-in living room with a television, magazines, and comfort. Turn left to the dining room. First you meet Emma, the resident ghost, at the piano. The food is very good, starting with appetizers like crabcakes, oysters, and tasty salads. Entrees include lobster and oyster dinner stew, sirloin and lobster tail, chicken, pork, and just plain lobster. The Sandy Bottom Pub offers lighter fare and a huge bar. The mother-daughter team really works. Come on up—you'll love it here.

HOW TO GET THERE: From the Maine Turnpike take exit 3. Follow Route 35 to Route 9 through Dock Square. Follow Route 9 east for 3 miles, to Cape Porpoise. Turn left on Route 9, continue 2½ miles, and turn right at "Clockfarm" onto Dyke Road to its end. Turn left to the inn.

# Seashore Trolley Museum

Take a trip back in time at the Seashore Trolley Museum (207–967–2800), which houses a collection of more than forty fully restored trolleys, streetcars, buses, and subway cars. Board an open-air car for a ride on the old Atlantic Shore interurban trolley line that linked Kennebunkport to Kittery and Biddeford. Visit the restoration shop and watch artisans and mechanics work on the vehicles stored in the car barns. Enjoy a treat at the snack bar or buy a souvenir at the gift shop. Children will especially enjoy the chance to sound the motorman's whistle or even operate the car itself. Special events are held on weekends and holidays throughout the season, from early May through October. Admission is charged, but you can ride all day if you want to. The museum is on Log Cabin Road, about 3 miles from Dock Square.

# White Barn Inn 📱
## Kennebunkport, Maine 04046

**INNKEEPERS:** Laurie J. Bongiorno

**ADDRESS/TELEPHONE:** Beach Street (mailing address: P.O. Box 560-C);
(207) 967–2321; fax (207) 967–1100

**WEB SITE:** www.whitebarninn.com

**ROOMS:** 16, plus 9 suites; all with private bath, some with phone, TV,
and Jacuzzi, 11 with fireplace.

**RATES:** $180 to $450, double occupancy, continental breakfast and tea.
Packages available.

**OPEN:** All year.

**FACILITIES AND ACTIVITIES:** Dinner, full license. Meeting room, bicycles. Nearby: beach, shops, galleries, golf, tennis.

**BUSINESS TRAVEL:** Located 25 minutes from Portland. Writing desk
and phone in room, conference room, fax and audiovisual equipment
available.

*A* pre–Civil War farmhouse and its signature white barn have
been transformed into this lovely inn, which is just a short
walk from the beach and the charming village of Kenne-
unkport, with its colorful shops, galleries, and boutiques. When you consider the inn's exquisite food and its warmth and graciousness, it comes as
no surprise that it is the only Maine member inn of *Relais et Châteaux* and one
of just twenty in the United States.

Hospitality is evident throughout the inn. When you enter your room,
you find a basket of fruit, flowers, luxurious toiletries, and a robe for you to
wear. At night your bed is turned down and a pillow treat is left.

The rooms in the inn itself are attractively decorated with antiques,
armoires, and brass and iron beds in a variety of sizes. The Gate House's
rooms are large, with cathedral ceilings, ceiling fans, dressing areas, queen-
sized beds, and wing chairs. May's Annex has six suites with king-sized four-
poster beds and large sitting areas with fireplaces. There are oversized
marble baths with whirlpool baths and separate showers. The towels are
large and lush.

The sun room is the boardroom, seating up to fourteen people; it's a perfect, sunny spot for small meetings, retreats, and reunions. The breakfast room is large and cheerfully decorated with flower arrangements. The main dining room is the barn; a lovely lounge and piano bar are here, too. Candlelight, linen, and soft music are nice touches. The menu changes weekly.

When I think about the food, I want to go back for more. The restaurant has received five diamonds and an AAA listing; these are prestigious awards and well deserved. The menu changes weekly in order to offer the freshest and finest of ingredients. I know the greens are fresh—I watched them being picked. Soups are amazing: A light cream soup of potato, leek, and watercress is scented with thyme; lobster minestrone comes with black beans, roasted tomatoes, olive oil croutons, and a bacon pistou.

The appetizer of homemade ravioli is glorious. Dinner choices the week I was here included pan-seared striped bass with sautéed eggplant, Niçoise olives, and basil oil in a roasted tomato broth. The veal rib chop came grilled with glazed baby turnips, Swiss chard, garlic-roasted Parisienne potatoes,

and an herb sauce. You can guess there are more seafood offerings from this Maine inn—lobster, halibut, and salmon were also on the menu.

No matter what size your party—two or eight—when your dinner is ready, that number of waiters arrives to stand behind each diner's chair and on cue serves everyone simultaneously. What a sight.

The little bar is copper, with eight upholstered chairs. The piano bar has a huge flower arrangement in its center.

After dinner, go relax in the living room with a glass of port or brandy, a book from the inn's well-filled bookshelves, or one of the many current magazines. Or you could be ambitious and go for a ride along the beach on one of the inn's bicycles. I took one and sure did enjoy it.

There's a new wine room, and it's a beauty for large parties or small, I'm sure. Please invite me, I'd love to come.

There's a new pool, and the area around it is grand. Sodas and lunch are served to guests out here. Also new is the fly-fishing school, offered in conjunction with Orvis—wonderful packages for anglers.

**HOW TO GET THERE:** From the Maine Turnpike, take exit 3 to Kennebunk. Follow Route 35 south 6 miles to Kennebunkport, then continue through the fourth traffic light onto Beach Street. The inn is in ¼ mile, on the right.

# The Inn on Winter's Hill
## Kingfield, Maine 04947

**INNKEEPERS:** Richard and Diane Winnick and Carolyn Rainaud

**ADDRESS/TELEPHONE:** RR 1, Box 1272; (207) 265–5421 or (800) 233–9687; fax (207) 265–5424

**WEB SITE:** www.sugarloaf.com/IWH

**ROOMS:** 20, in 2 buildings; all with private bath, phone, coffee machines, and cable TV, 1 specially equipped for handicapped.

**RATES:** $75 to $150, double occupancy, EP. Golf, skiing, and fly-fishing packages available.

**OPEN:** All year.

**FACILITIES AND ACTIVITIES:** Dinner for public daily, by reservation. Wheelchair access to dining room. Bar, lounge, meeting and banquet facilities. Hot tub, indoor and outdoor swimming pools, croquet court, tennis, cross-country skiing, ice skating. Nearby: downhill skiing, hunting, fishing, hiking, golf, canoeing, Stanley Steamer Museum, dogsled rides.

*T*he Inn on Winter's Hill, located in the midst of western Maine's Bigelow, Sugarloaf, and Saddleback Mountains, sits on top of a six-acre hill on the edge of town. This Neo-Georgian manor house was designed by the Stanley (steam car) brothers and built at the turn of the century for Amos Greene Winter as a present for his wife, Julia. It is listed on the National Register of Historic Places. Today it is owned by a brother and sister who are doing a great job as innkeepers, following a longtime tradition of casual elegance and warm hospitality.

Accommodations are varied and range from the turn-of-the-century luxury rooms in the inn to the modern rooms in the restored barn. Every one is very comfortable, with nice bathrooms, wonderful views, cable television, and telephone.

Julia's Restaurant is elegant, and the food served here is excellent. The night I was here, for appetizers I had crackers and garlic cheese spread and pineapple wrapped in bacon. My garden salad with house dressing was followed by a light sorbet and then Sole Baskets, which were superb. The other entrees were Drunken Duck, chicken cordon bleu, and beef Wellington. Salmon in phyllo, Atlantic salmon fillet baked in phyllo with a Parmesan-cheese cream sauce, is superb; I had this on my last trip. Desserts are grand. Oh, it's all so good, it's hard to choose!

In the lounge area is an old piano; it came by oxcart from Boston for Julia Winter. It took two and a half months to arrive.

Spring, summer, fall, or winter, there is so much to do up here. Winter brings cross-country skiing from the door, and downhill skiing at Sugarloaf is minutes away. Hunting, fishing, canoeing, and hiking along the Appalachian Trail welcome outdoors people in the other seasons. If those do not appeal to you, try the pool table in the bar area. Television is here, too. All is watched over by Chee Sai and Kismet, the Shih Tzu inn dogs.

**HOW TO GET THERE:** Kingfield is halfway between Boston and Quebec City, and the Great Lakes area and the Maritimes. Take the Maine Turnpike to the Belgrade Lakes exit in Augusta. Follow Highway 27 through Farmington to Kingfield. The inn is on a small hill near the center of town.

# The Newcastle Inn
Newcastle, Maine 04553

**INNKEEPERS:** Howard and Rebecca Levitan

**ADDRESS/TELEPHONE:** River Road; (207) 563–5685 or (800) 832–8669; fax (207) 563–6877

**WEB SITE:** www.newcastleinn.com

**ROOMS:** 15, including 1 suite; all with private bath, some with fireplace, suite with Jacuzzi. Inn suitable for older children. No smoking inn.

**RATES:** $90 to $210, double occupancy, EPB; Packages available.

**OPEN:** All year.

**FACILITIES AND ACTIVITIES:** Dinner served on Friday and Saturday from November through the end of May and daily (except Monday) from June through October. Pub. Nearby: walking trails, beaches, bicycling, birdwatching, boating, cross-country skiing.

**RECOMMENDED COUNTRY INNS® TRAVELERS' CLUB BENEFIT:** Complimentary room upgrade, subject to availability.

The Newcastle Inn is in the lovely Boothbay region, only 14 miles from Boothbay Harbor and 16 miles to Pemaquid, with its famous lighthouse, fort, and sandy beach. This is a very interesting and distinctive part of Maine.

The beautiful flower known as the lupine is the signature of the inn. A native to this part of Maine, it grows just two weeks in June. Make sure you see the watercolor painting of lupines on the wall in the stencil room.

A 40-by-16-foot cedar deck at the rear of the inn overlooks the gardens and Damariscotta River. It is used in season for the inn's multicourse breakfasts and very special Downeast lobster bakes. Every summer night on the deck and in the pub, the innkeepers host a reception for their guests, with hors d'oeuvres and beverages of every kind.

Dinner is served most evenings in the summer. Here's a sample of the menu's offerings: appetizers like Newcastle Inn crabcakes and mussels in saffron cream and entrees like baked salmon with horseradish crust, baked stuffed lobster, and breast of chicken. For dessert try the apricot almond tart or the chocolate mousse. The chef's cooking is glorious.

The pub is open every night, and the wine list features selections from around the world. This room has a gas fireplace and a deck and lovely water views.

Each of the inn's rooms is special. All are named after the lighthouses on the coast of Maine. Many have a canopied four-poster bed. Some have a fireplace. The new suite offers a king-sized bed, a Jacuzzi for two, and a fireplace in the sitting room. Every night guests are left a gift of Godiva chocolates as part of the inn's turndown service.

Howard and Rebecca have a goal for each visitor: "Come as our guests and leave as our friends." Very nice indeed. Do say hello to Jasper, the inn's Maine coon cat. There is much to see and do up here. All you have to do is ask.

**HOW TO GET THERE:** Going north on Route 1, take the Newcastle exit to the right. About 7 miles north of Wiscasset, take Newcastle River Road; the inn is ½ mile down, on the right.

# The Bradley Inn
# at Pemaquid Point 📱
## New Harbor, Maine 04554

**INNKEEPERS:** Beth and Warren Busteed

**ADDRESS/TELEPHONE:** 361 Pemaquid Point (mailing address: Route 130 HC 61); (207) 677–2105 or (800) 942–5560; fax (207) 677–3367

**ROOMS:** 12, plus 1 cottage, 1 carriage house, all with private bath. Rooms with phone and TV, 5 with gas fireplace.

**RATES:** $125 to $185 in season, double occupancy, EPB. Off-season $95 to $150 double occupancy, EPB. Special packages available.

**OPEN:** All year except Christmas Eve and Christmas Day.

**FACILITIES AND ACTIVITIES:** Dinner. Bicycles and helmets. Wedding facilities. Nearby: ocean, tennis, golf.

**BUSINESS TRAVEL:** Phone with private line in room, conference facilities.

*P*emaquid, an Indian word meaning "long finger," is an appropriate name for the point of land that extends farther into the Atlantic Ocean than any other on the rugged Maine coast. This information is from the inn's brochure. What a wonderful ride it is out here! And once you arrive, the terrain is breathtaking. You're just a short walk from the Pemaquid Lighthouse or the beach with its lovely white sand. In the nearby seaside village of New Harbor, you can watch the working boats. Fort William Henry is close by. I drove around the point, parked my car, and watched the surf beating on the rocks below. It was quite a sight.

On this visit I scrambled down to the water's edge and back up. It was a bit scary but well worth it.

The inn is more than eighty years old. There's an attractive living room with a fireplace and a baby grand piano. On Fridays and Saturdays, the piano is played by John Mantica, who has entertained here for years. A folk singer also performs on Friday nights. The taproom has a long, custom-made bar of Portland granite with a mahogany rail.

The Bradley Inn Restaurant is decorated with some beautiful ship models and a huge ship's wheel. Some of the appetizers are chilled Spiney Creek oysters and smoked salmon terrine. Entrees may be filet mignon, Maine lobster, and sea scallops. The menu changes monthly. The wine list is impressive, and the dessert that won my vote was Chocolate Decadence cake.

The rooms are charming and very comfortable. The view from some of the second- and third-floor rooms is of Johns Bay or the gardens. The cottage

has heat and a wood fireplace, a limited kitchen, a bedroom, and bath, living room, screened-in porch, and a TV. Chloe, a love of a yellow lab, is the inn dog.

The carriage house has three lodging options. On the second floor is a large apartment with a kitchen, bedroom, bath, and a loft—a great place for children. On the first level is a bedroom with a private bath and another bedroom with a private bath and sitting room. The carriage house is available in summer only.

There's also a nice yard with lounge chairs. There's much to do and see out here, so come on up.

On a slate around the fireplace in the common room with a lovely piano is this saying by Harry Emerson Fosdick: *Bestow upon us, Eternal God, the fine gift of friendliness, forgive us our angers, hatreds, grudges and vindictiveness. Below all our varieties teach us the common goal. Amen.*

HOW TO GET THERE: Take the Maine Turnpike to exit 9, Falmouth—Route 1 interchange. Take I-95 21 miles to Brunswick. Continue on Route 1 to Damariscotta, 27 miles, and from there follow Route 130, 14 miles to the inn.

# The Rangeley Inn
## Rangeley, Maine 04970

**INNKEEPERS:** David and Rebecca Schinas

**ADDRESS/TELEPHONE:** P.O. Box 398; (207) 864–3341 or
(800) MOMENTS (666–3687); fax (207) 864-3634

**E-MAIL:** rangeinn@rangeley.org

**WEB SITE:** rangeleyinn.com

**ROOMS:** 36; all with private bath, 5 have double whirlpool tubs,
2 specially equipped for handicapped.

**RATES:** $64 to $104, single; $69 to $110, double occupancy; EP. MAP
available.

**OPEN:** All year.

**FACILITIES AND ACTIVITIES:** Breakfast, dinner, bar, lounge, banquet
facilities. Dining room closed Easter to Memorial Day and Thanksgiving to Christmas. Pub open seven days with a pub menu. Wheelchair
access to dining room, lounge, and public restroom. Nearby: fishing,
boating, swimming, hiking, tennis, golf, hunting, skiing, snowmobiling.

What a wonderful trip it is just to get up here in this beautiful country. The first thing you see when you arrive at the Inn is their wonderful long verandah that gives a nice old-fashioned feel of a
long-ago summer hotel. Well, it's been here since 1907 and is on the shore of
Haley Pond.

The bar and lounge
area is quite large. A pool
table is in here, as is a huge
rock fireplace and several
comfortable bar stools. A
pub menu is offered seven
nights a week. The television room has a big screen

and a VCR—all very comfortable, good chairs and couches.

Almost all of the rooms are carpeted, and all are very clean. The baths
have wonderful claw-footed tubs. A bath in an old tub is heavenly. You can
be up to your neck in water. Try this in a modern one—no can do! Some
rooms have showers. Five rooms have double whirlpool tubs.

The dining room is large and very comfortable. Breakfast is huge—eggs any way, corned beef hash, all kinds of pancakes and waffles and French toast. Cold cereal, hot cereal, and tons of side things to order. A wondrous espresso machine, and what coffees and latte! Wish I lived closer. Dinner starters—how about ostrich? They serve grilled marinated strips of ostrich steak, served on a bed of braised greens. Wow. There are more goodies and entrees like pasta primavera, steak, chicken, salmon, rack of lamb. Save room for dessert, the food up here is glorious.

There are nature hikes. A sunrise canoe trip starts at 5:00 A.M. I'm told it's so beautiful it takes your breath away, but I don't think I'll try it.

Spring brings superb fishing for brook trout and landlocked salmon. Some brooks are open only to fly-fishing. Wildflowers and migrating birds are plentiful, so bring a camera. Summer is ideal for boating, swimming, hiking, tennis, and golf. Fall brings spectacular foliage and hunting. Winter, of course, brings snow activities. Saddleback Mountain is nearby for downhill skiing, and cross-country skiing and snowmobiling are everywhere.

In any season of the year, Angel Falls, 20 miles away, is impressive and worth a visit. It is a 50- to 60-foot fall. Beautiful!

**HOW TO GET THERE:** From the Maine Turnpike take exit 12 at Auburn. Pick up Route 4 and follow it to Rangeley.

# Capt. Lindsey House Inn  ♡
## Rockland, Maine 04841

**INNKEEPER:** Charles A. M. Childes; Capts. Ken and Ellen Barnes, owners

**ADDRESS/TELEPHONE:** 5 Lindsey Street; (207) 596–7950 or
(800) 523–2145; fax (207) 596–2758

**E-MAIL:** lindsey@midcoast.com

**WEB SITE:** www.midcoast.com/~lindsey/

**ROOMS:** 7 rooms and 2 suites, all with private bath, cable television, telephone, air conditioning, and hair dryer. 1 room specially equipped for the handicapped. No smoking inn.

**RATES:** In season, $95 to $160 EPB; off season $65 to $150 EPB; packages available. Gourmet continental breakfast and afternoon tea included.

OPEN: All year.

FACILITIES AND ACTIVITIES: Available for small conferences and retreats. Nearby: shopping districts of Rockland and Camden; the Farnsworth Museum; cross-country skiing; golfing at the Samoset golf course; six-day Windjammer cruises aboard the historic schooner *Stephen Taber* (22 passengers, no children under 14. For reservations call 800–999–7352).

BUSINESS TRAVEL: Access to fax machine and copying services; computer port in library.

RECOMMENDED COUNTRY INNS® TRAVELERS' CLUB BENEFIT: 10 percent discount each night, Monday Thursday, subject to availability.

*T*he Capt. Lindsey House Inn is located in Rockland's harbor district. Built in 1837, it was Rockland's first inn. It is certainly one of its best.

There is a story behind the inn's simple brick facade. You see, the bricks were hand-burned on site by the original owner. Imagine that! The inside is simply grand. The decor here is all in deep greens, wines, and creams, with polished oak floors and rich oriental rugs throughout. It is all tastefully decorated with fine antiques and family heirlooms.

The living room is quite inviting. It has a cozy fireplace and comfortable couches. There is also a library with a good selection of books. You're invited to take one home if you're still reading it when you're ready to leave.

Accommodations are bright and homey. Each bedroom is done right. There are wide beds, warm down comforters, tapestry bedspreads, and good pillows. My room had two comfortable reading chairs and original hardwood floors. The large sea trunk at the foot of my bed has been in the Lindsey family since anyone can remember.

In the morning there is a gourmet continental breakfast, with homemade granola, muffins and croissants, fresh fruit, juices, and more. What a nice way to start the day. It is served in the cheerful oak-paneled breakfast room.

Afternoon tea is an especially nice feature of the inn. You may choose tea, sherry, or port. In the summer there is a lovely selection of scones, fresh fruit, tea cookies, sweetbreads, and cucumber sandwiches. In the winter you'll find hot chocolate and an assortment of cookies.

I had a wonderful dinner with Ken and Ellen Barnes next door at their WaterWorks Pub and Restaurant. Dining is always a pleasure here, and it is quite a family affair. You see, their daughter, Susan, is the chef here. The *Boston Globe* called Waterworks a "place not to be missed in Midcoast Maine." I can understand why.

You'll enter the restaurant through large oak doors with leaded-glass windows. Notice the wide floor boards and beamed ceilings. The two funny wooden monkeys you see are genuine movie stars! They were once props on a Hollywood sound stage. Well, here you must make a choice. To your right is a casually elegant restaurant with intimate tables. To your left is an English-style pub with long oak trestle tables and a grand stone fireplace.

The menu? Where should I begin? I had pan-fried salmon with an oak crust and a leek and cider sauce. Simply divine. One popular entree is called "Whale Bones." These are very large prime rib bones slow-cooked in a rum barbecue sauce. And you must leave room for dessert. Susan's apple crisp with cinnamon ice cream is a special favorite. Oh boy, is it yummy!

Rockland is some area. Take a stroll around the lovely harbor, and you'll see the schooner *Stephen Taber*. It was built in 1871 and is the oldest merchant sailing vessel in continuous service. Ken and Ellen serve as captain and cook on six-day sails from Windjammer Wharf. Ken tells wonderful sea stories. Ellen cooks all of the schooner's gourmet meals on a vintage woodstove in the galley. Maine blueberry pancakes with warm maple syrup is a popular breakfast choice. If you sign up for a sail, you'll even feast on steamed lobsters with all the fixings on a mid-week stop on a deserted island. You can find Ellen's recipes in her book, *A Taste of the Taber*. The trips are very popular. You must reserve early.

HOW TO GET THERE: From the south, take the Maine Turnpike (I–95) to exit 22, coastal Route 1, into Rockland. From the north take coastal Route 1 through Camden to Rockland. Call the inn for directions once you reach Rockland.

# The Claremont
## Southwest Harbor, Maine 04679

INNKEEPER: John W. Madeira Jr.

ADDRESS/TELEPHONE: P.O. Box 137; (207) 244–5036 or (800) 244–5036; fax (207) 244–3512

**ROOMS:** 24 in the inn, 6 in Phillips House, 12 cottages; all with private bath.

**RATES:** In-season: $180 to $200, double occupancy, MAP; $155 to $175, double occupancy, EPB. Off-season: $167 to $187, double occupancy, MAP. No meals with cottages. No credit cards.

**OPEN:** Early June to mid-October. Cottages from mid-May to mid-October.

**FACILITIES AND ACTIVITIES:** Lunch in-season, dinner, full license. Tennis court, dock and moorings, croquet courts, badminton, bicycles, rowboats, library. Nearby: 3 golf courses, sailing, freshwater swimming, summer theater, Acadia National Park.

The Claremont has been a landmark on the shores of Somes Sound, the famous fjord of beautiful Mount Desert Island, for more than a century. It was entered in the National Register of Historic Places in 1978. I saw an ad that describes the inn well: "For over 100 summers, upholding the traditions of hospitality and leisure on the Maine coast."

There is so much to do and see up here. The Claremont Croquet Classic—the home of nine-wicket croquet—is held every summer.

You can sit in a cozy chair at a bay window upstairs and watch this event in sheer comfort. Bring your binoculars and you can see all the way to Northeast Harbor. Watch for all the lobster boats, sailboats, and yachts that sail by.

I was here in mid-June and boy, did the fireplace in the lovely living room feel good! The library-gameroom also has a nice fireplace. There are a lot of places to sit down and just relax at The Claremont. If you look hard, you can find a television, but why bother, with all of this beauty around you?

Most activities center on the boathouse and waterfront, where a dock, float, and deep-water moorings are available for guests. The boathouse is open June 25 through August and is nice for lunch and predinner cocktails. What a view you get from here!

The guest rooms in the inn are comfortable and decorated simply. There are also two guest houses. The Phillips House has six large rooms, including a suite, a large living room with a fireplace, and a veranda with views. The Clark House has an additional suite. There are also twelve housekeeping cottages, each of which has a Franklin stove or a stone fireplace. Most of these have views of the Sound.

The dining room is lovely, with candlelight, linens, fresh flowers, and attentive service. Gentlemen are asked to wear jackets. The food is excellent. You can order char-grilled salmon, Maine crabcakes, sautéed duck breast, and beef, but, of course, the king of all is lobster. The breakfast menu is extensive.

**HOW TO GET THERE:** Take the Maine Turnpike to Augusta, exit 15. Follow Route 3 east through Ellsworth to the Trenton Bridge and Mount Desert Island. Once over the bridge, take Route 102 to Southwest Harbor and follow signs to The Claremont.

# The East Wind Inn
## Tenants Harbor, Maine 04860

**INNKEEPER:** Tim Watts

**ADDRESS/TELEPHONE:** P.O. Box 149; (207) 372–6366 or (800) 241–VIEW

**ROOMS:** 26, including 3 suites and 1 apartment, in 2 buildings; 16 with private bath, all with phone.

**RATES:** $72 to $275, double occupancy, EP.

**OPEN:** All year. From December 1 to April 1, the inn is available only to groups.

**FACILITIES AND ACTIVITIES:** Breakfast, Sunday brunch, dinner. Wheelchair access to dining room and meeting room. Lounge with full liquor license, meeting room, deep-water anchorage for boats, sailboat charter. Nearby: golf, tennis, swimming, cross-country skiing.

**RECOMMENDED COUNTRY INNS® TRAVELERS' CLUB BENEFIT:** 10 percent discount on stays of two or more nights.

The inn was built in 1890 and stood vacant for twenty years. Tim, a native of the town, watched the old house deteriorate and dreamed of restoring it so others could share the charm of "the country of the pointed firs." He's been able to do just that.

Today you can sit on the wraparound porch of the inn and enjoy the view. Tenants Harbor should be on a postcard, it's so beautiful. The inn is within walking distance of the village, where you will find a library, shops, post office, and churches.

The Meeting House is so nice for a relaxed conference or seminar. The guest rooms are very clean. Some have oak bureaus and Victorian side chairs, while others have brass beds. Almost all the rooms have good views of the harbor.

The view and the food compete for your attention here. Dinner has marvelous specialties from the sea—fresh daily, as you'd expect. Desserts—of course, they are excellent.

The inn is open all year, so winter sports enthusiasts will find lots of snow for cross-country skiing. The Camden Snow Bowl is only a short drive away. The friendship sloop *Surprise* sails three times a day from the pier at The East Wind. These are three-hour cruises on a 33-foot ketch, with comfortable accommodations for up to six persons. The captain really knows these waters and can tell you all you want to know. Go and enjoy.

**HOW TO GET THERE:** From Route 1, just east of Thomaston, take Route 131 south for 9½ miles to Tenants Harbor. Turn left at the post office and continue straight to the inn.

# The Waterford Inne
Waterford, Maine 04088

**INNKEEPERS:** Barbara and Rosalie Vanderzanden

**ADDRESS/TELEPHONE:** P.O. Box 149; (207) 583-4037

**ROOMS:** 10; 7 with private bath.

**RATES:** $80 to $115, double occupancy, EPB.

**OPEN:** May 1 through February 28.

**FACILITIES AND ACTIVITIES:** Breakfast, dinner. BYOB. Nearby: hiking, hunting, fishing, swimming, bird-watching, golf, skiing.

**RECOMMENDED COUNTRY INNS® TRAVELERS' CLUB BENEFIT:** 10 percent discount, Monday–Thursday.

*T*his is a beautiful part of the world. It is secluded, quiet, and restful. The inn offers a fireplace in the parlor and a library full of books and good music for your relaxation. And when the weather is warm, you can while away your days in the rockers on the porch.

But if you're looking for activity, The Waterford Inne can offer that, too. The area provides hiking, hunting, fishing in the summer and winter, downhill and cross-country skiing, swimming, and bird-watching.

This is a first for me, a mother and daughter who are the innkeepers. They bought the inn in 1978 and have done a masterful job of restoring and renovating it. There are antiques in all the rooms, nice wallpapers, and some stenciling. For your comfort there are electric blankets in the winter, and for your visual pleasure there are fresh flowers

in the summer. The Country Fair room, all pine and posters, is the latest addition and very refreshing.

Rosalie, the mother, does the cooking. The dinner is a fixed price with one entree served each evening. She is a very good and creative chef. All baking is done right here, and all the vegetables are grown in the inn's garden. Barbara does the serving, and you may be seated at a table for four in the attractive dining room with a fireplace or in a secluded corner just for two.

Tansey and Teasel are the two inn cats lucky enough to live in this glorious part of the world.

**HOW TO GET THERE:** From Norway, Maine, take Route 118 west for 8 miles to Route 37. Turn left and go ½ mile to Springer's General Store. Take an immediate right up the hill. The inn is in about ½ mile.

# The Lawnmeer Inn
## West Boothbay Harbor, Maine 04575

**INNKEEPERS:** Jim and Lee Metzger

**ADDRESS/TELEPHONE:** P.O. Box 505; (207) 633-2544 or (800) 633-7645

**ROOMS:** 32, all with private bath, cable TV, and phone; some with sundeck.

**RATES:** $65 to $130, double occupancy, EP.

**OPEN:** Mid-May to mid-October.

**FACILITIES AND ACTIVITIES:** Full breakfast, dinner, Sunday brunch. Bar, lounge, boat dock. Nearby: Boothbay Harbor activities, boat tours, aquarium, theater.

**RECOMMENDED COUNTRY INNS® TRAVELERS' CLUB BENEFIT:** 25 percent discount, Monday–Thursday, excluding August, subject to availability.

The inn is nicely located on the island of Southport in the Boothbay Harbor region. As you sit on its porch or relax in the Adirondack chairs on the lawn, you are looking at Townsend Gut and watching the masts of the moored sailboats sway with the winds and tides.

The accommodations range from modern rooms in a new wing to comfortable inn suites and rooms. Lee's handiwork is evident in many rooms; her grapevine wreaths, potpourri, and stenciling are a pretty touch. Some rooms have a television and a sundeck overlooking the water. The views are really lovely and tranquil—nearly every room has a view to savor.

There are delightful sitting areas. One has a fireplace to ward off early spring or fall chills. The common room has a television and is full of wicker furniture and baskets of books. Rescued bears collected from far and wide and nearby also reside in baskets around the inn. Puss, the inn's coon cat, keeps them company. The bar and lounge add to the inn's charm. The two dining rooms are attractive,  with their nice napery and tall ladder-back chairs. One has a fireplace.

A breakfast of hot oatmeal is nice, and the inn offers a full breakfast, too. I had orange French toast made with a hint of Triple Sec. It was very good. The brunch menu has quiches, crepes, eggs prepared many ways, waffles, fresh-squeezed orange juice, fresh blueberry muffins, and more.

For dinner there are lobster and baked, broiled, and fried seafood selections and plenty of them. The native sea scallops are grand. Of course, there are meat and chicken dishes for the landlubbers. Lawnmeer's seafood pasta with four or five kinds of deep-sea catches over linguine with an Alfredo sauce is a winner. So is the sautéed veal in wine and mushroom sauce. If you're worried about your health or weight, Patrick will cook to order according to your dietary needs.

The inn has been operating since 1898. It is the oldest continually operated inn in the Boothbay area. Come see the puffins, craggy cliffs, coon cats, and lighthouses. It's all yours to enjoy.

The windjammers arrive every July, and I was lucky enough to be here then. What a treat!

HOW TO GET THERE: Take exit 22 from I–95 onto Route 1. Just north of Wiscasset turn on Route 27 south. Go through Boothbay Harbor onto the island of Southport. The inn is on Route 27, ³/₁₀ mile from the Southport Bridge.

# The Squire Tarbox Inn 🎔
## Wiscasset, Maine 04578

INNKEEPERS: Karen and Bill Mitman

ADDRESS/TELEPHONE: RR 2, P.O. Box 620; (207) 882–7693

ROOMS: 11; all with private bath.

RATES: $120 to $220, double occupancy, MAP; $80 to $160, double occupancy, EPB.

OPEN: Mid-May through October.

FACILITIES AND ACTIVITIES: Full license. Bicycles. Nearby: beaches, harbors, museums, antiques shops.

Everyone knows how I feel about inns and animals. Well, here they are really different. Among their farm animals Karen and Bill have Nubian goats, which are very pretty animals. Much of the inn's baking is done with the milk, and the goat cheese is shipped all over the country. The barns are scrupulously clean, as these goats are fastidious. Their names—well, they are Cinnamon, Lacey, Jalapeño, Sugar, Spice, and Nice, watched over by BC, the barn cat.

The inn is old, circa 1763, and is listed on the National Register of Historic Places. Many of the original boards and timbers remain today. There are eight fireplaces in the inn. Four are in the bedrooms, which are nicely furnished and comfortable. If you'd like to bring your children to the inn, the innkeepers suggest you telephone first.

A five-course dinner is served at 7:00 P.M. There is one entree, and the menu changes daily; so stay a week or so, and you will never tire of the food. One dinner featured pear or cucumber soup, whey buns, roast pork tenderloin, Parmesan potatoes, broccoli, acorn squash, and chocolate cake with brandied strawberries. Another night: potage Portugaise, orange and grapefruit nut salad, whey buns, scallops Rebecca (scallops in a wine-Parmesan sauce), cranberried red cabbage, and Sin Pie. As they say, it's the ultimate chocolate dessert. Other menus include fresh seafood, chicken, beef, and more. The inn caters to those on special diets, and alternative choices are offered each evening.

You wake up to a full breakfast, featuring really fresh eggs from the inn's own chickens. Count on some divine quiches and stratas.

The sitting areas are neat, with a wood stove, books, and puzzles. The music room has a player piano with lots of rolls. Really nice. You'll find much to do here. There are sand dunes, museums, and flea markets. I'd just sit and enjoy. It's beautiful here. (The inn cats are Ferdinand and Victoria.) I just love the deck, with its bird feeders—it's such fun to watch the many varieties of birds that come here. And there is a path to the water where a rowboat awaits you.

**HOW TO GET THERE:** From Route 1 between Bath and Wiscasset, turn onto Route 144 and follow it 8½ miles to the inn, which is on Westport Island.

# York Harbor Inn
York Harbor, Maine 03911

**INNKEEPERS:** Nancy and Gary Dominquez
**ADDRESS/TELEPHONE:** P.O. Box 573; (207) 363-5119 or (800) 343-3869; fax (207) 363-3545

**E-MAIL:** garyinkeep@aol.com

**WEB SITE:** www.yorkharborinn.com

**ROOMS:** 40, plus 2 suites in 2 buildings; all with private bath, air conditioning, and phone, some with TV and fireplace, 4 with Jacuzzi.

**RATES:** High season April 4 to November 1, $119 to $239, double occupancy, EPB; low season November 2 to April 1, $99 to $179. Harbor Cliffs, $159 to $229, double occupancy, EPB. Very special packages available.

**OPEN:** All year.

**FACILITIES AND ACTIVITIES:** Lunch in-season, dinner, Sunday brunch, bar, full license. Nearby: public beach, fishing, boating, golf, tennis.

**BUSINESS TRAVEL:** The inn offers more than 5,000 square feet of meeting space and has an inventory of state-of-the-art audiovisual equipment including a computer video data projector.

**RECOMMENDED COUNTRY INNS® TRAVELERS' CLUB BENEFIT:** 10 percent discount, subject to availability.

*W*ow! Three dining rooms with a view of the Atlantic. This is a cozy and comfortable inn, with good food and good grog. Sitting there looking over the Atlantic should be enough, but when you add the excellent food, it is heaven.

Everything is made to order and baked right here. Chef Gerry Bonsey, named chef of the year by the local chapter of the American Culinary Federation one year, by his own admission creates incomparable soups.

The appetizers, such as Portobello Pizza and Maine crabcakes (I had these on my last trip and they're delicious), are glorious. Entrees include baked stuffed haddock, orange and honey-glazed veal chop, stuffed breast of chicken, roast rack of lamb, beef tenderloin, and, of course, lobster and scallops. Do save room for the desserts.

The wine cellar, which once was a livery stable, is the lounge. The bar is a beauty, made of unstained cherry wood joined with holly and ebony woods. The carpenter even put an inlaid tulip in a corner—out of tulip wood, of course. Happy Hour is very happy, featuring good food and conversation with a lot of local people. There is entertainment here on Thursday, Friday, and Saturday.

Parts of the inn are very old; 1637 is the date of the cabin room. Originally a fisherman's house, it has sturdy beams in the ceiling—not for holding up the roof but instead for holding up wet sails to dry before the large fireplace. It was moved here.

The rooms are comfortable, and from some you can see the sea. On a quiet night you can hear the surf breaking on the generous beach below the inn. The carriage house next door is handsomely decorated. All rooms have private baths and two have working fireplaces. All are air-conditioned and have a complete sprinkler system.

The Harbor Cliffs next door is a real beauty, offering seven rooms, all with private bath, four with wood fireplaces, two with Jacuzzis, one with a large deck. You can see the ocean very well from here. The ocean is so beautiful, and so are these rooms.

The inn dogs, Annie and Sam, are handsome springer spaniels. Bring your camera—it's beautiful up here. Come up for York's Christmas Prelude—the first two weekends in December.

HOW TO GET THERE: Going south on I-95, take the Yorks/Berwicks exit; going north on I-95, take the Yorks/Ogunquit exit. Turn right at the blinking light, left at the first traffic light (Route 1A), and go through the village about 3 miles. The inn is on the left.

## Nubble Light

The town of York's most visited—and most photographed—site is the Nubble Light at Cape Neddick, the rocky promontory that stretches nearly a mile into the Atlantic Ocean. On its own little island at the tip—or "nubble"—of the peninsula, the 1879 lighthouse is at the end of Nubble Road off Route 1A at York Beach. English navigator Captain Bartholomew Gosnold landed at this site in 1602; Captain John Smith came to chart the area in 1614. It is he who coined the term "knubble." Now automated and maintained by the U. S. Coast Guard, the white iron-sheathed brick tower had a keeper until 1987. Its black-capped light is 88 feet above the high-water mark, still protecting seafarers off Maine's rugged coast.

# Select List of
## Other Maine Inns

## Mira Monte Inn & Suites

69 Mount Desert Street
Bar Harbor, ME 04609
(207) 288–4263 or (800) 553–5109
Fax: (207) 288–3115

*13 rooms in 1864 main building, 11 with fireplace, all with private bath;*
*3 suites in other buildings, all with private bath, fireplace, balcony.*

## John Peters Inn

Peters Point
Box 916
Blue Hill, ME 04614
(207) 374–2116
E-mail: jpi@downeast.net
Web site: www.johnpetersinn.com

*14 rooms, all with private bath; on 30-acre estate.*

## Spruce Point Inn

Atlantic Avenue
Boothbay Harbor, ME 04538
(207) 633–4152 or (800) 553–0289
E-mail: thepoint@sprucepointinn.com
Web site: www.sprucepointinn.com

*72 rooms, all with private bath; main inn has restaurant and lounge.*

## Maine Stay

22 High Street
Camden, ME 04843
(207) 236–9636; fax (207) 236–0621
E-mail: innkeeper@mainestay.com
Web site: www.mainestay.com

*8 rooms, all with private bath; 200-year-old farm complex.*

## English Meadows Inn B&B

Port Road
Kennebunkport, ME 04043
(207) 967-5766 or (800) 272-0698

*12 rooms, 10 with private bath; Victorian farmhouse.*

## Old Granite Inn

546 Main Street
Rockland, ME 04841
(207) 594-9036 or (800) 386-9036
E-mail: ogi@midcoast.com
Web site: www.midcoast.com/~ogi

*11 rooms, 8 with private bath; federal Colonial B&B.*

## The Surry Inn

Route 172
Surry, ME 04684
(207) 667-5091
Web site: www.surryinn.com

*13 rooms, 11 with private bath. A lovely 1834 inn on Contention Cove, chef-owned with dinner served seven days. Wonderful sunsets.*

## Edwards Harborside Inn

Box 866, Stage Neck Road
York Harbor, ME 03911
(207) 363-3037 or (800) 273-2686
Fax: (207) 363-1544

*10 rooms, 8 with private bath; Victorian waterfront estate.*

## Stage Neck Inn

Route 1A—Stage Neck Road
York Harbor, ME 03911
(207) 363-3850 or (800) 222-3238

*58 rooms, all with private bath; 2 dining rooms; indoor pool; Jacuzzi; fitness room.*

# Massachusetts

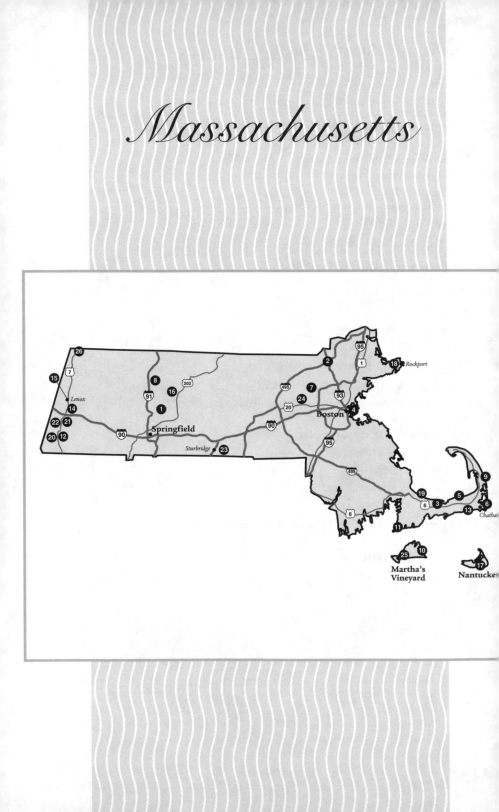

# Massachusetts

*Numbers on map refer to towns numbered below.*

*\* A Top Pick Inn*

# The Lord Jeffery Inn
## Amherst, Massachusetts 01002

**INNKEEPER:** Michael Maderia

**ADDRESS/TELEPHONE:** 30 Boltwood Avenue; (413) 253–2576

**ROOMS:** 40 rooms, 8 suites; all with private bath, TV, and phone.

**RATES:** $68 to $118, double occupancy; $98 to $148, suites; EP.

**OPEN:** All year.

**FACILITIES AND ACTIVITIES:** Breakfast, lunch, dinner, Sunday brunch. Elevator. Nearby: skiing, golf, tennis.

**RECOMMENDED COUNTRY INNS® TRAVELERS' CLUB BENEFIT:** 10 percent discount, subject to availability.

*T*he Lord Jeffery Inn, located on the historic common in Amherst, is named for Lord Jeffery Amherst, a hero of the French and Indian War. When you arrive here, you'll think the inn is so impressive with its whitewashed brick exterior.

The common rooms on the first floor are huge and comfortable. Cozy couches and chairs, beautiful flowers, and wonderful fireplaces are all around. An enormous walk-in fireplace is in the living room. There's a baby grand piano, circa 1876, a game table holding a backgammon board, and nice bookcases full of books. I also like the tavern, with its small bar, tables, and windows looking out over the gardens. A patio is off the tavern.

A comforting thing to know about this old building is that its halls have sprinkler systems and that smoke alarms are everywhere. The rooms here come in all sizes—small, medium, and large. Some are small suites. All have new mattresses and box springs, television, and telephone. Some of the rooms overlook the lovely Colonial gardens, and others have a view of the  Amherst common. Eight of the garden rooms have porches.

The two large private dining rooms have their own fireplaces. The dining room has wrought-iron chandeliers, windows that overlook the lovely gardens, nice napery, and fresh flowers. A beautiful pink rose was on my table. The dining room is air-conditioned for your comfort.

The food here is excellent! Breakfast here is the best way to start your day, and wow, what a start! Breads and baked goods, wonderful extras, berries, bacon, sausage, omelets, eggs, oatmeal, and more. Lunch is also a wow and in summer is served on the terrace; when I last visited, I had a delicious, rather thick tomato and spinach soup and a salad I could not finish. The menu is extensive—burgers, club sandwiches, and more. At dinnertime there are several appetizers and salads; entrees like pan-seared breast of duck, lobster, boneless pork chops, and Cornish game hens; and tableside entrees, such as chateaubriand—a yummy favorite of mine—and rack of lamb. Any room for dessert? These are also grand. Remember, menus change seasonally.

Room service is also available, and there is nightly turndown service.

There is much to do in this area. Besides Amherst College, many other colleges are in the area. Skiing, golf, tennis, and more are all nearby.

**HOW TO GET THERE:** Take I-91 to the Amherst exit (exit 19), then go east 8 miles on Route 9 to Amherst.

# Andover Inn 📱
## Andover, Massachusetts 01810

**INNKEEPER:** Henry Broekhoff

**ADDRESS/TELEPHONE:** Phillips Academy campus; (978) 475-5903; fax (978) 475-1053

**E-MAIL:** info@andoverinn.com

**WEB SITE:** www.andoverinn.com

**ROOMS:** 11, plus 4 junior and 2 executive suites; all with private bath, air conditioning, TV, phone, wheelchair accessibility.

**RATES:** $95, single; $110, double; $140 to $170, suite; EP.

**OPEN:** All year.

**FACILITIES AND ACTIVITIES:** Breakfast, lunch, dinner, Sunday brunch. Dining room closed on Christmas Day. Bar, elevator, barbershop.

**BUSINESS TRAVEL:** Located 30 minutes from Boston. Phone in all rooms, desk in some; conference room; fax available.

The Andover Inn is part of the campus of Phillips Academy. It is privately owned and offers twenty-four-hour desk service, an elevator, dry-cleaning services, photocopying, and box lunches. Room service is available, as are baby-sitters, medical services, safety deposit boxes, taxis, and wake-up service.

You expect ivy-covered buildings here, and you get them in abundance. Upon entering the inn you are in the reception area, with a fireplace and comfortable couches. The bar is in the right corner of this room, and it is one of the nicest I've visited. The stools with armrests are overstuffed, and honest, you hate to leave them.

The rooms have modern conveniences, such as color television, air conditioning, direct-dial telephone, radio, and full bath. All of them have nice views of the campus.

The dining rooms are lovely, and the china used is Villeroy and Boch. Siena is the pattern. It is porcelain and looks just like pink marble. The breakfast menu is extensive. Freshly squeezed orange or grapefruit juice is a nice way to start the day.

Dinner selections include hot and cold appetizers, salads, and entrees from the sea or land. Try the specialty of the inn, shrimp flambé.

From early May to the end of June, there is a white asparagus festival. The asparagus comes fresh from the Netherlands twice a week to the inn. Grown underground and harvested by hand, it's a rare treat.

Sunday brings rijsttafel, an original Indonesian dish served late in the day. It consists of dry steamed rice and an indefinite number of side dishes and sauces. The menu tells you how to eat it. I was overwhelmed and delighted by it. Do go and give it a try. It's worth a trip from anywhere, and reservations are a must.

Monday through Thursday and Saturday evenings, guests enjoy light classical music on the grand piano. Friday evening are dinner and dancing to the sounds of the big-band era. Sunday brunch features classical guitar music.

**HOW TO GET THERE:** The inn is 25 miles north of Boston on Route 28, near the intersection of I–93 and I–495.

# Cobb's Cove
## Barnstable Village, Massachusetts 02630

**INNKEEPERS:** Evelyn Chester and Henri-Jean

**ADDRESS/TELEPHONE:** Powder Hill Road (mailing address: P.O. Box 208); (508) 362–9356, same number for fax.

**ROOMS:** 6 suites; all with private bath.

**RATES:** $149 to $189, double occupancy, EPB.

**OPEN:** All year.

**FACILITIES AND ACTIVITIES:** Dinner by reservation only to houseguests. BYOB.

*T*he moment you walk in the door and are greeted by Evelyn and Henri-Jean, you know you have happened on a distinctive and delightful inn. You are taken to your suite, and what a marvelous view you have! The third-floor suites have an immense dormer with glass on three sides and a million-dollar view. There is a couch in front of this dormer where you can sit and see all of Cape Cod Bay, Sandy Neck, and all the way to Provincetown Light. The other suites also have grand views, deliciously comfortable beds, and all the extras you expect at an extraordinary inn. The baths all have whirlpools—so relaxing after a day of travel. The soaps and bubble bath are pear scented, a nice touch. There are plenty of big towels and good, soft pillows.

The inn is on a very secluded and scenic piece of property. The bay is right at hand. The inn was built of 12-by-12-inch rough-cut timbers, and many of the walls are done in rough burlap. The keeping room has a  large Count Rumford shallow fireplace, comfortable chairs, and wonderful smells that come from Henri's kitchen. There is a terrace full of bird feeders made by Harry Holl of the Scargo Pottery. Harry also made many of the kitchen things Henri uses, including a huge salad bowl that is a rare beauty. In summer breakfast is served on the terrace, and it's quite a sight with all the birds on the feeders.

# Cape Cod by Land and by Sea

Traffic on Cape Cod can be a real misery at the height of the tourist season. Let someone else do the driving whenever you can. Landlubbers can tour a part of the Cape by excursion train. The Cape Cod Scenic Railroad hooks up three vintage railway cars to make a 42-mile round trip from Hyannis (just south of Barnstable) to Buzzards Bay. The two-hour ride includes grand scenery and an interesting narrative on the various sights. A special three-hour Dinner Train is a romantic option; it includes a five-course dinner and a sunset stop at the world's widest sea-level canal. The CCSR also offers ecology discovery tours that include a stop for a marsh walk at the Talbots Point Conservation Preserve in Sandwich. For a schedule and reservations, call (508) 771-3788 or (800) 872-4508.

Lovers of the sea may want to leave the driving to a licensed captain. Walk down to Barnstable Harbor off Mill Way and book passage on a Hyannis Whale Watcher cruise (508–362–6088 or 800–287–0374). The four-hour trip to and from Stellwagen Bank may include a look at humpbacks, minkes, finbacks, and more. An on-board naturalist points out the sights. The 100-foot boat has both open and enclosed decks and a galley for snacks and drinks. Cruises are April through October.

The dining room—library has a long hutch table that seats fourteen quite comfortably. Dinner is served in three or five courses. One night I was there it started with delicious mussels, then a special cauliflower dish done Henri's way. This was followed by a fish (cod, I believe, and you can only believe because Henri reveals no kitchen information at all) so white and so tasty you wondered why you had ever eaten meat. Next came a salad, and finally a crème caramel for dessert, topped off by a great cup of espresso coffee, an Henri specialty.

This is fine dining, and believe me, the innkeeper who joins you for every course is the reason this inn is such a success. It also has the best view in Cape

Cod. I must add, however, that Henri cooks dinner only when he feels like it. You can walk to a ship in Barnstable Harbor for whale watching.

**HOW TO GET THERE:** Take exit 6 off Route 6. Turn left on Route 132 north to Route 6A. Turn right, go about 3 miles, and pass through the light in the middle of Barnstable Village. After you pass the church on your left, turn left onto Powder Hill Road. Take the first driveway on the left, marked EVELYN CHESTER.

# The Lenox Hotel
## Boston, Massachusetts 02116

**INNKEEPER:** Jeffrey Saunders, vice-president and managing director; Leszlie Purstell, general manager; the Saunders family, owners

**ADDRESS/TELEPHONE:** 710 Boylston Street, at Copley Square; (617) 536-5300 or (800) 225-7676; fax (617) 267-1237

**ROOMS:** 212, plus 6 suites; all with private bath, TV, phone, alarm clock, hair dryer, and iron and ironing board, some with fireplace. Some no smoking rooms.

**RATES:** $225 to $295, double occupancy; $450, suites; EP.

**OPEN:** All year.

**FACILITIES AND ACTIVITIES:** Breakfast, lunch, dinner, Sunday brunch. Grill room, function room.

**BUSINESS TRAVEL:** Located in the heart of Boston. Room with phone, some with desk; fax available; conference rooms; corporate rates.

The Lenox Hotel, almost a hundred years old, is located in the Back Bay section of Boston, close to Copley Square. This is a family-owned hotel, nice to find in a world of corporate ownership. The lobby is comfortable, with couches and chairs and a lovely fireplace. Three floors of the hotel are smoke-free. This is a delight, as is the glory of working fireplaces in a hotel in Boston—just grand. The rooms call to mind a country inn rather than a hotel. They are appointed with Colonial Ethan Allen or French Provincial furnishings, with spacious closets and nice touches like alarm clocks, hair dryers, irons and ironing boards. The rooms have all been refurbished and have Italian marble bathrooms: very nice. I think it's about time we had an in-town inn. Lord & Taylor is next door—we were in our glory, shopping until we were tired.

The hotel offers every service you could desire. Valet parking and limo transportation from Logan Airport by the hotel's private service are among the values here. The employees are very friendly. One doorman has been here more than fifty years; he is also the fire-tender. Two of the waiters in the Samuel Adams Brew House have been here twenty-five and twenty-six years, respectively. They are so caring.

Served in the Samuel Adams Brew House, breakfast for hotel guests features fresh-squeezed orange juice and, of course, lots more. Lunch offers soups, salads, sandwiches, burgers, and entrees like fish-and-chips or fresh Boston scrod. With lunch you might try one of the many different beers. I had a draft beer called a summer beer—cherry wheat, and you could taste the cherry. The upstairs grill room features dining in the setting of a Colonial inn—delicious. My friend Audrey Musgrave had fresh scrod; of course, I tasted it, and it was so fresh and nice. I had the Fisherman's Platter—scallops, shrimp, and scrod. Yum. Of course, there are meat and chicken dishes, and the desserts—well, now I'm going on a strict diet.

The hotel's four-star Anago restaurant offers fine, candlelight dining by reservation only. They offer lunch and dinner daily, plus Sunday brunch, which features the classic eggs Benedict, corned beef hash and eggs, smoked salmon, and more.

There are a lot of changes coming to Lenox—keep your eye on this one.

HOW TO GET THERE: Take exit 22 from the Massachusetts Turnpike, the Copley Square ramp, and turn left on Dartmouth Street for 2 blocks to Newbury Street. Take a left on Newbury Street for 1 block to Exeter Street, take a left on Exeter for 1 block, and the hotel is ahead at the corner of Exeter and Boylston streets. An airport limo service between Logan Airport and the Lenox is available for a nominal fee.

# High Brewster

Brewster, Massachusetts 02631

INNKEEPER: Brian Sheehan

ADDRESS/TELEPHONE: 964 Satucket Road; (508) 896–3636

ROOMS: 8, in 4 buildings; all with private bath.

RATES: $90 to $120, double occupancy, expanded continental breakfast. Weekly rates available.

OPEN: All year, except January and February, and Mondays and Tuesdays in March, April, May, November, and December.

FACILITIES AND ACTIVITIES: Dinner, wine, beer. Fishing. Nearby: biking, ocean, antiques stores, state parks with nature walks.

The grounds of High Brewster are beautiful. There are lush lawns, glorious flowers, and tables on the terrace overlooking Lower Millpond. There are three and a half acres in all. In spring the herring come up Herring Run Creek to spawn. There are walkways along the creek for you to walk on.

The original property had three houses, one of which stands today. Referred to as the Main House, it is circa 1762. That's old, folks; and the way the floors tip and tilt upstairs, you know it's old. There are two rooms upstairs—the Red Room and the Green Room.

There are guest rooms in three other buildings. Pond Cottage overlooks the pond and has one bedroom, a service kitchen, and a wonderful screened-in deck with a view of the pond. The living room in Brook House has a lovely fireplace, a dining table, and a picture window overlooking the pond. It also has two bedrooms and one bath, plus a deck where you can sit and listen to the creek on its way down to the pond. A really restful

sound for this inn creeper. Then there is the barn, which has a bedroom, a sleeping loft, one and a half bathrooms, a kitchen, and a fireplace.

You have a choice of three dining rooms. Fresh flowers are on the tables. The kitchen is spotless and the food is grand. The menu changes at least every six weeks and sometimes more often.

There were four of us on my last trip here, and we started our dinner with an array of appetizers. One I really liked was Portobello Pot Stickers, filled with chicken, goat cheese, and leeks, with a light Oriental glaze.

We all had lamb chops grilled with garlic mashed potatoes and vegetables and a good salad. Other menu choices include grilled leg of lamb with different sauces each day, medallions of veal, shrimp, scallops, and black Angus tenderloin of beef.

For dessert I had the best rhubarb and strawberry crisp with ice cream that I've had in many a country mile.

By the way, Brian, the innkeeper, is a doll.

**HOW TO GET THERE:** Take Route 6 to exit 11. Go left on Route 6A to a blinking amber light. Turn on Stony Brook Road and go about 1 mile. Just past the gristmill and creek, take the first left and turn into the inn's driveway.

# The Queen Anne Inn
## Chatham, Massachusetts 02633

**INNKEEPERS:** Guenther and Dana Weinkopf

**ADDRESS/TELEPHONE:** Queen Anne Road; (508) 945-0394 or (800) 545-4667; fax (508) 945-4884

**ROOMS:** 31; all with private bath, phone, and TV.

**RATES:** $172 to $295, per room double occupancy, continental breakfast.

**OPEN:** All year except January.

**FACILITIES AND ACTIVITIES:** Dinner. Tennis courts, swimming pool. Nearby: boating, fishing tours can be arranged.

*I*magine receiving this lovely place as a wedding gift. True. It happened in 1840. Now Guenther has a fine inn. The rooms are so very comfortable. On the garden side the rooms have private balconies, which are a nice addition to the inn. Rooms looking south have a good view of Oyster Pond Bay.

There is a very pleasant lounge to relax in. The artist James Parker has done a grand mural of Indians here in the lounge; there are others in various rooms and in the spa. And then there is the Earl of Chatham, the dining room, serving the most unbelievable food you can imagine. The waitstaff are beautifully trained. The chef has a briefing with them each night, so they can explain each course to their diners.

The appetizers are great—fried native oysters with roasted corn salsa and horseradish butter, or crispy shiitake mushroom and soft polenta sandwiches with basil-tomato fondue. The salads with field greens or arugula are so pretty and good. Entrees include roasted halibut with garlic mashed potatoes, spinach, fried onion rings, and red-wine butter sauce. There are also oven-roasted salmon, grilled tenderloin of beef, breast of chicken, and more.

Do remember, though, that the menus change, so you may find different choices.

I needed a walk, and there are pleasant places to go. The water is close at hand, and every Friday night band concerts are held in nearby Kate Gould Park. What a nice way to meet the other guests! Maybe you will also be lucky enough to meet Dana and Guenther's baby—a real beauty—so is Dana.

The spa downstairs has a stunning mural that surrounds the hot tub; a mermaid, fish, and plants are depicted in soft and very restful colors. There are lounge chairs and comfort in here. The next room has a large television and good books.

The inn also has three all-weather Har-Tru tennis courts in a beautiful parklike setting, a resident tennis pro, pro shop, and private lessons. There's a lovely swimming pool, and a service bar in the lower lounge. Add to all this the inn dog, Tip, who's a pip.

This is a beautiful area of the Cape. See the lighthouse and windmills, listen to the bells chiming from the church steeples, and watch the surf thundering on Nauset Beach and Monomoy Island.

# The Town House Inn
## Chatham, Massachusetts 02633

**INNKEEPERS:** Russell and Svea Peterson

**ADDRESS/TELEPHONE:** 11 Library Lane; (508) 945–2180 or (800) 242-2180

**ROOMS:** 26, plus 2 air-conditioned cottages; all with private bath, TV, refrigerator, and phone. No smoking inn.

**RATES:** $135 to $285, double occupancy, EPB.

**OPEN:** All year except January.

**FACILITIES AND ACTIVITIES:** Dinner May to the end of October. Full liquor license, lunch in-season. Heated pool, spa. Nearby: Friday-night band concerts, golf, tennis, beaches.

**RECOMMENDED COUNTRY INNS® TRAVELERS' CLUB BENEFIT:** Stay two nights, get third night free, subject to availability.

*T*he front porch that overlooks Main Street beckons me. The Fourth of July parade, one of the summer's biggest events, goes right by the front door. Best seat in town is the porch of this inn. The original structure dates back to the 1820s. Remains of the foundation can still be seen in the cellar, and some of the original woodwork is here. The carved moldings and wood trim depict harpoon and oar motifs. The floors are made of hemlock, and the original walls, recently exposed, have hand-painted scrolling. Check out the stencils in the rooms. Some of the shell stencils are really beautiful.

The rooms are immaculate; matter of fact, the whole inn is. The beds are queens and doubles. There are four-poster canopy beds in several rooms. All of the linens and towels are laundered right here by Svea. There are irons and ironing boards in each room.

Each room also has a television with HBO and a clock radio. Hair dryers, too, are in every room; this is a really nice touch. The cottages have a fireplace and air conditioning. Children are welcome in the cottages, and baby-sitters are available.

Breakfast is not a ho-hum thing here. Russ bakes the muffins and Svea does wonders with Scandinavian goodies. Favorites are Svea's Finnish pancakes with a fresh fruit mélange on top and her French toast with apricots.

The restaurant is called Two Turtles. Using her mother's recipes, Svea prepares Swedish pickled herring and Swedish meatballs as well as desserts.

Her son, David Peterson, is a certified chef and serves glorious food. There are nine choices of appetizers, followed by good soups and salads. He prepares entrees like baked scrod with lemon butter, Nantucket scallops, scampi, grilled lamb chops, salmon, and much more. The desserts are sinful. Two Turtles flourless chocolate cake with lightly sweetened whipped cream is just one.

David is also the restaurant manager and beverage coordinator. Son Russell oversees the cabana, with glorious frozen margaritas and lots more. The pool is really nice, and Russ—well, come on, girls, he's a real hunk!

Toole is a huge black-and-white Norwegian forest cat, and Chang is just a cat.

HOW TO GET THERE: Take Route 6 (Mid-Cape Highway) to exit 11, Route 137 south to Route 28 and east to the center of downtown Chatham. Watch for the Eldredge Library on your left. The inn is next door, at 11 Library Lane.

# Wequasset Inn
## Chatham, Massachusetts 02633

**INNKEEPER:** Mark Novata

**ADDRESS/TELEPHONE:** Route 28, Pleasant Bay, Cape Cod;
(508) 432–5400, (800) 352–7169 (in Massachusetts), or (800) 225–7125;
fax (508) 432–5032

**ROOMS:** 104, including 7 suites; all with private bath, some with private
patio or deck.

**RATES:** $170 to $480, single or double occupancy, EP.

**OPEN:** April to late November.

**FACILITIES AND ACTIVITIES:** Breakfast, lunch, dinner. Croquet court,
5 all-weather PlexiPave tennis courts plus pro shop and lessons, fitness
center, conference center, heated swimming pool, fishing, 18-hole
golf course.

*T*aking its name from the American Indian word meaning "Cres-
cent on the Water," Wequasset is a country inn resort that
includes eighteen separate buildings and is worth a trip from anywhere. Tucked between a secluded ocean cove and a twenty-two-acre pine
forest, the lands around Wequasset were once used by native peoples as a
summer campground.

A nineteenth-century sea captain's home now houses the inn's main dining room, the Square Top, named for the building's unusual roof line. There

is a spectacular view of
Pleasant Bay from here, a
nice complement to the
inn's glorious food, which
has been awarded Mobil
Travel Guide's four-star
rating and AAA's four-diamond rating. The break-
fast menu offers so many
choices that you could eat
all day. At lunch there are
six different salads, great

burgers, and a deli board. One sandwich I liked was the Yorkshire—thinly sliced roast beef, creamy horseradish, and lettuce and tomato piled high on a kaiser roll. Way to go, Elizabeth—right to the fat farm. Of course, they do have a fitness platter. Well, maybe next time. There's also a lovely selection of really different drinks on the lunch menu.

The dinners? Well, you can imagine. Four cold appetizers and six hot. I can taste the lump-meat crabcakes now. Soups, salads, and fresh pastas—one I tasted was spicy pepper fettucine and blackened shrimp. Oh my! The seafood is wonderful, as are the meat and poultry. It's nice to have half a rack of lamb on the menu. Desserts—are you ready? Wequasset Inn's chocolate truffle cake. I do not know where I put it, but it was all gone. There are eleven specialty coffees along with the regular ones.

The accommodations are unique. Each room has its own bath and entrance, simply styled pine furniture, traditional fabrics, and lots of charm. There are heating and cooling units, color television, and patios and decks. Suites feature fresh flowers, minibar, and VCR.

It would be hard to beat the serenity of sitting on the porch overlooking the bay at any time of the day, but oh, the early-morning calm!

HOW TO GET THERE: Wequasset Inn is on Pleasant Bay midway between Chatham and Orleans on Route 28. If you are driving from the north, take Route 6 east to exit 11. Turn left at end of exit ramp; go 25 yards to Pleasant Bay Road (your first left). Go straight through the first stop sign, and when you reach the second stop sign, you have arrived at Wequasset Inn.

# The Colonial Inn 📱
## Concord, Massachusetts 01742

INNKEEPERS: Jurgen and Rebecca Demisch

ADDRESS/TELEPHONE: 48 Monument Square; (508) 369–9200 or (800) 370–9200

ROOMS: 46, plus 4 suites; all with private bath, air conditioning, phone, and TV.

RATES: $95 to $200 per room, EP. Packages available.

OPEN: All year.

FACILITIES AND ACTIVITIES: Breakfast, lunch, dinner, Sunday brunch, afternoon tea. Tavern, lounge, gift shop, jazz or folk music daily.

**BUSINESS TRAVEL:** Located 18 miles from Boston, 20 miles from Logan Airport. Phone in room; conference room; corporate rates.

The history of The Colonial Inn (1716) ranks with the history of young America from famous Concord, Massachusetts. Here was fired the "shot heard 'round the world." Here lived some of the nation's literary greats—Henry David Thoreau, Ralph Waldo Emerson, Louisa May Alcott, Nathaniel Hawthorne. They are all laid to rest on Author's Ridge in Sleepy Hollow Cemetery, a short walk from the inn. There is so much history in Concord, it would take days to see it all.

High tea means sandwiches of cucumber and radish, cream cheese and chives, smoked salmon and watercress, plus crumpets and scones, cream and fresh berries, miniature cakes and fresh fruit tarts—afternoons here are done right.

The whole inn was refurbished a few years ago, and it's lovely. The main dining room is beautiful, with its white napery, windows full of plants, and beamed ceiling. The lunch menu is extensive with four different salads, good soups, and choices of hot sandwiches such as hot open-face turkey sandwich with giblet gravy, mashed potatoes, and vegetables. You'll also find shrimp scampi, steak au poivre, poached salmon, and cold sandwiches. Dinner, of course, is grand, as are the desserts. The staff is very nice.

The taproom and Liberty and Village Forge lounges are three rustic lounges that, until 1967, served men only. Women are welcome today but at their own risk. Ho, ho. I wasn't scared. Many years ago, however, I stayed in Room 24. Now they tell me it's haunted. Well, the lights came on in the wee hours and woke me. I knew I hadn't turned them on, but I certainly did turn them off—after a while. I wonder who it was?

**HOW TO GET THERE:** Take Route 2 east to Route 62 east to Concord Center to Monument Square. The inn is at 48 Monument Square.

# Deerfield Inn

## Deerfield, Massachusetts 01342

**INNKEEPERS:** Karl and Jane Sabo

**ADDRESS/TELEPHONE:** Main Street; (413) 774–5587 or (800) 926–3865; fax (413) 773–8712

**ROOMS:** 23; all with private bath, air conditioning, phone, and color TV. No smoking inn.

**RATES:** $122.00 to $156.50, double occupancy, EPB.

**OPEN:** All year except December 24 to 26.

**FACILITIES AND ACTIVITIES:** Lunch, dinner. Cocktail lounge, two bars, elevator, color TV in lounge. Nearby: Museums, Deerfield Academy, historic house tours.

**BUSINESS TRAVEL:** Phone in room; conference rooms; audiovisual equipment and fax available.

*S*ome years back a serious fire did extensive damage to this lovely old inn, but alumni of Deerfield and many others banded together and rebuilt the inn. They did such an exquisite job that the federal government has designated the inn a National Historic Site.

The rocking chairs on the front porch somehow let you know how lovely things will be inside. The parlors are beautifully furnished, with mostly twentieth-century copies or adaptations. The Beehive Parlor, done in shades of blue, is a restful place for a cocktail or two. The main dining room is spacious, serving the kind of food befitting the setting. The chef prepares a daily special, taking advantage of seasonal and local market offerings. He also does magical things with veal, chicken, and fish. Fresh fish is brought in three times a week.

The luncheon menu has some interesting and quite different offerings, such as a beautiful summer salad (the raspberry vinaigrette is glorious) and a very good casserole of fresh fish baked in wine and garden herbs. At dinnertime try the gravlax with a sauce of honey mustard and dill. I thought it was yummy. There's also broiled venison on the menu.

The bedrooms are true joys—Beautyrest mattresses, matching bedspreads and drapes, comfortable chairs, and good lights for restful reading or needlework. The baths have been color-coordinated with the rooms they serve. The towels are large and fluffy. Little to nothing has been left to chance in this restoration. Even European hair dryers have been added; they have magnifying mirrors on them.

A coffee shop on the lower level leads out to an outdoor garden: a perfect spot for informal meals and a place the children will love.

Take a carriage ride down the street and around Historic Deerfield. Browse through Memorial Hall Museum, one of the nation's oldest, and through the museum shop. Take time to tour the homes around here—they are lovely.

HOW TO GET THERE: From I-91 take exit 24 northbound. Go 6 miles north on Route 5. At the sign for Old Deerfield Village, take a left. The inn is on your left, just past Deerfield Academy.

## Historic Deerfield

The Deerfield Inn is smack-dab in the middle of one of the nation's best-preserved historic sites. The village of Deerfield was founded in the 1660s at the edge of the frontier claimed by the British. Attacked several times and nearly destroyed twice by Indian and French raids, the settlement was rebuilt throughout the eighteenth century. Now it stands as a monument to two centuries of colonial and early American life and architecture.

Along the mile-long Main Street of Old Deerfield are many beautiful private homes and more than a dozen museum homes. Visit the Hall Tavern Information Center at Historic Deerfield: A Museum of New England History and Art (413–774–5581) to see a lovely short film on the history of the village and its restoration, then buy tickets to tour the homes that are open to the public. There are also museums displaying colonial artifacts, textiles, silver and metalware, costumes, and much more. A charming museum store right next to the Inn offers beautiful reproductions, needlework, fabrics, books, and other gifts that you can buy as a memento of your visit here.

# Nauset House
East Orleans, Massachusetts 02643

**INNKEEPERS:** Diane and Al Johnson, Cindy and John Vessella

**ADDRESS/TELEPHONE:** 143 Beach Road (mailing address: Box 774); (508) 255–2195

**ROOMS:** 14; 8 with private bath.

**RATES:** $75 to $135, double occupancy, EP; afternoon refreshments.

**OPEN:** April 1 to October 31.

**FACILITIES AND ACTIVITIES:** Full breakfast. Dinner by special arrangement. BYOB. Nearby: ocean.

Nauset Beach at East Orleans is the first of the great beaches that rim Cape Cod. Rolling dunes, dashing surf, and wide swaths of sand run southward for more than 10 miles. Quiet, out-of-the-way coves offer the beachgoer an ideal place to sun and picnic or just relax and enjoy. If you prefer fresh water, dozens of inland ponds are at hand.

At Nauset House the conservatory, circa 1910, is from an estate in Greenwich, Connecticut, and was reassembled here in the late 1970s. Very charming with its dolphin fountain, plants and flowers, and nice wicker furniture, it is a pleasant place to while away a summer's evening.

The inn, which includes four guest rooms, dates back to the 1800s and was a farm in those years. The carriage house, with more guest rooms, is the farm's original barn. There is also a one-room cottage called Outermost House. All of the rooms are very comfortable, and many are enhanced by lovely hand-painted furniture. You might find irises on a wall and on a bookrack.

Breakfasts are good, and the innkeepers have printed a recipe book with loads of great ideas to take home. Every afternoon wine and cranberry juice are served with hors d'oeuvres. Diane has done spontaneous dinners such as lobster feasts and pasta by candlelight. In addition, there are good restaurants nearby.

The inn has a good map of the Cape, and the innkeepers are very helpful with arrangements. Boots the cat and Wiley the inn dog will be there to greet you.

**HOW TO GET THERE:** Take exit 12 (Orleans-Brewster) off Route 6. Turn right at bottom of ramp, then right at first traffic light. Proceed to the second traffic light and turn right onto Main Street. Proceed to the fork and bear left onto Beach Road. The inn is ⅘ mile on the right.

# The Charlotte Inn
## Edgartown, Massachusetts 02539

**INNKEEPERS:** Gery and Paula Conover

**ADDRESS/TELEPHONE:** South Summer Street; (508) 627–4751

**ROOMS:** 23, plus 2 suites; all with private bath, some with fireplace, air conditioning, and phone. TVs in most rooms.

**RATES:** In-season, $250 to $650; interim-season, $165 to $550; off-season, $145 to $395; suites, $495 to $650; double occupancy, continental breakfast.

**OPEN:** All year.

**FACILITIES AND ACTIVITIES:** In-season, dinner. Off-season, dinner on weekends. Reservations a must. Gift shop and gallery. Nearby: sailing, swimming, fishing, golf, tennis.

The start of your vacation is a forty-five-minute ferry ride to Martha's Vineyard. It's wise to make early reservations for your automobile on the ferry. There are also cabs if you prefer not to take your car.

When you open the door to the inn, you are in the Edgartown Art Gallery, with interesting artifacts and paintings, both watercolor and oil. This is a well-appointed gallery featuring such artists as Ray Ellis, who has a fine talent in both media. The inn also has an unusual gift shop, now located next to the Garden House.

On one of my visits here, four of us had dinner in the inn's lovely French restaurant, named L'Etoile. The food was exquisite. Capon breast stuffed with duxelles, spinach, and sun-dried tomatoes with coriander mayonnaise was the best I have had. I tasted everyone's food—nice occupation I have. Rack of lamb, served rare, with red wine—rosemary sauce and accompanied by potato and yam gratin was excellent. During my last visit I had grilled Angus filet mignon—it was glorious. My friend Audrey had a halibut fillet. They also have a special or two, but then everything is so special, the word does not fit. The menu changes weekly; desserts the week I was there included blackberry and lemon curd napoleon and rhubarb and raspberry tart—oh my! For breakfast I had a strawberry crepe that I can still remember vividly. Freshly squeezed juices and fruit muffins . . . heaven!

The rooms are authentic. There are fireplaces and Early American four-poster beds, and the carriage house is sumptuous. The second-floor suite has a fireplace I could live in. Paula has a touch with rooms—comfortable furniture, down pillows, down comforters, and all the amenities. As an example, the shower curtains are of eyelet and so pretty. As a finishing touch, there are plenty of large towels.

Across the street is the Garden House, and it is Edgartown at its best. The living room is unique and beautifully furnished, and its fireplace is always set for you. The rooms over here are just so handsome. The Coach House is magnificent, furnished with fine old English antiques, a marble fireplace, and a pair of exquisite chaise lounges in the bedroom. It is air-conditioned.

Paula, by the way, has green hands, and all about are gardens that just outdo one another.

Gery and Paula are special innkeepers, but they do need the help of Ozzie and Jezebel, a pair of goldens.

HOW TO GET THERE: Reservations are a must if you take your car on the ferry from Woods Hole, Massachusetts. Forty-five minutes later you are in Vineyard Haven. After a fifteen-minute ride, you are in Edgartown, and on South Summer Street is the inn.

# Ferrying to Martha's Vineyard

Sailing from "America," as the islanders call the mainland, to Martha's Vineyard is easily accomplished on one of the ferries that ply the waters between the island and Falmouth, Hyannis, Woods Hole, and New Bedford. All of the ferry services offer parking lots for both day-tripping and overnight travelers.

The **Steamship Authority** (508–477–8600 or 508–693–9130) out of Woods Hole offers the only car-and-passenger service to the island, sailing year-round to Vineyard Haven and from May to September to Oak Bluffs. The crossing takes forty-five minutes, and car reservations are required.

The *Island Queen* (508–548–4800) is a passenger ferry that makes daily trips from Falmouth Harbor on Cape Cod to Oak Bluffs on the Vineyard. This crossing takes only thirty-five minutes. From late May to mid-October, this open-air vessel offers a spacious sun deck and a complete snack bar on board as well as secure parking in a private lot not far from the Falmouth dock. Day-trippers and other seasonal visitors can bring bicycles aboard and cycle along the island's shore path and into Oak Bluffs, Vineyard Haven, and Edgartown. Island tours can also be arranged through this ferry service.

Also in season only, from May through October, the **Cape Island Express** (508–997–1688) sails from New Bedford to Vineyard Haven and the Hy-Line *Grey Lady* high-speed catamaran (508–778–2600) sails from Hyannis to Oak Bluffs. The 600-passenger ferry *Schamonchi* (508–997–1688) travels from Billy Woods Wharf in New Bedford to Vineyard Haven from mid-May to mid-October.

# The Daggett House
Edgartown, Massachusetts 02539

**INNKEEPER:** Stephen Warriner; John Chirgwin and Jim Chirgwin, owners

**ADDRESS/TELEPHONE:** 59 North Water Street; (508) 627–4600 or (800) 946–3400; fax (508) 627–4611

**WEB SITE:** www.mvweb.com/daggett

**ROOMS:** 31, plus 4 suites; all with private bath, TV, and phone. No smoking inn.

**RATES:** $80 to $225, double occupancy; $115 to $550, suites; EP.

**OPEN:** All year.

**FACILITIES AND ACTIVITIES:** Breakfast and dinner April through October; full license. Boating and swimming.

The Daggett House, built in 1660, has an interesting history. It was the first tavern on Martha's Vineyard licensed to sell beer and ale. It has been a store, a lodging for sailors, an accounting house in whaling days, and a privately owned mansion. In 1948 it was purchased by the Chirgwin family and became an inn.

The location on the water is splendid, and the ferry to Chappaquiddick Island is right here. Yachts and sailboats sail by the inn's private dock.

The inn consists of three buildings. The Garden Cottage is down by the water. It once was a schoolhouse and later became an artist's studio. It is open from April to November. One room has a large picture window and a comfortable chaise lounge. Another has white wicker furniture and a lovely white canopy bed. All of the beds are comfortable.

The Captain Warren House, which is also open April to November, is across the street. Built around 1850, it has lovely rooms, nice wallpapers, and interesting tiles in the tubs.

Some of the rooms have ceiling fans, and all have televisions and telephones. The third floor has a large suite, with two bedrooms and baths, living room, dining room, and kitchen. Up on the roof the widow's walk has a view that won't quit and a hot tub and chairs. Why go anywhere else? This is as close to heaven as you will get.

The dining room is in the main inn. It has a beehive fireplace that dates back to 1660 and a bookcase that swings open to reveal a hidden stairway leading to a guest room. Of course, it's named the Secret Staircase Room. The Chappaquiddick Suite looks at the island and has a hot tub. There's another room called the Red Canopy Room, which, of course, has a red canopy as well as a view of the harbor.

The breakfast menu is ample. There are omelets, waffles, eggs Benedict, and Grapenut French toast. The recipe for the Grapenut Bread is yours for the asking and came from the owner's mother. The dinner menu changes often. The entrees when I was there were scallops, salmon, pork loin, duck, and wonderful baked scrod. The first course had a new one for this inn creeper—littlenecks served five ways.

**HOW TO GET THERE:** Take the ferry to Martha's Vineyard. In Edgartown go down Main Street to North Water Street. Turn left and the inn is on the right.

---

# Coonamessett Inn
## Falmouth, Massachusetts 02541

**INNKEEPERS:** Linda and Bill Zammer, Jr.; Jim Underdah, general manager

**ADDRESS/TELEPHONE:** 311 Gifford Street; (508) 548–2300; fax (508) 540–9831

**E-MAIL:** cmi.cathi@aol.com

**WEB SITE:** www.capecod.com/coonamessett

**ROOMS:** 25 suites, plus 1 cottage; all with private bath.

**RATES:** $79 to $250, double occupancy, EP.

**OPEN:** All year.

**FACILITIES AND ACTIVITIES:** Lunch, dinner, bar. Parking.

**RECOMMENDED COUNTRY INNS® TRAVELERS' CLUB BENEFIT:** 10 percent discount, subject to availability.

In 1796, in a rolling field that sloped gently down to a lovely pond, Thomas Jones constructed a house and barn that was to become Coonamessett Inn (an Indian word for "the place of the large fish"). The framework of the house is finished with wooden-peg joints, and much of the interior paneling is original. Many of the bricks in the old fireplaces are thought to be made of ballast brought from Europe in the holds of sailing ships. Hanging in the inn are many paintings by the primitive American artist Ralph Cahoon. They represent much of the history of the Coonamessett.

The food is excellent, offered from a large, varied menu and served by friendly waitresses. Luncheons attract a lot of people, as the inn's food reputation travels far and wide. The famous Coonamessett Onion Rings are glorious. Dinner appetizers are many, including clams casino—my favorite after lobster—and baked imported brie with basil pesto. A real winner, and judged to be the best in the East, is the lobster bisque, and I'll second it. It's really almost better than I make! And dinner entrees are great, with fresh lobster meat, Cape Cod lobster pie, or cold boiled lobster. There are other seafood dishes, and meat eaters are not forgotten either. There are beef, lamb, and veal entrees, plus the chef's special homemade fresh pasta of the day. (Note: The innkeepers also own Bally's Restaurant in North Falmouth and the Flying Bridge Restaurant overlooking Falmouth Harbor.)

The Cape Cod Room is the newest addition at the inn, and it is large and grand, with windows along one wall overlooking the pond. The room seats 300 at a sit-down dinner, and the chandeliers—more than a dozen of them—are beautiful. Outside the Cape Cod Room and the main dining room is a deck large  enough for al fresco dining and glorious enough for a wedding ceremony.

The guest suites have a sitting room, bedroom, modern bath, color television, and touchtone telephone. They are furnished with period antiques and Colonial pine and cherry reproductions. These are cottage suites, as there are no guest rooms in the inn itself. At present all of the suites are being refurbished and the baths tiled; I can't wait till I see the improvements.

I love the Cape in the off-season, and it's good to know that no matter what day I decide to come, I will receive a cordial welcome here. The inn grounds are beautiful and are kept in mint condition year-round. All around you will see the loveliest array of grass, trees, flowers, shrubs . . . and peace. Don't forget the peace.

I wish I lived closer, because I like the whole thing, starting with the flower arrangements, fresh every other day, that are done by a woman who really knows how to arrange.

**HOW TO GET THERE:** Take Route 28 at the bridge over the canal, and go into Falmouth. Turn left on Jones Road, and at the intersection of Gifford Street, you will see the inn.

# Thornewood Inn
## Great Barrington, Massachusetts 01230

**INNKEEPERS:** Terry and David Thorne

**ADDRESS/TELEPHONE:** 453 Stockbridge Road; (413) 528–3828

**ROOMS:** 10; all with private bath and TV, 2 with fireplace.

**RATES:** $65 to $175, double occupancy, EPB.

**FACILITIES AND ACTIVITIES:** Dinner, Sunday brunch in summer only. Jazz entertainment on weekends only, taproom, swimming pool. Nearby: skiing, Tanglewood, summer theater, museums.

The inn, a Dutch Colonial built in 1920, has been restored with care. The rooms have twin, double, or queen beds, some of which are four-posters and canopies. All the rooms are comfortable and furnished with antiques and fine reproductions.

The library-taproom is nice and has its own light fare menu and music on Friday and Saturday nights by the Dave Thorne Trio. The full beer menu includes information about authentic world-class brewing styles. It's all about ales and lager. It's very interesting.

Dining at the Thornewood is quite elegant. The dining room has mauve and white napery, candles, and stained-glass panels in the entryway. The menu changes seasonally. When I was there, one of the appetizers was French goat cheese in puff pastry, baked golden brown and served on a bed of fresh spinach with lemon vinaigrette. Another was sea scallops in a sherry, lemon, and garlic sauce. Mussels are served steamed with wine, garlic, butter, and herbs.

Entrees of Norwegian salmon, Adams Apple Pork, pastas, duck, and grilled lamb steak are followed by grand desserts. A delicious country breakfast is served in the morning.

The inn is minutes away from Tanglewood, summer playhouses, museums, and antiques shops. Winter brings skiing, and summer is ideal for relaxing in the inn's own pool.

**HOW TO GET THERE:** The inn is at the junction of Routes 7 and 183 in Great Barrington.

# Windflower Inn 💟
## Great Barrington, Massachusetts 01230

**INNKEEPERS:** Barbara and Gerald Liebert, Claudia and John Ryan

**ADDRESS/TELEPHONE:** 684 South Egremont Road; (413) 528–2720 or (800) 992–1993

**ROOMS:** 13; all with private bath, many with fireplace and TV.

**RATES:** $110 to $180, double occupancy, EPB.

**OPEN:** All year.

**FACILITIES AND ACTIVITIES:** Swimming pool. Nearby: golf, tennis, downhill and cross-country skiing, music, theater. BYOB.

*G*reat Barrington was settled in the eighteenth century, and today it is a lovely resort town. The inn was built in 1820 and is Federal style.

I like the large living room. It has a white brick fireplace, couches, and a huge coffee table covered with magazines. Very conducive to loafing. There is also a reading or game room with a piano for anyone who knows how to play. There are tons of books to read.

The guest rooms are spacious. All the beds are queens, and some have canopies. Fireplaces are in some of the rooms. The room on the first floor

has its own entrance from the terrace and a large stone fireplace. It's a lovely room.

The dining room features Currier & Ives snow scenes on the walls and works done by local artists. One of them, by Gerald, is of his granddaughter holding a balloon. It's very dear.

The vegetable garden is a 70-by-90-foot spread of delights. John was ready to go out and pick raspberries when I saw him. He is the only one who picks them, because he's so careful that they don't get bruised.

The country club across the street is available for golf and tennis. The inn's own swimming pool is very relaxing, and in summer you have Tanglewood, Jacob's Pillow, and the Berkshire Theater nearby.

**HOW TO GET THERE:** The inn is on Route 23, 3 miles west of Great Barrington.

# Augustus Snow House
## Harwichport, Massachusetts 02646

**INNKEEPERS:** Joyce and Steve Roth

**ADDRESS/TELEPHONE:** 528 Main Street; (508) 430–0528

**ROOMS:** 5; all with private bath, TV, and ceiling fan.

**RATES:** $105 to $170, double occupancy, EPB and high tea.

**OPEN:** All year.

**FACILITIES AND ACTIVITIES:** BYOB. Lawn games, croquet, badminton. One block from private beach.

Built in 1901, the Augustus Snow House is a romantic Queen Anne Victorian mansion that's a real beauty. It has gabled dormers and a wraparound porch with a screened gazebo.

The parlor has a fireplace, nice couches, and an interesting old organ that doesn't work. A small dining room for inn guests is off this room. Guests are provided with a gourmet breakfast and an elegant high tea.

Up the stairs is a cabinet full of old Cabbage Patch dolls and five exquisite rooms that are named after the three daughters and their mothers: a nice idea. The wallpapers all through the inn are glorious. Three rooms have whirlpools. All have televisions and ceiling fans. One room has the most unusual commode I have ever seen, and I surely have seen a lot of them. This is Sara's Room.

Melissa's Room has beautifully curved bay windows, a fireplace, and a grand bath. Amy's Room is Country French, with yellow striped wallpaper, and has the house's original bathroom with a claw-footed tub. Belle's Room has a private entrance, a king-sized bed, and tons of charm. Rose's Room is soft pink and has a water view, a four-poster queen-sized bed, and abundant charm.

There's a patio with white iron furniture. In-season, dining is out here for those who wish. The grounds are beautiful, and a private beach is just 1 block away.

**HOW TO GET THERE:** Take exit 10 off the Mid-Cape Highway (Route 6). Proceed south on Route 124/39 to Main Street in Harwich Center. Turn left onto Main Street and then take your first right onto Bank Street. Follow Bank Street to Route 28 and turn right. The inn is about ½ mile on your right.

# The Morgan House
## Lee, Massachusetts 01238

**INNKEEPERS:** Lenora and Stuart Bowen; Pauline Lauden, manager

**ADDRESS/TELEPHONE:** Main Street; (413) 243–0181

**ROOMS:** 11; 6 with private bath

**RATES:** $50 to $160, per room, EPB.

**OPEN:** All year.

**FACILITIES AND ACTIVITIES:** Lunch, dinner, bar, and lounge. Nearby: Tanglewood, Jacob's Pillow, golf, tennis, swimming, hiking.

*T*he Morgan House is a great in-town inn. It has a long and interesting history dating back to 1817, when it was built as a private home. In 1853 it was converted into a stagecoach inn, and an inn it has remained.

The lobby is papered in old registration sheets, many of them showing the names of noted visitors over the past hundred years, such as Ulysses S. Grant, Robert E. Lee, "Buffalo Bill" Cody, Horace Greeley, and George Bernard Shaw. Many of the pages are beautifully decorated in flowing script advertising the bill at the local opera house.

Lenora is a fine chef and artist; she's a very multitalented lady. All the paintings in the dining room are hers. Neither Lenora nor Stuart looks old enough to have the extensive background each has.

Lunch features appetizers, soups, salads, and grand sandwiches, as well as entrees like Boston scrod, scallops, and baked stuffed shrimp.

One of the dinner appetizers sounds so good; it's a lobster, scallop, and sweet potato cake with roasted red pepper sauce. For main courses there are ample choices for everyone—pastas, chicken, salmon, scrod, cranberry pot roast, roast duckling, and a lot more. Save room for dessert, because they are grand.

All the rooms are being refurbished. Those that were finished when I was there are very comfortable and cozy, just what you'd expect at an inn that has welcomed such illustrious guests.

**HOW TO GET THERE:** From the Massachusetts Turnpike take exit 2. Follow Route 20 west 1 mile, to the center of Lee. The inn will be on your left.

# Jacob's Pillow Dance Festival

This ten-week summer festival celebrates the work of some of the nation's most talented and innovative dance companies. Performing in the rustic country setting of the world-class dance school named Jacob's Pillow, Paul Taylor, Alvin Ailey, Merce Cunningham, Meredith Monk, Twyla Tharp, Margot Fonteyn, and many other dance greats have wowed audiences at both indoor and outdoor theaters. On a hilltop former farm in the town of Becket, just east of Lee, are studios where you can watch rehearsals, a cafe where you can enjoy a light meal, and picnic areas where you can relax while you watch developing dancers practice their art. Performance tickets are $15 to $40. Call (413) 243–0745 for the schedule or tickets.

# The Gateways Inn
## Lenox, Massachusetts 01240

INNKEEPERS: Rosemary and Fabrizio Chiariello

ADDRESS/TELEPHONE: 51 Walker Street; (413) 637–2532; fax (413) 637–1432

E-MAIL: gateways@berkshire.net

WEB SITE: gatewaysinn.com

ROOMS: 11, plus 1 suite with fireplace; all with private bath, phone, TV, and air conditioning.

RATES: In-season, $120 to $185, room; $295, suite; off-season, $85 to $150, room; $260, suite; continental breakfast.

OPEN: All year.

FACILITIES AND ACTIVITIES: Restaurant closed Mondays and Tuesdays in winter. In summer dinner by reservation preferred. Open for lunch during Tanglewood season. Nearby: Berkshires attractions.

The Gateways began as a mansion built for Harley Procter of Procter and Gamble, the Ivory soap magnate. In the shape of his favorite product, a cake of soap, it is square and flat on top. The new owners have done extensive work on the Inn, and it sure shows. The dining rooms are glorious, and the menus are wonderful. The canopied terrace is neat; no bugs out here—there's a net to keep them out.

The chef, who trained under former chef-owner Gerhard Schmid for the past few years, learned his lessons well. The food is still as delicious as ever. The Gateways rates three stars in the *Mobil Travel Guide*.

Want a few hints of what to expect? Lobster cocktail, mussels vinaigrette, and smoked salmon are some of the appetizers. Chilled vichysoisse and bisques are some soups. These are followed by wonderful salads and entrees like veal sweetbreads, veal contadina, steaks, salmon continental, rack of lamb, fish, game, poultry, and specials of the house. The desserts are fabulous. I really cannot say enough about his creations. You'll have to try  them for yourself. In summer you'll enjoy dining on a lovely side porch.

The oval windows beside the front door and the magnificent stairway alone are worth a visit here.

Two bedrooms, with their high ceilings, are perfect for the massive furniture with which they are furnished. The other bedrooms, equally lovely, have Colonial-style furniture. Every room has its own temperature controls, and color-coordinated towels in the baths add just the right final touch. The suite is called the Fiedler Suite because Arthur Fiedler stayed in it so many times. It is lavish in its appointments and is worth all it costs to spend a night in. Double Jacuzzis are in here, too.

It is hard to believe that this lovely inn was once a girls' finishing school, a ballet school, a real estate office, and a boardinghouse. Lucky for us that it's now such a nice inn.

HOW TO GET THERE: Take Route 7 to Route 7A. The inn is on Route 7A, 1 block from the intersection of Routes 183 and 7A.

# The Village Inn
## Lenox, Massachusetts 01240

**INNKEEPERS:** Clifford Rudisill and Ray Wilson

**ADDRESS/TELEPHONE:** Church Street; (413) 637–0020

**ROOMS:** 32; all with private bath and phone, 6 with fireplace, 1 room for the handicapped.

**RATES:** $50 to $225, double occupancy, EP. MAP rates available.

**OPEN:** All year.

**FACILITIES AND ACTIVITIES:** Breakfast, afternoon tea, dinner Tuesday through Sunday in summer and fall. Village Tavern. Nearby: skiing, tennis, golf, swimming, horseback riding, fishing, hiking, Tanglewood, Jacob's Pillow.

There is a saying here at the inn: "If you can't be a houseguest in the Berkshires, be ours." This surely would be a fine choice. The rooms are so clean and cheerful. The inn's walls are covered with stenciled wallpapers, the maple floors have Oriental rugs, and antiques are found throughout the inn.

The Village Tavern, a British pub, was built in the old cellars of this 1771 house. It is furnished with seats made from church pews. On those blustery winter days, there is a cheery fire to go with your drink. The living room, called the Common Room, is a delightful place to sit and listen to the grand piano being played. There is a nice television and reading room for your comfort.

A real first is an authentic English tea, served from 2:30 to 4:30 P.M. every day, with homemade scones, pastries, and small tea sandwiches. To make it perfect, you are provided with Devonshire-style clotted cream.

The Village Inn is the name of the restaurant here at the inn. Breakfast includes choices like sourdough French toast and omelets you design yourself from a list of nine add-in ingredients. You can also choose a French breakfast or an English one. Very inventive. The dinner menu has a nice variety of first courses and entrees like veal chops poêle with bourbon and green pepper-corn sauce, beef sirloin, fillet of salmon, and rack of lamb. And the desserts—oh, my! Come pay a visit and try some.

The inn is near many activities, churches, shops, the library, and the bus stop.

**HOW TO GET THERE:** Take Route 7A off Route 7 and turn on Church Street in Lenox. The inn is on the right.

# Wheatleigh 💙
## Lenox, Massachusetts 01240

**INNKEEPERS:** Susan and Linfield Simon; Francois Thomas, general manager

**ADDRESS/TELEPHONE:** West Hawthorne; (413) 637–0610; fax (413) 637–4507

**WEB SITE:** www.wheatleigh.com

**ROOMS:** 17; all with private bath, air conditioning, and phone; 9 with working fireplace.

**RATES:** $175 to $625, double occupancy, EP.

**OPEN:** All year.

**FACILITIES AND ACTIVITIES:** Lunch for houseguests, dinner, Sunday brunch. Grill room, lounge. Swimming, tennis, cross-country skiing.

**RECOMMENDED COUNTRY INNS® TRAVELERS' CLUB BENEFIT:** Stay two nights, get third night free, subject to availability.

*I*n the heart of the picturesque Berkshires, overlooking a lake, amid lawns and gardens on twenty-two self-contained acres stands the estate of Wheatleigh, former home of the Countess de Heredia. The centerpiece of this property is an elegant private palace fashioned after an Italian palazzo. The cream-colored manse re-creates the architecture of six-teenth-century Florence. You must read the brochure of Wheatleigh, for it says it all so well.

Patios, pergolas, porticos, and terraces surround this lovely old mansion. The carvings over the fireplaces, cupids entwined in garlands, are exquisite. In charming contrast, the inn also has the largest collection of contemporary ceramics in the New England area. There are many lovely porcelain pieces on the walls. In the dining room are tile paintings weighing more than 500 pounds. They are Doultons from 1830; this was before it became Royal Doulton. They are just beautiful.

The portico is a prime dining room—all glass with glorious views. And the food—wow! The grill room, which is open in-season, provides an a la carte menu of light fare prepared to the same high standards of the dining room. Its casual ambience features an elegant black-and-white color scheme—the plates are beautiful.

There is a service bar in a lovely lounge, and boy, you sure can relax in the furniture in here! It has a wonderful fireplace, and the views from here are glorious. And imagine a great hall with a grand staircase right out of a castle in Europe. There are also exquisite stained-glass windows in pale pastels, plus gorgeous, comfortable furniture. From the great hall you can hear the tinkle of the fountain out in the garden.

The whole inn was done over very recently, and wow, the rooms are smashing! Do you long for your own balcony overlooking a lovely lake? No problem. Reserve one here. The facilities are not well suited to children under eight.

At the entrance to the dining room, the homemade desserts are beautifully displayed, along with French champagne in six sizes, from a jeroboam to a small bottle for one. This is very nice indeed. I chose grilled quail on young lettuce leaves and raspberries for a dinner appetizer; it was superb. Tartare of fresh tuna was strikingly presented, just like a Japanese picture, and delicious. I also had chilled fresh pea soup with curry and sorrel, followed by monkfish coated with pistachios, sautéed, with red wine sauce.

Homemade sorbets are very good, but then so is everything else here. The executive chef is Peter Platt. He has been here for years, and he offers cooking classes on Sunday through Thursday—a French immersion course!

Susan's description of the inn is "elegance without arrogance," and Lin's is "the ultimate urban amenity." Mine is "a perfect country inn."

There are very special weekend pacakges; do call and ask. Two that come to mind are a Burgundy Weekend with Louis Jadot and a Chocolate Lover's Weekend. Wow—wish I lived closer!

HOW TO GET THERE: From Stockbridge at the Red Lion Inn where Route 7 turns right, go straight on Prospect Hill Road, bearing left. Travel about 4 ½ miles, past the Stockbridge Bowl and up a hill to Wheatleigh.

From the Massachusetts Turnpike, take exit 2, and follow signs to Lenox. In the center of Lenox, take Route 183, pass the main gate of Tanglewood, and then take the first left on West Hawthorne. Go 1 mile to Wheatleigh.

# Hannah Dudley House
Leverett, Massachusetts 01054

INNKEEPERS: Erni and Daryl Johnson

ADDRESS/TELEPHONE: 114 Dudleyville Road; (413) 367–2323

ROOMS: 3, plus 1 suite; all with private bath, hair dryer, iron, and ironing board, some with fireplace.

RATES: $125 to $185, double occupancy, EPB. $560, whole inn, first night; $530 subsequent nights.

OPEN: All year except Christmas Eve, Christmas Day, and one week in midwinter.

FACILITIES AND ACTIVITIES: Dinner by reservation in summer and fall. Wintertime hot hors d'oeuvres. Swimming pool, hiking, fishing, skating, ponds.

RECOMMENDED COUNTRY INNS® TRAVELERS' CLUB BENEFIT: 20 percent discount, Monday–Thursday, or stay five nights, get sixth night free, subject to availability.

*T*his one is a rare find—it's in the woods. As the innkeepers say, it is "secluded on a quiet country road in the most scenic area of the Pioneer Valley." No matter where you look out the windows, there are trees and lush landscaping on the 110-acre property.

You will find privacy, quiet, and beauty at the Hannah Dudley House. There are just three rooms and one suite, but the inn has places to sit and fireplaces in abundance. All of the guest rooms have their own small refrigerators, and two also have fireplaces.

The inn is old, built, they think, about 1797. It has been modernized but not spoiled. It's truly lovely.

The Kitty Korner is the suite, with its own fireplace and a queen-sized bed. I wish I could take the bedframe home, it's such a beauty. The sitting room is the Mouse Hole with a couch. Its bath is grand, with a very deep tub and a separate shower.

Hannah's Room, done in Colonial decor, is sunlit and lovely. The Dragon's Lair was created for the innkeeper's collection of dragons and wizards. It has a queen-sized bed and fireplace. This is your own private castle.

Frog Hollow is very bright and froggie—you'll see one outside the door, holding up a wall. It has two double beds and a double sink in the bathroom.

Take a walk on one of the many walking trails. They are well marked, and there's a trail map. Daryl makes giant wind chimes, and you'll see a few. The meadow above the 20-by-40-foot in-ground pool is a delight for any sort of outdoor function. As you can imagine, a wedding here would be grand.

Breakfast is the big thing here. It starts with fruit, and on the table are cold cereals, granola, juices in nice pitchers, and hot water for coffee, tea, or hot chocolate. Then Erni and Daryl produce muffins. I had glorious blueberry ones. And pancakes of all kinds. Hot apple crisp, too. You will not go away hungry.

Dinner is served by reservation in the summer and fall. If you're lucky enough to be here, you'll find they do it well. I had a lobster dinner that was a wow.

Erni and Daryl miss the ocean, so they've given their gameroom, the Captain's Quarters, a nautical feeling.

You'll also find a small gift shop, Bart the Bear, Dudley Bear at the front door, and some smaller bears. There are a refrigerator for guests to use and a microwave, paper products, coffee, tea, and hot chocolate. Both Erni and Daryl beat me at bumper pool; oh well. Outside are porches, patios, hammocks, picnic tables, ponds, fish, a barbecue, and more.

**HOW TO GET THERE:** From I–91 take Route 116 south 2 miles. Then go left onto Route 47 and go north 5 miles. Cross over Route 63 to North Leverett Road. Travel 3⁷⁄₁₀ miles. On the right is the village co-op; Dudleyville Road is a right fork just beyond the co-op. Follow it 1 mile. Go left at the sign, into the inn.

# Jared Coffin House
## Nantucket, Massachusetts 02554

**INNKEEPERS:** Philip and Peg Read; Jonathan P. Stone, general manager

**ADDRESS/TELEPHONE:** 29 Broad Street; (508) 228–2400 or
(800) 248–2405; fax (508) 228–2400

**E-MAIL:** jchouse@nantucket.net

**WEB SITE:** www.nantucket.net/lodging/jchouse

**ROOMS:** 60; 11 in main house, 16 simpler rooms in Eben Allen Wing, 3 rooms in Swain House connected to the Eben Allen Wing, 12 rooms in Daniel Webster House across the patio, 18 rooms in 2 houses across the street.

**RATES:** $60 and up, single; in-season, $150 to $200, double occupancy; off-season $100 to $120, double occupancy; EPB.

**OPEN:** All year.

**FACILITIES AND ACTIVITIES:** Breakfast, lunch, dinner, taproom. Eben Allen Room for private parties. Nearby: swimming, tennis.

**BUSINESS TRAVEL:** Meeting rooms; fax, e-mail, overhead projector available.

*I*t is well worth the 30-mile trip by ferry, or the plane trip from Boston or New York, to end up at the Jared Coffin House. Built as a private home in 1845, the three-story brick house with slate roof became an inn only twelve years later. The inn passed through many hands before it came to the extremely capable ones of Philip and Peg Read.

The public rooms at the inn reflect charm and warmth. The furnishings are Chippendale and Sheraton; showing the results of the worldwide voyaging by the Nantucket whalemen are Chinese and Japanese objets d'art and furniture.

To add to the charm are many fabrics and some furniture that have been made right here on the island. In addition to the main house, there are several other close-by houses that go with the inn. All are done beautifully for your every comfort. The size and the quantity of the luxurious bath towels in the guest rooms please me greatly. The housekeeping staff does a wonderful job, and the exquisite antiques reflect their loving care.

The taproom, located on the lowest level, is a warm, happy, fun place. Here you meet the local people and spin yarns with all. Old pine walls and hand-hewn beams reflect a cozy atmosphere. Luncheon is served down here, with good burgers and great, hearty soups. During the winter this is a nice spot for informal dinners.

The main dining room, papered with authentic wallpapers, is quiet and elegant. Wedgwood china and pistol-handled silverware make dining a special pleasure and reflect the good life demanded by the nineteenth-century owners of the great Nantucket whaling ships.

The inn is located in the heart of Nantucket's Historic District, about ⅛ mile from one public beach and 1 mile from the island's largest public beach and tennis courts. It's a very pleasant 3-mile bicycle ride through the district to superb surf swimming on the South Shore.

HOW TO GET THERE: To get to Nantucket, take a ferry from Hyannis (April through January) or Woods Hole (January through March and summer months). First call (508) 540–2022 for reservations. Or take a plane from Boston, Hyannis, or New York. The inn is located 2 blocks north of Main Street and 2 blocks west of Steamboat Wharf.

# Wauwinet
## Nantucket, Massachusetts 02554

**INNKEEPERS:** Russ and Debbie Cleveland; Steven and Jill Karp, owners

**ADDRESS/TELEPHONE:** P.O. Box 2580; (508) 228–0145 or (800) 426–8718; fax (508) 228–6712

**ROOMS:** 32, plus 3 suites; all with private bath, TV, phone, and air conditioning. No smoking inn.

**RATES:** Spring and fall, $165 to $590, single or double occupancy; $410 to $1,170, cottage suite; summer, $310 to $710, single or double occupancy; $610 to $1,400, cottage suite, EPB.

**OPEN:** Mid-May through October.

**FACILITIES AND ACTIVITIES:** Lunch and dinner daily; Sunday brunch. Lounge, pro shop, tennis, bocce, boating, sailing, swimming, biking, croquet, harbor cruises.

The inn opened in the middle nineteenth century as the Wauwinet House, a restaurant serving "shore dinners." It was named for a seventeenth-century Indian chief. The Karps, who bought and restored the property, were longtime Nantucket visitors.

The rooms and suites are lovely, with grand views. There are king- and queen-sized beds, all very comfortable. The bathrooms even have a clothesline in the tub area, good fluffy towels, and a nice pair of robes.

There are Har-Tru clay tennis courts and pro shop, swimming, sailboats, rowing sculls, kayaks, eighteen-speed mountain bikes, croquet, bocce, and beach chess for adults only. Or take a harbor cruise. The captain will take you to a secluded spot for swimming or loafing. A picnic lunch is also provided. This is a nice way to spend a vacation.

For quiet entertainment you'll be given a key to the lovely library. It has a huge fireplace, good overstuffed chairs and couches, tables, classical music, and hundreds of New England books. The fireplace in here is the original one.

Toppers, the restaurant, provides a casual but sophisticated setting indoors and on a seaview deck. For breakfast there are many choices, including eggs Benedict or eggs Argyle (which have salmon instead of ham). I had a favorite of mine one morning—Grapenuts with raspberries. If you are a hearty eater, there are Wauwinet Wild Turkey Hash, two-poached eggs, and hollandaise sauce. Lunch is really different. The menu is designed so you can sample several items in small portions. I tried grilled curried chicken salad with banana chips and the sautéed sirloin with mushrooms. My friend Audrey tried the salmon horns with chive sour cream. Wow, were they good! The presentation is grand. You can also opt for a picnic-basket lunch—this is a great area for a picnic.

The dinner appetizer of lobster and crabcakes with smoked corn, jalapeño olives, and mustard sauce is a winner. Salads are good, and dinner entrees include saffron linguine with local lobster and herb butter, loin of lamb, salmon, and turkey. The desserts are glorious. Come on out and try them.

A really neat little bar and lounge serves a really hot Bloody Mary and a

## Getting to Nantucket

Flying and ferrying are the two preferred methods of traveling to Nantucket, unless you happen to have your own sturdy boat or the means to charter one. To fly from the mainland to Nantucket Memorial Airport (508–325–5300), call Business Express/Delta Connections (800–345–3400) for flights from Boston year-round and from New York's La Guardia Airport in season. Call Cape Air/Nantucket Air (508–771–6944 or 800–352–0714) for flights from Hyannis and Providence year-round. Call Colgan Air (800–272–5488) for flights from Hyannis and Newark year-round. Call Continental Express (800–525–0280) for nonstop flights from Newark in season.

Ferries run year-round from Hyannis only. The Steamship Authority (508–477–8600) offers car-and-passenger, two-and-a-quarter-hour-trips. Hy-Line (508–778–2600) sends its high-speed cat *Grey Lady* on one-hour crossings year-round and its slower MV *Great Point* ferry on two-hour crossings from mid-May to late October. Reservations for cars are a must.

great Painkiller. The staff is very gracious. The inn has won awards for its extensive wine list.

A guest library and tennis courts are also here; it's a lovely walk to the latter. Inn guests also have access to more than 20 miles of quiet, unspoiled Atlantic Ocean and bay beaches. Among summer activities are boating and cruises on Nantucket Bay, organized bird-watching outings, and four-wheel-drive natural history excursions; amenities include beach towels and lounge chairs. Sunrises on the Atlantic Ocean, sunsets on Nantucket Bay, and more—what are you waiting for?

**HOW TO GET THERE:** Take the ferry or fly over. Call for the jitney from the inn to pick you up.

# The Woodbox Inn
## Nantucket, Massachusetts 02554

**INNKEEPER:** Dexter Tutein

**ADDRESS/TELEPHONE:** 29 Fair Street; (508) 228–0587

**ROOMS:** 3 queens, plus 6 suites in 2 buildings; all with private bath.

**RATES:** $150 to $260, double occupancy, EP. No credit cards.

**OPEN:** Memorial Day to Columbus Day. Weekends only from Columbus Day to January 1.

**FACILITIES AND ACTIVITIES:** Full breakfast, dinner, beer and wine license. Wheelchair access to sunrooms, dining rooms. Nearby: swimming, boating, biking, tennis.

**RECOMMENDED COUNTRY INNS® TRAVELERS' CLUB BENEFIT:** Stay two nights, get third night free, Monday–Thursday, from late October to end of May, excluding holidays.

For forty-five years there has been a Tutein running this inn. Built in 1709, it is the oldest inn on Nantucket Island. What a treat to be here!

The suites are unique. In an old building like this, you cannot change the structure to modernize it, so the bathrooms have been very inventively fit in.

Very pretty and comfortable. The suite I was in had a fireplace in the living room, two bedrooms, one with a huge canopy bed, and a lovely little private patio. It was hard to leave.

There are three dining rooms in the inn. I'm sure I had dinner in what must be the oldest public dining room in New England. The room has two "king's boards" on the wall of the immense, almost walk-in fireplace. Today the fireplace holds an old cradle with dried flowers. The china is old, and there are nice touches on the tables, like your own pepper mill. Tall candlesticks add to the charm of this inn.

The inn is famous for its popovers, and I can understand why, having devoured quite a few. The food is truly gourmet. Naturally, the entrees include the catch of the day; I had fresh sea bass that was delicious. My dinner companion had the veal chop, saffron rice, and glazed pear chutney. The house salad dressing is excellent. And for dessert, well, the best crème brûlée I have ever had.

The inn's breakfast is a great way to start the day—choose Belgian waffles or pancakes or the eggs Benedict—an inn tradition. The pancakes and waffles come with pure maple syrup, blueberries, strawberries, peaches, or apples. Those wonderful popovers come with any egg dish. The chef has cooked several times at the James Beard Founda-tion in New York City. One night during our stay, Dexter took us to a real Nantucket hot spot for a very unusual dinner at Black Eye Susan's (508-325-0308) at 10 India Street—do go try this one.

The powder room must be seen. There are no words to describe it.

**HOW TO GET THERE:** Take the ferry to Nantucket or fly from Hyannis. The inn is at 29 Fair Street. You can walk to it from the ferry.

# Yankee Clipper Inn
## Rockport, Massachusetts 01966

**INNKEEPERS:** Bob and Barbara Wemyss Ellis

**ADDRESS/TELEPHONE:** 96 Granite Street; (978) 546–3407 or
(800) 545–3699; fax (978) 549–9730

**E-MAIL:** info@yankeeclipperinn.com

**ROOMS:** 26, including 6 suites, in 3 buildings; all with private bath,
air conditioning, cable TV, and phone. Some baths have Jacuzzis.

**RATES:** $99 to $279, double occupancy, EPB; MAP is available.

**OPEN:** March 1 to December 15.

**FACILITIES AND ACTIVITIES:** Dinner. Small function room, heated
saltwater pool. Nearby: fishing, boating, shopping, whale watching.

When you are lucky enough to be here and see a sunset, you will be overwhelmed. It's a golden sea and sky, with the town of Rockport in the distance. No camera could truly capture this scene. Wait a while longer, and the moonlight on the sea is an awesome sight.

Three buildings make up the Yankee Clipper. The inn is an oceanfront mansion. Here the rooms have antique furniture, Oriental rugs, and some canopy beds. Some rooms have porches. You're sure to enjoy the television lounge, with cable television and a really big screen. All meals are served in this building.

The Quarterdeck has large picture windows, providing a panoramic view of the ocean. Upholstered chairs are placed in front of the windows. Sit back and relax; it's almost like being on a ship that does not move. All of the rooms in this building are beautifully furnished. Some of the rooms in the Bullfinch House have water views.

The special occasion room is a lovely spot. For any sort of function from small weddings to executive meetings, it has a wonderful water view, a big-screen TV and VCR, and everything you'd need for your meeting.

The Veranda dining room has marvelous views that are matched by the marvelous food. David Pierson is a chef with imagination. I started my dinner with a taste of one appetizer—lobster polenta, which was a baked blend of cornmeal and native lobster, served with boursin cheese sauce—and the soup of the day—cold zucchini soup.

I went on to the seafood au gratin, which was shrimp, scallops, and haddock, baked in cream and herbs, and topped with cheddar cheese and bread crumbs. Vegetarian Wellington was new to me; a medley of fresh vegetables was baked in puff pastry with boursin cheese. Delicious.

The Captain's Quarters is a private, fully furnished house. Rented by the week, it sleeps six. It costs $2,400 without housekeeping, $2,700 with.

To work off some of the calories, you might want to swim in the heated saltwater pool at the inn. In the area there are whale-watching trips, fishing, and, in the town of Rockport, fantastic shopping. It really is fun to walk around here.

**HOW TO GET THERE:** Take Route 128 north and east to Cape Ann. Route 128 ends at traffic lights. Turn left onto Route 127. Drive 3 miles to where Route 127 turns left into Pigeon Cove. Continue on Route 127 for 1²/₁₀ miles to Yankee Clipper in Pigeon Cove.

# The Dan'l Webster Inn
## Sandwich, Massachusetts 02563

**INNKEEPER:** Steve Catania

**ADDRESS/TELEPHONE:** Main Street; (508) 888–3622 or (800) 444–3566

**WEB SITE:** media3.com/dan'lwebsterinn/

**ROOMS:** 47, in 3 buildings; all with private bath, phone, TV, and air conditioning, some with whirlpool tub and fireplace.

**RATES:** $139 to $209, double occupancy, EP per person. $226 to $412 double occupancy, MAP.

**OPEN:** All year except Christmas Day.

**FACILITIES AND ACTIVITIES:** Breakfast, lunch, dinner, Sunday brunch. Bar, lounge, swimming pool, gift shop. Nearby: doll museum, glass museum, Heritage Plantation, beaches.

A 250-year-old linden tree, complete with bird feeders, stands outside the Conservatory, one of the inn's three lovely dining rooms, and a new aquarium filled with beautiful fish is in the wall on the way to the Conservatory dining room. This is a glassed-in room, overlooking a beautifully landscaped courtyard and swimming pool. The dining menu is a bit different. There are half dinners, and, believe me, you will not go away hungry.

The Webster Room has china cabinets to display old Sandwich glass on loan from the museum. There's a portrait of Daniel Webster's second wife in here. The Heritage Room has a huge open fireplace and a grand piano on the stage for your entertainment. A dance band is here on weekends, and they surely sounded good to me.

These dining rooms provide the perfect atmosphere for the excellent food. Breakfasts are hearty, with eggs, six different omelets, sausage, croissants, fruit, and much more. The lunch menu lists salads, sandwiches, and quite a few hot choices. Dinner is an adventure. The hors d'oeuvres list is extensive. I had clams casino and also tasted the escargots, which were served en croute with  mushrooms, garlic, and herb butter. There are four veal offerings, chicken, ten different seafood specials, and, of course, beef. I had chateaubriand—very nice because it was served for one. It was very good. Desserts are sinful, and there are special coffees.

New to the inn is the D. W. Aqua Farm, a state-of-the-art greenhouse aqua farm in which the Catania family is hydroponically growing salad greens, herbs, and flowers for use in the inn. They use no pesticides.

The Devil 'n Dan Tavern is a cozy spot, with stained-glass windows and very nice wooden bar stools. There are tables and chairs here for those who are not barflies.

All the guest rooms are a little different. Most have Hitchcock furniture. Some have canopy beds. All the beds are comfortable. The Webster Suite on the third floor of the inn has two bedrooms and two bathrooms. One bath has a Jacuzzi, and the other has a steam tub.

In the lovely Fessenden House next door are four suites. I was in the Captain Ezra Nye Suite. A whirlpool tub is in each of these suites, as is a marble fireplace. They are beautifully furnished with classic antiques. I had to go up two steps to get into bed. Oh my, I do like it here.

A split of sparkling water is provided in each guest room. The beds are turned down in the evening, and a chocolate is left on the pillow. What nice touches!

The John Carver Inn, in Plymouth, Massachusetts, is sister inn to this one. Steve's brother Bill Catania is innkeeper. It's larger, and there's only a short walk to the "rock" (25 Summer Street; 508–746–7100 or 800–274–1620).

HOW TO GET THERE: Go over the Bourne Bridge to a rotary; go three-fourths of the way around it, taking the Route 6A exit that parallels the canal. Stay on this road until you come to the third set of lights. This is Jarves Street. Go right, then right again onto Main Street. The inn is on the right, close to the corner.

# The Egremont Inn
## South Egremont, Massachusetts 01258

INNKEEPERS: Karen and Steve Waller

ADDRESS/TELEPHONE: Old Sheffield Road (mailing address: Box 418); (413) 528–2111 or (800) 859–1780; fax (413) 528–3284

WEB SITE: www.egremontinn.com

ROOMS: 17, plus 3 suites; all with private bath, some with whirlpool and phone. No smoking in rooms.

RATES: $90 to $190 double occupancy; $130 to $215, suites; EPB on weekends.

OPEN: All year.

FACILITIES AND ACTIVITIES: Dinner Wednesday through Sunday in summer and fall. Live entertainment on Thursday and Saturday. Discounted greens fees and fitness center at nearby country club. Discounted ski tickets. Group rates for bikes.

uilt in 1780, this inn is true New England. It is in the quiet corner of the Southern Berkshires. When you walk in, you are in a huge living room, called the Pine Room. There are a large fireplace, good couches and chairs, and the start of a stuffed animal collection that you'll find all over the inn. I sort of relate to this as I've got tons of bears. Albert the Duck and Winston A. Bear are there waiting. Yes, Karen has named them all.

To the right of this room is another lovely room with a fireplace. There are also a sitting room with another fireplace, a couch right in front of it, and a television. This is where you'll find a lot of board games and a toy chest for children.

The main dining room is warm and attractive. The napery is white, and there are lots of green and flowering plants.

Another fireplace is in here. The food is grand. Among the five appetizers, wild mushroom soup rings a bell. The roast vegetable lasagne is a new entree for me, and there are also pork chops, salmon, lamb chops, and game hen. The menus change often and seasonally.

There's a really nice bar, and the tavern has its own menu, with beer-battered scallops or shrimp, Caesar salad, pastas, burgers, and more.

A very nice summer brunch menu is glorious, with French toast, omelets, eggs Benedict, pasta, spinach salad, and lots more. I wish I lived closer. I had a look at the Easter menu—wow!

Accommodations are delightful. There are several whirlpool tubs, and some floors tilt. This is a wonderful old building.

Do take the walking tour through town, because there is a lot to see. The lovely village is on the National Register of Historic Places. The inn is, too.

**HOW TO GET THERE:** From New York go north on Route 22 or the Taconic Parkway to Route 23 east. After the town of South Egremont, turn right at the small island. The inn is 200 yards ahead. From Boston take the Massachusetts Turnpike to exit 2. Follow Route 102 west to Route 7 south. After going through Great Barrington, take Route 23 west to South Egremont. In $3^3/_{10}$ miles, bear left at the small island. The inn is straight ahead.

# The Weathervane Inn
## South Egremont, Massachusetts 01258

**INNKEEPERS:** Jeffrey and Maxine Lome

**ADDRESS/TELEPHONE:** Main Street (Route 23); (413) 528–9580 or
(800) 528–9580; fax (413) 528–1713

**E-MAIL:** innkeeper@weathervaneinn.com

**WEB SITE:** www.weathervane.com

**ROOMS:** 11, including 1 suite with fireplace, all with private bath, air
conditioning. 2 rooms with wheelchair accessibility. No smoking inn.

**RATES:** $135 to $165 ($245 suite), double occupancy, EBP. On week-
ends, $115 to $150, double occupancy, EBP. Minimum of two nights'
stay on weekends, three nights on holiday weekends and in the summer.
Special seasonal or group packages available, some with dinner.

**OPEN:** All year except Christmas Day.

**FACILITIES AND ACTIVITIES:** Breakfast and afternoon tea; optional
catered dinner for small groups. Swimming pool, outside games.
Nearby: Antiques stores, fishing, hiking, bicycling, golf, tennis, skiing.

**BUSINESS TRAVEL:** Fully appointed meeting room; audiovisual equipment; copying, faxing, Internet access available.

The Weathervane began its existence as a farmhouse in 1785. The
original fireplace, which served as a heating and cooking unit,
boasts a beehive bake oven. These are rarely seen today but were a
real necessity in those early times. The inn has been included in the National
Register of Historic Places.

What better way to cele-
brate the old farmhouse's
history than with a hearty
country breakfast? Innkeepers Jeff and Maxine Lome
offer a homemade French
toast with maple syrup from
local farmers. It's to die for!
Or you can savor fresh-
baked muffins, like their

applesauce strudel muffins, in addition to other hot-off-the-griddle breakfast
fare. Don't miss the homemade preserves prepared from fruit grown on the

premises. Talk about flavorful! You'll enjoy this feast while looking out over 10 beautifully landscaped acres of gardens and trees.

After a day of sightseeing, sports, shopping, or even snoozing (!), don't miss the afternoon tea put out each day. Have a cup of your favorite tea, or try spiced cider or hot chocolate in season. There are always homemade goodies to tempt you, maybe Toll House cookies or fresh banana bread. Dinner is available only by special arrangement, usually for groups of ten or more, although the inn sometimes offers family packages that include a family-style dinner. Ask ahead of time if you're interested.

Guest rooms feature cheerful flowered wallpapers, colorful patchwork quilts, comfortable reading chairs, and queen- or king-sized beds, some of them four-poster. A new suite has a king-sized bed, in-room fireplace, and television with VCR. Luxurious!

All the public rooms are comfortable, and there is so much to do in this area all year that you could stay and stay. Be sure to visit the antiques dealer in the barn. In winter downhill or cross-country skiers will not have far to go. Bicycling or hiking in the area is awesome. Riding horses or fishing the lakes is also a nice thing to do in this beautiful countryside.

HOW TO GET THERE: Follow Route 7 to Route 23 west. You are now 3 miles from South Egremont. The inn will be on your left.

# Federal House
## South Lee, Massachusetts 01260

INNKEEPERS: Robin and Ken Almgren

ADDRESS/TELEPHONE: Main Street; (413) 243–1824

ROOMS: 10; all with private bath and air conditioning.

RATES: $95 to $195, double occupancy, EPB.

OPEN: All year.

FACILITIES AND ACTIVITIES: Full breakfast; dinner Thursday through Sunday. Bar, lounge. Nearby: private club with golf and tennis privileges, skiing.

*K*en is the innkeeper-chef of Federal House. He worked for one of my favorite people, Albert Stockli, of the Stonehenge Inn in Ridgefield, Connecticut, who has gone to his reward.

The Federal House was built in 1824 by Thomas O. Hurlbut, whose family came to America in 1635. It remained in this family until 1948, when it became a summer home for family members who resided in New York City. Today it has been restored to the original country elegance it once had. Its architectural style is Greek Revival.

The rooms are spacious and air-conditioned and have large windows. The wallpapers are lovely, and so are the Victorian couches. Some of the antiques came from the original Hurlbut home, and some were handed down in the innkeepers' families.

Dinner, as well as Sunday brunch, is served in a choice of three lovely rooms—the original dining room, the front parlor, or the billiard room. No matter which one you choose, the tables are set with fine silver, tall candles, and fresh flowers that are just beautiful.

The food, as you would expect in this elegant atmosphere, is glorious. No prepared foods are used. All the sauces and condiments are made right here. There are appetizers like seared yellowfin tuna with horseradish and soy sauce, Federal House smoked duckling with fresh peach chutney, and rabbit terrine. Dinner entrees always  include fresh fish, duckling, chicken, sweetbreads, beef, and rack of lamb prepared in different ways depending on the season. To accompany your meal, choose a wine from the fine wine cellar. The inn also has a full license for other drinks.

Both Ken and Robin have had extensive training, mostly in four-star restaurants, so it is no wonder that this is a grand inn.

**HOW TO GET THERE:** South Lee is 4 miles from Lee and 1 mile from Stockbridge. The inn is on Main Street (Route 102).

# The Red Lion Inn
## Stockbridge, Massachusetts 01262

**INNKEEPER:** Brooks Bradbury; Dennis Barquinero, director of lodging

**ADDRESS/TELEPHONE:** Main Street; (413) 298–5545,
fax (413) 298–5130

**ROOMS:** 111, plus 20 suites; 90 with private bath, most with wheelchair accessibility.

**RATES:** $65 to $300, winter; $75 to $350, summer; double occupancy, EP.

**OPEN:** All year.

**FACILITIES AND ACTIVITIES:** Breakfast, lunch, dinner, bar. Heated outdoor swimming pool. Elevator. Pink Kitty Gift Shop.

*T*he Red Lion Inn is a four-season inn. In summer you have the Berkshire Music Festival at Tanglewood and the Jacob's Pillow Dance Festival, both world-renowned. The inn's own heated outdoor swimming pool is a nice warm-weather attraction. Fall's foliage is perhaps the most spectacular in New England; in winter there is snow on the hills; in spring come the lovely green and flowers. All go together to make this a great spot any time of year. And right down the street is the Corner House, the museum of Norman Rockwell's works.

The inn is full of lovely old antiques. The halls are lined with antique couches, each one prettier than the last. From a four-poster canopy bed to beds with great brass headboards, all the rooms are marvelously furnished and comfortable as sin. Whether in the inn itself or in one of the inn's adjacent houses—Stafford House, Ma Bucks, or 2 Maple Street—you will love the accommodations. The wallpaper in Ma Bucks is a delight. All rooms have extra pillows, which I love.

During one visit, I stayed in a turn-of-the-century village firehouse. This also was the subject of a Norman Rockwell painting, which hangs here in the Old Stockbridge firehouse (1899) that has been coverted into a spacious suite. The firemen used to gather around their antique pool table; now the place is furnished with a beautiful king-sized bed, part of a lovely wicker set from an old estate. The bathroom has a double whirlpool bath and a huge shower. Downstairs the doors for the fire engines are still here.

2 Maple Street is a newer old house (circa the 1940s), where I was lodged on my most recent visit. It has a living room, fully equipped kitchen, bedroom, bath, a porch, and private parking. Very nice.

The Lion's Den is downstairs in the main inn, with entertainment nightly and its own small menu. In warm weather the flower-laden courtyard, with its Back of the Bank Bar, is a delightful place for food and grog. There's a wonderful collection of old birdcages out here. And the chef really knows what to do with scrod.

Another place to eat is the Widow Bingham's Tavern. There is an almost hidden booth designed for lovers in here.

More excellent food is served in the lovely dining room. The poached salmon is divine. The vegetable plate is a very nice touch. The inn also serves New England favorites like old-fashioned chicken pot pie and roast native turkey. The menu changes with the seasons. Do you still want to know more? Well, in the morning you'll find many breakfast choices, starting with freshly squeezed orange juice.

Be sure to find an opportunity to visit The Red Lion Inn and listen to the authentic country inn cricket in the lobby. Honest, he lives here.

HOW TO GET THERE: Take exit 2 from the Massachusetts Turnpike and follow Route 102 west to the inn.

# Norman Rockwell Museum

Overlooking the Housatonic River in Stockbridge is a museum honoring one of America's most beloved illustrators. Norman Rockwell was a resident of the town for fifty years while he painted magazine covers for *Saturday Evening Post, Look, McCalls*, and *Colliers*. In this beautiful museum, see permanent displays of Rockwell's original artwork, his own studio, and changing exhibitions of other noted illustrators. Stroll the 36-acre grounds to see sculptures by son Peter Rockwell. The museum is open year-round. Call (413) 298-4100 for hours and admission.

# Colonel Ebenezer Crafts Inn
## Sturbridge, Massachusetts 01566

**INNKEEPER:** Albert Cournoyer

**ADDRESS/TELEPHONE:** Fiske Hill Road (mailing address: P.O. Box 187); (508) 347–3313

**ROOMS:** 7, plus 1 suite; all with private bath.

**RATES:** $79 to $99, double occupancy; $109 to $145, suites; continental breakfast.

**OPEN:** All year.

**FACILITIES AND ACTIVITIES:** Afternoon tea. Publick House nearby for other meals. Small swimming pool. Nearby: Old Sturbridge Village.

*I*n Colonial times the finest homes were usually found on the highest points of land. Such a location afforded the owners commanding views of their farmland and cattle. It also set them above their contemporaries. So in 1786 David Fiske, Esquire, a builder, built this house high above Sturbridge. The house was magnificently restored by the management of the Publick House and named after the inn's founder, Colonel Ebenezer Crafts.

Accommodations are wonderful. There are two queen-sized canopy beds that are real beauties. Some beds are four-posters. Terrycloth robes are placed in your room for your comfort. The wallpapers are subtle and elegant. The suite joins the main inn by a short breezeway. It has a living room, bedroom, bath, and color television.

Provided for your relaxation is a nice living room with a baby grand piano, a color television with a VCR and movies, and a good library of books and the *National Geographic* magazines that are always a pleasure to read or look through.

Your breakfast of freshly baked muffins, fresh fruit, juice, and coffee comes with a copy of the morning paper. In the afternoon, tea, sherry, and sweets are served. Or you can go 2 miles down the road to the famous Publick House in Sturbridge for a full breakfast. Here, too, you can have lunch and dinner and enjoy the lovely bar and cocktail lounge. You will find a gift shop and an incredible bake shop. Do not miss taking some treats home.

If you want to plan a business conference or family gathering, the entire house is available for up to twenty-two people.

Ask someone to show you the Underground Railroad of Civil War days. The slave hole is still here.

**HOW TO GET THERE:** Take exit 3 from I–86, and bear right along the service road into Sturbridge. Continue to Route 131, where you turn right. Turn left at Hall Road and then right on Whittemore Road, which becomes Fiske Hill Road.

# Publick House
## Sturbridge, Massachusetts 01566

**INNKEEPER:** Albert Cournoyer

**ADDRESS/TELEPHONE:** P.O. Box 187; (508) 347–3313 or (800) PUBLICK 782–5425; fax (508) 347–1246

**E-MAIL:** bdion@gnn.com

**WEB SITE:** www.publickhouse.com

**ROOMS:** 17, plus 9 suites; all with private bath, air conditioning, phone.

**RATES:** $90 to $135, double occupancy; $130 to $155, suites; EP. Package rates available.

**OPEN:** All year.

**FACILITIES AND ACTIVITIES:** Breakfast, lunch, dinner, bar. Wheelchair access to restaurant. TV in lounge, gift shop, swimming pool, tennis courts, jogging trail, shuffleboard, children's play area, petting farm. Nearby: Old Sturbridge Village, golf, fishing, cross-country skiing.

**BUSINESS TRAVEL:** Meeting rooms, phone in all rooms, fax available, corporate rates.

*I*t's a real pleasure to me to keep coming back to the Publick House and finding it always the same, always excellent. As a matter of fact, very little has changed here in the past 200 years. The green still stretches along in front of it, and the trees still cast their welcome shade. The Publick House is still taking care of the wayfarer, feeding him well, providing a comfortable bed, and supplying robust drink.

The Publick House calendar is fun to read. Throughout the year there are special celebrations for holidays. They do keep Christmas here. All twelve days of it. The Boar's Head Procession is truly unique, complete with a roast young suckling pig, a roast goose, and plum pudding. Wow!

Winter weekends are times for special treats, with chestnuts roasting by an open fire, and sleigh rides through nearby Old Sturbridge Village, a happy step backward in time. During the Yankee Winter Weekends, celebrity chefs give demonstrations and lessons.

The guest rooms are decorated with period furniture, while the penthouse suite has the modern conveniences of a television and king-sized bed. The wide floorboards and beamed ceilings have been here since Colonel Ebenezer Crafts founded the inn in 1771.

The barn, connected to the main house with a ramp, has been transformed into a restaurant. Double doors, topped by a glorious sunburst window, lead into a restaurant that serves hearty Yankee cooking, such as delicious lobster pie. There is a little musician's gallery, still divided into stalls, that overlooks the main dining room. Beneath this is an attractive taproom where a pianist holds forth, tinkling out nice noises.

A blueberry patch and a garden that covers more than an acre of land provide the inn with fresh fruit and vegetables and beautiful roses during the summer.

I found my way by following my nose to the Bake Shoppe, where every day fresh banana bread, sticky buns, deep-dish apple pies, corn bread, and muffins come out of the ovens to tempt me from my diet! Take some along for hunger pangs along the road.

And from home you can order the inn's good jams, mustards, relishes, chowders, and more. They are beautifully packaged and mailed to you wherever you wish. A country village picnic can also be arranged.

HOW TO GET THERE: Take the Massachusetts Turnpike to exit 9. The Publick House is located on the Common in Sturbridge, on Route 131. From Hartford, take I–84 to I–86, exit 3, which brings you right into Sturbridge.

# Longfellow's Wayside Inn ▣
## Sudbury, Massachusetts 01776

**INNKEEPER:** Robert Purrington

**ADDRESS/TELEPHONE:** Wayside Inn Road; (508) 443–1776

**ROOMS:** 10; all with private bath, air conditioning, and phone.

**RATES:** $65 to $95, single; $90 to $130, double; EP.

**OPEN:** All year except Christmas Day and July 4.

**FACILITIES AND ACTIVITIES:** Breakfast for houseguests only, lunch, dinner, bar. Horses boarded. Gift shop, museum.

**BUSINESS TRAVEL:** Located 22 miles from Boston. Phone, table, and chairs in room; conference room; fax available.

*E*ight generations of travelers have found food and lodging for "man and beast" at the Wayside Inn. Route 20 is the old stagecoach road to Boston, now well off the beaten track. The inn looks much as it did 280 years ago and still supplies the traveler with hearty food and drink and a comfortable bed.

As with many old buildings, "improvements" were made to the inn in the nineteenth century, but a complete restoration in the 1950s afforded the opportunity to put many things back the way they were in the beginning. Now part of the inn serves as a museum with priceless antiques displayed in their original settings.

There are a large dining room and several smaller ones, a bar, a gift shop, and a lovely walled garden. At the end of the garden path is a bust of Henry Wadsworth Longfellow, who was inspired by the inn to link a group of poems known to all schoolchildren as *Tales of a Wayside Inn*.

Henry Ford bought 2,995 acres surrounding the inn in 1923, and since then this historic area has been preserved. A little way up the road stand a lovely chapel, the little red schoolhouse that gained fame in "Mary Had a Little Lamb," and a stone gristmill that still grinds grain for the rolls and muffins baked at the inn. I bought some of their cornmeal because the muffins I ate at the inn were exquisite. This is a most interesting building to visit, as all of the equipment in the mill is water-powered.

As a final touch, the inn boasts of the oldest mixed drink in America. It is called Coow Woow. You must taste it to discover how well our forefathers lived.

**HOW TO GET THERE:** From Boston take the Massachusetts Turnpike west to Route 128 North. Take exit 26 west onto Route 20. Wayside Inn Road is 11 miles west, just off Route 20. From New York take the Massachusetts Turnpike to Route 495, and go north to Route 20 East. It is approximately 8 miles to Wayside Inn Road.

# Lambert's Cove Country Inn
## West Tisbury, Massachusetts 02568

**INNKEEPERS:** Katherine and Louis Costabel

**ADDRESS/TELEPHONE:** Lambert's Cove Road (mailing address: Box 422, RFD, Vineyard Haven, MA 02568); (508) 693–2298; fax (508) 693–7890

**ROOMS:** 15; all with private bath.

**RATES:** In-season, $145 to $185; off-season, $75 to $120; double occupancy, EPB.

**OPEN:** All year.

**FACILITIES AND ACTIVITIES:** Dinner daily in-season, Thursday through Sunday interim season. BYOB. Tennis court. Nearby: swimming, cross-country skiing, ice skating.

At the end of a tree-shaded country road, you will find this gem of an inn. The original house was built in 1790. Over the years it was enlarged and a carriage house and barn added. Today the carriage house and barn have been beautifully renovated for guest use, and half of the rooms are here.

One of the rooms in the carriage house has a greenhouse sitting room at one end. Nice to have your cocktails in here and look up at the stars. All of

the rooms in the inn are done with imagination. There are plenty of pillows and lush towels.

When you enter the inn, you are in an elegant center hall. Up a magnificent staircase and you are in a restful sitting area, with an overstuffed couch and chair and bookcases full of books. There is also a delightful library, a huge room with walls lined with volumes of books and furnished with tables for games and really comfortable furniture. On a cold day a fire in the fireplace here feels great.

A big deck opens from the library and dining room and looks out on an apple orchard. There are five decks in all at this inn. The English garden is lovely, and flowers are everywhere you look. Princess, the inn cat, watches over it all.

Maybe you'd like to come for dinner. Roast duckling is glazed with honey and Grand Marnier. Breast of chicken Francis comes with pine nuts and lemon butter. All the desserts are made right here. The one I had on my last visit was white chocolate mousse with fresh raspberries. It is hard to make a choice, because they also serve key lime pie and strawberries Romanoff. No matter what you order, it will be good.

This is real country. Walk twenty minutes to the Lambert's Cove beach, or just walk anywhere. It's just a beautiful part of the world, and it would be a wonderful spot for a wedding.

HOW TO GET THERE: Take the ferry to Martha's Vineyard from Cape Cod. After driving off the ferry, take a left, then a right at the next stop-sign intersection. Stay on this road for 1½ miles to Lambert's Cove Road, on your right. Three miles from this point, look for the inn's sign, on the left.

# Le Jardin
## Williamstown, Massachusetts 01267

**INNKEEPER:** Walter Hayn

**ADDRESS/TELEPHONE:** 777 Cold Spring Road; (413) 458–8032

**ROOMS:** 6; all with private bath.

**RATES:** $75 to $95, double occupancy, EP.

**OPEN:** All year.

**FACILITIES AND ACTIVITIES:** Breakfast, dinner, Sunday brunch, bar, trout pond.

The grounds are so pretty at this inn. The backyard has picnic tables, and in front are Hemlock Brook and a nice pond. There are a lot of sugar maples on the property, and Walter taps them and then makes his own maple syrup.

The rooms are lovely. There are four working fireplaces with glass doors for safety. One of the rooms, the one where I always want to stay, has a whirlpool tub. What heaven it is to relax in! Another room has a deck extending into the woods.

There is also a nice bar and lounge. It's a most attractive room, with comfortable bar stools and tables.

Terry is the manager of the dining rooms, and she does a superb job. They are real beauties. Fresh, crisp napery, a fresh flower on each table, and plants hanging in the windows provide the perfect cozy, but still elegant, atmosphere for the magnificent food. The cuisine is French. Some of the hors d'oeuvres are snails in garlic butter, oysters baked with spinach and Pernod, and beluga malossol caviar. I had the onion

soup baked in a tureen. Very hot and good. The frog legs were done to perfection. There are also jumbo shrimp baked with a hint of garlic and crisp

Long Island duckling with apples. A real zinger is sirloin flamed in Cognac and laced with coarse black pepper. Rack of lamb is beautifully served with tender vegetables and fresh mint sauce. There's a wonderful and extensive wine list. It's so nice when both the food and the wine are exceptional.

And the desserts . . . well, just imagine a French restaurant. I'm not about to spill the beans and tell you what to expect. Come on up and see for yourself.

A nice feature on the property is the trout pond. You may try to catch your own. Can't get them much fresher than that. Yum.

HOW TO GET THERE: The inn is right on Route 7, just 2 miles south of Williamstown, on the right.

## Sterling and Francine Clark Institute

Here in the hollows of the Berkshires, far from big-city museums, is one of the finest art collections in the nation. The French Impressionists are among the most notable works—see Monet, Pissarro, Degas, and Renoir. American paintings and sculpture by Sargent, Homer, and Remington are here along with European pieces dating back to medieval times. The museum itself is grand, and admission is free. Lectures, concerts, poetry readings, and outdoor musical performances in the summer are on the yearlong calendar of special events. A gift shop and seasonal cafe are also here. Call (413) 458-2303.

# Select List of
# Other Massachusetts Inns

## The Captain House Inn

369–371 Old Harbor Road
Chatham, MA 02633
(508) 945–0127 or (800) 315–0728
Fax: (508) 945–0866
E-mail: capthous@capecod.net
Web site: captainshouseinn.com

*19 rooms, all with private bath; 13 with fireplace, TV/VCR; 4 with whirlpool tub; 1839 Greek Revival B&B decorated in Williamsburg style.*

## Walker House

64 Walker Street
Lenox, MA 01240
(413) 637–1271 or (800) 235–3098
Fax: (413) 637–2387
E-mail: phoudek@vgernet.net
Web site: www.walkerhouse.com

*8 rooms, all with private bath; B&B in 1804 federal Colonial decorated with antiques; each room named for a composer.*

## Spray Cliff on the Ocean, a B&B Inn

25 Spray Avenue
Marblehead, MA 01945
(781) 631–6789 or (800) 626–1530
Fax: (617) 639–4563

*7 rooms, all with private bath, 3 with fireplace; B&B in early 1900s oceanfront house 1 mile from town.*

## Seven Sea Street Inn

7 Sea Street
Nantucket, MA 02554
(508) 228-3577 or (800) 651-9262
Fax: (508) 228-3578
E-mail: seast7@nantucket.net

*11 rooms, 2 suites, all with private bath; serves breakfast; thirteen-year-old inn with red oak post and beam construction.*


## Fernside B&B

162 Mountain Road
P.O. Box 303
Princeton, MA 01541
(978) 464-2741 or (800) 545-2741
Fax: (978) 464-2065

*4 rooms, two suites, all with private bath; 1835 federal mansion.*

# New Hampshire

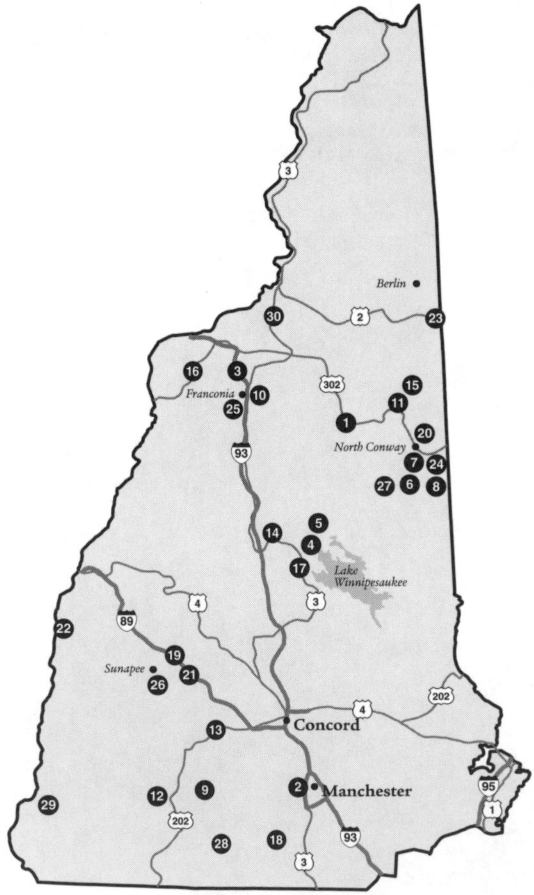

Berlin

3

2

23

30

302

16  3
Franconia  10
25

15
11

1

20

93

North Conway

7  24
27  6  8

14

5
4

17
Lake
Winnipesaukee

3

22

89

4

Sunapee

19
26  21

202

13

Concord

12  9

2  Manchester

95

29

202

28  18

1

93

3

# New Hampshire

*Numbers on map refer to towns numbered below.*

*A Top Pick Inn

*A Top Pick Inn

# The Notchland Inn
## Bartlett, New Hampshire 03812

**INNKEEPERS:** Les School and Ed Butler

**ADDRESS/TELEPHONE:** Route 302; (603) 374–6131 or (800) 866–6131; fax (603) 374–6168

**WEB SITE:** www.notchland.com

**ROOMS:** 7, plus 5 suites; all with private bath and fireplace, 1 specially equipped for handicapped.

**RATES:** $185 to $275, double occupancy, MAP. B&B is available.

**OPEN:** All year.

**FACILITIES AND ACTIVITIES:** Full liquor license. Hot tub. Hiking, canoeing, swimming, fishing, bicycling, cross-country skiing, sleigh rides, snowshoeing, and ice skating. Nearby: downhill skiing. Dinner is not served on Mondays.

The inn was built in 1862 by a wealthy Boston dentist, Samuel Bemis. He used native granite and timber, and you can bet that the construction of this building was some job. Seventeen fireplaces are in the inn, and all of the rooms have a working fireplace. Some of the suites have a two-person spa bath. One suite has an exquisite Japanese wedding kimono posted on a wall, and a few suites are in the carriage house and schoolhouse. The Carter Suite is grand; it has a deck, a wood-burning fireplace, a Jacuzzi tub in a large bathroom, a queen-sized bed, and a nice living room.

There are high ceilings and beautiful mountain views. The front parlor was designed by Gustav Stickley, a founder of the Arts and Crafts movement. The music room is inviting with its piano and stereo, and the sunroom is full of beautiful plants and a fountain. The dining room dates back to 1795, has a raised hearth fireplace, and looks out onto the pond and gazebo.

Every evening dinner is served at 7:00, and patrons are offered a choice of two soups, two appetizers, three entrees, and three desserts. To give you an idea of the varied menu, soup might be lightly curried sweet potato and butternut squash, orange-scented tomato with a fresh herbed yogurt, or Szechwan carrot. Appetizers might be crabcakes or three-tier vegetable pâté with a red pepper coulis. Entrees might be filet mignon with béarnaise sauce, chicken champagne, poached catfish, or poached salmon stuffed with scallops and herbs. And dessert might be very lemon pie, apricot cheescake, or chocolate walnut tart. If you can even think about breakfast after such a dinner, you'll delight in the full country breakfast that will start your day right.

There's so much to do in this area that you may have a hard time deciding where to start. Hiking is by far the nicest you'll find almost anywhere. There are beautiful waterfalls and granite cliffs to scale. The Saco River is the place for swimming, fishing, or canoeing, and two swimming holes are on the inn's property. White-water Class III and IV are here in the spring, so come on up with your canoe. Or bring your bicycle, as biking is fun here. Skiing of all kinds is very close by (there are 45 miles of ski trails)—or do you want to try snowshoeing? This is the place for it, or you can go ice skating on the inn's pond. If more sedentary activities suit your fancy, rocking chairs on the porch are ideal for reading and needlework.

The innkeepers love animals as much as I do. Mork and Mindy are the miniature horses, and Dolly is a Belgian draft horse. DC and Sid are the llamas. Coco, their Bernese mountain dog, is a love and even has "Coco Loco" cookies to give to guests—boy, are those good! Coco's Corner is in the Inn's newsletter, and what a wag he is! He reports on all of the animals that visit— ducks, bears, and birds. Keeps him busy.

While you are here, do read the history of the Inn; it's a fascinating story. When you come in the door of the inn and turn left, there is a living room with a puzzle going at all times; it's always fun to work on it. By the fireplace is a slate marker about Nancy Barton—be sure to read it—it's a riot.

HOW TO GET THERE: Follow Route 302 from North Conway to the inn. It is 20 miles north of North Conway.

# Attitash Bear Peak

Outdoor recreation lovers will enjoy the multiseason activities at Bartlett's Attitash Bear Peak (603–374–2368) on Route 302. This year-round recreation area and ski mountain has forty-five downhill ski trails, including a vertical drop of 1,750 feet for thrillseekers and a novice trail for beginners. There are complete snow-making capabilities, pay-by-the-run lift tickets, a ski school with classes for ages four to adult, and instruction for snowboarding at the site's snowboarding park and halfpipe.

In the warm months visitors can enjoy the mountain's ¾-mile alpine slide with rider-controlled sleds. Waterslides and kiddie pools are also part of the fun here. For a breathtaking view of the countryside, you can take the chairlift to the 2,350-foot summit of the mountain, then climb to the top of the White Mountain Observation Tower. In addition, the downhill ski trails are opened to mountain bikers. A 3-mile downhill trail challenges experienced bikers. A less difficult trail traces the banks of the beautiful Saco River and includes interpretive information stops and picnic areas. Bike rentals are available. A base lodge has a cafeteria and restroom facilities. Fees are charged for all the mentioned activities.

# The Bedford Village Inn ♥
## Bedford, New Hampshire 03102

INNKEEPER: Jack Carnevale

ADDRESS/TELEPHONE: Route 101; (603) 472–2602 or (800) 852–1166; restaurant, (603) 472–2001; fax (603) 472–2379

ROOMS: 12 suites, plus 2 apartments; all with private bath and phone.

RATES: $135 to $275, double occupancy, EP.

OPEN: All year.

FACILITIES AND ACTIVITIES: Breakfast, lunch, dinner, Sunday brunch, tavern. Elevator.

"Country elegant" is the way to describe this inn. It was a farmhouse built before the American Revolution, and it still retains the original wide fireplaces and wide pine boards.

In what was once the hayloft, there are sumptuous suites, each with a bathroom of Spanish marble and a Jacuzzi. The fixtures are gold finish—very pretty. The suites are well furnished. There are nice lamps with three-way switches, a too-often-forgotten detail. Each suite has three telephones, one at the desk, one by the bed, and one in the bathroom. A deck off the luxury suite in the barn's peak overlooks the meadow. One of the apartments has two bedrooms.

The original milking room has become a common area for inn guests, furnished with couches, lounge chairs, and a nice table for games or whatever. It is a very comfortable room.

Breakfast at the inn includes all of the usual items plus banana pancakes, frittered French toast, and a different poached egg every day from an inventive chef. The sticky buns are beautiful and come straight from the inn's own bakery. The tavern has its own menu.

There are eight dining rooms, each one lovely. The oldest dates back to around 1700 and has a huge fireplace. Lots of windows make it light and airy. The luncheon and Sunday brunch are ambrosia, and dinner is a delight. Traditional New England foods are served here, and the menu changes every two weeks. Special dinners at the inn include a Christmas Eve feast and wild game feasts.

Oriental carpets, antique four-poster beds, comfortable chairs, and old fireplaces all add up to a wonderful country inn.

**HOW TO GET THERE:** The inn is on Route 101, just west of Manchester.

# Adair

## Bethlehem, New Hampshire 03574

**INNKEEPERS:** Pat, Hardy, and Nancy Banfield

**ADDRESS/TELEPHONE:** Old Littleton Road; (603) 444–2600 or
(800) 441–2606; fax (603) 444–4823

**ROOMS:** 7, plus 2 suites; all with private bath. No smoking inn.

**RATES:** $135 to $220, double occupancy, EPB.

**OPEN:** All year. Restaurant closed in April and November and on Mondays and Tuesdays.

**FACILITIES AND ACTIVITIES:** Dinner. Beer and wine, or BYOB. Tennis.
Nearby: hiking, skiing, golf, boating, fishing.

*A*dair was built in 1927 as a gift to Dorothy Guider from her father. She lived in this hilltop mansion until her death in 1991. The house was converted into a glorious inn the next year. It is surrounded by 200 acres of sheer beauty in a picture-postcard setting.

The landscaping, designed by the Olmsted brothers of Boston Common and Central Park fame, is magnificent. The walking paths offer grand views of the Presidential and Dalton mountain ranges. A very nice patio overlooks the tennis court.

You enter a formal entry hall. On one side is a large, beautifully furnished living room with a fireplace, bellpulls, and a game of chess at the ready. To the left is a lovely dining room.

At 8:45 in the morning, piping-hot popovers are served, followed by Irish French toast, eggs Benedict, orange juice, and more.

The Tim-Bir Alley restaurant's menu changes every week. Beer and wine are served, but you can bring other beverages. The restaurant is separate from the inn, so you must pay in here. Two of the appetizers are cream of mushroom and sherry soup and chilled pasta rolls filled with smoked salmon mousse on horseradish cream. Entrees may be catfish with basil,

Brie, and walnut pesto, or tournedos of beef. Chocolate ricotta strudel with caramel sauce is one of the desserts that caught my eye.

The Granite Taproom is a good spot for relaxing or playing a game of pool. Television and a VCR with a variety of movies are here, too, as is a private telephone.

On the way upstairs to the luxurious guest rooms is a library. The rooms are named for the mountain ranges, and all of them have a view of either mountains or the beautiful grounds. The furniture consists of nice antiques. In the attic is a collection of great hats.

**HOW TO GET THERE:** From I–93, take exit 40, which takes you directly to Adair's driveway. From Route 302 Adair is 3 miles west of the center of Bethlehem village.

# Red Hill Inn
## Center Harbor, New Hampshire 03226

**INNKEEPERS:** Rick Miller, Don Leavitt, and Gerre Strobel

**ADDRESS/TELEPHONE:** Route 25B and College Road; (603) 279-7001

**ROOMS:** 26, in 5 buildings; all with private bath. Air conditioning in all, Jacuzzi in 11, fireplace in 19.

**RATES:** $105 to $175, double occupancy, EPB.

**OPEN:** All year.

**FACILITIES AND ACTIVITIES:** Lunch, dinner, Sunday brunch. Television and VCR, gift shop, cross-country skiing, hiking. Nearby: sailboat rentals, swimming, tennis, golf, heated pool. Wheelchair access to dining room.

**RECOMMENDED COUNTRY INNS® TRAVELERS' CLUB BENEFIT:** Spend two weekend nights, get 50 percent discount off third night.

*T*raveling along Route 25B, you glance up a hill, and sitting there is this lovely old restored country inn. Not very long ago Rick Miller and Don Leavitt waded through waist-high snow to begin a project that was destined to become a showplace of New Hampshire's Lakes

Region. What they had to do to make the inn what it is today is just incredible. Rick and Don alone sanded the floors of twenty-five rooms.

Oak paneling is in the living room. A huge bay window affords you a view of Squam Lake and the Squam mountain range, the foothills of the White Mountains. There is an immense fireplace here that sure felt good one cool July night.

The rooms in the main inn, all named after mountains, are different. Two of them have a sun room and balcony, and three have their own fireplace. That same July night I lit a fire in the fireplace in my room; it felt and looked great.

Most of the rooms are large and very comfortable, with grand views. During the inn's restoration they discovered nursery-rhyme characters that had been painted on the walls and covered by panels. Of course, they are now here for you to see.

One of their buildings has hand-hewn beams, brick hearths, and fifteen rooms with fireplaces and telephones (five with Jacuzzis). The Runabout Lounge is very interesting; half of a 22-foot Chris Craft is the bar. Don's collection of license plates adorns the walls.

The farmhouse down the hill from the main inn is glorious, an 1850 barn now redone for this time. There are two-bedroom suites with air conditioning, fireplaces, and decks, phones, Jacuzzis, and wow!

The stone cottage has a bedroom with a queen-sized bed, a living room with a fireplace, cathedral ceilings, sky lights, and is oh so romantic.

The dining rooms are lovely. Both have a fireplace and view, and the food that is served here is sumptuous. I had a garlic night—first escargots, then garlic dressing on my salad, and finally the best shrimp scampi around. Of course I had to taste my dinner companion's lamb, and boy, was it good. Sunday brunch's menu is unusually large. Something for everyone, from lamb chops and Long Island duckling with fruit dressing to omelets and cool salads. The luncheon menu is the same, just a joy—lobster salad, diet tuna salad, and on and on. The desserts at every meal are glorious. All are baked here. I had the best lemon meringue pie I've had in many a country mile.

The herb path lies outside the sunporch–dining room. All hearty for the cold New Hampshire weather, all used in the kitchen, and so pretty to see.

There are more than 150 acres for cross-country skiing or hiking. It's a nice ten-minute walk down a hill and through the woods to the beach on Squam Lake. All this plus an inn cat named Smokey, the innkeeper's collections, and utter peace. Do I like it here? You bet!

**HOW TO GET THERE:** Take exit 23 off I-93. Follow Route 104 east toward Meredith. At Route 3 go left, and follow Route 3 north about 4 miles to its junction with Route 25B. The inn is ⅛ mile off Route 3 at the corner of 25B and College Road.

# Corner House Inn
## Center Sandwich, New Hampshire 03227

**INNKEEPERS:** Jane and Don Brown

**ADDRESS/TELEPHONE:** Route 113 (mailing address: P.O. Box 204); (603) 284-6219 or (800) 501-6219

**ROOMS:** 3; all with private bath.

**RATES:** $80, double occupancy, EPB.

**OPEN:** All year.

**FACILITIES AND ACTIVITIES:** Lunch, dinner, full liquor license. Portable wheelchair ramp to dining room. Nearby: skiing, hiking, swimming, art gallery, museums, antiques shops.

*T*his is a very interesting and different town. The inn is centrally located so you can walk to everything. The New Hampshire League of Arts and Crafts is here, as are pottery shops, galleries, and museums. Five major ski areas are within a short driving range, as is Squam Lake (where *On Golden Pond* was filmed) for swimming and fishing.

The inn has been in business for more than one hundred years. To keep pace with its history, the waitresses are in colorful period pinafores. The food they serve is excellent. The kitchen is famous for its crepes, and several different ones are prepared each day. I have tried a few and, wow, are they good! They also do fabulous things with soups. Another great inn specialty is dessert; apple crisp and apple pie stand out, and I dare you to eat a piece of the Grand Marnier or chocolate truffle cake and not go back for more.

Of special note is the inn's house salad dressing. It is a buttermilk-dill combination. One of my party usually hates salad, but he ate it down to the last wisp of lettuce.

Roast duck is unusual; it is glazed with a variety of fruit sauces. And a new one on an old inn creeper like me is a seafood mixed grill of salmon, shrimp, and crabcakes. Well, that tells enough about this good New Hampshire food.

The rooms are very comfortable. Queen canopy beds and a single or double bed in addition are a plus. Bay windows in the living room, a spinning wheel, and plants give that touch of comfort you love in an inn. The carriage house is now the main dining room.

Good inn animals are here; the dogs are golden retrievers named Maya and Charlie.

**HOW TO GET THERE:** Up I–93 to exit 24, thence Route 3 to Route 113. Route 113 goes directly to Center Sandwich.

# Stafford's in the Fields
Chocorua, New Hampshire 03817

**INNKEEPERS:** Ramona and Fred Stafford

**ADDRESS/TELEPHONE:** P.O. Box 270; (603) 323–7766 or (800) 446–1112

**ROOMS:** 11 in main building, 6 with private bath; 3 to 4 cottages, all with bath, depending on season.

**RATES:** $120 to $240, per person, double occupancy, MAP.

**OPEN:** All year.

**FACILITIES AND ACTIVITIES:** Liquor license; trail lunches available. Function barn for weddings, parties, concerts. Sleigh rides, cross-country skiing. Wheelchair access to dining room and cottage.

*A*t the end of a quiet country lane sits a really lovely country inn. It comes with a babbling brook, has forests at hand, and overlooks rolling fields. You will also find a barn with truly unusual acoustics. It can hold up to 250 people; what a great spot for a wedding! The inn's Oliver Twist Tap Room is an intimate place to relax in an Old English atmosphere.

Ramona Stafford likes to cook in a sort of French country–style with wine and herbs and spices and, best of all, great imagination: pork tenderloin with prunes, and stuffed chicken breast with almonds and raisins.

Breakfast is the way to start your day. Omelets are different—sour cream with green chives, mild country cheddar, or cheddar and salsa. You will not go wrong trying the huevos rancheros or fresh sweet rolls. Ramona serves well-balanced meals. Smoking is not permitted in the dining room.

The inn is immensely comfortable, with cross-country skiing right on the fields, and just utter peace. As Fred Stafford says, there is an inexhaustible supply of "nature things to do." Just sitting, watching the swallows swoop or a leaf spin slowly to the ground, restores what you may have lost in the hustle and bustle of today's world.

Turn in the lane some snowy evening and see Stafford's glowing in the field, waiting to welcome you from a world well left behind. Pita, the inn dog, and Celeste, the goose, will be waiting to greet you. So will Buddy the Bear—he's stuffed, of course—who wears Fred's father's World War I helmet.

**HOW TO GET THERE:** Take Route 16 north to Chocorua Village, then turn left onto Route 113 and travel 1 mile west to the inn. Or, from I-93, take exit 23 and travel east on Route 104 to Route 25, and then to Route 16. Proceed north to Route 16 to Chocorua Village.

# Darby Field Inn

## Conway, New Hampshire 03818

**INNKEEPERS:** Marc and Maria Donaldson

**ADDRESS/TELEPHONE:** Bald Hill Road (mailing address: P.O. Box D); (603) 447–2181 or (800) 426–4147 (outside New Hampshire); fax (603) 447–5726

**ROOMS:** 15, plus 1 suite; 14 with private bath.

**RATES:** $70 to $118, per person, double occupancy, MAP; $50 to $90, per person, double occupancy, EPB. Package plans available.

**OPEN:** All year except April.

**FACILITIES AND ACTIVITIES:** Bar, TV, library, swimming pool, 12 miles of cross-country ski trails, hiking.

**RECOMMENDED COUNTRY INNS® TRAVELERS' CLUB BENEFIT:** 15 percent discount, minimum two-night stay, Sunday–Thursday, excluding foliage season and Christmas vacation.

*S*et high atop Bald Hill in New Hampshire's White Mountains with spectacular views of this wonderful country is Darby Field Inn. Located 1,000 feet above Mount Washington Valley and only 3 miles from Conway Village, the inn delights wanderers adventurous enough to leave the beaten path.

The inn borders the White Mountain National Forest, where guests are welcome to cross-country ski, snowshoe, hike, or walk to nearby rivers, waterfalls, and lakes. The inn dog, Gorby, and the bunny, Fluffy, love this beautiful country.

Rooms are charming, some with four-poster beds and wall-to-wall rugs. Most rooms have private baths, and they are tucked away wherever space was available. How do you feel about an L-shaped shower stall? The suite has a Jacuzzi and a wonderful view.

The inn's huge cobblestone fireplace is the center for warm conversation. The pub has a wood-burning stove.

Candlelit dinners begin with fine wine and a smashing sunset view up the valley. The food reflects the careful preparation of the chef. You'll always find a chef's special and fresh fish du jour. Whatever you order up here will be excellent. Desserts are interesting. You must try Darby cream pie, quite different. The Irish Revolution will really end your day nicely.

Darby Field, a notorious Irishman, was the first white man to ascend Mount Washington. Had the inn been here in 1642, it is doubtful whether Mr. Field would ever have passed the pub.

**HOW TO GET THERE:** Turn on Bald Hill Road, a half-mile south of the Kancamagus Highway, off Route 16, then go 1 mile up the hill and turn right onto a dirt road. The inn is 1 mile beyond.

## *Conway Scenic Railroad*

You can't beat the scenery and the sense of adventure when you board the excursion trains at North Conway's grand Victorian railroad depot for a ride on the Conway Scenic Railroad (603–356–5251 or 800–232–5251). Choose from a 55-minute ride or a 105-minute ride on the Valley Train, which stays in the Mount Washington Valley for trips to Conway and Bartlett and back to the depot. You can also take the Notch Train; buy a ticket for this five-hour round trip, then hop on for the most beautiful ride of your life. This route passes through Crawford Notch on the Frankenstein Trestle, a remarkable structure that carries the train through one of the most awesome landscapes in New England.

Live narration is given on all trips; snack bars are on both trains. At least one train each day offers dining service. Coach and first-class seats are available on both trains; fares vary with the age of the passenger, the length of the trip, and the season. The Valley trips run from April through October; the Notch train runs from mid-June through October, weather permitting. Reservations are highly recommended during September and early October when the foliage is at its peak.

# Rockhouse Mountain Farm Inn

## Eaton Center, New Hampshire 03832

**INNKEEPER:** John R. Edge, Jr, and Alana

**ADDRESS/TELEPHONE:** Rockhouse Mountain Road; (603) 447–2880

**ROOMS:** 18; 8 with private bath.

**RATES:** $56 to $64, per person, double occupancy; $70 to $80, single;
MAP. Children's rates.

**OPEN:** Mid-June to November 1.

**FACILITIES AND ACTIVITIES:** BYOB. Private beach on Crystal Lake,
450 acres to roam, animals. Nearby: golf, tennis, weekly hayrides for
kids, canoe trips down the Saco River.

Memorable summer and fall vacations have been had at Rockhouse since 1946. There are 450 acres of pastures, woodlands, mountains, and ponds, so bring your camera. It's all just so beautiful.

The private beach on Crystal Lake has rowboats, canoes, and sailboats. A nice added attraction is the once-a-week luncheon barbecue at Frog Rock on Swift River. Take a swim under the waterfall.

And there are animals—llamas, piglets, horses, dogs, cats, peacocks, geese, an Arabian stallion, and prize steer.

The inn provides ice, glasses, and refrigeration and hopes you will join the adults at Happy Hour under the big maple tree or around the fireplace.

Rooms here are plain but clean. There are reduced rates for children, and even a children's dining room for dinner. And speaking of dinner, one entree is served each evening. It may be roast lamb, baked ham, fish, or turkey if it's Sunday, chicken or barbecued beef at the Sugar House on Wednesday, and a steak cookout on Saturday. All breads and pastries are homemade.

The view from the living room of the mountains and trout pond is spectacular. The recreation room has Ping-Pong and shuffleboard, and the barn is a major attraction.

The Carriage House has three rooms, and another building, called the 20's House, has three bedrooms and a living room with fireplace. These are great accommodations for a family.

Have a reunion up here; you will never forget it.

**HOW TO GET THERE:** From I–95 take Route 16 to Conway. Turn right on Route 153 to Eaton Center. At the Inn at Crystal Lake, take a sharp right up the road to the inn.

# The Inn at Crotched Mountain
## Francestown, New Hampshire 03043

**INNKEEPERS:** John and Rose Perry

**ADDRESS/TELEPHONE:** Mountain Road; (603) 588–6840

**ROOMS:** 13; 8 with private bath, 4 with fireplace.

**RATES:** $60 to $70, per person, double occupancy, EPB

**OPEN:** All year except first three weeks in November, weekdays in winter, and after ski season until Mother's Day.

**FACILITIES AND ACTIVITIES:** Wheelchair access to inn and dining rooms. Bar, tennis, swimming pool, cross-country skiing. Nearby: golf, fishing, summer theater.

This 150-year-old Colonial house is located on the northern side of Crotched Mountain. There is a 40-mile view of the Piscataquog Valley, complete with spacious skies. Both innkeepers have gone to school to learn their trade, and what a charming house to practice it in. They are both pretty special themselves. Rose is from Singapore, and John is a Yankee.

Come and stay: There are many things to do. There are three golf courses in the nearby valley, the fishing is great, and there is a wading pool for the young, as well as a 30-by-60-foot pool for real swimmers. Two areas pro-

vide skiing—one at the front door and another down the road. Two clay tennis courts eliminate that tiresome waiting for a playing area. And come evening there are two summer theaters, one at Peterborough and another in Milford.

Any house that has nine fireplaces needs a wood lot and a man with a chainsaw. Four of the bedrooms here have a fireplace, so remember to request one when you reserve.

Two English cockers live here, Winslow and Lucy. There are numerous streams, ponds, and lakes for fishing and mountains for hiking. Golf is nearby. Come and enjoy this wonderful countryside with the dogs. They would love to have you.

**HOW TO GET THERE:** Take 101A from Nashua to Milford, Route 13 to New Boston, and Route 136 to Francestown. Take Route 47 2½ miles, then turn left onto Mountain Road. The inn is 1 mile up the road.

# Franconia Inn 🏨
## Franconia, New Hampshire 03580

**INNKEEPERS:** Richard and Alec Morris

**ADDRESS/TELEPHONE:** Route 116 (mailing address: 1300 Easton Road); (603) 823–5542

**ROOMS:** 31, plus 2 family suites and 1 "inn" suite; all with private bath, 2 with Jacuzzis.

**RATES:** $145 to $205, double occupancy, MAP. $165 to $225 during foliage season (September 25 to October 13) and Christmas week. EP rates available.

**OPEN:** All year except April 1 to Mother's Day.

**FACILITIES AND ACTIVITIES:** Bar, lounge, gameroom, airfield, hot tub, swimming, four tennis courts, cross-country ski center, ice skating, sleigh rides, soaring center, horseback riding. Nearby: downhill skiing, golf.

This is an inn in the fine tradition of old New England hostelries. The inn is the fourth for the Morris family. It is run by third-generation innkeepers. The inn welcomes children. Never a dull moment any season of the year. While the children play or watch a movie, you can relax in the lounge and listen to selected classical and popular music by the glow of the fireplace.

A card room and a library are here for your enjoyment, as is a screened porch overlooking the pool and the mountains. And they have something a bit unique: a gameroom for children, no adults allowed.

Another entertainment for you is horseback riding. There are trail rides through Ham Branch stream and around the hay fields.

The living room is paneled with old oak and, with the fireplace, is very warm and cozy. A lovely candlelit dining room, with pink and white napery, serves glorious food. The chef has treated escargots in an innovative way. They are marinated, baked in butter, garlic, and ouzo, and sealed in a puff pastry shell. Superb! Bouillabaisse a la Provençale is really a winner, and so is spicy ginger and soy sauce sauté. A vegetarian pastry is delightful for vegetarians.

There are 30 miles of cross-country trails right at hand, and they also have facilities so that you can ski from inn to inn on connecting trails. Downhill skiing is but 10 miles away. Horse-drawn sleigh rides in this beautiful winter wonderland are my idea of heaven. Do come and enjoy.

**HOW TO GET THERE**: Take I–91 north to the Wells River–Woodsville exit. Go right on Route 302 to Lisbon, New Hampshire. A few miles past Lisbon, go right on Route 117 to Franconia. Crossing the bridge into town, go right at the Exxon station onto Route 116, and you're 2 miles from the inn, which is on the right. Or, if you have a single-engine plane, the inn has its own FAA-listed airfield with a 3,000-foot-long runway.

# The Horse and Hound
## Franconia, New Hampshire 03580

**INNKEEPERS:** Bill Steele and Jim Cantlon

**ADDRESS/TELEPHONE:** 205 Wells Road; (603) 823–5501 or
(800) 450–5501

**ROOMS:** 6, plus 2 two-bedroom units; all with private bath and phone.

**RATES:** $79.95, double occupancy; $115 for two bedrooms; EPB. MAP
rates also available.

**OPEN:** All year except April 1 to Mother's Day, and sometimes November.

**FACILITIES AND ACTIVITIES:** Dinner. Bar, lounge. Skiing, soaring,
biking, hiking. Nearby: swimming, boating, fishing, golf, tennis.
Wheelchair access to bar, lounge, and dining room. Well-behaved
pets welcome.

**RECOMMENDED COUNTRY INNS® TRAVELERS' CLUB BENEFIT:** Stay
two nights, get third night free, subject to availability.

The Horse and Hound is located at the base of Cannon Mountain
just north of Franconia Notch. Tucker Brook rushes down from
the top of the mountain just past the edge of the inn's property.
In winter you can set off from the door of the inn on your cross-country skis.
In other seasons bicycling is a big thing here at the inn. There is a 7-mile circuit for you to try. Should be fun up here in these beautiful mountains.

You can also go soaring in a plane or just take an airplane ride. What a
way to enjoy the fall foliage. I did it once in a helicopter, and it was sublime.

There are three fireplaces to warm you, whether you are in the living
room or the dining rooms.
The library lounge has lots
of books, which are well
organized in categories
such as bike books, chil-
dren's books, and classics.
There is music in here also.
A miniature pool table is
tons of fun, or you can
enjoy checkers and other
games. You might enjoy
playing with Gus and Max, the inn's cocker spaniels, or Boris and Igor, the
inn's cats.

Comfortable accommodations are here. The rooms are bright and airy and have lovely views.

The terrace in summer is so lovely for cocktails. The menu is good and the food is excellent. Under appetizers, escargots en croûte are good. I liked the baked French onion soup, but there is also a soup du jour. Entrees include filet mignon, Trafalgar Grill (a petite fillet with two scampi-style jumbo shrimp), lamb chops, veal, fish, the chef's Vegetarian Fancy, and daily specials. The desserts and pastries all are made here and are so good.

**HOW TO GET THERE:** From Boston take I–93 north, exit at Route 18, and turn left. Go 2½ miles to Wells Road, take a left onto Wells; inn is on the left. Coming south on I–93, take exit 38 from Franconia, go left on Route 18, travel 2½ miles to Wells Road, and take a right onto Wells.

# Lovett's by Lafayette Brook
## Franconia, New Hampshire 03580

**INNKEEPERS:** Sharon and Anthony Avrutine

**ADDRESS/TELEPHONE:** Route 18; (603) 823–7761 or (800) 356–3802; fax (603) 823–8578

**ROOMS:** 23, in inn, barn, cottages; all with private bath. No smoking inn.

**RATES:** $90 to $150, double occupancy, MAP. EP rates available.

**OPEN:** End of June to mid-October, and December 26 to March 15.

**FACILITIES AND ACTIVITIES:** Bag lunches available. Wheelchair access to dining room, living room. Bar, gameroom, heated swimming pool, spa. Nearby: tennis, golf, horseback riding, bicycling, fishing, skiing.

There are lots of reasons for coming to the White Mountains and Franconia Notch, and one of the reasons is this inn. It was constructed circa 1784, even before a road was built through Franconia Notch.

Sharon and Anthony are the innkeepers at this fine inn. They work hard to have the best table and the best cellar in the North Country. The chef spent four years at a five-star Palm Beach hotel and now creates an ever-changing slate of temptations, country-style. On my most recent visit, I had Wild White Mountain Blueberry Soup, and it was glorious. Other appetizers were cold black bean soup with Demarara rum and Snaffles mousse. I also

had a moist and yummy Boston scrod. Guests at the next table ordered tenderloin of beef stroganoff, and they reported it to be excellent. The next time I visit here, I hope to have the breast of chicken in apples, Calvados, and cream, or maybe I'll choose the mild curried lamb with Lovett's chutney. A special children's menu includes milder but equally tasty favorites like southern fried chicken and pasta. The chef also puts up his own pickles, and they are great.

The inn has its own herb garden. At last count there were thirty-seven different herbs at hand—no wonder the food is so good! Desserts, as you would expect, are heavenly.

There is a lovely terrace overlooking the mountains and the pool. Actually, there are two pools. One is to the rear of the inn, and the other is fed from mountain springs. Oh, to be that hale and hearty for the latter!

And the bar, the bar! From the staircase in a Newport mansion, the marble bar is the most inviting spot I've run into in a month of Sundays.

Try to visit the New England Ski Museum, an excellent review of a sport that goes back 5,000 years. It is important to preserve these rare artifacts. The museum is right in the area.

There is no smoking in this inn. Bogart and Bentley, the inn dogs, do not like smoke. Neither do I.

HOW TO GET THERE: Take I-93 north, take exit 3 at Route 18, and turn left. The inn is on the left, 2 miles down the mountain.

# Sugar Hill Inn
Franconia, New Hampshire 03580

**INNKEEPERS:** Kelly and Stephen Ritarossi

**ADDRESS/TELEPHONE:** Route 117; (603) 823–5621 or (800) 548–4748 for reservations

**ROOMS:** 10, plus 6 cottage rooms; all with private bath. No smoking inn. Gas fireplaces in four of the cottages.

**RATES:** $145 to $255, double occupancy, MAP.

**OPEN:** All year except April.

**FACILITIES AND ACTIVITIES:** Dinner, full license. Nearby: skiing, riding, fishing, canoeing, tennis, golf, hiking, museums, antiques shops, summer theater, hot-air ballooning.

The White Mountains are so beautiful and majestic, it is a joy to find the Sugar Hill Inn tucked into this loveliness. This charming inn was built in 1789 as a farmhouse by one of Sugar Hill's original settlers, and it was converted to an inn in 1929.

The inn has been carefully restored. The innkeepers have made the most of the beautiful old beams and floors and the handsome fireplaces. They have two charming common rooms, each with original fireplaces. Each has comfortable furniture, reading materials, board games, and puzzles. A television is in one of these rooms.

In the living room is an antique player piano with a lot of rolls. Really fun for a sing-along. A recent addition to the inn is a lovely pub dubbed "Squier's Pub."

Guest accommodations in the inn and in the country cottages are lovely. Handmade quilts, good mattresses, lovely antiques, stenciled walls, and all superclean. The closets are scented with potpourri. The rooms in the inn are not well suited to children under twelve. The cottages are open all year and are ideal for families. Each cottage has two bedrooms, two bathrooms, and a front porch.

Stephen prepares all the meals. The breakfasts are full country ones and may include super walnut pancakes or Swiss eggs with croissant. Be sure to try the fresh muffins. I had the pumpkin raisin muffins.

Dinner starters might include a choice of mushroom dill soup or New England clam chowder. Try the chicken Washington (chicken breast stuffed with crabmeat and covered with hollandaise) or veal Oscar with béarnaise sauce. Four entrees are always offered each evening. Oven-baked salmon is a winner; tenderloin of beef is grilled to order and served with bordelaise sauce. Desserts are delicious; raspberry pie, pecan bourbon pie, and chocolate mousse might be available when you're here.

A tea cart, laden with scones and sweet breads, is in the parlor at 4:00 P.M. during the fall only. And the hot cider on the wood-burning stove for skiers is so nice.

HOW TO GET THERE: Follow Route 18 through Franconia. Turn left on Route 117. The inn is ½ mile up the hill, on the right.

# Bernerhof Inn
Glen, New Hampshire 03838

INNKEEPER: Sharon Wroblewski; Mark and Ruth Prince, general managers

ADDRESS/TELEPHONE: Route 302; (603) 383–9131 or (800) 548–8007 (out-of-state and Canada)

ROOMS: 9, all with private bath, 6 with Jacuzzi; all with TV, phone, and air conditioning.

RATES: $69 to $139, double occupancy, EPB.

OPEN: All year.

FACILITIES AND ACTIVITIES: Breakfast and dinner served to house-guests year-round, bar. Wheelchair access to dining room. Hiking trail. Nearby: golf, tennis, canoeing, fishing, cross-country and downhill skiing.

**RECOMMENDED COUNTRY INNS® TRAVELERS' CLUB BENEFIT:** 25 percent discount, Monday–Thursday, November 1–June 30, on standard room; upgrading available upon check-in. Excludes foliage season and holidays.

The Black Bear Pub at the Bernerhof Inn welcomes guests with a cozy atmosphere. It's a lovely oak room done in the style of a European pub. A true haven for beer lovers, it also serves good food from its own menu at affordable prices. You can sip some real Gluh Wein or espresso made from freshly ground beans.

As the brochure says so well, this is "an elegant small hotel in the foothills of the White Mountains." Rooms are light and airy and individually decorated. There are three king-sized brass beds and six Jacuzzis. One is in a sensational window alcove. There is a sitting room with games and puzzles.

A Taste of the Mountains, a cooking school hosted by the innkeepers, is designed for lovers of fine food. If you want to know more, do call or write for a brochure.

Food here is something else, as you might expect from anyone who runs a cooking school. The *delices de Gruyère*—a smooth blend of Swiss cheeses, delicately breaded and sautéed and accompanied by a savory tomato blend—is superb. Swiss entrees include *emince de veau au vin blanc*, Wiener schnitzel, and, of course, fondues. You might also try the sautéed rainbow trout with almonds, brandy, amaretto, and tarragon butter, or the basil cannelloni with roasted red pepper and tomato sauce. The portions are very generous.

You'll want to leave room for dessert, it's so good. Pot de crème, chocolate fondue, linzertorte, or profiteroles au chocolat—tiny pastries filled with ice cream and topped with chocolate. The Grand Marnier mousse is outrageously good. I could go on, but I'm getting hungry.

A free champagne breakfast in bed is yours on the third morning of your stay. It comes with eggs Benedict and fresh flowers. My, my!

**HOW TO GET THERE:** From North Conway take Route 16 north. At Glen, turn left onto Route 302. The inn is on your right.

# The Hancock Inn
## Hancock, New Hampshire 03449

**INNKEEPERS:** Joe and Linda Johnston

**ADDRESS/TELEPHONE:** Main Street; (603) 525–3318 or (800) 525–1789
(outside New Hampshire); fax (603) 525–9301

**E-MAIL:** innkeeper@hancockinn.mv.com

**WEB SITE:** www.hancockinn.com

**ROOMS:** 11; all with private bath, air conditioning, cable TV, and
phone. 1 suite for handicapped. No smoking inn.

**RATES:** $98 to $150, double occupancy, EPB. Special package rates.

**OPEN:** All year.

**FACILITIES AND ACTIVITIES:** Dinner, lounge. Wheelchair ramp into
the inn. Parking. Nearby: swimming, hiking, antiquing, summer
theater, skiing, tennis.

Operated as an inn since 1789—it is the oldest inn in New Hampshire—The Hancock Inn is now in the competent hands of old
friends and good innkeepers, Joe and Linda Johnston.

This is a nice old inn. Carefully preserved is The Mural Room, believed to
date back to the early years of the inn. The recently remodeled Carriage
Lounge is a comfortable and very unusual common room and bar. The name
of the inn stems from the fact that John Hancock, the founding father, once
owned most of the land that
composes the present town
of Hancock. Set among
twisting hills and featuring a
weathered clapboard facade,
graceful white pillars, and a
warm red door, the inn represents all that is good about
old inns.

At the end of the day, you
will retire to the comfort of a
four-poster bed, where the sound of the Paul Revere bell from a nearby
steeple will gently lull you to sleep. This is a town that hasn't changed much
in the past two centuries.

The dining rooms are lovely, and the food is superb. The inn has been awarded the best of the best award: four diamonds, designating this to be one of the top one hundred restaurants in the country in the category of American food. Appetizers like cranberry shrub, Maryland crabcake, and baked brie are followed by good soups and an excellent house salad. The famous Shaker cranberry pot roast is alone worth the trip, but perhaps you'd like to try the roasted maple duck, rainbow lake trout, or summer garden linguine.

Swim in summer in Norway Pond, within walking distance of the inn. Climb mountains, or just sit and listen to the church chimes during foliage time. Alpine and cross-country skiing are nearby in winter. Or browse in the antiques shops on a cool spring morn.

The governor, Stephen Merrill, has given a commendation to the inn for its 200-plus years of being a country inn—1789 was George Washington's first year in office and the year the inn was built.

The inn dogs are Duffy, a springer spaniel, and Maggie, his niece.

The TVs are under cozies, and on top of each one is a saying—Caution! Do not remove unless you wish to return to the twentieth century.

HOW TO GET THERE: From Boston take I–93 north to I–293, then Route 101 to Peterborough. Take a right onto Route 202, then a left onto Route 123. Turn left at the stop sign.

# Colby Hill Inn 🗇
## Henniker, New Hampshire 03242

INNKEEPERS: Ellie, John, and Laurel Day

ADDRESS/TELEPHONE: P.O. Box 778; (603) 428–3281 or (800) 531–0330; fax (603) 428–9218

ROOMS: 16; all with private bath and phone, 2 with working fireplace. Entire inn is air conditioned. No smoking inn.

RATES: $85 to $185, double occupancy, EPB.

OPEN: All year.

FACILITIES AND ACTIVITIES: Breakfast, dinner. Swimming pool, ice skating, tennis, badminton. Nearby: canoeing, kayaking, fishing.

BUSINESS TRAVEL: Phone in rooms, fax available, meeting space.

his is a no smoking inn; I just love it. Built more than 200 years ago as a farmhouse, it leans and dips here and there, but that only adds to its charm. The wide floorboards are authentic. Over the years it has been a tavern, a meetinghouse, and a church. What a history!

In one living room is an Edison Standard phonograph that's almost a century old. It's a rare gem. Ask John to run it for you. The records are round, the size of a can of soup, and play for four minutes. I never saw one of these before.

The sixteen guest rooms are filled with antiques and have their own telephones and numbers. A very nice touch. The parlor has a fireplace, good magazines, a television, and a VCR. If you come in the summer, be sure to go see the pool. You go through the barn, turn right through a tunnel, and there it is. The barn is also fun to explore.

Colby Hill also offers cross-country skiing and tennis, and nearby are canoeing, kayaking, and fishing. It's a perfect spot for vacations, weddings, and conferences.

Now to the good stuff—dinner. Among the appetizers during a recent visit were seafood crepe, marinated tenderloin tips, and lobster ravioli. The lobster bisque was divine. Entrees range from loin of venison and roast lamb loin to baked scrod and vegetarian medley. Then there are those like me who can't wait for dessert. Apple crumb pie, brownie sundae, dessert specials—oh boy!—and then warm up with spirited coffees. This is just a sample of what to expect.

Breakfast is great, with pancakes, crepes, eggs many ways, and all so good.

I've never met dogs before that were half Labrador and half Great Dane, but there are two of them here, Bertha and Deliah, that are loves.

**HOW TO GET THERE:** Take I–91 to Brattleboro, then Route 9 east to Henniker.

# The Fiber Studio

One of the most charming aspects of journeying through New England is finding artists' studios and crafters' workshops tucked in the small towns we visit. A restored barn overlooking Henniker's Pat's Peak mountain is the home of the Fiber Studio (603–428–7830), a glorious riot of color and texture hidden in the hills. Workshops are offered year-round in weaving, dyeing, spinning, basketry, and knitting. Hand-dyed woolens, mohairs, alpacas, cottons, linens, and silks for weaving and knitting are for sale here, as are beads from around the world, buttons galore of every description, hand-crafted jewelry and jewelry-making supplies, and much more. Looms, spinning wheels, and books—you name it.

The shop is open year-round Tuesday through Saturday from 10:00 A.M. to 4:00 P.M. and on Sunday by chance. It's located at 9 Foster Hill Road in Henniker off Route 202/9.

# The Meeting House
## Henniker, New Hampshire 03242

**INNKEEPERS:** June and Bill Davis; Cheryl and Peter Bakke

**ADDRESS/TELEPHONE:** Flanders Road; (603) 428–3228; fax (603) 428–6334

**ROOMS:** 6; all with private bath and air conditioning.

**RATES:** $65 to $105, double occupancy, EPB.

**OPEN:** All year.

**FACILITIES AND ACTIVITIES:** Dinner. Bar, hot tub, sauna (available at extra charge). Nearby: white-water canoeing, sailboarding, tennis, golf, hiking, indoor ice skating, cross-country skiing, downhill skiing, antiquing, summer theater.

**RECOMMENDED COUNTRY INNS® TRAVELERS' CLUB BENEFIT:** 10 percent discount, Monday–Thursday.

*Y*ou can sit in the bar area of this inn and watch the skiers coming down the hill. Now that's fun. This old barn that houses the restaurant and bar is 200 years old.

Hanging on the walls are plastic bags in which people from all over the world have collected shells, stones, sand, and volcano dust and sent them here for display. A nice thing to do. Little white Christmas lights are all over this area. They are so pretty and unique. Only in a country inn.

When you want breakfast, it is delivered to your room in a basket, and what a surprise awaits you! (No, I'm not going to tell; you'll have to see for yourself.)

And dinner . . . well, there is fillet de Cassis, beef Wellington, duck, and lamb. Add to those choices seafood offerings you don't find very often and veal and chicken dishes, all of which looked great. Their salad dressings are super. I had an excellent hot bacon dressing. The fried cinnamon apples with ice cream, flavored with apple brandy, were the perfect ending to my dinner.

The rooms are filled with treasures from June's and Bill's former homes. I was delighted to find plenty of books and magazines and plump pillows for reading in bed, a favorite pastime of mine. Grensel, a Maine coon cat, is the inn cat.

After a day of skiing, try the sauna and hot tub in the greenhouse. Sheer luxury! In summer, stroll around to view the flower gardens.

White-water activities are on the Contoocook River. Antiques shops are nearby, and a summer theater is in a neighboring town. This really is a nice area.

**HOW TO GET THERE:** In Henniker take Route 114 south for about 2 miles to Pat's Peak sign. Turn right onto Flanders Road. The inn is in about ½ mile on the right.

# The Manor

## Holderness, New Hampshire 03245

**INNKEEPERS:** David and Bambi Arnold

**ADDRESS/TELEPHONE:** Route 3, Box T; (603) 968–3348 or
(800) 545–2141; fax (603) 968–2116

**ROOMS:** 25, plus 2 cottages; all with private bath.

**RATES:** $210 to $350, double occupancy, EPB.

**OPEN:** All year.

**FACILITIES AND ACTIVITIES:** Afternoon tea. Bar, lounge, swimming
pool, tennis, boating, ice skating. Nearby: downhill and cross-country
skiing. Wheelchair access to first floor.

From the moment you drive up the long driveway to the inn, you are
enchanted with the surroundings. Then The Manor comes into
view and your enchantment is complete, the inn is just so lovely.
Built in 1903 by a wealthy Englishman, Isaac Van Horn, the house still has
its original rich wood paneling, beautiful doors (some with mirrors), magnificently carved moldings, marble fireplaces, and old pedestal sinks. Thank-
fully, all details have remained unscarred over the years.

The inn is smoke-free, and its broad lakefront gives you a 65-mile view of
Squam Lake and the mountains.

The lovely Three
Cocks Pub has four bar
stools, beautiful tables,
and a baby grand piano.
Formal tea is served at
4:00 P.M. with the appro-
priate accompaniments.

The dining rooms are
lovely and air condi-
tioned. A huge two-sided
fireplace divides the space. Some appetizers are honey-glazed scallops
wrapped in bacon, fresh Maine crabcakes, and baked brie in phyllo. These are
followed by good soups and salads. One entree I especially enjoyed was the
roast duckling, served on a bed of wild rice with a choice of orange Grand

Marnier sauce or cranberry Chambord sauce. Perhaps you'd prefer the filet mignon, roast rack of lamb, or pasta. I hate to mention the desserts; they are sinfully good. The inn has received from AAA a four-diamond rating for the dining room and guest rooms and an award of excellence from the *Wine Spectator* magazine.

Breakfast may bring English country eggs, omelets, French toast, pancakes, and much more. I think I'll lose ten pounds and go back for a week.

The guest rooms are exceptional, with handsome wall coverings and good beds and chairs. Some have lovely old pedestal sinks, and nine have fireplaces. The cottages are elegant.

There is everything to do here: swimming pool, tennis, shuffleboard, croquet, Ping-Pong, and much more. The *Lady of the Manor* is a luxurious 28-foot pontoon craft that is available for guided tours of "Golden Pond," parties, picnics, and transportation to Church Island for Sunday services in an outdoor setting. There are thirteen acres for you to play in and 300 feet of sandy beach frontage for you to sunbathe on. If it rains, there are many games to play inside and many places to just relax in this beautiful mansion.

**HOW TO GET THERE:** Take Route 3 into Holderness. Cross the bridge, and on the right you will see the signs for The Manor.

# Christmas Farm Inn
## Jackson, New Hampshire 03846

**INNKEEPERS:** William Zeliff; Bill and Sydna Zeliff, owners

**ADDRESS/TELEPHONE:** P.O. Box CC; (603) 383–4313 or (800) HI–ELVES; fax (603) 383–6495

**ROOMS:** 35, including suites and cottages; all with private bath. Phones, TV in cottages.

**RATES:** $78 to $110, per person, double occupancy, MAP. Special weekly and package rates.

**OPEN:** All year.

**FACILITIES AND ACTIVITIES:** Wheelchair access to inn and dining room. Pub, complimentary movies, gameroom, putting green. Nearby:

80 kilometers of cross-country trails, golf, tennis, sauna. Nearby: downhill skiing, alpine slide, canoeing on Saco River.

*Y*es, Virginia, there is a Christmas Farm Inn, and they have the Mistletoe Pub and the Sugar Plum Dining Room to prove it. The food is fit for any Santa and his helpers, from the hearty, full country breakfast, which includes homemade doughnuts, muffins, and sticky buns, to gracious dinners featuring a full menu of entrees, soups, salad bar, and fresh breads and desserts made by an on-site baker. Children age twelve and under have their own special menu.

The food is excellent. The medallions of pork MacIntosh are glorious and have a hint of brandy. The veal and chicken are so tender. Entrees from the seas are real treats. The desserts do indeed make visions of sugarplums dance in your head. How about apple pie, carrot cake, or the Christmas Farm special sundae? From here take a quick trip to the Mistletoe Pub for a nightcap.

Separate from the main building is the Christmas Farm function center, a perfect spot not only for medium to small business meetings but also weddings, anniversaries, and the like. At one side of the room is a 12-foot-wide fieldstone fireplace. There are games of all sorts, a wide-screen television, a sauna, a bar, and four nice suites that are ideal for families.

Also separate are the cottages, each with living room, fireplace, two bedrooms, and two baths. The rooms in the main building have Christmas names: Holly, Dasher, Prancer, Vixen, Donner, Cupid, Comet, and Blitzen. There are two deluxe rooms with Jacuzzi tubs.

Sugar House has air conditioning. Honeymoon Cottage has a wood fireplace in its living room, a bedroom, and a huge bath with a two-person Jacuzzi and a shower. Five cottages have two bedrooms and baths, coffeemakers, TV, and refrigerators, plus air conditioning. They are grand.

Jackson is in the heart of the White Mountains, so bring your skis, or come in the summer for the annual Christmas-in-July party, which features an outside buffet and Christmas tree, as well as live entertainment, dancing, shuffleboard, and golf tournaments. Santa must live nearby, because he never fails to arrive in a most unusual manner.

Making memories is something Bill and Sydna and their staff know all about.

HOW TO GET THERE: Go north on Route 16 from North Conway. A few miles after Route 302 branches off to your left, you will see a covered bridge on your right. Take the bridge through the village and up the hill ¼ mile, and there is the inn.

## Jackson Ski Touring Foundation

One of the best such operations in the entire Northeast, the Jackson Ski Touring Foundation maintains nearly 160 kilometers of cross-country ski trails over 60 square miles of this region. Skiers can use the trail system to ski from inn to inn; some trails are easy and others suited to experienced skiers. Races and workshops are held on these trails every winter weekend. Trail fees help to maintain the trails, and they were recently used to build a covered bridge to provide access to the Ellis River Trail, a 10-kilometer route from the village of Jackson to one of the inns in the area. Call (603) 383-9355 for more information.

# Ellis River House ♥
## Jackson, New Hampshire 03846

**INNKEEPERS:** Barbara and Barry Lubao

**ADDRESS/TELEPHONE:** Route 16 (mailing address: P.O. Box 656); (603) 383–9339 or (800) 233–8309; fax (603) 383–4142

**E-MAIL:** innkeeper@crhinn.com

**WEB SITE:** www.crhinn.com

**ROOMS:** 13, plus 4 suites and 1 cottage; all with private bath, air conditioning, phone, and TV, 11 with fireplace, 3 with two-person Jacuzzi.

**RATES:** $69 to $129, spring; $99 to $229, fall foliage; $89 to $199, winter; double occupancy, EPB.

**OPEN:** All year.

**FACILITIES AND ACTIVITIES:** Dinner, full license. Wedding and anniversary functions. Cross-country skiing, fishing, vineyard, swimming pool. Nearby: shopping, downhill skiing, and much more.

Calling all snow people: Have I found an inn for you! The inn's River and Mountain View Atrium is a glass-enclosed 24-by-24-foot room with an eight-person spa in the center. Imagine sitting in hot water in this heated room and watching the snow coming down and cross-country skiers going by. That's the way for this inn creeper to go.

In warm weather the heated outdoor pool or trout pond will beckon you. Or perhaps you'll enjoy the new gazebo off the dining room and overlooking the Ellis River and the inn's well-landscaped grounds.

The rooms here are wonderful. Eleven of them have a fireplace. Three have two-person Jacuzzis. All are air-conditioned and have cable television, classic antiques, good beds, and a ton of comfort.

A wedding here is handled beautifully. From the church, florist, photographer, horse-drawn carriages, lake, entertainment, and dinner, it's complete.

The menu changes daily, so you can keep coming here and enjoying new and excellent food every day. Some of the kitchen's first-course offerings are butternut squash soup, escargots in puff pastry, and tomato and wild mushroom soup. They also prepare roast tenderloin of pork, prime ribs, good pastas, and fish. Roast goose is really different. Garlic mashed potatoes make my mouth water. Desserts? Why ask? They're glorious.

Breakfasts are a treat. In addition to the usual, there are homemade breads—cinnamon, oatmeal, molasses, beer, or French.

The inn has a wonderful history. It's been here since 1893, starting as a farmhouse. There's much to do in this area—factory outlet shopping, skiing, fishing, you name it.

**HOW TO GET THERE:** Take I–95 north to Route 16 north to Jackson. The inn is on the left, ¼ mile past the historic covered bridge.

# The Inn at Thorn Hill
## Jackson, New Hampshire 03846

**INNKEEPERS:** Jim and Ibby Cooper

**ADDRESS/TELEPHONE:** Thorn Hill Road; (603) 383-4242 or (800) 289-8990; fax (603) 383-8062

**WEB SITE:** www.innatthornhill.com

**ROOMS:** 19, in 2 buildings, plus 3 cottage suites, all with private bath and phones; 7 Jacuzzis and 1 soaking tub. No smoking inn.

**RATES:** $150 to $250, double occupancy, MAP. Higher in peak season.

**OPEN:** All year.

**FACILITIES AND ACTIVITIES:** Bar, swimming pool, hot tub, cross-country skiing. Nearby: downhill skiing, golf club, tennis, horseback riding, canoeing, ice skating, sleigh rides.

Over the Honeymoon Bridge to The Inn at Thorn Hill you go, and when you get there you will find a Victorian beauty. Mountains are everywhere you look from this inn. Relax on the porch in a New England rocking chair and enjoy the view. Even on a bad day, it is spectacular.

I loved the Victorian parlor, with a baby grand piano, and the spacious drawing room, with a wood stove and an unbelievable view. There are board games, cards, and books for you to enjoy. A cozy pub with a fireplace and five bar stools has lots of cheer.

Elegant country dining by candlelight is what you get, and the food is good. The menu changes nightly, offering the freshest and most innovative ingredients the season has to offer. Casually elegant service, an extensive wine list, and a full-service pub are to be found here.

Sautéed almond- and Parmesan-crusted shrimp served with a grilled pineapple, radish, and caper salad with fresh tarragon dressing is just an example of the appetizers—there are more.

The soups and salads are interesting. And the entrees are grand. Lobster Pie Thorn Hill, served with brandy Newburg sauce in a puff pastry shell. Crisp roast duckling, served with Cointreau sauce and sautéed orange slices.

Lamb chops stuffed with tomato, feta cheese, and fresh mint. The list goes on. The desserts that follow are excellent.

There is a Victorian flair to all the inn rooms. A variety of beds are available—canopies, singles, doubles, kings, and queens—and all rooms have wonderful views of the mountains. The Katharine room has two Victorian mannequins; they're beauties. The carriage house next door has a 20-by-40-foot great room with a fireplace and seven guest rooms, so bring a gang and have some fun. This is the place to be. The cottages are very nice and just great for those who want more privacy. The three cottages have just been beautifully refurbished, each with a Jacuzzi, front porch, wet bar, television, gas fireplace, and air conditioning. Some have a deck and view. I stayed in one of the cottages, and, believe me, you could move right in and be very comfortable.

The inn's facilities are not well suited to small children.

There is much to do here. The inn has its own swimming pool; hiking and downhill skiing are close at hand. Cross-country skiing begins at the doorstep and joins the 146-kilometer Jackson touring network. Say hello to Gizmo, the inn cat, and Snuggles, the inn dog.

No wonder the inn was one of ten winners of Uncle Ben's Best Country Inn awards! I was one of the judges.

HOW TO GET THERE: Go north from Portsmouth, New Hampshire, on the Spaulding Turnpike (Route 16) all the way to Jackson, which is just above North Conway. At Jackson is a covered bridge on your right. Take the bridge, and two roads up from the bridge on the right is Thorn Hill Road, which you take up the hill. The inn is on your right.

# Whitney's Inn 🖼
## Jackson, New Hampshire 03846

INNKEEPERS: David Linne; Bob and Barb Bowman, owners

ADDRESS/TELEPHONE: Route 16B (mailing address: P.O. Box W); (603) 383–8916 or (800) 677–5737

E-MAIL: whitneyinn@aol.com

WEB SITE: www.mountwashingtonvalley.com

ROOMS: 30, plus 2 cottages; all with private bath, 13 with air conditioning; cottages with living room, fireplace, and TV. Nonsmoking rooms available.

RATES: $35 to $65, per person, double occupancy, EPB. $55 to $85, per person, double occupancy, MAP.

OPEN: All year.

FACILITIES AND ACTIVITIES: Bar, lounge, TV and VCR with movies, children's play yard, skiing, ice skating, tennis, swimming pond, badminton, shuffleboard, paddleboat.

*T*his is an authentic mountain hideaway nestled at the base of Black Mountain ski area. You can't get much closer than this. It's pretty nice to be able to crawl out of bed, have a sumptuous breakfast, and walk across to the lifts, trails, ski shop or ski school, all just a snowball's throw away.

Another very nice feature of the inn is the children's dinner table, available at 5:30 P.M. during busy times. It's nice to know you can spend some time alone while your children are well supervised. On Tuesdays and Thursdays in the summer, children are supervised in the children's play yard and picnic area. There is a good video library, along with board and card games and crossword puzzles. The recreation room has a Ping-Pong table. All this and fourteen acres, tennis courts, shuffleboard, badminton, and a brook-fed pond with a sandy beach and paddleboat.

The Greenery Lounge is neat. There are six original tractor seats at the bar, and on winter weekends the Shovel Handle Pub, a 250-seat après-ski bar, is open with live entertainment.

The dining room is a casually elegant one, and the food is grand. Asparagus with tomato vinaigrette and smoked scallops are but two appetizers. Entrees include sole, scampi, roast duck, and the chef's veal (this was really good), chicken, turkey, and marinated pork. All come with a house salad.

In the morning breakfast consists of fresh eggs (egg substitutes are available), French toast, pancakes, homemade corned beef hash, omelets. . . .

There is much to do up here, and when you arrive you will receive a map listing what is going on.

HOW TO GET THERE: Go north from Conway 22 miles on Route 16. Take a right on Route 16A through a covered bridge into Jackson Village. Take Route 16B to the top of the hill to the inn.

# The Wildcat Inn
## Jackson, New Hampshire 03846

**INNKEEPERS:** Pam and Marty Sweeney

**ADDRESS/TELEPHONE:** Route 16A; (603) 383–4245 or (800) 228–4245

**ROOMS:** 14; 12 with private bath and air conditioning, TV, and phones. 1 cottage.

**RATES:** $40 to $45, per person, EPB.

**OPEN:** All year.

**FACILITIES AND ACTIVITIES:** Lunch daily in-season, weekends off-season; no lunch served in April or May. Dinner, bar. Wheelchair access to dining room and tavern. Music in lounge. Nearby: downhill and cross-country skiing, golf, hiking, tennis, riding.

The brochure here at Wildcat says it so well that I'm just going to repeat it: "Everything you need for a perfect vacation is within walking distance of the inn, so leave your car out back and save gas, money, and time. Begin in the Tavern Gardens, where you will be well fed and properly wined from breakfast through last call. Tennis, your choice of one hard and three clay courts. Golf at the beautiful Wentworth Hall course. Riding lessons, shows, and trail rides through mountain forests. There are package deals for all of the above. Fishing, hiking, or just meandering through town; good shopping is up here. And both downhill and cross-country skiing are nearby."

The tavern has two big fireplaces and nice couches, and on weekends and holidays there is music. Accommodations are comfortable. All the rooms are different, and each one has a view and is air-conditioned.

The Wildcat is a very popular dining spot. In fact, some years ago the big old front porch had to be converted into a dining room to make more dining space for all the people who wanted to eat here. The food will titillate your taste buds. All meals are made to order and, as the chef says, patience is a virtue.

Breakfasts are full, with all pastries baked right here. There are tavern specials at lunch. Lobster Benedict is different. I had it for lunch one day. Another day I tried one called Salmagundi; enough food for an army and delicious. Also, lovely lox on a bagel! Marvelous salads, six of them, all accompanied by homemade breads. Be sure to read the sign with the rules of the tavern. It's very funny. There are a lot of inns in Jackson, but only this one serves lunch.

And at dinnertime there are good appetizers and soups. One entree is baked seafood platter, which is different every day. Wildcat chicken is chicken wrapped in puff pastry. A few of their desserts are sour cream apple pie, rhubarb pudding cake, and frozen raspberry soufflé. So what are you waiting for? Inn dog Quido is a German shepherd. He likes the desserts because they are all made here.

**HOW TO GET THERE:** Take Route 16 north from North Conway. Take Route 16A to your right, through a covered bridge, and into Jackson. The inn is in the center of town.

# The Ammonoosuc Inn
## Lisbon, New Hampshire 03585

**INNKEEPER:** Glen McCosham

**ADDRESS/TELEPHONE:** Bishop Road; (603) 838–6118

**ROOMS:** 9; all with private bath.

**RATES:** $79, double occupancy, EPB. MAP rates available.

**OPEN:** All year.

**FACILITIES AND ACTIVITIES:** Dinner, full license; call for reservations. Wheelchair access to dining room. Privileges at Lisbon Village Country Club—golf, swimming pool, cross-country skiing, sledding, tennis. Nearby: fishing, canoeing, downhill skiing.

*T*he inn was constructed as a farmhouse in 1888. It has been restored and remodeled into an inn with a fine restaurant called Cobblers.

The inn sits up high and overlooks the Ammonoosuc River, which flows peacefully along. Fishing is great. Tubing down the river would be fun. The Lisbon Village Country Club is right next door and offers many activities. Its golf course was designed by Ralph M. Bartin, a renowned golf course designer. The club has its own clubhouse and lounge.

Relaxing at the inn after a day of fun is easy. The lounge has a wood stove, and the parlors are comfortable. Everything is aimed at your comfort. There is satellite television for you to enjoy, or you might have drinks on the porch. The guest rooms are lovely and very tastefully decorated.

The dining room has its original wood paneling and beams. Breakfast provides Danish and other pastries. For dinner there are traditional New England entrees and a lot more. Baked artichokes, stuffed mushrooms, calamari, and good soups are nice for a start. There are four chicken dishes. Chicken Grand Marnier gets my vote. Barbecued pork ribs is another good dish. The seafood medley is served on linguine, and the combos take care of two taste treats— ribs and shrimp or steak and shrimp. Of course, there are veal dishes and steak. This is a really nice menu.

There is so much to do here that you should be sure to come for more than one day. If you like skiing, the inn is fifteen minutes from Cannon Mountain. I, for one, would love to go sledding on the golf course. In warmer weather the porch with rockers is my idea of peace. Just sit back and rock and watch the river.

**HOW TO GET THERE:** From I-91 take exit 17 (Woodsville–Wells River). Go east on Route 302 to Lisbon. Two miles past Lisbon take a left on Lyman Road for about ½ mile, then left onto Bishop Road for about ¾ mile. The inn is on the right.

# Inn at Baypoint
## Meredith, New Hampshire 03253

**INNKEEPER:** Rusty McLear

**ADDRESS/TELEPHONE:** Route 3; (603) 279–6455 or (800) 622–6455

**ROOMS:** 24, all with private bath, phone, and TV.

**RATES:** $69 to $249, double occupancy, EP. Packages with meals available.

**OPEN:** All year.

**FACILITIES AND ACTIVITIES:** Breakfast, lunch, and dinner. Bar and lounge. Sunday brunch. Boating, swimming, and fishing in the lake at the sister inn. Indoor pool, sauna, spa, shops, and a choice of restaurants.

The Inns at Mills Falls are a wonderful collection of three inns: The Inn at Mills Falls, the Chase House at Mill Falls, and this beauty on the shores of Lake Winnipesaukee. Sure wish I lived closer. The Inn at Baypoint is surrounded by more than 2,000 feet of manicured lakefront park. The views of the lake and mountains are awesome. Many of the guest rooms offer private lakeside balconies, fireplaces, and personal whirlpools. The lake, "Granddaddy Lake" (the smile of the Great Spirit) is 72 miles square, with 200 islands and a 300-mile shoreline. As they say up here where the mountains and blue water meet sky, bring your water wings!

The M.S. *Mount Washington* is 230 feet long; there are a lot of choices for cruises. Special theme and dinner dances, special functions, and smaller boats that go where the big one can't.

This inn is spectacular, as are the others. You can sit on the dock and watch the boats. Try the Boathouse Grill; lunch was lovely. There are several appetizers and entrees. Well, I had lobster salad, and it was so good. Other choices may be rock crab cakes, pizza of the day, soup and half a sandwich—

maybe the Baypoint Club. Then, after a day of delightful wandering all over the marketplace at the sister Inn at Mill Falls—just across the street—I was back in the Boathouse for dinner. I had the chef's suggested soup, and I was so glad I did. It had beef and chicken stock, shallots and garlic, lemon, pepper, heavy cream, and veggies. There are about ten different appetizers, and dinner entrees are a grand variety—something for everyone. Desserts? Well, just save room. The other restaurants at the other inns are great. Giuseppe's has such a menu you could almost eat it while reading it! Mame's is very unusual, too. They are all here waiting for you.

**HOW TO GET THERE:** From I–93 take exit 23, go east on Route 104 to its end. Go left on Route 3 north. The inn is 1 mile down the hill on the right.

# The Inn at Mill Falls
## Meredith, New Hampshire 03253

**INNKEEPER:** Rusty McLear; Sandra L. Quinney, front desk manager

**ADDRESS/TELEPHONE:** Route 3; (603) 279–7006 or (800) 622–MILL (6455)

**ROOMS:** 54; all with private bath, cable TV, phone; some with a fireplace. One inn room equipped for handicapped.

**RATES:** $69 to $249, EP. Packages with meals available.

**OPEN:** All year.

**FACILITIES AND ACTIVITIES:** Full breakfast, lunch, dinner, Sunday brunch, bar and lounge. Indoor pool, sauna, whirlpool spa, shops, art gallery. Boating, swimming, and fishing in lake. Nearby: tennis, racquetball, golf, skiing.

The inn is in what was once an old mill. It straddles an underground canal that runs from Lake Waukewan in the hills above to Lake Winnipesaukee below. Through a window near the lobby, you will see a sluice that is solid ice in winter.

The inn can accommodate banquets, seminars, conferences, and special events. Everything is here: mooring for your boat, newspapers, indoor pool,

whirlpool spa and sauna, video rentals, safety deposit boxes, and boating on beautiful Winnipesaukee, the sixth-largest natural lake entirely within the United States. It is 28 miles long and 9 miles wide. The M.S. *Mount Washington* is an excursion ship that will take you on a 50-mile cruise. Or sail the *Queen of Winnipesaukee*, a 46-foot sloop. There are others to choose from. You prefer sports on solid ground? Golf, jogging, skiing, hiking, tennis, and racquetball are all in the area, too. And some twenty shops and an art gallery are right here if you'd rather do something less active.

The enclosed walkway leading from the lobby spans the tumbling falls and connects the inn with the Mill Falls Marketplace. This 180-year-old restored mill building is the setting for the inn's full-service tavern and restaurant. Millworks has great breakfasts, both large and small ones. At luncheon there is a good selection of sandwiches. The French onion soup offered at dinner is glorious. The salads are very choice, and the entrees are excellent. You must try it here. Mame's is a small restaurant with many interesting dishes on the menu. Sunday brunch is served here; the eggs Benedict are perfect.

The accommodations are yummy, with wall-to-wall carpeting, telephones, and cable television. Well-lighted areas are provided for reading or for work (if you must). This whole inn is a wonderful vacation spot.

**HOW TO GET THERE:** From I–93 take exit 23. Go east on Route 104 to its end. Go left on Route 3 north. The inn is in 1 mile, down the hill on the left.

# Chase House at Mill Falls
## Meredith, New Hampshire 03253

**INNKEEPER:** Rusty McLear, Sandra L. Quinney, front desk manager

**ADDRESS/TELEPHONE:** Route 3, (603) 279–6455 or (800) 622–6455

**ROOMS:** 20, plus 3 suites, all with private bath, phone, TV, fireplaces, and balconies.

**RATES:** $69 to $249, double occupancy, EP. Packages with meals available.

**OPEN:** All year.

**FACILITIES AND ACTIVITIES:** 150-seat conference and function center, Camp restaurant.

The newest addition to the collection of inns here is the luxurious Chase House. The rooms and suites all offer lake views, fireplaces, and romantic sitting areas, and most offer private balconies and whirlpool spas. They are beautifully decorated.

The restaurant, called "Camp" and also known as The Common Man, has a huge fieldstone fireplace and views of the lake. The innkeepers say, and I quote, "We're not very big, our kitchen is tiny, so we go to market every day,

we may add an item or not have something—keeps things interesting!" The menu is fun and has lighter fare. Swasey's Back Porch over at the sister inn (see the Inn at Mill Falls) is the one for room service. Breakfast is served till 2:00 P.M.—the way to go when on vacation. Come on up here and try the inns.

**HOW TO GET THERE:** From I–93 take exit 23 and go east on 104 to its end. Turn left on Route 3 and in less than a mile on the left is the inn.

# The Ram in the Thicket
## Milford, New Hampshire 03055

**INNKEEPERS:** Andrew and Priscilla Tempelman

**ADDRESS/TELEPHONE:** Maple Street; (603) 654–6440; fax (603) 654–6440

**ROOMS:** 9; 3 with private bath.

**RATES:** $60 to $75, double occupancy, continental breakfast.

**OPEN:** All year.

**FACILITIES AND ACTIVITIES:** Dinner, bar. Hot tub, indoor swimming pool, horseback riding, hiking. Nearby: summer theater.

*T*he unusual name of the inn is taken from the old bible story of Abraham and Isaac. As a substitute for his dear son Isaac, Abraham finds "a ram caught in the thicket," sent by the Lord. Andrew and Priscilla founded the inn as a substitute for a life in the Midwest from which they wanted a change.

Luckily for all inn lovers, the Tempelmans' move has resulted in another better-than-nice inn. This old Victorian mansion has been carefully restored and now has lovely dining rooms with crystal chandeliers, a hand-carved fireplace, and many other Victorian touches. One dining room has lovely blue delft tiles. The innkeepers are Dutch. The New Hampshire lounge has plants hanging from the ceilings.

You will surely love the inventive and interesting dinners. Pasta e Fagioli is corkscrew pasta tossed with tomatoes, onions, favas, garbanzos, and kidney beans, seasoned with fresh oregano, thyme, and rosemary. Umeboshi Pork is Japanese. Veal Tiera del Fuego—go and see what it is. There are good soups, salads, and desserts. The menu changes quite often.

This fine inn is set in eight acres of wonderful country for roaming. Mandy is the inn dog, and Mogley is the inn cat.

**HOW TO GET THERE:** Take Route 3 and just about at Nashua take exit 7 west on 101A to 101 about 15 miles to Wilton. Watch for the inn's signs. The inn is 200 yards from the Wilton line.

# New London Inn
New London, New Hampshire 03257

**INNKEEPERS:** Kimberly and Terrance O'Mahony

**ADDRESS/TELEPHONE:** P.O. Box 8; (603) 526-2791 or (800) 526-2791; fax (603) 526-2749

**ROOMS:** 29, plus 1 suite; all with private bath, 1 with wheelchair access.

**RATES:** $85 to $125, single; $110 to $140, double occupancy; EPB.

**OPEN:** All year.

**FACILITIES AND ACTIVITIES:** Dinner, bar. Wheelchair access to dining room and bar. Nearby: skiing, theater, golf, two public beaches, water sports, shopping.

his college-town inn has been restored to the grandeur it had in 1792 when it began serving the traveler. The innkeepers have been faithful to detail, even right down to the Federal-period sign that hangs in front of the inn. This restoration has been a tremendous job for them, and I applaud them for their effort. And their gardens are lovely.

As you enter the inn, you immediately appreciate the long veranda. There's also another one upstairs with the rooms. Do come up and try the rockers. Rooms in the inn are large, airy, and comfortable. Each one is decorated differently, and one is specially equipped, bathroom and all, for handicapped guests.

Cool cream and green are the colors of the dining room. It has large windows and the original fireplace is still working. For an almost 200-year-old fireplace, that's a lot of fires! The dining room's gracious ambience is well suited to the wonderful food.

The dinner menu changes seasonally and features such enticing appetizers as warm asparagus strudel with light wine and herb sauce, and lemon pepper pasta with fresh vegetables and Italian bacon. For soups they have bisque of New England spring vegetables and chilled tomato lime and scallop soup, among others. Oh, I love interesting soups! Entrees are innovative, like grilled marinated monkfish served with red- and-yellow-pepper coulis, grilled smoked duck breast served with spicy white beans and corn crepes, and spiced beef medallions with lime-cilantro butter and avocado sauce. Boy, it's hard to choose which one to eat! Desserts are very good and prepared daily. Breakfasts feature freshly squeezed orange or grapefruit juice.

The town of New London, home of Colby-Sawyer College, still conveys the feeling of a nineteenth-century village. From its wide main streets, fields, fences, and gracious houses to the beautiful mountains, it's just a lovely place to be. Its location in the Mount Sunapee Lake Region means that there are three lakes close by that offer all the water sports. The golf is nice because there is no waiting, and there is good skiing.

This is a beautiful part of the world at any time of the year, so come on up.

HOW TO GET THERE: Take exit 8 at Ascutney, Vermont, from I-91. Follow signs to Claremont, New Hampshire. Take Route 11 east to Newport, Sunapee, Georges Mills, and New London. There is bus service via Vermont Transit from Boston and from White River Junction, Vermont.

## New London Barn Playhouse

In the summer months the stage of the New London Barn Playhouse is lit for a full season of dramatic and musical entertainment suitable for the whole family. Well-known on the summer-stock circuit, the theater is one of the oldest in New England. Special events and children's shows are also staged here from June through August. Regular performances are at 8:00 P.M during the week, at 5:00 P.M. on Sunday afternoons, and at 2:00 P.M. on Wednesdays. Call for information on the the full schedule. Tickets are reasonably priced; call the box office at 603–526–4631 or 800–633–2276.

# Pleasant Lake Inn
## New London, New Hampshire 03257

**INNKEEPERS:** Linda and Brian Mackenzie

**ADDRESS/TELEPHONE:** 125 Pleasant Street (mailing address: P.O. Box 1030); (603) 526–6271 or (800) 626–4907

**ROOMS:** 10, plus 1 suite; all with private bath. No smoking in bedrooms.

**RATES:** $95 to $145, double occupancy, EPB.

**OPEN:** All year.

**FACILITIES AND ACTIVITIES:** Dinner 6 nights a week by reservation. Bar. Swimming, boating, fishing, 2 canoes, 1 rowboat, and all winter sports.

*P*leasant Lake Inn is the oldest operating inn in this area. It began as a farm in 1790 and became an inn a century ago. Inn guests today are given privileges at the Slope and Shore Club on Pleasant Lake, just across the road, which offers tennis, boating, fishing, and swimming. There are iceboating and cross-country skiing here in the winter. The inn also has a nice pond for ice skating on the property, and downhill skiing is close at hand. King Ridge is five minutes away. Mount Sunapee and Whaleback are fifteen minutes away, Pat's Peak is twenty-five minutes away, and many more are within an hour's drive. Back at the inn spend some time at the bumper pool table in the family room. It's a favorite game of mine.

The view from the inn's front windows is magnificent, and in the fall, it's spectacular. The inn looks right out onto Pleasant Lake, and beautiful Mount Kearsarge is just on the other side of the lake.

There are antique furnishings, warming fireplaces, nice views, and very comfortable guest rooms throughout the inn. Andy, a border collie, lives here.

The food served in the pleasant dining rooms is good. Breakfast is hearty and includes a longtime favorite of mine, blueberry pancakes. Dinners are delicious. All the sauces and soups are prepared with the freshest ingredients, no artificial agents, and sauces are thickened by natural reduction instead of with heavy starches. Entrees include chops, chicken, and fish. For dessert they serve a family-recipe chocolate icebox cake, and, as they say, if you have a favorite, they will try to make it.

**HOW TO GET THERE:** From I–89 take either New London exit. Halfway through New London, turn at the New London Trust Company. This is Pleasant Street. Go about 2 miles, and the inn is on your left.

# The Scottish Lion Inn
## North Conway, New Hampshire 03860

**INNKEEPERS:** Michael and Janet Procopio

**ADDRESS/TELEPHONE:** Route 16; (603) 356–6381; fax (603) 356–4802

**ROOMS:** 8; all with private bath.

**RATES:** $59, off-season; $85, midweek summer; $110, foliage-season and summer weekends; double occupancy; EPB.

**OPEN:** All year except Christmas Eve and Christmas Day.

**FACILITIES AND ACTIVITIES:** Lunch, dinner, bar. Wheelchair access to first floor. Parking. Full country breakfast. TV in lounge.

*W*hen you come down the road and see the magnificent flag streaming out in the wind, you just can't go by. Stop for a drink if you can't stay the night. You'll love it.

The rooms at The Scottish Lion Inn are cozy. One has an eyelet-trimmed canopy bed, another a spool bed with a patchwork quilt. All are charming. The whole inn is full of fine Scottish paintings. Do not miss any of them.

Food, of course, features the best of Scottish touches. A hearty Scottish breakfast is served to houseguests. Dinner is rated three stars in the Mobil Travel Guide. Highland game pie, which is venison, beef, hare, and fowl

simmered in wine and baked in puff pastry, may sound strange, but a gentleman who had had it the night before reported to me, "Delicious." Chicken Dijonnaise, prime rib, and Scottish steak and mushroom pie are among the dishes offered. Hot Scottish oatcakes are served instead of bread or rolls. A marvelous dish named Rumble-dethumps is one of the potato choices; what a taste! I must tell you one more: Lobster Lady Tweedsmuir, tender pieces of lobster in a delicate cream and Drambuie sauce, stuffed in the shell. You must try this dish.

For dessert Scottish trifle or Scots crumpets with fresh fruit and honey are but a few of the choices available. The inn also serves a very special coffee. The pub has a long list of tantalizing pleasures, such as Hoot Mon cocktail, St. Andrews Hole-in-One, or Loch Ness Monster.

HOW TO GET THERE: Take Route 16 to North Conway. The inn is 1 mile north from the center of town, on the left.

# The 1785 Inn
## North Conway, New Hampshire 03860

INNKEEPERS: Charles and Rebecca Mallar

ADDRESS/TELEPHONE: Route 16 (mailing address: P.O. Box 1785); (603) 356-9025; fax (603) 356-6081

E-MAIL: the1785inn@aol.com

WEB SITE: www.the1785inn.com

ROOMS: 16, plus 1 suite; 12 with private bath.

RATES: $69 to $199, double occupancy, EPB.

OPEN: All year.

FACILITIES AND ACTIVITIES: Dinner, bar, lounge. Wheelchair access to dining room. Swimming pool, cross-country skiing. Nearby: golf, tennis, canoeing, fishing, skiing.

The 1785 Inn is one of the oldest houses in all of Mount Washington Valley. It was built in 1785 by Captain Elijah Dinsmore. Records indicate that Captain Dinsmore received a license to "keep a Publik House" in 1795. In addition to being a public house, the lovely old inn served as a stagecoach stop. The chimney and dining room fireplace with brick oven are original to the house. They form a beehive structure the size of an entire room in the center of the inn.

Guest accommodations are ample. The Mallars have completely refurbished the inn. What a large undertaking! They have done such a fine job. There is a sink in all the rooms. I find this a very nice feature in rooms with shared baths.

There are two living areas; both have fireplaces, and one has a television set. They are furnished with attractive chairs and couches for your comfort. An old oak icebox is in here. It surely makes a beautiful piece of furniture. The tavern has a large bar, a wood-burning stove, and good sitting areas. There is light classical music here at times.

The views from the porch–dining room are just lovely. The food is inventive and very good. One dinner dish is raspberry duck: duck roasted with a brandy-laced raspberry sauce and served on wild rice. There are several veal selections, and, of course, seafood and chicken. The desserts are wild. Chocolate velvet. Coffee butter-crunch pie, as featured in *Bon Appétit*. Becky's wondrous raspberry desserts.

Candlelight casts a romantic glow throughout the evening, so take your time and enjoy your meal and fine wines. The wine list has been called "one of the finest in the world" by *Wine Spectator* magazine.

This is a nice inn, surrounded by many activities and serving good food— what more can you want?

HOW TO GET THERE: Take Route 16 north. The inn is on the left just before you come to Route 16A.

# Stonehurst Manor
## North Conway, New Hampshire 03860

**INNKEEPER:** Peter Rattay

**ADDRESS/TELEPHONE:** Route 16; (603) 356–3113 or (800) 525–9100

**ROOMS:** 14 in the manor, 10 in the annex adjoining the manor; 22 with private bath, air conditioning, cable TV, radio.

**RATES:** $80 to $160, double occupancy, EP. MAP and package rates available.

**OPEN:** All year.

**FACILITIES AND ACTIVITIES:** Breakfast, dinner. Wheelchair access to dining room. Bar, meeting room for up to 50 persons. Pool, tennis. Nearby: swimming, hiking, fishing, skiing.

This turn-of-the-century mansion is a fine country inn. Set back from the highway among stately pine trees, it makes you think you are going back in time, and in a way you are.

The front door is huge. Once inside, you see beautiful oak woodwork and a wonderful wall-to-wall carpet. The room to the left is all wicker and all comfort. Ahead of you is the warm living room, with walls full of books and a huge fireplace. The unusual screen and andirons were made in England. To the right of the fireplace is a 12-foot, curved window seat of another era. The lounge area has a two-seat bar, just the right size.

Relax in a high-back wicker chair in one of the inn's four dining rooms, which have been awarded three stars in the *Mobil Travel Guide* and also won the Silver Spoon Award. Enjoy the fine gourmet dining. There are many appetizers; the escargots are divine, as is the smoked  salmon. Choose from the good soups and salads—the Caesar, prepared tableside, is glorious. The eighteen entrees are all so good. Chicken with wood-baked maple yams, roast duck with blackberry sauce, and rack of lamb for two. Oh my! There is a special wood-fired stone oven for pizzas. They are sensational, and there are a dozen different ones.

The manor staircase is a beauty, and the large rooms are meticulously appointed. Fantastic wallpapers and beautiful carpets all add to this great inn. The third-floor rooms have windows at odd angles, dictated by the roof line of the house. Some rooms have porches, and one has a stained-glass door going out to its porch. There is a lot of lovely stained glass throughout the inn. On the second floor, in one of the hall bathrooms, is a wood-enclosed steel bathtub. Be sure to take a look at it; it is quite a sight. Seven guest rooms have fireplaces. The inn was the country estate of the Bigelow carpet family, so of course the inn cat's name is Mrs. Bigelow.

Cocktails are served around the pool in the summer. Swimming or playing tennis will keep you busy, or, like me, you might want to just sit and relax.

There are a variety of walking and hiking experiences near to the inn. More than 1,100 miles of maintained trails await you.

**HOW TO GET THERE:** The inn is on Route 16 just a short distance north of North Conway Village.

---

# Follansbee Inn
## North Sutton, New Hampshire 03260

**INNKEEPERS:** Sandy and Dick Reilein

**ADDRESS/TELEPHONE:** P.O. Box 92; (603) 927–4221 or (800) 626–4221

**ROOMS:** 23; 11 with private bath. No smoking inn.

**RATES:** $75 to $95, double occupancy, EPB.

**OPEN:** All year except parts of April and November.

**FACILITIES AND ACTIVITIES:** Dinner for houseguests by reservation. Beer and wine license, for inn guests only. Cross-country skiing from the inn, swimming, boating, Ping-Pong, bicycles. Nearby: downhill skiing, golf, antiquing.

The Follansbee Inn is an 1840 New England farmhouse located on Kezar Lake. It has its own pier and private beach. A sailboard, paddleboat, rowboat, and canoe are provided for your pleasure.

Or perhaps you'd like to take a swim in this lovely lake? The innkeepers are always willing to pack a lunch for a secluded picnic on the lake's island or for hiking up Mount Kearsarge.

A wood-burning stove makes the living room cozy and homey. One sitting room has a well-stocked service bar for houseguests, and a Ping-Pong table is ready for use. Guests are encouraged to play the piano or guitar. The rooms are recently refurbished and are nice. The innkeepers have thoughtfully purchased very good mattresses. The upstairs halls are wide enough to have space for some interesting furniture. There are plants all over the inn, no televisions, and lots of good books. The inn's facilities are not well suited to children under ten.

## Muster Field Farm Museum

Farming in the New Hampshire mountains wasn't easy in the 1800s—still isn't easy now. By the late nineteenth century many farmers in the area realized they'd make a bit more money if they opened their farmhouses to paying guests, and the villages of North Sutton, Sutton, Sutton Mills, and all the other Suttons became popular destinations for travelers. The circa 1780 Matthew Harvey Homestead was one of the homes opened as a tavern of sorts, and today it and the 265-acre Muster Field Farm are open to the public as a museum.

Dedicated to educating visitors about agriculture and farm life, the museum includes farm implements and domestic utensils, an 1881 springhouse, a blacksmith shop, an 1810 schoolhouse, and demonstration flower and vegetable gardens. Activities are common throughout the summer season—you might be able to take a hay ride, for instance. Fresh eggs, milk, and locally grown berries and other produce are often here for sale. Admission is $3 for adults, $1 for children 6 to 12, and free for younger children. A craft show with more than 100 exhibitors is held here on the weekend before Labor Day. Traditional crafts and farming methods and tasks are demonstrated at this special Farm Day. Call (603) 927-4276 for hours and other information.

The dining room has comfortable captain's chairs and touches of chintz and linen. These are very pleasant surroundings in which to relax and savor the food. Breakfast, served around large tables with other guests, includes homemade granola, fresh fruit, muffins, and a hot dish such as an egg casserole or pancakes. A chalkboard menu for the night's dinner is shown at breakfast each day. One entree is served each evening. It might be rack of lamb, a chicken dish, roast pork, their special crab-and-shrimp casserole, a pasta dish, or something else equally delicious. The desserts are homemade. How about some chocolate cheesecake, chocolate eclair tart, or baked Alaska pie?

There is much to do in the area. You can go play a game of tennis or golf, take a hike or bicycle ride, or go picnicking. Maps are provided for interesting day trips, or you can just sit and relax on the front-porch rockers. In winter alpine skiing is nearby, and cross-country skiing is from the door of the inn.

North Sutton's old church is right next door. You might want to set your watch by its chiming clock.

**HOW TO GET THERE:** Take I–91 north to Route 9 in Brattleboro, Vermont. Continue to Henniker, New Hampshire, and go north on Route 114 for 18 miles to North Sutton. The inn is behind the church. From Boston take I–93 North to I–89 at Concord. Follow I–89 to exit 10, turn left off exit; follow 2 miles to North Sutton.

# Home Hill Inn 💛
## Plainfield, New Hampshire 03781

**INNKEEPERS:** Victoria, Gordon, and Stephan du-Roure, owners

**ADDRESS/TELEPHONE:** River Road; (603) 675–6165; fax (603) 675–5220

**WEB SITE:** www.homehillinn.com

**ROOMS:** 7, plus 2 suites; all with private bath, 4 with working fireplaces.

**RATES:** $150 to $225, double occupancy, continental breakfast. Fall season and holidays slightly higher.

**OPEN:** All year except Mondays and Tuesdays.

**FACILITIES AND ACTIVITIES:** Dinner, bar, lounge. Swimming pool, tennis court, cross-country skiing, fishing in Connecticut River, walking trails. Nine-hole golf course for guests only.

The brochure said Home Hill Country Inn and French Restaurant, and I could hardly wait to get here. At the inn's authentic French restaurant, the food presentation is picture-perfect and the taste is elegant. No gravies, only sauces, and no flour, cornstarch, or fillers are allowed.

The contemporary menu changes every day. You might try the cream of onion soup, then veal slices, very thin and young with French mushrooms. You may have the salad before, with, or after dinner, and the house dressing is gorgeous. At dinner I had duck prepared with white plums; it was very moist and delicious. Another dish served occasionally is veal with fresh wild mushrooms. Grilled New England sea scallops with red-pepper coulis sounds great. Desserts, as would be expected, are superb. The wine list features both French and California wines.

In the kitchen is a lovely, long pine table where breakfast is served. What a homey spot at which to enjoy the continental breakfast of juice, croissants, butter, jams, and coffee!

The rooms are charming. The cottage is large enough for eight persons. There are French and American antiques, reproductions, and comfort. The lounge-library is lovely; in fact, you will find it hard to find any fault with this inn.

The carriage house, also on the property, has three bedrooms, each with a bath. This is a nice addition to the inn. I stayed in one of these rooms during my last trip.

The inn is on twenty-five acres, only 500 yards from the Connecticut River. There are a swimming pool (a bar is out here), tennis courts, and cross-country skiing. Any season, any reason, head for Home Hill. Herman, the automatic tennis ball shooter, is a neat exercise encourager.

**HOW TO GET THERE:** Take I–89 to exit 20. Follow Route 12A south 3 miles to River Road and turn right. In 3½ miles you'll find the inn on the left.

# Philbrook Farm Inn
## Shelburne, New Hampshire 03581

**INNKEEPERS:** Connie Leger and Nancy Philbrook

**ADDRESS/TELEPHONE:** 881 North Road; (603) 466–3831

**ROOMS:** 19, plus 7 cottages with fireplaces; 10 rooms and all cottages with private bath. Five cottages have housekeeping arrangements. Pets welcome in cottages. Cottages open in summer only.

**RATES:** $125 to $155, double occupancy, MAP (private bath); $115, double occupancy, MAP (shared bath); $575 per week, housekeeping cottages; $145 per night, MAP, one-room cottages. No credit cards.

**OPEN:** All year except April and October 31 to December 26.

**FACILITIES AND ACTIVITIES:** BYOB. Wheelchair access to dining room and first floor but not to restrooms. Library, pool table, Ping-Pong, swimming pool, cross-country skiing, snowshoeing, hiking. Nearby: downhill skiing.

When you're traveling along Route 2, take a look across the fields, and there you'll see this lovely inn that is listed on the National Register of Historic Places. And rightly so. In 1861 Philbrook Farm started as an inn. Today it is still an inn and still has Philbrooks living here, running it in fine New England tradition.

Everything you eat here is prepared from scratch in their kitchens. The baked goods are made daily. A huge garden provides good vegetables. One entree is served each night. Roasts of everything you can want—pork, beef, turkey—and on and on. The New England boiled dinner is a favorite, as is baked

bean supper on Saturday nights and baked chicken dinner on Sundays.

The downstairs playroom has Ping-Pong, a pool table, shuffleboard, puzzles, and fun. A lot of reading material can be found all over the inn. Fireplaces are also all over the inn. The inn has a wonderful selection of Philbrook Farm puzzles made by Connie's grandfather. They have large, ¼-inch-thick pieces and are just beautiful. A player piano, an old pump organ—where else can you find such unique things except in an inn?

Rooms are furnished with a lot of old family treasures. There are some nice four-posters and a wonderful collection of old bowl and pitcher sets. All the cottages are different. They sure are nice if you want to linger here awhile. Some have dining rooms, some have fireplaces, and some have porches. If you are staying in a cottage, you can bring along your pet.

With more than 1,000 acres, the inn has plenty of room for you to roam any season of the year. Look across their fields to the Carter-Moriah and Presidential mountain ranges. Behind the inn rises the Mahoosuc Range. This is the Androscoggin Valley. The inn cats are Sugar and Spice, and the inn dog, Liebschen, is a German shorthair pointer.

**HOW TO GET THERE:** The inn is 1½ miles off Route 2. From Route 2 take Meadow Road. Cross the railroad tracks and then a bridge. Turn right at the crossroads and go ½ mile to the inn, which is on North Road.

# Snowvillage Inn 💟
## Snowville, New Hampshire 03849

**INNKEEPERS:** Barbara and Kevin Flynn

**ADDRESS/TELEPHONE:** P.O. Box 176; (603) 447–2818 or (800) 447–4345

**WEB SITE:** www.snowvillageinn.com

**ROOMS:** 18; all with private bath, 4 with fireplace.

**RATES:** $79 to $189, per person, double occupancy, MAP available.

**OPEN:** All year.

**FACILITIES AND ACTIVITIES:** Bar, lounge, sauna, cross-country skiing, tennis, nature trails. Nearby: swimming, fishing, canoeing, hiking, downhill skiing.

**RECOMMENDED COUNTRY INNS® TRAVELERS' CLUB BENEFIT:** 10 percent discount, Monday–Thursday, subject to availability.

In the winter Snowville lives up to its name. It snows, and it is pristine and beautiful all around. The view from the inn is breathtaking. Mount Washington and the whole Presidential Range greet your eyes wherever you look. In summer at the top of Foss Mountain, right at the inn, you can eat your fill of wild blueberries.

The guest rooms are comfortable and spacious, with tons of towels in luscious colors. The rooms are named after writers (funny, I did not find an Elizabeth Squier room), some have fireplaces, and all have private baths.

The living room, with its huge fireplace and nice couches, makes this an inn for rest and relaxation. There are a service bar, a lounge area, and books everywhere. A huge porch surrounds part of the inn. I could sit here all day and enjoy the incredible views.

Dinner is a delight in the very nice dining room. I enjoyed the home-baked sour cream rolls, but there is also oatmeal bread. The Mediterranean fish soup is delicious and leads the way to such entrees as poached salmon, grilled shrimp with roasted red pepper sauce, veal with lemon and capers, duck with port wine sauce, or—this one is my favorite—duck a l'orange.

Can you still find room for dessert? Why not, when it's cheesecake with raspberry sauce, or profiterole, or chocolate mousse?

Cross-country ski right on the inn's trails, sled on its hill, and play tennis on its court. Crystal Lake is nearby for swimming, fishing, and canoeing. Remember, though, shopping is nearby.

HOW TO GET THERE: Outside of Conway on Route 153, go 5 miles to Crystal Lake. Turn left, follow the sign to Snowville, and go about 1½ miles. Turn right at the inn's sign, and go up the hill ¾ mile to the inn.

# Foxglove
Sugar Hill, New Hampshire 03585

**INNKEEPERS:** Janet and Walter Boyd

**ADDRESS/TELEPHONE:** Route 117 at Lovers Lane, Sugar Hill; (603) 823-8840; fax (603) 823-5755

**ROOMS:** 6, all with private bath.

**RATES:** $85 to $165, double occupancy, EPB. MAP available in foliage season.

**OPEN:** All year.

**FACILITIES AND ACTIVITIES:** Breakfast, dinner, BYOB. Conference room for small executive retreats. Nearby: tennis, swimming, hiking, cross-country and downhill skiing, snowshoeing, and much, much more.

*S*ugar Hill is a wonder. When the lupine is in bloom, it's one of the most beautiful sights I've seen—the fields are a blaze of color. This is the village you must see to believe it's real. The meeting house was built in 1831, and the post office has one room.

Foxglove, at Lovers Lane, is made for all ages of lovers. I just spoke to Walter, and he reported a lot of snow has fallen. To be up here with it all white has to be just beautiful. There are local cross-country trails nearby. Also not too far away are four major ski areas. Anyone for ice skating? There are ponds for this. There's a glass porch that's really a picture window looking out at wildlife and sheer beauty—apple trees and maybe a deer. The fireplaces are warm and so inviting. So is dinner; some unusual choices for seating are offered in a sitting room for two, in the innkeepers' library with a stone fire-place, on the porch, or, how about the dining room? Try the good soups—black bean, cream of cauliflower, Belgian carrot, and more. There are good salads; entrees may be grilled corn-cob smoked ham steak with apple cream sauce and fresh chives served with whipped sweet potatoes and corn

bread. Maybe tenderloin of beef, shrimp, or poached salmon. The desserts are awesome; home-baked fruit pie or tart, strawberry rhubarb or maybe bittersweet chocolate torte. Way to go, Elizabeth! Eating my way through New England. What a life.

Accommodations are grand. Rooms are named so you won't get lost, laughs Walter. The Garden Room has a deck, indoor and outdoor shower, hot tub, king-sized bed, and sitting area, all looking at the forest. Oh my. The Paisley Room is lovely; the artwork in the inn is glorious. The Gingham Room is on a corner; Mrs. Harmes is a turret with magnificent views; the Blue Room is a favorite for honeymooners; and Serengheti speaks for itself. A small sitting room with a TV is between Gingham and Blue.

Breakfasts are well served. Extra-thick orange French toast is a winner, but there are also steamed eggs, pancakes, and more.

Do ask to see their beautiful cat.

**HOW TO GET THERE:** Take I–93 to exit 38. Go right on Route 18 for ½ mile. Go left on Route 117 to inn, 2³⁄₁₀ miles on right. From I–91, take Exit 17. Follow Route 302 east 16 miles. Turn right onto Route 117 to inn, 5⁶⁄₁₀ miles on the left.

# Sunset Hill House
## Sugar Hill, New Hampshire 03585

**INNKEEPERS:** The Coyle Family—Michael, Retsy, Frank, and Gloria Korta

**ADDRESS/TELEPHONE:** Sunset Hill Road; (603) 823–5522 or (800) 786–4455; fax (603) 823–5738

**E-MAIL:** sunsethh@aol.com

**ROOMS:** 27, plus 3 suites; all with private bath, 2 with Jacuzzi, some with fireplace.

**RATES:** $80 to $155, double occupancy, EPB. MAP rates available.

**OPEN:** All year except two weeks in April.

**FACILITIES AND ACTIVITIES:** Dinner daily from mid-May to November 1 and Thursday through Sunday the rest of the year. Full license. Meeting room, art gallery, swimming pool, cross-country skiing. Nearby: almost anything you might want to do.

he Sunset Hill House is perched on a 1,700-foot ridge with unparalleled views of New Hampshire's Presidential Mountain Range to the east and Vermont's Green Mountains to the west.

The inn was built in 1832, in an era of grand hotels and resorts, and is Victorian in style. The living rooms have a view as well as fireplaces and an old piano.

There are many rooms and suites. Two have Jacuzzis, and all have private baths and views no matter which way you look. They're very nicely furnished and comfortable. Some have a fireplace, and some have a bow window.

The tavern, Rose Magee's, offers a lighter pub fare than you'll find in the dining room. It features pizza of the day and stir-fry of the day. My favorite dish was rotini and hot linguine salad tossed in a puree of olive oil, green onions, peas, garlic, sun-dried tomatoes, and cheese, and topped with marinara sauce, mixed greens, and a creamy parsley dressing. Oh my!

But there's more. A salad with apple and maple walnut vinaigrette dressing sounds wonderful. I'll have to order it the next time I come here.

The dinner menu opens with crispy duck with an Asian plum sauce, grilled crabcakes, and good soups and salads. The entrees include roast pork loin, sautéed chicken breast, broiled trout, and tenderloin of beef, or the chef will accommodate any dietary preference. All you have to do is ask.

I like what Mike Coyle calls his 3 Ms—the Majesty of the Mountains, the Magic Nature of a Country Inn, and the Management of Every Detail.

I especially liked the art gallery in a wide hall. All the works are by local artists and are for sale. On the terrace level is a huge room for business meetings, weddings, and receptions. There are a lovely heated swimming pool and much more to do up here.

HOW TO GET THERE: From I–93 take exit 38 to Route 117 to the top of Sugar Hill. Turn left on Sunset Hill Road. From I–91 take exit 17 to Route 302 east. Proceed approximately 18 miles to Route 117. Drive to the top of Sugar Hill and turn right on Sunset Hill Road.

# Dexters
## Sunapee, New Hampshire 03782

**INNKEEPERS:** Holly and Michael Durfor

**ADDRESS/TELEPHONE:** P.O. Box 703S; (603) 763–5571 or (800) 232–5571

**ROOMS:** 17, plus 1 cottage; all with private bath. Wheelchair access to specially equipped room and bath for handicapped.

**RATES:** $135 to $175, double occupancy, MAP. Package rates offered in off-season. $385 per day for 4 guests in cottage, MAP; $1,250 weekly (no meals).

**OPEN:** May 1 to October 31.

**FACILITIES AND ACTIVITIES:** Bar. Tennis, swimming pool, recreation barn, English croquet, horseshoes, shuffleboard.

The main house was built in 1801 by an artisan, Adam Reddington. He earned his living by carving, from the huge knurls of the many fine maples on the grounds, the bowls in which sailing ships carried their compasses. In 1948 the house became a small country inn.

Dexters is a nice family inn that welcomes children. Holly and Michael run the inn with the help of two young innkeepers, Hartwell and Hayley-Marie, born in 1985 and 1988. Never too soon to start learning.

Your day starts with juice and coffee served in your room at a time you set the night before. Or you can be really spoiled and have a New England breakfast tray in bed. How about some eggs Benedict, French toast, or pancakes to start your day right? These are rooms you'll want to linger in. They are a bit above average, with marvelous wallpapers, heavenly pillows made of feathers, fresh fruit and flowers, and antique beds.

The living room-library has more than 500 books, magazines, and newspapers. It offers lots of comfort and charm, along with a fireplace. There are two television rooms and a breezy screened porch. For dinner one special is poached salmon with dill hollandaise, or try chicken piccata, swordfish, lamb chops, or steak.

Outdoor sports? You name it. Tennis is taken seriously here. Three all-weather Plexicushion tennis courts with a pro and shop are provided for your enjoyment. Tournaments for seniors are just a few of the happenings going on up here. After a game there is a lovely outdoor swimming pool to cool off in. Croquet, a horseshoe pit, and shuffleboard are also available. In springtime the lake trout and salmon are close to the surface and hungry, so come all you fishers. Spring is always late up here, so you have a longer season. For a good summer or fall activity, some of the loveliest walking and hiking trails are right on the inn's property.

There is a special recreation room in the barn for all ages, but it is keyed to those under seventeen who need a place of their own when the 5:00 P.M. cocktail hour begins.

HOW TO GET THERE: Take I-89 out of Concord and follow exit 12 to Route 11 west for 5½ miles. Turn left on Winn Hill Road for 1½ miles to inn. Or take I-91 out of Springfield and follow exit 8 to Claremont, New Hampshire, to Route 103/11 east for 18 miles to Newport. Follow Route 103 left onto Young Hill Road for 1²/₁₀ miles to inn.

# League of New Hampshire Craftsmen's Fair

The oldest continual crafts fair in the nation, dating from the 1930s, is held annually at the base of Mount Sunapee during the second week of August. For nine splendid days, the fair features craft demonstrations, artists' workshops, displays and sales of hand-crafted clothing, furnishings, jewelry, weaving, basketry, metalsmithing, and much more. A fabulous collection of the region's finest juried craftspeople are an inspiration to the thousands of visitors who come to the fair. The talent—well, let me just say, WOW. Live theater and musical performances are a part of the excitement here.

The fair runs from 10:00 A.M. to 5:00 P.M. daily. Call for this year's exact dates. Admission (about $7 per adult, $4 for seniors, and free to children under twelve) includes all the exhibits and performances—and a return trip the next day so you can see anything you missed the first time. For information, call (603) 224-3375.

# The Inn at Sunapee

## Sunapee, New Hampshire 03782

**INNKEEPERS:** Ted and Susan Harriman

**ADDRESS/TELEPHONE:** Burkehaven Hill Road (mailing address:
P.O. Box 336); (603) 763–4444 or (800) 327–2466

**ROOMS:** 16, plus 5 suites; all with private bath.

**RATES:** $60, single; $80, double; $110 to $130, suite; EPB.

**OPEN:** All year except two weeks in November and April.

**FACILITIES AND ACTIVITIES:** Dinner every night but Tuesday. Wheelchair access to dining room but not restrooms. No smoking in dining room. Bar, lounge, full license. Pool, tennis, hiking. Nearby: downhill skiing, cross-country skiing.

The Inn at Sunapee, an 1800s farmhouse with a classic wraparound porch, is nicely situated on a hilltop that overlooks beautiful Lake Sunapee and historic Sunapee Harbor. The lake is the second largest in New Hampshire, and it's a great spot for sailing, fishing, and waterskiing. The inn is also located at the base of Mount Sunapee. You can go skiing for the day or you can sit and watch the skiers from the warmth of the inn.

Attached to the house is a barn that has been turned into a lounge with a fieldstone fireplace and good couches. The views from the windows in here and in the dining room are spectacular any season of the year. If you like animals, you'll especially like watching the cows in the field across the road.

Most of all you'll enjoy the good food served here. The menu changes quite often. When I was here, there were Maryland crabcakes and Vietnamese spring rolls with spicy dipping sauce as appetizers. Grilled tuna, a daily veal special, beef, and chicken are but a few of the foods served here. Holidays, I'm told, are really special.

Ted and Susan lived in the Far East and Southeast Asia for more than twenty-five years, and their wonderful collection of furnishings is used throughout the inn. Rooms are decorated with oak and iron furniture. Some rooms have wide-board pine floors. There is a separate honeymoon cottage, and it is cute and small. Everything about this inn is very gracious.

Children are welcome here. They'll enjoy the swimming pool, tennis court, and ten acres of woodland for hiking. They will also want to curl up with the inn Labrador or the cats—all six of them, including a calico and a coon cat. A sign on the door reads: DON'T LET THE INN CATS OUT.

HOW TO GET THERE: From Boston, take I–93 north to Concord, New Hampshire. Then take I–89 north to exit 12 and follow Route 11 west to Sunapee. At the blinking light turn toward Sunapee Harbor. At the harbor you will see a park with a bandstand. Take the first right after the bandstand and go ½ mile up the hill to the inn.

# The Tamworth Inn
## Tamworth Village, New Hampshire 03886

INNKEEPERS: Phil and Kathy Bender

ADDRESS/TELEPHONE: Main Street; (603) 323-7721

E-MAIL: tamworth@nxi.com

ROOMS: 15, including 5 suites; all with private bath.

RATES: $95 to $130, double occupancy, EPB. $120 to $160, double occupancy, MAP.

OPEN: All year except April.

FACILITIES AND ACTIVITIES: Sunday brunch, dinner. Pub, swimming pool, fishing, skiing, hiking. Nearby: downhill skiing, Barnstormer's Theater.

RECOMMENDED COUNTRY INNS® TRAVELERS' CLUB BENEFIT: 10 percent discount on stays of three or more days, subject to availability.

Built in 1833, The Tamworth Inn is a rambling building in a lovely New England town across from the Congregational Church and a thoroughbred horse pasture.

The Swift River flows swiftly behind the inn. If you're looking for a memorable spot for your wedding, the riverside gazebo is great; if you're inclined toward fly-fishing, this is the place for you. The hale and hearty might want to walk about a quarter-mile to the swimming hole. Anyone less adventuresome will find the inn's swimming pool just right.

The main attraction in the summer is the Barnstormer's Theater down the street, the oldest summer theater in New England. An "equity house," the theater offers eight different professional performances each summer. It certainly is nice to stay at the inn, have a tasty dinner, and walk to good theater.

There are lots of hiking trails in this area, and they are maintained by the Appalachian Mountain Club, the Tamworth Outing Club, and the Wonalancet Outing Club. They are within walking distance of the inn. In winter these trails become cross-country ski trails.

Back at the inn, guests enjoy sitting by the fireplaces, reading a book, patting Misty the cat, or watching a movie from the extensive video collection. The pub has a dartboard—anyone for a game of darts?—as well as a large collection of old sleds on display. You can order a meal in here. Full dinners are served in the lovely dining rooms. The menu changes monthly and is quite extensive. You might find chilled cucumber soup and crab bisque among the appetizers and fettucine Alfredo, sole Florentine, beef, and veal among the entrees. Do save room for dessert; they're delicious. The porch has been screened in as an addition to the pub.

The guest rooms are all different, and all of them are comfortable. One room has a huge canopy bed, so high it needs steps to climb into it. As Phil says, Kathy is the key person here and takes charge of the rooms beautifully. She makes sure that all the amenities are here, including fresh flowers in the summer and fresh fruit in the winter.

HOW TO GET THERE: Tamworth is on Route 113, 3 miles northwest of the intersection of Routes 25 and 16.

# The Birchwood Inn
## Temple, New Hampshire 03084

**INNKEEPERS:** Judy and Bill Wolfe

**ADDRESS/TELEPHONE:** Route 45; (603) 878–3285

**ROOMS:** 7; 5 with private bath.

**RATES:** $65 to $70. No credit cards.

**OPEN:** All year except two weeks in April and one week in November.

**FACILITIES AND ACTIVITIES:** Dinner served Tuesday through Saturday. Wheelchair access to dining room. BYOB. Nearby: antiquing, downhill and cross-country skiing, hiking, hunting, golf, summer theater, lakes.

The inn is in the Mount Monadnock region of New Hampshire, so there is plenty to do and see here. From the top of the mountain you can see four states, a nice reward for you hikers. There are trout waiting for the fisher, much game for the hunter, plus golf, summer theater, horseback riding, and walking.

Bill and Judy are the owner-chefs and are very good at what they do. Roast duckling, chicken piccata, and shrimp Parmesan served on green noodles are three examples of their good food. They have she-crab soup, which is hard to find north of South Carolina. It is excellent. Homemade breads and desserts

are created daily. The dining-room walls are covered with simply beautiful Rufus Porter murals.

Bill is an avid collector of model trains. I'm a train buff myself, so I got a real kick out of seeing Bill's collection all over the inn.

The inn has an 1878 square Steinway grand piano that is kept in perfect tune. The inn history stretches back some two centuries to circa 1775. During this time many people have come and gone, one notable personage being Henry David Thoreau. A room at the inn is named for him. Other rooms have different themes and rather different sorts of names, such as "The Bottle Shop" and

"The School Room." The innkeepers will entertain you with the stories of how the rooms became so named. Say hello to Barney the bassett hound when you visit.

**HOW TO GET THERE:** Take Route 3 out of Boston to Nashua, New Hampshire, exit 8. Follow Route 101 to Milford to Route 45 to Temple.

# The Chesterfield Inn ♥

## West Chesterfield, New Hampshire 03466

**INNKEEPERS:** Judy and Phil Hueber

**ADDRESS/TELEPHONE:** Route 9; (603) 256–3211 or (800) 365–5515; fax: (603) 256–6131

**E-MAIL:** chstinn@sover.net

**WEB SITE:** distinctiveinns.com/chst/

**ROOMS:** 11, plus 2 suites; all with private bath, air conditioning, refrigerator, phone. Many rooms have a fireplace and/or a garden terrace; one has wheelchair access. Pets are welcome.

**RATES:** $120 to $175, double occupancy, EPB.

**OPEN:** All year.

**FACILITIES AND ACTIVITIES:** Dinner Monday through Saturday. Wheelchair access to dining room. Full license. Ice skating. Nearby: fishing, boating, skiing, swimming.

The inn was a tavern from 1798 to 1811, and then it became a farm. In 1984 the inn opened after extensive renovations by architect Rod Williams of The Inn at Sawmill Farm, and he is the best around. Exposed beams, many of them part of the original structure, and walls paneled with boards that came from an old barn make for a warm and friendly atmosphere.

The guest rooms are spacious. Some rooms have balconies or garden patios, others have a fireplace, and all are scrumptious. They are done in soft shades of blues, greens, and pinks. They are air-conditioned and have clock radios and telephones (all different), including one in the bathroom. Good fluffy towels and an assortment of toiletries are here. To top it all off, each room has a refrigerator with juice, bottled spring water, beers, and wine. I found a welcoming split of champagne in mine. Oh my!

The foyer has a large fireplace holding a bright red wood stove, and nice couches. It's a good place for cocktails.

Off the foyer is the parlor with a fireplace and good couches. A window seat overlooks an outdoor patio.

The dining room is down the hall from here. The chef is a four-star one, and when you dine here you will believe it. The menu changes often. First courses might include crab cakes with a remoulade sauce; asparagus, tomato,

olive, and roasted garlic salad; or good soups. Entrees may be duck—grilled breast and braised leg with ginger and soy sauce—or penne with basil pesto and grilled vegetables. Or maybe veal rib chop with wild mushroom sauce or beef tenderloin with garlic, parsley, and jalapeño relish. There are always more, and these are only a sample of the good food served here.

The chef always has a fish of the day. Desserts are wonderful. Come and try this food. There are three dining rooms to choose from, all with wonderful views.

The inn's grounds are full of perennial, herb, and vegetable gardens. The beautiful Connecticut River is a short walk from the inn, so bring along your canoe or fishing pole. Lake Spofford has boats for rent. Pisgah Park has hiking trails and two spring-fed ponds for swimming. In winter, skiing is close at hand, and the inn's pond is lighted for night skating under the stars. (Watch for Ellie, the inn cat.) And all year you'll find good antiques shops and arts and crafts shops.

HOW TO GET THERE: Take exit 3 off I–91. Take Route 9 east, going over the border from Vermont to New Hampshire. The inn is 2 miles on your left.

# Spalding Country Inn
## Whitefield, New Hampshire 03598

**INNKEEPERS:** April and Diane Cockrell and Michael Flinder

**ADDRESS/TELEPHONE:** Mountain View Road (mailing address: RR 1, Box 57); (603) 837–2572 or (800) 368–VIEW; fax (603) 837–3062

**WEB SITE:** www.nettx.com/spalding.htm

**ROOMS:** 36, plus 6 cottages; all with private bath and phone, cottages with fireplace.

**RATES:** $169 to $189, double occupancy, MAP; $109 to $139, double occupancy, EPB; $89 to $109, double occupancy, EP. Packages available. Six two-bedroom suites, $150, EPB; $200 MAP.

**OPEN:** Memorial Day through October.

**FACILITIES AND ACTIVITIES:** Bar, lounge, TV room, library, function rooms, exercise equipment, swimming pool, clay tennis courts, croquet lawn, putting green and executive golf course, lawn bowling. Nearby: Weathervane Theatre, 9-hole Mountain View Golf Course.

*I*f you care to see how our parents and grandparents might have spent their summers years ago, come to the Spalding Country Inn. It's been welcoming people since the early 1800s.

The rooms and cottages are tastefully appointed, with direct-dial telephones and extra pillows and blankets. The cottages have a living room, up

to four bedrooms, and a bath. They each have their own fireplace, and some have their own porch.

White linen in the dining room is always a sign of good things to come, and starting with breakfast the choices are grand. Fresh juice, seasonal fruit, granola and yogurt, hot and cold cereals, pancakes, French toast, eggs any style, home fries, bacon, ham, omelets—the list goes on.

The dinner menu changes nightly, except on Friday, when it's lobster night. Thai coconut soup sounds good. The salads are made of locally grown greens. Entrees range from the very popular Duck Bombay—a roasted duck covered with bacon and toasted almonds—to roasted tenderloin of beef with rosemary and madeira butter; grilled salmon fillet; shrimp scampi; roast loin of pork; and grilled lamb chops. These are but a few of the many choices. Did I hear dessert? Come on up and try some.

Michael is the chef, Diane is the baker, and April runs the front desk.

There is no dress requirement at the inn other than to be comfortable. And that's easy here. This is a glorious spot, inside and out, so do come up and enjoy a taste of yesteryear.

There's a bear or two—stuffed, of course—in the inn. Look for them. The children's corner is great; Buttermilk, the rocking cow, is here along with small wicker chairs and games.

HOW TO GET THERE: Take I–93 north to exit 41. Follow Route 116 through the village of Whitefield. Continue 1½ miles north of town and turn right on Mountain View Road.

# Select List of
# Other New Hampshire Inns

## Rosewood Country Inn

67 Pleasant View Road
Brandford, NH 03221
(603) 938–5253 or (800) 938–5273

*7 rooms and 3 suites, all with private bath; 1896 Victorian B&B inn. Special event weekends held year-round.*

## Three Chimneys Inn/ffrost Sawyer Tavern

17 Newmarket Road
Durham, NH 03824
(603) 868–7800 or (888) 399–9777
Fax: (603) 868–5011
E-mail: chimney3@threechimneysinn.com
Web site: www.threechimneysinn.com

*23 rooms, all with private bath, four-poster bed; 4 rooms with Jacuzzi and some with two-person tub; inn built in 1649 on the Oyster River.*

## Maple Hill Farm Country Inn B&B

200 Newport Road
New London, NH 03257
(603) 526–2248 or (800) 231–8637
Web site: www.maplehillfarm.com

*10 rooms, 6 with private bath; B&B in 1824 farmhouse. Six-person hottub spa, indoor basketball court, farm animals. Full-service country inn in winter; B&B in summer. Specializes in group and family package deals with meals.*

## Nereledge Inn

River Road
P.O. Box 547
North Conway, NH 03860
(603) 356–2831
E-mail: info@nereledgeinn.com
Web site: www.nereledgeinn.com

*11 rooms, 5 ½ with private bath; full breakfast; game room, fireplace in sitting room; B&B in 1787 farmhouse.*

## The Inn at Kinney Hill

96 Woodman Road
South Hampton, NH 03827
(603) 394–0200 or (888) 687–4455
E-mail: dsoconnor@aol.com

*3 rooms plus 1 suite, all with private bath; full breakfast, afternoon tea, gourmet French dinner on request; indoor heated lap pool, eight-person hot tub, and workout area; billiard room.*

## The Wolfeboro Inn

90 North Main Street
Wolfeboro, NH 03894
(603) 569–3016 or (800) 451–2389
Web site: www.wolfeboroinn.com

*44 rooms, all with private bath; original part of inn dates from 1812; banquet facilities, swimming beach, boat on Lake Winnepesaukee.*

# Rhode Island

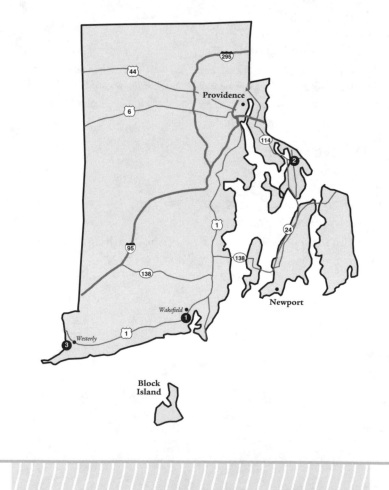

295

44

6

Providence

114

2

95

1

24

138

138

Wakefield

1

Newport

1

Westerly

1

3

Block
Island

# Rhode Island

*Numbers on map refer to towns numbered below.*

*\* A Top Pick Inn*

# Larchwood Inn
## Wakefield, Rhode Island 02879

**INNKEEPERS:** Francis and Diann Browning

**ADDRESS/TELEPHONE:** 521 Main Street; (401) 783–5454 or
(800) 275–5450; fax (401) 783–1800

**ROOMS:** 19, in 2 buildings; 12 with private bath, some with phone.

**RATES:** $65 to $130, double occupancy, EP.

**OPEN:** All year.

**FACILITIES AND ACTIVITIES:** Breakfast, lunch, dinner, bar, tavern.
Nearby: swimming, fishing, skiing.

**RECOMMENDED COUNTRY INNS® TRAVELERS' CLUB BENEFIT:** 10 percent discount, Sunday–Thursday, November–April.

Over the fireplace in the homey bar is carved "Fast by an Ingle Bleez-
ing Finely," a quotation from the Scots' Robert Burns. The Tam
O'Shanter Cocktail Lounge serves up a delectable lunch that
includes huge sandwiches, good salads, hamburgers, and quiche.

There are four other lovely rooms for dining or private entertaining. Dinner ideas are rack of lamb for one or two, lots of fresh fish, and a beefeater's
special: a thick slice of prime rib Angus. Breakfast is very ample. I really like
the special French toast topped with either sour cream or whipped cream
and warmed strawberries.
Perhaps you'd enjoy croissants or poached eggs with
hollandaise and mushrooms
and artichoke hearts. Come
summer, the meals are served
on the covered patio in the
garden.

Some of the rooms are in
the Holly House across the
street. It is the same age as
the inn; both were built in the 1830s. It is so well done. Diann has a real
touch. The wallpapers are glorious, and one room is an especially lovely
salmon color. All the inn's guest rooms have been individually decorated and

are beautifully furnished. Butch, the inn cat, is a beauty; maybe you can rent him for a night.

The inn is situated in the heart of Rhode Island's beautiful South County. Saltwater beaches for bathing, fishing, and sunning are close by. In the winter it is only a short drive to Pine Top and Yawgoo Valley for skiing. Monday night is cabaret night in summer—this is a really fun time and includes a sing-along.

Rhode Island isn't all that big, you know, so it's never very far from anywhere to the Larchwood Inn.

HOW TO GET THERE: Take I-95 to Route 1. Exit from Route 1 at Pond Street, follow it to the end, and the inn will be immediately in front of you.

---

# *South County Museum*

Not far from Wakefield is the town of Narragansett on the western side of beautiful Narragansett Bay. Take Route 1A to the Narragansett Town Beach and Pier. A bit north of the pier, opposite the beach pavilion, you'll find Canonchet Farm and the South County Museum (401-783-5400). It holds a collection of more than 10,000 artifacts that demonstrate the history and culture of this area and its varied settlers. From farm tools and domestic implements to a gentleman's study and children's dolls, dollhouses, and trains, the museum imaginatively presents a real sense of the passage of time through three centuries. Next to the main museum building is a barn with displays of carriages and wagons; on the property are hiking trails, a fitness course, and lots of pretty places to picnic. The museum is open from May through October. A small admission fee is charged; parking is free. The Farm and Museum host frequent festivals throughout the summer; call for a schedule of such events as a quilt show, an herb gardening day, a children's fair, and an antique car show.

# Nathaniel Porter Inn
## Warren, Rhode Island 02885

**INNKEEPERS:** Viola and Robert Lynch

**ADDRESS/TELEPHONE:** 125 Water Street; (401) 245–6622

**ROOMS:** 3; all with private bath.

**RATES:** $80, single or double occupancy, continental breakfast.

**OPEN:** All year except Christmas Eve, Christmas Day, July 4, and Labor Day.

**FACILITIES AND ACTIVITIES:** Dinner. Tavern. Nearby: boating and swimming at town beach.

*T*he inn is named after Nathaniel Porter, who, at the age of twelve, established his place in history when he was among the seventy-seven Minutemen who stood on Lexington Green and fired the first shots of the American Revolution in 1775. The current owners are direct descendants of that young man.

The restored inn dates back to 1795, when it was built by a wealthy sea captain. Some of the earliest documented stencils were discovered under numerous layers of paint and wallpaper. The parquet floors, dating back to the early 1800s, are just beautiful, and so are the wide-board floors. The inn is listed on the National Register of Historic Places. The French mural in one of the parlors dates from about 1810, and all the window glass was hand-blown in Germany.

The front parlor has nice romantic tables for two, and there are five fireplaces in the dining rooms. The waitresses here are called hostesses. They describe everything on your plate to you. Very professional. The menu changes twice a year and is extensive, offering more than enough choices for all tastes. There are seven appetizers as well as a soup of the day. I had grilled shrimp in a strawberry-thyme sauce. What a nice and different flavor it had! I also tasted the smoked mussels and the excellent seafood chowder.

I get hungry just thinking about the entrees. I had filet mignon with roasted hazelnuts, flamed with cognac. It was tender and delicious. The next time I visit the inn, I'm going to try the whiskey cream shrimp. The shrimp are sautéed in butter, flamed with Jim Beam, finished with cream and Dijon mustard, and served in puff pastry.

Everything is spectacular and well presented. Need I mention desserts? Ambrosia. Add to this a wonderful wine list with some interesting Australian wines.

So off to bed. Two rooms have canopied double beds with lovely antiques, and the other has twins. At night the inn is lighted by window candles and chandeliers.

HOW TO GET THERE: From Providence take I–195 east to Route 114. Go south on Route 114 to Warren. At the first traffic light in town, go right onto Water Street. The inn is in 4 blocks on the right.

## A Colonial Christmas Celebration

Each December at the Nathaniel Porter Inn dinner guests can join the colonial yule log festivities. Five or six such evenings are planned within the second and third weeks of the month, and each of these full-evening events begins about 6:00 P.M. and ends around 10:00 P.M. The Pawtuxet Rangers fife-and-drum corps performs outside the inn, and guests parade into the inn under their crossed swords when their initial performance ends. Cocktails and fruits and cheese are served in one of the inn's pretty dining parlors, then a full four-course dinner is served while the corps performs inside throughout the evening and toasts the guests at tableside. After dinner the corps plays the Christmas hymn *Joy to the World* as they carry in the traditional yule log, which is set ablaze in the inn's fireplace. Each guest makes a wish for the New Year on a sprig of holly and tosses it into the flames. A Christmas carol singalong follows, and the evening ends with the sharing of wassail. A night to remember.

If this event ($45 per person, by reservation only) is fully booked, perhaps you could make arrangements to come to the inn in early January to join in the Twelfth Night celebration. This single-night event ($35 per person by reservation only) includes a traditional roast goose dinner with all the trimmings and a light-hearted appointment of the King and Queen of Misrule from among the guests.

# Shelter Harbor Inn
## Westerly, Rhode Island 02891

**INNKEEPER:** Jim Dey

**ADDRESS/TELEPHONE:** Route 1; (401) 322–8883; fax (401) 322–7907

**ROOMS:** 23; all with private bath, TV, and phone, some with fireplace and private deck.

**RATES:** $92 to $136, double occupancy, EPB.

**OPEN:** All year.

**FACILITIES AND ACTIVITIES:** Lunch, dinner, Sunday brunch, bar. Private ocean beach, two paddle tennis courts with night lighting, hot tub, croquet court. Nearby: golf, boat-launching area, tennis, summer theater, Block Island ferry, Mystic Seaport, Mystic Marinelife Aquarium.

**BUSINESS TRAVEL:** Desk and phone in all rooms, conference room, fax available, corporate rates.

*I*f you would like a 3-mile stretch of uncluttered ocean beach located just a mile from a lovely old country inn, find your way to Rhode Island and the Shelter Harbor Inn. Bring the children. When they're not playing in the ocean surf, there's a salt pond near the inn for them to explore.

Eight of the guest rooms are in the restored farmhouse, and ten more are located in the barn. The rest of the rooms are in the coach house, which is a lovely addition to the inn. There is a large central living room here that opens onto a spacious deck—how ideal for families! Or, if your business group is small, have a meeting right here. There is also a library with comfortable leather chairs where you can relax with a book.

The menu reflects the location of the inn, and at least half the items offered are from the sea. The finnan haddie is specially smoked in Narra-

gansett. You can choose your place to eat—the formal dining room, the small private dining room with a fireplace, or the glassed-in terrace room. The sunporch has been turned into a pub bar, and plants are everywhere. If weather permits, take a drink out to the secluded terrace. On a clear day you can see Block Island from the third floor of the inn. There's a hot tub up here, plus a barbecue grill.

If you can tear yourself from the beach, there is much to see around here. You are about halfway between Mystic and Newport. The ferry to Block Island leaves from Point Judith. It is an hour-long ride, and when you arrive on Block Island, you will find it a super spot for bicycling. You can charter boats for fishing or stand at the edge of the surf and cast your line into the sea. In the evenings there are Theater by the Sea in nearby Matunuck and the Colonial Theatre in Westerly.

HOW TO GET THERE: Take I-95 to Route 1. Follow Route 1 out of Westerly for about 5 miles. The inn is on the right side of the road when you're heading northeast.

## Colonial Theatre

Theater lovers may want to make plans to see an Actor's Equity professional performance at Westerly's Colonial Theatre (401–596–0810) in the Greek Revival former First Congregational Church on Granite Street. Contemporary musicals, dramas, and comedies are on the bill from late April through Labor Day, and a special annual performance of Charles Dickens' *A Christmas Carol* or a similar holiday show suitable for whole family is the traditional fare between Thanksgiving and Christmas. Tickets for the regular season are reasonably priced between $15 and $25; all seats for the holiday show are $10.

Also popular is the theater's Shakespeare in the Park summer festival for three weeks each July. These outdoor performances at nearby Wilcox Park are free; bring a picnic and enjoy.

# Select List of
# Other Rhode Island Inns

## The Atlantic Inn
P.O. Box 1788
High Street
Block Island, RI 02807
(401) 466-5883 or (800) 224-7422
Fax: (401) 466-5678

*21 rooms, all with private bath and phone; children welcome.*


## The Blue Dory Inn and the Adrian Inn
P.O. Box 488
Dodge Street
Block Island, RI 02807
(401) 466-5891 or (800) 992-7290
Fax: (401) 466-9910

*30 rooms, 4 suites, and 6 cottages; all in a 100-year-old Victorian inn.*


## The 1661 Inn and Hotel Manisses
1 Spring Street
Block Island, RI 02807
(401) 466-2421 or (401) 466-2063
Fax: (401) 466-2858
E-mail: BIRESORTS@aol.com

*38 rooms, most with private bath, some Jacuzzis; breakfast and dinner, conference area.*

## Spring House Hotel

Spring Street, Old Harbor
Block Island, RI 02807
(401) 466–5844 or (800) 234–9263

*49 rooms, all with private bath; 1862 hotel.*

# Vermont

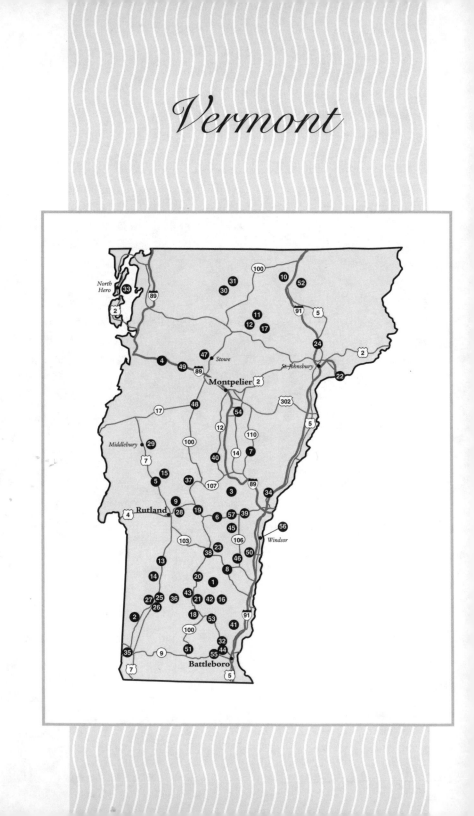

# Vermont

*Numbers on map refer to towns numbered below.*

*\* A Top Pick Inn*

*A Top Pick Inn*

* A Top Pick Inn

# The Inn at High View
Andover, Vermont 05143

**INNKEEPERS:** Greg Bohan and Sal Massaro

**ADDRESS/TELEPHONE:** RR 1, Box 201A; (802) 875–2724; fax (802) 875–4021

**ROOMS:** 6, plus 2 suites; all with private bath.

**RATES:** $95 to $135, double occupancy, EPB. Packages available.

**OPEN:** All year except the first two weeks in April and November.

**FACILITIES AND ACTIVITIES:** Dinner on weekends, BYOB. Conference room, swimming pool, dry sauna. Nearby: skiing, theater, antiquing, golf.

*T*felt like a mountain goat getting up to The Inn at High View, but once up there I was overwhelmed with the breathtaking views. I would love to see it in the winter, surrounded by snow. It must be truly beautiful.

Once you get to the inn, you enter through a screened porch into a large living room with a huge fireplace and a large, curved, gray sofa. It's very cozy and comfortable. There's a checkerboard laid out on a table inviting you to play a game of checkers, but you play with apples instead of checkers. Also in the room are lots of books, an old Victrola with vintage records that sound really great, and a piano, just waiting for someone to play it.

The dining room has a fireplace and a large rectangular table and a smaller square one. The kitchen is very open and the views are superb, no matter which direction you look.

Once a month on a Thursday night is a sort-of-private party for the neighbors; however, if you're here, you are invited to join in. The only other

nights dinner is served are during the weekend. Then it's a four- or five-course affair prepared by Sal. He might offer you salmon mousse on cucumber slices, stuffed mushrooms, prosciutto and melon, or Sal's Memorable Italian Olives. After salad and the pasta course, the main course might feature stuffed pork chops, chicken florentine, or saltimbocca. Greg's famous cheesecake is not to be missed.

The basement boasts the conference room. It is fully equipped, and the inn is a perfect location for productive, private meetings. They even offer word processing, reproduction, and other support for your needs. Also in the basement is a dry sauna and a television/movie room for all ages. The pool-house has a waterfall, and all of this is watched over by Brenda, a cocker spaniel.

The rooms are named. Ask for Ozzie and Harriet or the Cheshire Cat.

**HOW TO GET THERE:** Take I–91 north to exit 6 (Route 103 north) to Chester. Follow Route 11W to Andover-Weston Road. Watch for signs to the inn; turn right. It is the second farmhouse, ½ mile up the hill on the left.

# The Arlington Inn  ♥ 📱
## Arlington, Vermont 05250

**INNKEEPERS:** Bill and Sherrie Noonan

**ADDRESS/TELEPHONE:** Route 71 (mailing address: P.O. Box 369); (802) 375–6532 or (800) 443–9442; fax (802) 375–6534

**WEB SITE:** www.discover.vermont.com

**ROOMS:** 19, in 3 buildings; all with private bath and air conditioning; 8 with fireplace, 1 with whirlpool tub.

**RATES:** $70 to $195, double occupancy, EPB.

**OPEN:** All year.

**FACILITIES AND ACTIVITIES:** Dinner. Tennis. Nearby: fishing, hiking, skiing, shopping, and much more.

**RECOMMENDED COUNTRY INNS® TRAVELERS' CLUB BENEFIT:** 25 percent discount, Sunday–Thursday, November–April, excluding holidays, 10 percent discount otherwise, subject to availability.

*Y*ou can recapture the gracious living of the Victorian period in this historic Greek Revival mansion. It was built in 1848 by Martin Chester Deming. The lovely rooms in the inn are named after Deming's family members. There are Sylvester's Study, Pamela's Suite, Martin Chester's Room, Sophie's Room, Mary's Room, and (I love this name) Chloe's Room.

They are all beautifully furnished and very comfortable. Eight have fireplaces, and one has a whirlpool tub. A handsome addition to the inn, the Parsonage has six rooms with televisions and phones, really beautiful beds, and delightful peace.

It matters not what season you are here; there is much to do year-round. Tennis is right on the inn grounds, the famous Battenkill river nearby is loaded with fish, and you can find opportunities for hiking, biking, golf, swimming, and canoeing. Winter brings cross-country  and downhill skiing just a short drive away. If you'd prefer to go shopping, it's very close by.

Dining at The Arlington is very gracious. Start your dinner right with Maine crab croquettes or a selection of other first courses. Move on to entrees like chicken Sundance, grilled peppercorn pork, Black Angus steak, seafood du jour, veal, duck or egg and spinach fettuccine—a new one for me. The Deming Tavern has its own delightful menu. The house salad is a winner.

Move on to roast duck, pork tenderloin, medallions of Vermont-raised buffalo, or smoked trout. The inn uses authentic Vermont products whenever possible.

Breakfasts are ample. You'll find omelets, eggs any style, blueberry and strawberry pancakes, French toast, huge blueberry muffins, and fresh fruit cup.

When looking for the ideal spot to host your management retreat or workshop, look no farther. Weddings, rehearsal dinners, anniversaries, and parties are done very well here at The Arlington. All are watched over by Zig the inn dog—a bichon like mine—and B.J. the cat. I sure like it here.

**HOW TO GET THERE:** The inn is located on Historic Route 7A between Bennington and Manchester in the center of Arlington.

# West Mountain Inn

## Arlington, Vermont 05250

**INNKEEPERS:** Mary Ann and Wes Carlson; Paula Maynard, manager

**ADDRESS/TELEPHONE:** P.O. Box 481; (802) 375-6516;
fax: (802) 375-6553

**E-MAIL:** info@westmountaininn.com

**WEB SITE:** www.westmountaininn.com

**ROOMS:** 10, plus 6 suites and 2 cottage rooms; all with private bath;
1 specially equipped for handicapped.

**RATES:** $156 to $234, double occupancy, MAP; $104, per room, EPB.
Corporate rates available.

**OPEN:** All year.

**FACILITIES AND ACTIVITIES:** Wheelchair access to all common rooms.
Bar, hiking, cross-country skiing, fishing, canoes, swimming. Nearby:
antiquing.

Wes and Mary Ann are really the ideal innkeepers. From the minute you arrive until you leave, you feel at home. The inn is always being updated. There is a recently added lovely suite of rooms with a fireplace. There is also a room and bath with complete facilities for the handicapped. The nicest touch is the thought. There are too few people who care enough to spend a bit more for other people's comfort. The cottage rooms have housekeeping facilities.

Wes loves exotic goldfish. They are in the ponds around the inn and in a huge aquarium inside that is so nice to watch. In addition, there are three llamas and one goat in residence. Wes also raises African violets. He puts one in each room and invites you to take it home with you. The bowl of fruit, the chocolate llama, and the trail map are also for your pleasure.

The rooms, all named for famous people, are quite different. I have stayed in the Norman Rockwell Room, which is up in the treetops. Icelandic comforters and wool blankets are provided to keep you toasty warm.

There's a separate children's room with its own television, huge stuffed animals, books, and games. The aquarium is in here. So nice for parents that the children have their own place.

Across the lounge area are tables set with games, rockers, and a view of the birdfeeders and beyond.

There are three millhouse suites in a separate house. In each are two bedrooms and a bath upstairs and a living room and kitchen downstairs. Two of the suites have private decks, and two have open-hearth fireplaces.

The inn prepares great dinners. Wes has some excellent wines in an extensive wine cellar. They are the perfect complement to the meal. The crab cakes are delicious, and the pasta primavera is excellent—all of the food is. There are specials nightly. Desserts, well, I gained a pound—but it was worth it.

This inn is truly in the country, with 150 acres of trees, trails, pastures, and ponds, all on the mountainside overlooking the village of Arlington. Cross the trout-filled Battenkill; wind your way over the bridge, which is flower-laden in summer; go by the millhouse, up past the main cottage and spring-fed rock quarry, to the seven-gabled inn. The grounds around the inn are reputed to have more species of evergreens than any other place in New England. There are lovely trails for hiking, jogging, or cross-country skiing, depending on the season.

HOW TO GET THERE: Midway between Bennington and Manchester, the inn is ½ mile west of Arlington on Route 313. Turn onto River Road, cross the river, turn left and go up the hill until you come to the inn.

# Twin Farms  💙
## Barnard, Vermont 05031

INNKEEPERS: Shaun and Beverly Matthews; Thurston Twigg-Smith, owner

ADDRESS/TELEPHONE: Barnard; (802) 234–9999 or (800) 894–6327; fax (802) 234–9990

ROOMS: 4 suites, 8 cottages, 2 suites in lodge; all with private bath, phone, TV, air conditioning, minirefrigerator, and CD player.

**RATES:** $800 to $1,500, double occupancy; all inclusive. $14,500 per day for the whole property.

**OPEN:** All year except April.

**FACILITIES AND ACTIVITIES:** Full license, spa, all winter sports, mountain bikes, tennis, croquet, swimming, canoeing, fitness center.

Twin Farms is a 235-acre hideaway estate that was owned by novelist Sinclair Lewis and given to his wife, Dorothy Thompson, as a wedding present. During the 1930s and '40s, they came here to rest and entertain many literary figures of the time.

You arrive at the entry gate and dial a number indicating who you are. Then you enter an unbelievably unique property. Drive down the lane and along a circular drive to the main house.

The gameroom, with a beautiful fireplace, has many games and Stave wood puzzles. Off this is the Washington Suite, where my friend Audrey and I stayed. It has beautiful quilts and down-filled beds, two televisions, a CD player, and a bathroom with a large skirted antique tub and a huge shower. The sitting room has a bay window with a nice view, good couches, and a beautiful fireplace. There's a fireplace in the bedroom, too.

Dorothy's Room, on the second floor, is where she preferred to read and write. Red's Room, the original master suite, is glorious, with a view of Mount Ascutney. Red was Sinclair's nickname.

The guest room's walls and curtains are covered in toile de Jouy, a green-and-ivory French linen that tells a story. It's just beautiful.

The cottages have fireplaces, sumptuous baths, very private screened porches, and lots of comfort. They all have names. The studio is splendid and

has a huge copper soaking tub and front and back porches; a porch overlooks a stream, and a lot of fish-related items decorate the interior. The Treehouse is a wow, with Chinese fretwork in the bedroom. Orchard Cottage is set amid the old apple orchard and features two handcarved granite fireplaces. The two-story Barn Cottage offers grand views, and the Meadow, with its Moroccan interior reminiscient of a desert king's traveling palace, is stunning; the tent ceiling is something you'll just have to see. Wood Cottage has an Italian oak writing table and much charm. And the Log Cabin is an authentic old Tennessee log cabin refurbished the Twin Farms way. It's very hard to choose here, so come a lot of times—you won't be disappointed.

A covered bridge takes you to the pub. Here are a self-service bar, pool table, fireplace, and television. Below this is a fully equipped fitness center. In-room massages are available. Up the road is a Japanese Furo. There are separate tubs for men and women, separated by fragrant pine walls, and one larger one for both men and women.

The main dining room is rustic; however, you can dine wherever you choose. We were in the original dining room, and both the food and the service were incredible. Cocktails are at 7:00 P.M. There are two bars for you to help yourself from any time of the day or night. Lunch may take any form, and you can have it anywhere. Tea is glorious.

There is much to do here, whatever the season. Tennis and croquet; a lake for swimming, canoeing, or fishing; walking; biking. You can use the inn's mountain bikes. The inn also has its own ski slopes, ski trails, snowshoes, toboggans, and ice skating.

This is an experience few may be able to afford, but what a wonderful trip. The inn was awarded five stars by the *Mobil Travel Guide*. Say hello to Maple, the golden inn dog.

HOW TO GET THERE: Take I-91 north to I-89 north. Take exit 1 off I-89. Turn left onto Route 4 to Woodstock, then Route 12 to Barnard. At the general store, go right and follow this road for about 1½ miles. As the road changes from blacktop to dirt, you will see two stone pillars and a wrought-iron gate on your right, marking the driveway entrance.

# The Black Bear Inn
## Bolton Valley, Vermont 05477

**INNKEEPER:** Ken Richerdson and Suzanne Wallace

**ADDRESS/TELEPHONE:** Bolton Valley Road (mailing address: P.O. Box 26, Richmond 05477); (802) 434–2126 or (800) 395–6335

**E-MAIL:** blkbear@wctv.com

**ROOMS:** 24; all with private bath and color TV, 15 with Vermont stove or a fireplace.

**RATES:** $69 to $109, double occupancy, EP.

**OPEN:** All year.

**FACILITIES AND ACTIVITIES:** Breakfast, dinner, lounge. Heated swimming pool, cross-country skiing, downhill skiing, hiking. Nearby: tennis, fishing, golf.

Four miles up twisting, curving Bolton Valley Road, you come across this contemporary country inn, nestled in the mountainside as if it had been here forever. Once inside, you are greeted by the warmth of a wood-burning stove and the aroma of freshly baked breads and muffins that fills the air.

Everything is homemade. You could stay here for two weeks and not be served the same thing twice, and that even includes the breads and muffins. You can begin your dinner with some good soups, like cream of broccoli, chilled gazpacho, or a roasted onion, corn, and sweet potato chowder. Yum. There are always three entrees offered, one of which is seafood. You might find rack of lamb, sea scallops baked with

mushrooms and herbs, and vegetarian pasta on the menu one evening. For a happy ending, try the blueberry raspberry cobbler.

The rooms are well appointed, with color televisions, good beds, and lovely balconies where in summer you may sit and smell the good clean air and enjoy the views of the grounds, covered with wildflowers. The heated pool beckons you, comfortable lawn furniture is all around, and the beautiful blue skies are yours to enjoy. They are spectacular this far up in the mountains.

Some of the rooms have a fireplace and some a Vermont stove. The inn's 54 miles of cross-country ski trails make good paths for a hike. When you return to the inn, there's a nice cozy bar with four barstools and a sign behind the bar that says "Teddy Bear Crossing."

In cold weather Bolton Valley's nearby indoor sports center, with swimming, exercise rooms, saunas, and tennis, is the place to be when you're not skiing. There is so much to see and do in the area in all seasons, you'll find it a great place to bring your children.

There are a lot of bears up here (stuffed, of course) in many different poses. There is Burt Bear sitting on a chair, and he's huge. A real live bassett hound called Oscar also lives here.

HOW TO GET THERE: Coming west on I–89, take exit 10 at Stowe–Waterbury. Turn left, then turn right onto Route 2 and follow it 7 miles. Turn right onto Bolton Valley Road in Bolton where I–89 passes over Route 2. The inn is 4 miles up the mountain.

# The Brandon Inn
## Brandon, Vermont 05733

INNKEEPERS: Sarah and Louis Pattis

ADDRESS/TELEPHONE: 20 Park Street; (802) 247–5766 or (800) 639–8685; fax (802) 247–5768

E-MAIL: slpattis@sover.net

WEB SITE: www.historicbrandoninn.com

ROOMS: 24, plus 4 suites; all with private bath and phone.

RATES: $70 to $85, per person, double occupancy, MAP; $55 to $70, per person, double occupancy, EPB.

OPEN: All year.

FACILITIES AND ACTIVITIES: Lunch in summer only, Tuesday through Saturday. Wheelchair access to dining room. Bar, lounge, elevator, meeting facilities, TV rooms, swimming pool, trout fishing, summer theater.

*F*acing the village green in lovely Brandon is this Queen Anne–style brick inn, which is listed on the National Register of Historic Places. The inn has been here since 1786.

The rooms at the inn all come with private bath. There are king, queen, double, and twin beds. The choice is yours. Each room is different and has a charm of its own, perhaps created by a cozy easy chair for curling up in with a book or an intimate corner desk perfect for letter writing.

Your room is not the only place to relax. There are cheery, comfortable sitting rooms on each floor, just right for watching television on a rainy day. The main floor also offers various spots where you can unwind: the main foyer, for example, where you can enjoy a roaring fire in the winter and gentle breezes in the summer. There are puzzles and chess and books.

The inn has excellent facilities for weddings, meetings, and conferences. The mirrored ballroom is perfect for an elegant reception.

The five acres of inn grounds provide outdoor recreation. The swimming pool is great, and the Neshobe River on the inn's grounds is perfect for trout fishing. The lower barn is the home of the Vermont Ski Museum.

Luncheon has a goody. At dinner try tortellini Alfredo. Doesn't it sound great? Go on to the special house salad with black pepper dressing. It's excellent. Breast of chicken is prepared many different ways. The Brandon Inn's mixed grill is of quail, Cajun duck breast, smoked wild boar sausage, and venison bratwurst sausage. Ginger-crusted salmon is a different way of serving it and very good. A nice selection of desserts is also offered. In winter there is a tavern menu. Very nice.

The oldest elevator in Vermont is here; it's checked very regularly, so it's safe. Sarah has it decorated in checks, and it looks like a bird cage.

**HOW TO GET THERE:** The inn is on Route 7 in Brandon, on the village green.

# Walking Around Brandon

Established two hundred years ago between the Neshobe River and Otter Creek, Brandon has one of the most unusual town layouts in New England. Distinguished by its two greens, one on each bank of the Neshobe, the town also boasts a collection of nearly 250 nineteenth-century homes, ranging in styles from late Georgian through Federals, Greek Revivals, and Queen Anne Victorians. Almost every one of these homes is on the National Register of Historic Places. The Brandon Chamber of Commerce (802-247-6401) has published a walking tour around the village. You might see the birthplace of Stephen A. Douglas, U.S. senator famed for his debates against Abraham Lincoln.

Brandon also borders the Green Mountain National Forest, which has miles and miles of hiking and cross-country ski trails. Ask at the inns for the best access routes to these trails or pick up a copy of the Green Mountain Club's *Day Hiker's Guide to Vermont.*

# The Churchill House Inn
Brandon, Vermont 05733

INNKEEPERS: Lois and Roy Jackson

ADDRESS/TELEPHONE: RD 3, Box 3265; (802) 247–3078

ROOMS: 8; all with private bath, 3 with whirlpool tub.

RATES: $75 to $110, per person, MAP.

OPEN: All year except April and November.

FACILITIES AND ACTIVITIES: BYOB. Swimming pool, sauna. Guided tours for treks, hikes, bikes. Nearby: fishing.

*T*his is an inn for active people. The inn sits at the edge of the Green Mountain National Forest and provides numerous recreational opportunities, such as hiking, biking, skiing, and fishing. All are right here at the door, and the inn has a nice pool to relax in during the summertime.

The Churchill House participates in an activity that originated here with Lois and Roy—the Trail for Bikes, from country inn to country inn. These self-guided bicycling vacations are custom-planned according to your wishes. Hiking begins in mid-May and lasts through October; these treks are guided, and all of them are great. There is also cross-country skiing from inn to inn—wonderful. The Catamount Trail runs the length of the Green Mountains, with inns along the way, beautiful scenery, and quiet everywhere except for your skis. As the saying goes, this one's for me.

Twenty-five kilometers of cross-country trails are maintained by the inn, including the 17-kilometer loop to Silver Lake. Ski rentals are available at the inn. An old-fashioned sleigh ride is available by advance reservation.

Fishermen, do not despair. Native and rainbow trout exist in nearby Neshobe River, Furnace Brook, and the Middlebury and White Rivers. A guide can be provided for fishing trips, too.

Churchill House has a great reputation for fine food. My spies tell me that the cottage-cheese pancakes at breakfast are sinful, and a favorite at dinner is the New England pot roast. The French bread and desserts are all made here. What a treat after a busy day!

**HOW TO GET THERE:** Go up Route 7 to Brandon and turn right on Route 73 east; the inn is in about 4 miles.

# The Lilac Inn 🎗 📱
## Brandon, Vermont 05733-1121

**INNKEEPERS:** Melanie and Michael Shane

**ADDRESS/TELEPHONE:** 53 Park Street; (802) 247-5463 or
(800) 221-0720; fax (802) 247-5499

**E-MAIL:** lilacinn@sover.net

**WEB SITE:** www.lilacinn.com

**ROOMS:** 9; all with private bath, 1 with whirlpool tub, 3 with fireplace.
Phone available.

**RATES:** $100 to $250, double occupancy, EPB. MAP rates available.

**OPEN:** All year. Restaurant closed to public between Easter and
Mother's Day.

**FACILITIES AND ACTIVITIES:** Sunday brunch, dinner Wednesday
through Saturday. Catering and room service. Winter Arts Festival on
Friday and Saturday nights in February and March. Jazz and classical
concerts in summer.

**BUSINESS TRAVEL:** Ballroom for meetings. Function planning, secretarial services, telephone, computer, fax, and modem available.

Wow! This is a beauty. It's a 10,000-square-foot Georgian Revival mansion that was built in 1909 as a summer cottage. Adorned with yellow and white paint, it is a lovely country inn today. Michael and Melanie have recaptured the charm of the era in which it was built.

To the left of the coach entrance is the library, which has a nice fireplace, books galore, chess, and a ton of comfort and charm. On the right is a stupendous butler's pantry hall leading to the tavern. Here is a beautiful copper-topped bar with six leather chairs with backs. Boy, are they comfortable!

The tavern has its own menu, full of glorious food. How about a Loaf of Soup—a freshly baked mini-boule, filled with the soup of the day?

The dining room menu changes weekly. Usually there are four appetizers and soup du jour. A few of the choices when I visited were grilled Angus sirloin, baked cheddar scrod, raspberry lamb, and baked stuffed salmon. Two of the desserts take thirty minutes to prepare. I won't tell you what they are. Come up and find out; they are wonderful.

The staircase is grand. In 1991 a time capsule was inserted into its newel post. At the top of the stairs is an ornate Chinese chest from the 1850s.

The rooms are spacious and well appointed. The bridal suite has a two-person whirlpool tub and wedding dolls on the fireplace mantel. Televisions are in armoires, and there also are VCRs. Melanie makes the dolls. There is one of her in her wedding dress when you first enter the inn.

What a talented pair of innkeepers we have here! They're assisted by three inn cats—Brown Nose, White, and Sebastian, a wonderful Himalayan. The inn dogs are pugs called Dr. Watson, Winston, Carmel, and Bella.

**HOW TO GET THERE:** Follow Route 7 to Brandon. Turn right on Route 73 east (Park Street). The inn is about the fourth building on the right.

# The October Country Inn
## Bridgewater Corners, Vermont 05035

**INNKEEPERS:** Richard Sims and Patrick Runkel

**ADDRESS/TELEPHONE:** Upper Road Route 4 (mailing address: P.O. Box 66); (802) 672–3412; fax (800) 648–8421

**E-MAIL:** oci@vermontel.com

**ROOMS:** 10; 8 with private bath.

**RATES:** $140 to $170, double occupancy, MAP.

**OPEN:** All year except April and two weeks in November.

**FACILITIES AND ACTIVITIES:** Pool. Nearby: downhill and cross-country skiing, antiquing, horse shows.

There are a lot of comfortable things about this inn. It has a very cozy living room, with overstuffed furniture and a fireplace at one end and an old, old wood stove at the other. The fire is usually blazing, and the library offers an extensive supply of books as well as a great selection of games and puzzles. The innkeepers are always buying new books and games for you to enjoy. This room is a nice place for guests to relax and meet each other.

The rooms are also comfortable, with good beds and mattresses. Some rooms have skylights, which I always like.

On a summer day you can sit by the pool and a glass of lemonade will be brought out to you. The pool is in a peaceful meadow, and the view is great. If you want to stay out of the sun, relax under an apple tree or on the secluded deck.

Of course, if you can tear yourself away from all the comfort and relaxation, there are lots of things to do in this area. The Quechee Hot Air Balloon Festival is in June, and the Scottish Festival is in August; there are horse shows, antiquing, and Calvin Coolidge's birthplace. Winter brings a winter carnival, and downhill and cross-country skiing are nearby.

Dinner is a real experience. The French menu has onion soup, French baguette, sole au gratin, vegetable strudel, oven-roasted potatoes, salad, and apple cheese torte. The Italian menu offers summer-garden minestrone soup (the inn has its own vegetable and herb gardens), Italian bread, garlic-baked chicken, eggplant parmigiana, homemade pasta with garlic and olive oil, salad, and chocolate cake with raspberry cassis sauce. Also here are African, Greek, Scandinavian, Mexican, and good old American menus. I'm impressed that the innkeepers are so inventive. Breakfast includes fresh fruit, homemade granola, freshly baked small muffins, breads, and something hot, such as pancakes with Vermont maple syrup.

There are lots of reasons why I like it here, but one more is Zoe, the inn's beautiful cat.

HOW TO GET THERE: From I–91 north take exit 9 to Route 12, then go west on Route 4. From I–89 north take Vermont exit 1 to Route 4. The inn is at the junction of Routes 4 and 100A, halfway between Killington and Woodstock.

# *Bridgewater Mill Mall*

Built in 1825 as a cotton mill, the Bridgewater Mill Mall on Route 4 also had a long history as a woolen textile mill. For many years it processed the fine wool from the 9,000-plus sheep that lived in Bridgewater in the 1840s, and during World War I and World War II, uniforms and blankets for soldiers were made here. In 1925, the owners of the Bridgewater Mill changed its name to Vermont Native Industries.

The mill was closed in 1973 because flood waters from the Ottauquechee River destroyed the dye room, but in 1978 the mill building was reopened for a new life as the Bridgewater Mill Mall, also known as the Old Mill Marketplace. Home again to Vermont native crafters and artists, it also houses the Sun of the Heart Bookstore, a furniture workshop, a ski/sports outlet, and the Mountain Brewery. Visit such artists as David Crandall, born in Springfield, Vermont, and a jewelry maker since the age of fourteen! His beautiful work in gold, platinum, diamonds, and gemstones is glorious. The mall is open seven days a week, but some artists have hours by chance or by appointment only. See what's open on the day you visit or call (802) 672–3332 for more information.

# Shire Inn 🖤
## Chelsea, Vermont 05038

**INNKEEPERS:** Jay and Karen Keller

**ADDRESS/TELEPHONE:** Box 37; (802) 685–3031 or (800) 441–6908

**E-MAIL:** shireinn@sover.net

**WEB SITE:** www.innbookcom/shire.html

**ROOMS:** 6; all with private bath, 4 with working fireplace, 1 with wheelchair access. No smoking inn.

**RATES:** $145 to $205, double occupancy, MAP. On weekdays, $95 to $145, double occupancy, EPB. Two-night minimum stay on weekends in fall and on all major holidays.

**OPEN:** All year.

**FACILITIES AND ACTIVITIES:** Bicycles and cross-country skis available. Meeting facilities for small parties and social events; fishing, biking, snowmobiling. Nearby: downhill and cross-country skiing, swimming, boating, theaters. Dinner served with twenty-four-hour notice.

**RECOMMENDED COUNTRY INNS® TRAVELERS' CLUB BENEFIT:** 10 percent discount, October 26–September 14, excluding holidays, subject to availability.

Constructed in 1832 of Vermont brick, this inn was truly built to last. It is situated in a lovely part of the state. The White River is close by—actually, it's in the backyard. It's a paradise for fisherfolk. Cross-country skiing is in Chelsea, and downhill skiing is good at the Sonnenberg Ski Area near Woodstock. Lake Fairlee is the place to be for swimming and boating in the summer and ice skating in the winter. Hanover, New Hampshire, the home of Dartmouth College, isn't far and offers theaters, art, and more.

The living room/library with its neat fireplace beckons all who pass through the door. Lots of books and a good collection of *National Geographic* magazines make this room very enticing on a cold or rainy day. Be sure to ask about the history of the antique French buffet in the

living room. A circular stairway goes up to some of the rooms, and they are lovely. Four rooms have working fireplaces. They are furnished with period antiques. A canopy bed is in one room; a king-sized bed is in another. Good feather or foam pillows assure you of a good night's sleep. The inn is not well suited to children under five.

Climb the hill to the Adirondack chairs under the apple tree and just sit and enjoy the view of the town. If you want to take a walk, there's a bridge over the river leading to an open field. In the wintertime this is a great spot for sledding or skiing—or take a ride on the skimobile trail. There is also a nature trail about 1 mile above the inn.

Breakfast is not to be missed. There are six different muffins and all sorts of fresh fruits, Maine blueberry or apple pancakes, waffles, French toast, omelets, and quiche. I hope you like to start your day with a stupendous breakfast.

Dinner means such goodies as spinach, sweet pea, and mint soup; oven-baked crusty mustard chicken; Italian stuffed flank steak; scallops with mushrooms and tomato cream sauce served on angel hair pasta; apple-cranberry crumble topped with French vanilla ice cream; chocolate raspberry cake; and chocolate mint cheesecake. Oh my! This is a fine inn.

**HOW TO GET THERE:** From I–89 take the Sharon exit via Route 14 to South Royalton, then Route 110 north to Chelsea.

---

# Chester House Inn
## Chester, Vermont 05143

**INNKEEPERS:** Randon Guy and Paul Anderson

**ADDRESS/TELEPHONE:** 266 Main Street; (802) 875–2205 or (888) 875–2205; fax (802) 875–6602

**WEB SITE:** www.chesterhouseinn.com

**ROOMS:** 7, all with private bath, phones, modems; 3 with wood-burning fireplaces; 2 with Jacuzzi.

**RATES:** $89 to $149, double occupancy, EPB. Packages available.

**OPEN:** All year.

**FACILITIES AND ACTIVITIES:** Full breakfast, dinner by reservation for house guests only, wine and beer license. TV in the bar area.

The inn was built in 1780, and the rooms are named for the king, his wife, and children. There's a booklet in each room with a short biography of the person for whom that room is named. I was in the room named for Prince Oclavious; he was the thirteenth child of King George and Queen Charlotte-Sophia, born on February 23, 1779—my birthday, but not the year. Ho ho. He died only four years later. The rooms are all very different. One has a table made from English stove pipes, canopies, and a sleigh bed; all are very comfortable.

The inn is on the village green, where there are good shops and restaurants also. Dinner at the inn is served in the keeping room by a colonial fireplace, and I enjoyed their spring menu. Antipasto and breadsticks, garden salad, a choice of shredded pork tenderloin with lime sauce (it

was excellent), gorgonzola ravioli with butter herb sauce, or chicken Wellington, plus vegetable du jour. Tea or coffee and ice cream or rhubarb ice finished that wonderful meal.

For winter activities, the inn is close to the major ski mountains, cross-country-skiing touring center, ice skating, and sleigh rides.

There are three lovely inn cats named Purrsistence, Tom-E-Cat, and Suki. I love cats.

**HOW TO GET THERE:** From I–91 take exit 6 and watch for Chester signs; the inn is on the green.

# Mountain Top Inn
Chittenden, Vermont 05737

**INNKEEPERS:** Margaret and Michael Gehan

**ADDRESS/TELEPHONE:** Mountain Top Road; (802) 483–2311;
(800) 445–2100 from out of state

**WEB SITE:** www.mountaintopinn.com

**ROOMS:** 35, plus 22 cottage and chalet units; all with private bath,
chalets with kitchenette. No smoking in chalets or dining room. Two
rooms specially equipped for handicapped.

**RATES:** $134 to $246, double occupancy, EP. MAP is available.

**OPEN:** All year except April and November.

**FACILITIES AND ACTIVITIES:** Lunch, bar, lounge. Wheelchair access to
dining rooms. Heated pool, tennis, lawn games, 5-hole pitch and putt
with full-sized greens, gameroom, horseback riding, sauna, whirlpool,
exercise room, cross-country skiing, horse-drawn sleigh rides, sailboarding, canoeing, ice skating, sledding, golf school, fly-fishing clinics.
Nearby: downhill skiing, horseback riding and lessons.

*I*n the 1870s the Mountain Top property was part of the Long family's turnip farm. In 1940 William Barstow, an engineer and philan-
thropist from New York, purchased the farm and converted the
barn into a wayside tavern as a hobby for his wife.

Today, the inn is just beautiful, with views that no money can buy. At a
2,000-foot elevation, the inn overlooks Mountain Top Lake, which is surrounded by fantastic mountains. When you enter the inn, you are in a very
inviting living area with a large fireplace. Ahead of you are the view and a
spectacular two-story glass-enclosed staircase that leads to the "Charlie
James" cocktail lounge, presided over by a regal fox, and the dining room.
The food served here is superb, beginning with appetizers like scallops
sautéed with chutney and Dijon mustard, and seviche. One entree that I love
here is New England seafood au gratin. Medallions of pork loin are also delicious. On my most recent visit here, I ordered veal piccata, which came with
a baked potato and salad. It was very good.

The rooms, most overlooking the lake and mountains, are large and luxuriously furnished. All have spacious baths. A nice touch is your bed turned down at night with a maple sugar candy on the pillow. So is an electric pot for boiling water for your early morning coffee.

The inn has an excellent ski touring program. With more than a thousand acres to ski on, the views are awesome. The sugarhouse, a wooden structure, is well located near several of the inn's ski touring trails. It has been turned into a ski-warming hut where skiers in the spring have the added bonus of watching the sap boiling-down process firsthand. There are two other warming huts on the property. The inn has a ski shop with instructors and all the latest equipment. Ice skating and toboggans are also fun, and downhill skiing is nearby at Pico and Killington.

Summer brings walking or hiking through the lovely countryside, and in fall the color show of the trees is breathtaking. And in winter, riding in sleighs drawn by draft horses is a wonderful yesteryear experience.

**HOW TO GET THERE:** From Rutland head north on Route 7. Pass the power station, turn right on Chittenden Road, and follow it into Chittenden. Follow the signs up to the inn.

# Tulip Tree Inn 🖤
## Chittenden, Vermont 05737

**INNKEEPERS:** Ed and Rosemary McDowell

**ADDRESS/TELEPHONE:** Chittenden Dam Road; (802) 483-6213 or (800) 707-0017

**E-MAIL:** ttinn@sover.net

**WEB SITE:** www.tuliptreeinn.com

**ROOMS:** 8; all with private bath, 5 with Jacuzzi, 2 with fireplace.

**RATES:** $130 to $289, double occupancy, MAP.

**OPEN:** All year except April, most of May, and part of November.

**FACILITIES AND ACTIVITIES:** Full license. Fishing. Nearby: swimming, hiking, golf, tennis, canoeing, bicycling, skiing.

In 1989 this inn was selected as one of the top ten country inns in the nation. You can't beat that! You arrive and a lovely front porch with wicker chairs beckons you at once. Beautiful woods surround you. You hear a brook babbling, and a feeling of sheer peace comes over you. Cara, the Bernese mountain dog, or Hoover, the cat, may greet you. Inside you find a nice living room with a fireplace, a small bar and library, a den with a fireplace, and a great assortment of chairs, love seats, and couches throughout.

The rooms are the sort you never want to leave. Puffy comforters on the beds are inviting to curl up under, and the Jacuzzi tubs in five of the rooms feel so great after a long day. There are nice antiques, including a huge pine bed with a pineapple on top.

Dining is very special here at the inn. Pretty, too, with yellow and white napery in the summer and red, white, and blue in the winter. Rosemary's breakfasts are full

Vermont style. That means you'll find cold cereals; yogurt; juices; sweet breads; and apple, cheese, or blueberry pancakes or French toast, all with pure maple syrup.

If you think that's good, come back at dinnertime, when Rosemary really shines. There are homemade breads and soups like zucchini and curried carrot. Salads are interesting, especially with Rosemary's dressings. A sorbet is brought to you to cleanse your palate, and then it might be medallions of pork with apricot-orange sauce or chicken with curry sauce or fillet of beef with béarnaise. Oh my, and her desserts! . . . Well, just save some room, because they are so good.

The inn is only a mile from the Chittenden Reservoir, where the fishing and swimming are superb. East Brook runs right by the house. Trout anyone? There's a saying up here—by Mr. Ed, I'm sure—a traffic jam in Chittenden is one farmer with one tractor towing two wagons.

**HOW TO GET THERE:** From Rutland drive north on Route 7. Just outside Chittenden you will see a red brick power station on the left. Just beyond it is a Y in the road, with a red country store in the middle. Keep right of the store and follow the road approximately 6 miles. Just past the fire station, go straight ahead ½ mile to the inn, which will be on your left.

---

# Heermansmith Farm Inn
## Coventry, Vermont 05825

**INNKEEPERS:** Jack and Louise Smith

**ADDRESS/TELEPHONE:** Heermansville Road, Box 7; (802) 754–8866

**E-MAIL:** Heermansmith@connriver.net

**ROOMS:** 6, all with private bath; 1 cottage with 3 bedrooms, 1 bath, kitchen, TV, washer and dryer.

**RATES:** $65, double occupancy, EPB; cottage, $125 a night, $500 a week.

**OPEN:** All year, except April in mud season.

**FACILITIES AND ACTIVITIES:** Breakfast and dinner, extensive music library, wonderful walking and hiking, cross-country skiing from door, and fishing in the Black River

*A*long with simplicity of life in the valley, life within the inn is equally low key. A gravel road meanders by the inn. Street lights don't exist—the twinkle of stars is spectacular and the clean fresh country air is shared by plants, animals, and guests. Innkeepers Jack and Louise are not in the forefront directing the ebb and flow of guests at the Inn. At Heermansmith you're simply enjoying a home that has been in their family for generations without a bit of pretense. This is from their brochure, and I could not say it any better.

There's a cottage that dates back to 1809. It has wide-board floors, a slate fireplace, three bedrooms, a bath, a kitchen with washer and dryer, a TV in the living room, and cross-country skiing from its door or the inn next door.

The inn has been here since 1807, and it's lovely. When you come in the door and turn left you are in the bar area; the living area and dining room are close by. The food up here is glorious. A few ideas for appetizers are New England codfish cakes, baked stuffed mushrooms, and good soups. An entree may be duck, a house special, roasted crisp with a strawberry and chamborg sauce—oh my, I wish I lived closer—or shrimp Louise or Delmonico steak. Or sample the chef's choices: Cajun

grilled scallops, fresh veal cutlets, or fresh salmon. Save room for dessert.

There's a nice library and a model of a four-masted schooner named *Maude Ritter*—it's a beauty. The rooms are spotless and very comfortable.

Do go wandering while you are up here. Visit country stores, walk through acres of wildflowers. Northern Vermont has autumn colors better than any place. Winter is a picture, so are spring and summer. Do yourself a favor and come on up.

HOW TO GET THERE: Take I–91 to exit 26 (Orleans) and pick up Route 5 north. Go about 6 miles to Coventry. At the sign COVENTRY VILLAGE SCHOOL, take a left into Coventry Village. Take the next left onto Heermansville Road. Go uphill ⁶/₁₀ mile; the inn is the fourth place on the right.

# The Craftsbury Inn
## Craftsbury, Vermont 05826

**INNKEEPERS:** Blake and Rebecca Gleason

**ADDRESS/TELEPHONE:** Main Street; (802) 586–2848 or (800) 336–2848

**ROOMS:** 10; 6 with private bath. No smoking inn.

**RATES:** $140 to $160, double occupancy, MAP; $90 to $110, double occupancy, EPB. EP rates available.

**OPEN:** All year except April and November.

**FACILITIES AND ACTIVITIES:** Dinner for public, by reservation, Wednesday through Sunday. Bar, cross-country skiing. Nearby: canoeing, swimming, fishing, horseback riding, tennis, golf.

**RECOMMENDED COUNTRY INNS® TRAVELERS' CLUB BENEFIT:** 10 percent discount, Monday–Thursday, subject to availability.

*T*he inn is a lovingly restored Greek Revival house that was built circa 1850. The little town of Craftsbury, said by the *Boston Globe* to be Vermont's most remarkable hill-town, was founded in 1788 by Colonel Ebenezer Crafts and lies in what is called the Northeast Kingdom. The population today is something less than 700, and that includes Craftsbury, East Craftsbury, and Craftsbury Common.

One year I arrived here on a chilly day in the middle of June and was greeted by a lovely fire in the television room. Boy, did it feel good! Speaking of fireplaces, the one in the living room is the original fireplace that warmed the first post office in Mont-pelier, Vermont's capital.

The rooms here are filled with antique wicker, and the beds have handsome heirloom quilts. Fresh paint and paper have made this lovely old inn even nicer.

All ice creams, breads, and pastries are prepared here. They also make their own stocks, and this does make a difference in the taste of food.

The food is very good and inventive. You'll find appetizers like wild game soup, cream of mushroom soup, and duck en croûte. And for your entree consider sautéed pheasant with a Frangelico sauce or poached salmon with a cucumber dill sauce. Baked partridge is served with a sage stuffing and a white wine–fresh rosemary sauce. The desserts are yummy—Black Forest cake, apple flan, wild-berry pie, and more.

There is much to do in this area. A cross-country ski trail is connected to the Craftsbury Sports Center, very near the inn. In the summer you can rent a canoe, swim, or fish in the center's lake. You can also ride horseback, play tennis, or play golf at Vermont's oldest course in Greensboro, where the greens are fenced to prevent intrusion of the grazing cattle. Throughout July and August the Craftsbury Chamber Players perform every Thursday evening. Come and enjoy.

HOW TO GET THERE: Take I–91 to St. Johnsbury, pick up Route 2 west, and at West Danville take Route 15 to Hardwick. Follow Route 14 north to Craftsbury. Take a right off Route 14 onto Main Street. The inn is 2 miles down on the right, across from the general store.

# The Inn on the Common
## Craftsbury Common, Vermont 05827

INNKEEPERS: Penny and Michael Schmitt

ADDRESS/TELEPHONE: Main Street; (802) 586–9619 or (800) 521–2233; fax (802) 586–2249

ROOMS: 17, in 3 buildings; all with private bath, 5 with fireplace or wood stove.

RATES: $110 to $140, per person, double occupancy, MAP. Ski touring and ski packages available. B&B rates available.

OPEN: All year.

FACILITIES AND ACTIVITIES: Food and drinks to the public by reservation. Solar-heated swimming pool, clay tennis court, English croquet, boating, cross-country skiing.

*I*t is a long way up here, but it's worth every mile you travel to be a guest of the Schmitts. There are three buildings that make up the inn. The north annex is on the common, with a lovely picket fence around it. All of its rooms are beautifully appointed. The wallpapers are Scalamandre reproduction from a South Carolina historic collection. The sheets throughout the inn are brand-new and Marimekko. There's a very unusual sofa; try to figure out how the arms go down. Two of the bedrooms in the north annex have a fireplace. One of the bathrooms has such a cute, tiny bathtub. There's a lovely canopy bed in one room. In the main house are three luxurious rooms that Penny loves to show off.

Across the street is the south annex. The guest lounge has a fireplace, comfy sofas, and a large television. You can fix lunch, make tea, or concoct whatever else you may wish in the guest kitchen. Two Jøtul wood-burning stoves keep the rooms warm and cozy.

In the main house is the dining room with a glass wall overlooking the rose gardens. All the gardens are lovely. Penny has green hands and is a faithful gardener. The dining room has the perfect atmosphere to savor the sumptuous food. Iced purple plum soup and grilled scallop bisque were two offerings on my most recent visit here. Rabbit was one of the entrees, braised in a rich broth of stock, beer, fresh herbs, and cloves.

Salads are so good. I never had a vegetable baklava before, and it is delicious. The menu changes all the time, and the choices are really spectacular and tasty. Off the dining room a new deck is where will summer dinner will be served. The inn has had AAA's four-diamond rating for years.

There is a superb wine cellar with many wines to complement your meal. Cocktail hour in the library is a fun, social time. The inn has won the *Wine Spectator* Award of Excellence for three years in a row.

The solar-heated swimming pool has a little waterfall to let the water in. It disturbs nothing in its peaceful location behind the south annex. Sam, the inn dog, enjoys watching it.

A staff of naturalists runs a sports complex near the inn. One hundred and forty acres include lake swimming, sculling, canoeing, cross-country skiing, nature walks, and bird-watching. There is a summer walking map of Craftsbury, with walks along the appropriate ski trails, logging roads, and back roads. Come on up. There is something for everyone.

Are you a sculler? There's a well-known sculling center up here with all aspects of sculling or sweep rowing covered.

**HOW TO GET THERE:** Follow I–91 to St. Johnsbury, take Route 2 west, and at West Danville take Route 15 to Hardwick. Take Route 14 north to Crafts-bury, and continue north into the common. The inn is on the left as you enter the village.

# Silas Griffith Inn
Danby, Vermont 05739

**INNKEEPERS:** Paul and Lois Dansereau

**ADDRESS/TELEPHONE:** South Main Street; (802) 293–5567

**ROOMS:** 17, in 2 buildings; 14 with private bath.

**RATES:** $72 to $94, double occupancy, EPB.

**OPEN:** All year except April.

**FACILITIES AND ACTIVITIES:** Dinner. Wheelchair access to dining room. Bar, swimming pool. Nearby: five ski areas, biking, horseback riding, golf, tennis, hiking, fishing, hunting, factory outlets.

In 1891 lumber baron Silas Griffith built this large, stately mansion on a bluff overlooking the town of Danby as a gift for his wife. The workmanship is grand. I was really taken with the round, cherry pocket door that leads into the music room. Oak, cherry, maple, and other woods have been used throughout the inn.

When you are past the foyer of the inn, you are in a huge living room–library full of books, chairs, couches, and a welcoming fireplace. A small antiques shop is off this room. Another, smaller living room has a television and is a good spot to meet the other guests.

Eight of the rooms are in the carriage house, and nine are in the inn itself. Most of them have queen-sized beds with fluffy quilts. Lois says she had a lot of fun—but I bet it was also hard work—visiting auctions and antiques shops to find the lovely old beds and Victorian furniture for the rooms. Then she had the double beds extended to fit queen-sized mattresses. Apples in the rooms add a nice, welcoming touch.

The restaurant is in the carriage house. You'll find a good-sized bar, a fireplace, and attractively set tables. Every night there is a new dinner menu. The night that I visited the inn, guests were able to start their dinner with brie baked with peach chutney or Vermont cheddar-cheese soup. A choice of marinated pork tenderloin served with a delicate cherry wine sauce, boneless breast of chicken  stuffed with crabmeat, steak, shrimp, or salmon was offered. There are fresh vegetables in season and assorted homemade desserts.

This is a nice area of Vermont with many activities to enjoy. Hikers like the inn's proximity to the Appalachian Trail; shoppers enjoy the factory outlets for bargain shopping; skiers think it's super to have five ski areas to try; and historians like the nearby marble museum. The world's largest underground marble quarry is inside Dorset Mountain; marble from here was used to build the Jefferson Memorial and most of the other marble buildings in Washington, D.C. Even if you're not a historian, you will find the museum worth a visit.

Do say hello to Violet, the inn cat. She is part calico and part Himalayan and with this mix, very different.

**HOW TO GET THERE:** On Route 7 about 12 miles north of Manchester, look for the inn's sign on the right. It's a left turn into the inn.

---

# Barrows House

Dorset, Vermont 05251

**INNKEEPERS:** Jim and Linda McGinnis

**ADDRESS/TELEPHONE:** Route 30; (802) 867–4455 or (800) 639–1620; fax (802) 867–0132

**E-MAIL:** innkeepers@barrowshouse.com

**WEB SITE:** www.barrowshouse.com

**ROOMS:** 18, plus 10 suites, in 9 houses, all with private bath and air conditioning; 5 with fireplace; 1 room specially equipped for handicapped. Pets welcome.

**RATES:** $200 to $250, double occupancy, MAP. EPB and off-season rates available.

**OPEN:** All year.

**FACILITIES AND ACTIVITIES:** Wheelchair access to dining room. Cross-country ski shop, rentals, heated swimming pool, tennis courts, bicycles. Nearby: golf, skiing, shopping, hiking, horseback riding.

**BUSINESS TRAVEL:** Meeting facilities, fax available, corporate rates.

The Barrows House is an inn for all seasons and all reasons. The unique facilities and extensive grounds make the inn a special place for a family gathering, honeymoon, small business meeting, or spur-of-the-moment vacation.

There is a story to every Barrows House room or cottage. Each is a furnished unit with its own restful style, antiques, old family pieces, and modern bedding. Each of the nine houses has its own sitting room and porch or

terrace, as well as its own fire control system.

Sitting on twelve acres, the Barrows House is a 200-year-old estate. The house was built for the pastor of the Dorset Congregational Church (you can walk there from the inn), and in 1888 it became an inn. The first innkeepers were Theresa and Experience Barrow. Don't you love his name? The front living rooms and entryways have some of the original stenciling, which was found after removing thirteen layers of wallpaper.

The menu changes nightly. The chef and sous chef do a fine job. Two of the appetizers are sweet potato, leek, and garlic soup, and batter-fried mushrooms with honey-mustard dipping sauce. There are entrees like pork medallions or grilled venison medallions, calves' liver, Vermont-raised trout, lamb medallions with honey-thyme sauce, and grilled peppered tuna with tomatoes, olives, garlic, and feta cheese. For "finishers," well, come on up and taste. Just a hint—the Maine crabcakes Chesapeake-style are a house specialty. Heart-healthy cuisine is available here.

There's so much to do in this area. The skiing is superb, antiques shopping is near, and the Dorset Playhouse is here. Horseback riding and hiking or golf are available in nearby Manchester. And when you're tired of all the activity, come back to the inn to enjoy the cozy tavern, the glowing fire in the main living room, or the eleven acres of grounds. Bring the whole family— children of all ages are welcome.

HOW TO GET THERE: The inn is 6 miles northwest of Manchester, Vermont, on Route 30.

---

# Cornucopia of Dorset
Dorset, Vermont 05251

INNKEEPERS: Linda and Bill Ley

ADDRESS/TELEPHONE: Route 30 (mailing address: Box 307);
(802) 867–5751 or (800) 566–5751

E-MAIL: cornucop@vermontel.com

WEB SITE: www.cornucopiaofdorset.com

ROOMS: 4, plus 1 cottage, all with private bath, phones, and air conditioning. No smoking inn.

RATES: $125 to $165, double occupancy, EPB; cottage, $210 to $245, double occupancy, EPB.

FACILITIES AND ACTIVITIES: Full breakfast only meal served. Nearby: good restaurants, theater, art centers, shopping, and more.

RECOMMENDED COUNTRY INNS® TRAVELERS' CLUB BENEFIT: Complimentary bottle of wine. With midweek stay of two or more nights, guests receive either a dining gift certificate or tickets to professional theater in season. Not valid during peak periods.

*I*n the living room is a small size Tracker organ circa 1840, painted pine case with cedar and pewter pipes, American made, probably in New York State. I like finding these old organs in inns, since I play one.

There's a large solarium overlooking the lovely landscaping, wonderful full-length windows, couches, plants, games, and books. A pillow on a couch says it so well: "Gardeners know the best dirt." The dining room is in this area. Breakfast is served in here on nice tables. And what a breakfast. It includes fresh fruit juice, a fruit course, entrees like baked apple butter French toast, fresh berries and cream crepes, Florentine eggs, grilled tomatoes, and apple turnovers. These are just a few of the treats you may find here.

Complimentary light hors d'oeuvres are served in the afternoon with wine or champagne or steeped or iced tea.

There are four lovely rooms in the inn. The cottage named Owl's Head is a restored carriage house and has a large wood-burning fireplace and a full kitchen. Upstairs is a carpeted loft with skylights, a queen-sized bed, and comfort. Downstairs, French doors open to a private patio facing the back lawn, very nice. They will put a television in the cottage if you want one.

The inn dog is Kitt. He is 100 percent Vermont mutt and a sweet dog.

Dorset is old and lovely. The marble quarries at the edge of Dorset are said to be the oldest in the country. They provided marble for the New York City Library, the sidewalks in town, and the all-marble church next to the village green. Yesterday's quarries are today's swimming holes.

**HOW TO GET THERE:** The inn is 6 miles northwest of Manchester, Vermont, on Route 30.

# Dorset Inn
## Dorset, Vermont 05251

**INNKEEPERS:** Sissy Hicks; Amanda McLean, manager

**ADDRESS/TELEPHONE:** Route 30; (802) 867–5500

**ROOMS:** 31; all with private bath.

**RATES:** $145 to $210, single; $210 to $230, double occupancy; MAP; suites $225 to $350.

**OPEN:** All year except March 15 to April 15.

**FACILITIES AND ACTIVITIES:** Breakfast, lunch, dinner, bar. Wheelchair access to dining room. Nearby: golf, theater, hiking, bicycling.

Built in 1796, this is the oldest inn in Vermont, and it has been continuously operated as an inn. Today the inn has been completely restored and is listed in the National Register of Historic Places. There are wide-board floors, and beautiful Vermont pine is around the fireplace in the living room.

While the inn has retained the feeling of the eighteenth century, it is modern in its conveniences. It has been completely insulated. The bathrooms have been redone, some of the rooms have been air-conditioned, and firm mattresses have been purchased. The whole inn is clean and neat.

The breakfast and luncheon room has a lovely old lion fountain. I love the sound of the water. The bar-lounge is spacious. There is no crowding in this large and rambling inn. Sissy Hicks presides over the kitchen and is a very well-known lady. Some of the luncheon items are curried mussels and noodles on spinach, beef and scallions with rice, and biscuit-crust apple and turkey pie. Sounds great! At dinner the appetizers are numerous. One is New England cheese chowder. Sissy's entrees are really different. Sautéed breast of chicken stuffed

with Brie and coriander. Fresh Atlantic salmon with creamy fennel and leek sauce. The breakfast menu is pure ambrosia.

I like it here. I think you can tell.

The recently restored tavern has its own menu from Sunday through Thursday in the summer and every night in the winter. It's lovely in here. Try the baked eggplant crepe or the grilled marinated shrimp.

A fine golf course is nearby for anyone who likes to play. Swimming is a lot of fun in a huge marble quarry up the road. If culture turns you on, the Southern Vermont Arts Center and the Dorset Playhouse will provide the comedy and drama of good theater. There are four inn dogs—three Labs and a bassett hound. Christmas is special up here, and the inn is glorious with lights.

HOW TO GET THERE: Leave I–91 at Brattleboro and go left on Route 30 to Dorset. Or take Route 7 to Manchester Center and go north on Route 30.

# Inn at West View Farm
## Dorset, Vermont 05251

**INNKEEPERS:** Helmut and Dorothy Stein

**ADDRESS/TELEPHONE:** Route 30; (802) 867–5715 or (800) 769–4903; fax (802) 867–0468

**E-MAIL:** westview@vermontel.com

**WEB SITE:** www.vtweb.com/innatwestviewfarm/

**ROOMS:** 10; all with private bath, 1 with wheelchair access.

**RATES:** $80 to $130, double occupancy, EPB; $155 to $190, double occupancy, MAP.

**OPEN:** May through October and mid-November through March.

**FACILITIES AND ACTIVITIES:** Breakfast, dinner, tavern. Dining room closed on Monday and Tuesday. Nearby: tennis, golf, swimming, skiing.

This is an authentic Vermont country inn. Informal and relaxed is the style of the innkeepers, who have thought of everything to make your stay here comfortable.

The living rooms, with their glowing fireplaces and good couches and chairs, are restful after a day of skiing or shopping. The guest rooms are warmly furnished with four-poster beds and antique dressers. One room has facilities for handicapped guests.

The dining room, which is done in shades of warm green, is just beautiful. It is highlighted by a tin ceiling and a broad bay window. The room seats forty-five people. The stunning place plates are a floral pattern from Villeroy and Boch, and Botanica made in Luxembourg. Need-less to say with such magnif-icent surroundings, the food served here is extravagant, with hors d'oeuvres and soups such as terrine of pheasant, a fish pâté, or hot or cold cream of mustard soup. This was a first for me and very good. There are

entrees like quenelles of scallops, fillet of salmon, or rack of lamb for two. A real favorite is chateaubriand flambé au cognac et poivres verts, also for two.

Ready for dessert? A pastry tray has an enticing variety of tarts, tortes, and pastries. Or you can order crème caramel, homemade sorbet, or homemade ice cream. What a way to go!

A lovely stained-glass window separates the dining room from the bar. The bar is done in rich, warm wood and is a real beauty. Clancy's Tavern, named for Clancy, an Irish setter, has its own menu. Some ideas are chef's soup of the day, salads, Tavern crabcakes (made with fresh Maine crabmeat), New York strip steak, shrimp, tagliatelle, and more and oh so good.

The inn is only 5 miles north of Manchester, where there are shops for your every wish. Three downhill ski areas and cross-country skiing are all nearby, and the Dorset Playhouse is less than a walk around the block from the inn.

To see this beautiful inn in the snow is a picture to remember. And in the warm weather, the porch with its wicker furniture beckons. What a great view from here!

HOW TO GET THERE: Take I-91 north to Brattleboro, then take Route 30 to Manchester. At the blinking lights, take a right and an immediate left, which brings you back on Route 30 north. Go about 5½ miles north of Manchester. Look for the inn on your right.

# Blueberry Hill
## Goshen, Vermont 05733

INNKEEPERS: Tony Clark and Shari Brown

ADDRESS/TELEPHONE: Blueberry Hill, RD 3; (802) 247-6735, (802) 247-6535 or (800) 448-0707; fax (802) 247-3983

WEB SITE: www.blueberryhillinn.com

ROOMS: 12; all with private bath, 1 specially equipped for the handicapped. No smoking inn.

RATES: In summer, $95 to $120 per person; in winter, $110 per person; double occupancy, MAP.

OPEN: All year.

FACILITIES AND ACTIVITIES: Packed lunch available, BYOB. Sauna across the pond. Cross-country skiing, swimming, fishing.

he inn is a cross-country skier's dream come true. It is nestled at the foot of Romance Mountain in the Green Mountain National Forest and is surrounded by good clean air and well-groomed snowy trails. From the inn brochure I quote: "The Blueberry Hill Ski Touring Center, across from the inn, devotes itself to cross-country skiers of all ages and abilities. Inside the fully equipped Ski Center are retail and rental departments, a waxing area, repair shop, and an expert staff to see that you are skiing better with less effort. Upstairs you can relax, make friends, and share the day's events in our lounge with its large windows, comfortable seating, and old wood stove. Surrounding the Ski Center are 75 kilometers of both challenging and moderate terrain. A loop around Hogback, a race to Silver Lake, or just making tracks in a snow world all your own . . . the activities never cease—from seminars, waxing clinics, night and guided tours, to the 60-kilometer American Ski Marathon."

In the summer the ski trails are used for hiking, walking, and running. There are a pond for swimming and streams and lakes for fishing.

The inn is a restored 1813 farmhouse. Dinner is served family-style in a lovely candlelit dining room. There are four courses served in an unhurried, comfortable way. While I was here, dinner included such delicious things as cold cantaloupe soup, scallion bread, broiled lamb chops with mint butter, stir-fried asparagus, lemon meringue tarts, and homemade ice cream. Tony's son made strawberry ice cream, and it was so good. The greenhouse just off the kitchen is full of glorious plants. Three of the guest rooms and a new wing are out here, just beyond the greenhouse.

Their upside-down gardens hanging from the ceiling beams are a colorful and imaginative use of strawflowers, and the brick patio overlooking Dutton Brook is so restful and nice. There are plenty of books to read, and the rooms are comfortable, with many antiques, quilts, and hot water bottles on the backs of the doors. Honest, they are there.

In honor of the inn's twenty-fifth anniversary, celebrated in 1996, the innkeepers have begun making Blueberry Hill chocolate chip cookies 303—pure good eating. Call and they'll ship you some—and boy, are they good.

**HOW TO GET THERE:** From Rutland take Route 7 north to Brandon, then Route 73 east for 6 miles. Turn left at the inn's sign, and follow the signs up the mountain on a dirt road to the inn.

# The Old Tavern  ♥ 📱
## Grafton, Vermont 05146

**INNKEEPER:** Kevin O'Donnell

**ADDRESS/TELEPHONE:** Route 121; (802) 843–2231 or (800) 843–1801; fax (802) 843–2245

**E-MAIL:** tavern@sover.net

**WEB SITE:** www.old-tavern.com

**ROOMS:** 66, in 7 houses; all with private bath.

**RATES:** $125 to $165, double occupancy, EPB and afternoon tea. Higher in fall foliage season. Senior citizen discounts.

**OPEN:** All year except April, Christmas Eve, and Christmas Day.

**FACILITIES AND ACTIVITIES:** Breakfast, lunch, dinner, bar. Wheelchair access to inn, bar, lounge, and dining room. Television in lounge, parking, elevator, conference facilities for up to forty, swimming. Nearby: tennis, nature walks, cross-country skiing, bicycle rentals.

*I*f you're looking for perfection in a country inn, go to a charming Vermont village called Grafton, where you'll find The Old Tavern. It has been operated as an inn since 1801. Since the inn was purchased by the Windham Foundation in 1965, it has been restored and is now one of those superb New England inns we are all seeking.

When you turn your car off pounding interstate highways to the tree-shaded route that winds to this quaint village, you step back in time. The loveliest of the old combined with the comfort of the new makes this an unbeatable inn. No grinding motors can disturb your slumber when you are in the best beds in all New England. The sheets and towels are the finest money can buy, and there are extra pillows and blankets in each room. The

# Grafton's Renaissance

In the early nineteenth century, Grafton's fourteen hundred or so citizens managed pretty tidily from the profits derived from the 75,000 yards of wool produced annually from the 10,000 sheep that grazed in Grafton pastures. Thirteen soapstone quarries produced sinks, stoves, and other household goods. The Phelps Tavern—now known as the Old Tavern—was upgraded with innkeeper Marlan Phelps's Gold Rush profits and entertained illustrious guests from poets to presidents.

Unfortunately, Grafton lost scores of its citizens in the Civil War, sheep farmers went looking for bigger pastures out West, and floods and new highways changed the look and the lure of this once-properous village. By 1940, the town's economy had trickled down to nearly nothing. Along came the Windham Foundation in 1963, and suddenly Grafton had new life in its center. Find out the history of the remarkable transformation of Grafton in its "new" Old Tavern Inn and in its three museums dedicated to the human and natural history of the town. Call the Grafton Historical Society (802-843-2564), the Grafton Museum of Natural History (802-843-2111), and the Windham Foundation (802-843-2211) for information about historical exhibits and tours. You can also visit the Grafton Village Cheese Co. (802-843-2348) for a look at its cheese-making operation, and you can see "demonstration" flocks of sheep at the village's sheep barn viewing area. Horse-drawn sleigh rides are offered in the village in the winter time, and the village's many walking paths, also popular in summer, are opened to cross-country skiers. Inquire at the Old Tavern about bicycle rentals and the Windham Foundation's horse stable.

spacious rooms are filled with antiques, all in mint condition. The guest houses across the street that are also part of the inn are enchanting.

There is no "organized activity" at The Old Tavern. The swimming pool is a natural pond, cool and refreshing. There are tennis courts nearby and marked trails in the woods for walkers. This is the place to calm your spirits and recharge your batteries.

The cocktail barn is charming, connected to the inn by a covered walk. There are flowers everywhere, in hanging baskets, in flower boxes, and on various tables in the gracious public rooms. The New England cuisine is excellent, with unusual soups and varied entrees, all cooked well and served by pleasant waitresses.

Up the street a bit, there is a six box-stall stable that will accommodate guest horses, plus a four-bay carriage shed, if you care to bring your own carriage. All this is for the exclusive use of Old Tavern guests.

The Old Tavern has a heritage that goes back almost as far as our country's. It first opened twelve years after America's independence. The Old Tavern looks very much as it did in former days, when, over time, it accommodated the likes of Daniel Webster, Oliver Wendell Holmes, Ulysses S. Grant, Rudyard Kipling, Ralph Waldo Emerson, and Henry David Thoreau.

**HOW TO GET THERE:** From I–91, take exit 5 at Bellows Falls. Take Route 5 north to Route 121, on which you will get to Bellows Falls (12 miles from I–91) and the inn. As you come down the exit ramp, watch for Route 121, which you'll take to the inn.

# Highland Lodge
## Greensboro, Vermont 05841

**INNKEEPERS:** Wilhelmina and David Smith

**ADDRESS/TELEPHONE:** RR 1, Box 1290; (802) 533–2647; fax (802) 533–7494

**E-MAIL:** HLodge@connriver.net

**WEB SITE:** www.pbpub.com/vermont/hiland.htm

**ROOMS:** 11 rooms, plus 14 cottages, all with private bath; 1 cottage equipped for handicapped.

**RATES:** $190 to $230, double occupancy, MAP. Off-season rates.

**OPEN:** All year except March 15 to Memorial Day and October 15 to December 20 (or nearest weekend thereto).

**FACILITIES AND ACTIVITIES:** Lunch, dinner, and Sunday brunch, beer and wine license. Wheelchair access to dining room. Tennis, bicycle rentals, lawn games, hiking trails, swimming, boating, fishing, cross-country ski touring center. Nearby: working dairy farm, golf.

When the snow starts falling up here, it has to be one of the most beautiful places in the world. And you can bet that it's popular with cross-country skiers. There is a complete ski touring center with daily instruction, ski shop (sales, rentals, and repairs), guided tours, marked trails, and skier's lunch. All this is at an altitude of 1,500 feet, a mini-snowbelt where there are miles of ski touring through the wonderful scenery.

Winter isn't the only fun time of year to be here. Caspian Lake, with the lodge's own beach house, is just across the road for swimming, canoeing, and sailing. Fishing is good in June and from September to mid-October for salmon, lake trout, rain-bow trout, and perch. Tennis, golf, and riding are available for those so inclined.

Any inn that sends its chef to France to train for the kitchen surely gets my nod. The food has always been outstanding here and now it is even better. The menu is inventive, and there are great grilled black Angus sirloin steaks to prove it. The innkeepers grow all their own herbs in a lovely herb garden.

I love the desserts. They have great names, and taste equally great. Ish-kabibble is a brownie topped with ice cream and homemade hot fudge. For-gotten Dessert is a meringue with ice cream and strawberries. It's nice to find these old favorites on a menu.

Children of all ages are welcome here. Baby-sitters are available. In July and August a play lady comes in for the four-to-nine set when there are enough children. The playroom offers amusement for kids of all ages, and the playhouse has a supervised play program for youngsters. With the children happily occupied, the living room and library remain free and quiet for you.

This is the place to get away from it all. The views and utter peace are so wonderful, they are hard to describe. Come and enjoy.

HOW TO GET THERE: Greensboro is in the Northeast Kingdom of Vermont, 35 miles northeast of Montpelier. From the south take I–91 to St. Johnsbury and follow U.S. 2 west to West Danville. Continue west on Vermont 15 to the intersection with Vermont 16, about 2 miles east of Hardwick. Turn north on 16 to East Hardwick and follow signs west to Greensboro, at the south end of Caspian Lake. Highland Lodge is at the north end of the lake, on the road to East Craftsbury.

# Three Mountain Inn 📱
## Jamaica, Vermont 05343

INNKEEPERS: Charles and Elaine Murray

ADDRESS/TELEPHONE: Route 30; (802) 874–4140

ROOMS: 16, in 3 different buildings, plus 1 suite and 1 private cottage; all with private bath.

RATES: $150 to $230, double occupancy, MAP; $95 to $175, double occupancy, B&B.

OPEN: All year except April to May 15 and November 1 until December 15.

FACILITIES AND ACTIVITIES: Pub, lounge, swimming pool. Nearby: cross-country skiing, downhill skiing, tennis, golf, fishing, horseback riding.

BUSINESS TRAVEL: Located 30 minutes from Brattleboro. Seminar room with fireplace, fax and audiovisual equipment available, corporate rates for groups.

The inn is well named, since it is within a few minutes of Stratton, Bromley, and Magic mountains. Mount Snow is also within easy range. Skiers should love this location. Cross-country buffs will find a multitude of trails beginning at the inn's doorstep, including a dramatic trail along the long-defunct West River Railroad bed. Tennis is available both indoors and out at nearby Stratton. Horseback riding is superb on lovely trails in the area, or go swimming in the inn's own beautifully landscaped pool.

This small, authentic country inn was built in the 1780s. The living room has a large, roaring fireplace, complete with an original Dutch oven. The floors and walls are of wide, planked pine, and there are plenty of comfortable chairs. A picture window offers views of the Green Mountains to complete the scene.

A cozy lounge and bar area makes you feel very comfortable for sitting back to enjoy good conversation and a before- or after-dinner drink. A good wine selection is at hand.

The rooms are tastefully decorated. One room has a four-poster king-sized bed in it. Another has a private balcony overlooking the swimming pool and garden. A charming Hansel and Gretel cottage is also available. The beds have lovely sheets, and the bathrooms have color-coordinated towels. Perfect for honeymooners, especially since the inn can host small weddings.

The inn was featured several years ago in *Gourmet* magazine, so you can safely guess that the food served in the lovely dining rooms is good—served by candlelight, of course. Dinners are carefully prepared to order, and the menu changes frequently to bring you the most seasonal foods available. Cucumber soup is excellent. They have locally smoked fish, broiled trout, and yummy crisp hash brown potatoes. Strawberry shortcake is always in demand. Elaine also does wonders with berry pies. Be sure to order a piece.

There are guided tours for fly fishermen on the West River and the Battenkill. Write for these package deals, and remember, you will eat what you catch.

Angus, the inn dog, is a nice one.

HOW TO GET THERE: Follow I–91 to Brattleboro and take the second exit to Route 30, to Jamaica.

# Mountain Meadows Lodge 👪
## Killington, Vermont 05751

**INNKEEPER:** Michelle Werle

**ADDRESS/TELEPHONE:** 285 Thundering Brook Road; (802) 775–1010 or (800) 370–4567; fax (802) 773–4459

**WEB SITE:** www.mtmeadowslodge.com

**ROOMS:** 18 rooms, including 2 suites, all with private bath, some with phones and television. 1 handicapped accessible room. No smoking inn.

**RATES:** $142 to $300, double occupancy, MAP; $106 to $250, double occupancy, EBP. Children ages 3 and under stay free, ages 4 to 10 are an additional $10 per night per child, ages 11 and above are an additional $20 a night.

**OPEN:** All year except the end of March to June 15 and mid-October to Thanksgiving.

**FACILITIES AND ACTIVITIES:** Handicapped-accessible dining room; full-license bar. Gameroom, hot tub, pool, sauna; hiking, swimming, boating, fishing, cross-country skiing. Nearby: tennis, alpine slide, downhill skiing.

*T*his inn welcomes families with children. Mountain Meadows Munchkins is the name of their state-licensed program. It introduces children to farm animal care, nature, outdoor activities, and art. A playroom includes games, books, craft supplies, and dress-up clothes for those rainy days. The inn also has a petting zoo.

The Appalachian Trail is close by. Many years ago I met Bear, a mostly red setter who had just come off the trail carrying his own backpack. If you are hiking inn to inn, this is the southernmost inn on the trail and a good place to start.

The inn is very casual and relaxed and overlooks 110 acres of lovely Kent Lake. The lake is stocked with rainbow trout and largemouth bass. You can borrow a fishing pole if you haven't brought one. There are rowboats, canoes, and sailboats for your pleasure, and you can swim in the lake or the inn's pool.

The food served here is delicious. Vegetarians are well taken care of, and us meat and fish people will have plenty to chose from, with items like prime rib, apple and cheddar–stuffed chicken, vegetarian pasta, and all sorts of fish. Salmon in puff pastry comes to mind! Do you enjoy a good breakfast? The inn is famous for its sky-high blueberry griddle cakes.

Children may dine at 5:30 P.M. with other youngsters in the children's

center, and they can select from a special kid's menu. There are also theater nights for children.

Right next door to the inn is the largest ski touring center in the area. The alpine skiing areas at Killington and Pico mountains are but five minutes away.

**HOW TO GET THERE:** The inn is 10 miles east of Rutland, just off Route 4. Follow Route 4 from Rutland for 12 miles, and at Thundering Brook Road you will come to the inn's sign. Turn left. The inn is ¼ mile beyond.

# The Vermont Inn
## Killington, Vermont 05751

**INNKEEPERS:** Megan and Greg Smith

**ADDRESS/TELEPHONE:** Route 4; (802) 775-0708 or (800) 541-7795 (outside Vermont); fax (802) 773-2440

**E-MAIL:** vtinn@aol.com

**WEB SITE:** www.vermontinn.com

**ROOMS:** 18, all with private bath, some with fireplaces; 1 specially equipped for handicapped.

**RATES:** In summer, $45 to $75, per person; in winter, $60 to $110, per person. MAP.

**OPEN:** All year except mid-April to Memorial Day.

**FACILITIES AND ACTIVITIES:** Dinner every day, bar. Wheelchair access to dining room. TV, gameroom, sauna, hot tub (not in summer), pool, tennis, lawn games. Nearby: gondola ride, alpine slide, summer theater, Norman Rockwell Museum, farmers' market, skiing.

*Y*ou may be greeted at the door of this friendly red house by a pair of inn cats, Sunshine and Autumn. Innkeepers Megan and Greg are always here, and a nicer couple you'd have to travel a long way to find. The Vermont Inn is well known locally for the fine food it serves in its lovely dining room. As a matter of fact, three years in a row the restaurant was awarded the Killington Champagne Award for fine dining. To give you an idea of what awaits you: There are six appetizers, including mussels Dijon. There are excellent entrees, with rack of lamb persillé, Delmonico steak au poivre, and Vermont Inn baked stuffed chicken some of the best known. There is a fine wine cellar to enhance the good food, and a special children's menu.

The inn's guests are a mixed bag and include many Canadian visitors. You'll run into young professional people from Boston or New York, a grandparent or two, families—anyone from honeymooners to golden oldies.

The room for handicapped guests has a ramp, a queen-sized bed, a beautiful daybed, a specially equipped bathroom, and air conditioning.

This old house has sturdy underpinnings. Some of the original beams still have the bark on them, and how the rocks of the foundation were ever put in place I cannot imagine. Everything was changed around—the old dining room became a lounge to make the inn cozier—so take advantage of the glorious view of Killington, Pico, and Little Killington, straight ahead across the valley. The bar was handmade locally of Vermont cherry wood, and it's a beauty. Couches and a wood stove make this room a great spot for relaxing. There is also a room that houses a hot tub, exercise machines, and lots of plants, and offers a wonderful view. It's handsome and is ideal for anyone who wants to unwind after a day on the slopes.

HOW TO GET THERE: The inn is 6 miles east of Rutland, on Route 4. It is also 4 miles west of the intersection of Route 4 and Route 100 north (Killington Access Road).

# The Landgrove Inn

## Landgrove, Vermont 05148

**INNKEEPERS:** Jay and Kathy Snyder

**ADDRESS/TELEPHONE:** Weston Road (mailing address: RR 1, Box 215); (802) 824–6673 or (800) 669–8466

**E-MAIL:** vtinn@sover.net

**WEB SITE:** www.innbook.com/land.html

**ROOMS:** 18; 16 with private bath.

**RATES:** $85 to $130, double occupancy, EPB.

**OPEN:** All year except April 1 to May 22 and October 20 to mid-December.

**FACILITIES AND ACTIVITIES:** Dinner, except Monday through Wednesday during the summer. Pool, tennis, stocked pond, ice skating, hiking trails, hay and sleigh rides, bumper pool, Ping-Pong, volleyball, cross-country skiing. Nearby: downhill skiing, alpine slide, summer theaters, and golf.

**RECOMMENDED COUNTRY INNS® TRAVELERS' CLUB BENEFIT:** Complimentary bottle of wine with dinner.

This is a family-run inn that especially welcomes families. Yes, that does mean you can bring your children. They will be well entertained, and so will you. Indoors is a fun gameroom, and outside are playthings, a heated swimming pool, two Plexipave tennis courts, and a volleyball court. A hike through the National Forest is unbelievably scenic, and summer theater is nearby.

Winter means snow, and there is plenty of it. It's only a short hop by car to Bromley, Stratton, Snow Valley, or Okemo. Cross-country skiing begins at the inn's door, or try your skills at snowshoeing or ice skating. After a long day revive yourself in the whirlpool spa, and then enjoy the fireside warmth

in the Rafter Room lounge. As the Snyders say, the lounge's provocatively supine couch is the ideal relaxation! A room near the lounge holds a big-screen television with a VCR.

The architectural style of the inn is peculiar to Vermont, with one building added onto another building. It turns out to be charming. The first part was built in 1810. It has been an inn since 1939. The rooms are spick-and-span, spacious, and very comfortable. The common rooms, dining room, and just everything about this quiet spot are relaxing. And the Snyders, who are cordial and welcoming innkeepers, make you want to return year after year.

The food is excellent. Just a few choices are angel hair pasta with sun-dried tomatoes, basil, artichokes, pine nuts, garlic, olive oil, and goat cheese; a wonderful seafood strudel, consisting of puff pastry filled with shrimp and scallops in a light clam sauce; and beef roulades. Desserts? Well, do save room.

From horse-drawn sleigh rides in winter to the blueberry pancakes, this is a nice place to be—with Chelsie, the inn dog, a beautiful shelty.

**HOW TO GET THERE:** From I–91 use exit 2 and take a left to Route 30 to Bondville. Take a right onto Route 100 to Londonderry, then go left on Route 11 and right on Landgrove Road. Go 4 miles to the inn, on your right.

From Manchester take Route 11 past Bromley Ski Area, and turn left into Peru Village. At the fork in Peru, bear left and continue 4 miles through the National Forest to the crossroads in Landgrove. Turn left toward Weston, and the inn will be on your right.

# The Meadowbrook Inn
Landgrove, Vermont 05418

INNKEEPERS: Tony and Madeline Rondella

ADDRESS/TELEPHONE: RR 1 Box 145, Route 11; (802) 824–6444 or (800) 498–6445; fax (800) 824–4335

E-MAIL: tony@meadowbinn.com

WEB SITE: www.meadowbinn.com

ROOMS: 7, all with private bath, 3 with two-person whirlpool, 4 with fireplace.

**RATES:** $85 to $175, double occupancy, EPB. MAP is available.

**OPEN:** All year except April.

**FACILITIES AND ACTIVITIES:** Full breakfast and dinner, mid-June to end of October and December through March, Wednesday through Saturday. Full license, bar and lounge, 26 kilometers of trails for all seasons, hiking, skiing, cross-country skiing rentals and instructions on the property.

**RECOMMENDED COUNTRY INNS® TRAVELERS' CLUB BENEFIT:** 10 percent discount, Monday–Thursday, excluding holiday weeks.

*N*ice to have this inn back in the book. The new owners changed the name from Nordic to Meadowbrook (for a meadow here on the property), refurbished the old inn, freshened the tavern, and added some comfortable sofas and chairs. The old stone fireplace is still here and wonderful. The bar is also still here. The solarium dining room has had a fireplace added for warmth and romance. And their good food is served in the terrace dining room with the beautiful oak floors. Some food ideas are miso soup and, the chef's selection, grilled shrimp and mozzarella. A few more entrees may be rack of lamb, seared duck breast, or salmon pasta. Breakfast is served in the glass-enclosed solarium, where the views any time of year are awesome.

Landgrove is on the Catamont Trail and near the Long and Appalachian trails; trout streams are in the area. Playhouses and shopping are close by.

The rooms are very lovely. Some have two-person whirlpool tubs and fireplaces; all are nice. Foxglove's iron bed is a beauty.

**HOW TO GET THERE:** The inn is between Bromley and Londonderry on Route 11, 14 miles east of Manchester.

# The Highland House
## Londonderry, Vermont 05148

**INNKEEPERS:** Roger Rice and Mimi Lloyd Rice

**ADDRESS/TELEPHONE:** Route 100; (802) 824–3019

**ROOMS:** 13, plus 4 suites, in 2 buildings; 16 with private bath, 1 specially equipped for handicapped.

**RATES:** $71 to $93, midweek; $81 to $103, weekends; double occupancy, EPB.

**OPEN:** All year except mid-April to mid-May and two weeks in November.

**FACILITIES AND ACTIVITIES:** Dinner Wednesday through Saturday, beer and wine license. Heated swimming pool, all-weather tennis court. Nearby: skiing, fishing, golf, horseback riding.

The Highland House has really grown. In the wonderful addition in the back of the inn, there is a living room with a fireplace that is just lovely. The suites are out here, but no matter where you put your head, you'll have a good night's sleep in this very quiet inn.

The heated swimming pool was built up on a hill. There are great views from here. The tennis court is also a nice addition to the property. The inn's grounds are just beautiful.

There is much to do here, no matter what season of the year you come. Trout fishing, golf, and horseback riding are nearby. Go picnicking and hiking in the Green Mountain National Forest. Weston is close by, and its summer playhouse is fun. Fall foliage is spectacular throughout the area, or you can sit right here and watch  the inn's 150-year-old maples turn color. Winter brings cross-country skiing in the area and downhill skiing at Bromley, Stratton, or Okemo. All are within twenty minutes of the inn.

The dining room is charming, and the food is glorious. Among the appetizers are warm goat cheese salad, butternut squash ravioli, and soups.

Entrees may include crusted trout, roasted game bird, filet mignon, duck Shrewsbury, poached salmon with dill, shrimp Corsica, veal pecan, veal scaloppine, or braised lamb shank. Desserts wow—warm chocolate cake with vanilla ice cream and chocolate sauce, or maybe warm tartlet of apple. Do give this inn a try.

**HOW TO GET THERE:** Take exit 2 from I–91 at Brattleboro. Take Route 30 north to Route 100, and the inn is just north of town on Route 100.

# Rabbit Hill Inn  ♥
## Lower Waterford, Vermont 05848

**INNKEEPERS:** Brian and Leslie Mulcahy

**ADDRESS/TELEPHONE:** Lower Waterford Road; (802) 748–5168 or (800) 76–BUNNY; fax (802) 748–8342

**E-MAIL:** info@rabbithillinn.com

**WEB SITE:** www.rabbithillinn.com

**ROOMS:** 21 rooms: 8 luxury (fireplace and whirlpool tub for two), 4 fireplaced rooms and suites, and 9 classic rooms; all with private bath, radio/cassette player, hair dryer, robes, coffeemaker. 1 room specially equipped for handicapped (wheelchair access to dining rooms). No smoking inn.

**RATES:** $235 to $370, double occupancy, MAP, includes all gratuities. Mid-week, winter rates available.

**OPEN:** All year except first two weeks of April and first two weeks of November.

**FACILITIES AND ACTIVITIES:** Breakfast and dinner served. Bar, gameroom, library, video den. Snowshoeing, sledding, cross-country and downhill skiing, hiking, biking, swimming, and canoeing. Nearby: ice skating, golf. Two quaint towns are within a ten-minute drive.

**BUSINESS TRAVEL:** Access to fax machine and copying services; two guest phone rooms.

*R*abbit Hill Inn is one of the lovingly restored crisp white buildings that make up Vermont's "White Village." This Historic District is one of the state's prettiest and most photographed places.

The inn was built by Samuel Hodby in 1795 as a tavern, general store, and lodging for those traveling between Canada and the ports of Boston and Portland. In 1825 Jonathan Cummings built his home and workshop here (it is now part of the foyer and front dining room). The two properties have operated as one since the 1830s. In the 1930s the inn was renamed the Rabbit Hill Inn for the many rabbit warrens then found on the property. The inn's present owners have preserved the charm of this lovely old inn. And what a job they've done!

Accommodations are grand. Every room or suite has its own enchanting theme. Some of them are the Toy Chamber (inspired by *The Velveteen Rabbit*), the Music Chamber (with a 1857 pump organ and antique victrola), and  Top of the Tavern (a real beauty with a grand four-poster bed, fireplace, and Victorian dressing room). I was in Victoria's Chamber, a lovely room with a king-sized 1850s reproduction bed, empire sofa, and glorious mountain view. A diary is in each room for people to write in during their stay. What fun they are to read! In every room you'll find pretty things, wonderful touches, and a stuffed rabbit sitting on the bed.

The first and second floor porches face the Presidential Range. It is a special place to just sit and rock with Zeke, the inn cat.

Do spend some time in the inviting common rooms. Afternoon tea and pastries are served in the Federal Parlor. The old crane in the fireplace here is still used in the winter for hearth cooking on Saturday afternoons. The Snooty Fox Pub is modeled after Irish pubs of the eighteenth century. Oh boy, what a place! There's also a comfortable library full of books and games to enjoy.

Everything is very nice indeed at the award-winning restaurant. The intimate, candlelit dining rooms feature good Windsor chairs and polished tables set with crystal and fine china.

Five-course gourmet dinners here are a true joy. It takes two hours to dine; it is all done right. The menu changes seasonally and frequently, each time bringing new delights. Everything is prepared from scratch. Try the seared Nantucket scallops or venison and pork pâté to start. Then sample the grilled tenderloin of beef with a maple molasses sauce; roasted chicken breast stuffed with shrimp, basil, and pine nuts; or sautéed monkfish. There are always heart healthy and vegetarian options available. Be sure to savor the homemade sauces, mustards, and salsas prepared with herbs and edible flowers from the inn's garden. Save room for dessert. Chocolate hazelnut cheesecake and espresso crème caramel are a sampling of the goodies you might find.

In the evening while you're dining, your bed is turned down, your radio is tuned to soft music, and your candle is lit. A hand-crafted fabric heart is placed on your doorknob. You are invited to use it as your do-not-disturb sign and then to keep it as a memento of your visit.

You'll wake in the morning to a full candlelit breakfast of homemade granola (not to be missed), fruits, yogurts, juices, and hot entrees. Delicious!

The inn is splendid. So is the pretty little village. You will not be disappointed.

**HOW TO GET THERE:** From I–91 (north or south): exit 19 to I–93 south. Exit 1 onto Route 18 south, 7 miles to inn. From I–93 north: exit 44 onto Route 18 north, 2 miles to inn.

# The Andrie Rose Inn
## Ludlow, Vermont 05149

**INNKEEPERS:** Jack and Ellen Fisher

**ADDRESS/TELEPHONE:** 13 Pleasant Street; (802) 228–4846 or (800) 223–4846; fax (802) 228–7910

**E-MAIL:** andrierose@aol.com

**WEB SITE:** www.members.aol.com/andrierose

**ROOMS:** 9, plus guest house with 11 suites; all with private bath, all suites and 5 rooms with whirlpool tub; steam showers in 2 suites. No smoking inn.

**RATES:** $80 to $280, double occupancy, EPB.

**OPEN:** All year.

**FACILITIES AND ACTIVITIES:** Picnic lunches available, dinner only on Saturday, full liquor license. Meeting facilities, special theme weekends, bicycles. Nearby: skiing.

*A*ndrie Rose was the former owner of this lovely inn, built in 1829. She would be pleased to have her name connected with this very gracious inn.

When you arrive, a personalized welcome card is in your room, highlighting area activities and events. If you are celebrating a special event, you may receive chilled champagne, flowers, or a Vermont specialty product. You can help yourself at any time to the cookies and candies found throughout the inn. In the fall and winter, guests enjoy hot chocolate, cider, tea, or coffee; in the summer lemonade and iced tea are served. Complimentary hors d'oeuvres are served during cocktail hour. All of these are very nice, thoughtful touches.

The front porch is a great place to just relax, have a cocktail, or read a book. A fireplace is in the living room, and games are in the front room. Bombay paddle fans are in all of the common rooms and guest rooms. These are lovely at any time of the year. The innkeepers are always thinking about what will make your stay memorable. Guests can choose "anytime specials," with themes such as a lovers' weekend, which includes roses, candlelight, champagne, and a horse-drawn carriage ride for two.

The rooms are decorated beautifully. Some are done in Laura Ashley prints. Caswell-Massey almond-scented bath accessories are in all the bathrooms. Soft pastel colors are used on the walls, towels, and linens. I found them very restful. There are eleven whirlpool tubs, so nice after a day of skiing. The beds are turned down in the evening, and soft music plays through the stereo system in each room.

On Saturday night a six-course dinner is served, with a choice of three entrees. When I visited here in June, the appetizer was mushroom caps stuffed with crabmeat. The soup was chilled summer fruit medley. The third course was a good salad. The entrees were filet mignon, veal or chicken roulade, and fillet of salmon Dijon, accompanied by vegetables and bread. The desserts are homemade.

My last trip was made during the week, when dinner is not available, so the innkeepers sent me to a nearby restaurant called Cappuccino's at 41 Depot Street. The food was so good. It was a wonderful recommendation.

When you return to your suite for the night, your bed is turned down, a cordial is waiting, soft music is playing, and clean towels and a candle in a glass have been set out. It's beautiful.

Breakfast comes in a basket by your door, ordered the night before. One highlight is broiled grapefruit.

Ludlow is a wonderful town. It is home to Okemo, a very popular downhill ski area. During the rest of the year, the inn has bicycles for your use, so go and have a Vermont adventure. Be sure to take along a picnic lunch.

The entire inn is available for a small business retreat or other function. Murder mystery weekends are offered during the summer and late fall. What great surroundings you'd have! The inn has been awarded AAA's four diamonds for their efforts.

HOW TO GET THERE: From I–91 or Route 131, follow Route 103 west to Ludlow.

# Echo Lake Inn
## Ludlow, Vermont 05149

INNKEEPERS: John and Yvonne Pardieu and Chip Connelly

ADDRESS/TELEPHONE: Route 100 (mailing address: P.O. Box 154); (802) 228–8602 or (800) 356–6844; fax (802) 228–3075

E-MAIL: echolkinn@aol.com

ROOMS: 21; 11 with private bath.

RATES: $60 to $130, double occupancy, EPB. MAP available.

OPEN: Closed first three weeks in April and November.

FACILITIES AND ACTIVITIES: Lunch in-season, dinner, full license. Swimming, tennis, boating, and activities suited to all four seasons.

RECOMMENDED COUNTRY INNS® TRAVELERS' CLUB BENEFIT: Stay two nights, get third night free, subject to availability.

Built in 1840, the Echo Lake Inn is one of the few inns remaining in Vermont that were originally constructed to operate as an inn. This is an authentic "old Colonial inn." But you do not have to worry; it has an automatic fire-alarm system.

There are family suites and deluxe rooms with queen-sized beds and ceiling fans. All the accommodations are comfortable.

The Basketcase Lounge is on the right as you enter the inn. On the left is a nice living room with good chairs, television, and books.

Now for my favorite pastime—food—which I certainly enjoyed in the cozy dining room. The menu changes twice a year, and there are always specials. The daily soup selections are really good. I have some of the recipes so I can make them at home. Among the entrees are grilled sirloin, sautéed fresh rainbow trout, and roast country duckling. I had veal, which was yummy. In July and August a buffet is served in the evening.

Be sure to save room for breakfast. It's yummy, too. A 2-2-2 Scramble is two eggs scrambled with two kinds of cheeses and two herbs. It comes with toast. There's more, of course.

The Stoned Tavern is open in the winter only. It has a fireplace, pool table, Ping-Pong, darts, and video games.

On a warm day you're sure to enjoy the lighted tennis courts, the pool, the steam bath, and the old-fashioned porch with rockers. You must see the chipmunks to believe them. They eat peanuts right from your hand, and one called Stripes will take a peanut from your pocket.

Take a walk and pan for gold. It was found near here years ago. The inn will lend you pans so you can try your luck. There are also boats on the lake, good fishing, secluded waterfalls, golf, skiing, and much more nearby. But if you decide to stay in, there are a six-person Jacuzzi and an exercise bike.

Any season here is beautiful, but the lakes mirror the brilliant colors of fall like nowhere else in New England. Spectacular! Echo is the middle lake of the three-stream, spring-fed Plymouth Lakes.

HOW TO GET THERE: From I–91 take exit 6 to Route 103 to Ludlow. One and a half miles north of Ludlow, turn right on Route 100. The inn is in 3½ miles on the left.

# The Governor's Inn
## Ludlow, Vermont 05149

INNKEEPERS: Charlie and Deedy Marble

ADDRESS/TELEPHONE: 86 Main Street; (802) 228–8830 or (800) GOV–ERNO (468–3766)

WEB SITE: www.vermontlodging.com

ROOMS: 7, plus 1 suite; all with private bath. No smoking inn.

RATES: $190 to $325, double occupancy, MAP.

OPEN: All year.

FACILITIES AND ACTIVITIES: Afternoon tea, picnic hampers available for lunch. Bar. Summer cooking seminars (send for brochure). Nearby: skiing, boating, fishing, golf, historical attractions.

RECOMMENDED COUNTRY INNS® TRAVELERS' CLUB BENEFIT: 10 percent discount, Monday–Thursday, excluding holidays and foliage season.

*D*eedy is the chef, and she really does justice to the title. All the food is prepared each day for that day. She does not buy any prepackaged portion-control-type foods, and there is no microwave oven. Breakfast may feature The Governor's special breakfast puff or Charlie's nearly world-famous rum raisin French toast. In the picnic hamper for lunch, you may find The Governor's braised quail, or cucumber and dill butter sandwiches with Pacific smoked salmon. Sounds so nice and

tastes so great by the side of a bubbling brook or any other spot in this marvelous countryside. On my last visit here, I had a great picnic; it included a sandwich of tenderloin of beef pâté.

Dinner is a grand, six-course affair. I do not care for bluefish, but if I did, I'd surely have it here—it's flambéed with gin! Salads are different. One I like is strawberry chardonnay with champagne. The after-dinner coffees and Victorian tea are also special.

The inn's "Collection of Recipes" includes several that you may find in your picnic basket. *P.M. Magazine* and *Vermont Life* have discovered the inn. It's no wonder, because both Charlie and Deedy are graduates of the Roger Vergé Gourmet Cooking School, and Deedy also attended cooking school in northern Italy.

I think you get the message: The food is excellent.

The dining room where you enjoy this good food has restful blue tablecloths and a beautiful collection of ornate teacups, added to quite often by contented guests. The parlor has a magnificent 1895 marbleized slate corner fireplace, a real work of art. The governor of Vermont who lived here surely had a beautiful home.

Deedy has opened her kitchen and is revealing culinary secrets to small groups of cooking enthusiasts. Wish I lived closer! Chef Deedy is a great teacher and a wonderful chef. Call for the next seminar.

The bedrooms are so attractive, with lovely wallpapers. The beds have all new linen and a flannel top sheet to boot. There's one brass bed that's more than one hundred years old. You will find miniature cordials in your room. There are also welcome gifts, parting gifts, and turndown gifts. Nice touches like this make it no wonder this inn was selected as a *Mobil Travel Guide* four-star accommodation in 1991–92.

The Governor William Wallace Stickney Suite has a living room, a large bedroom with a seating area, a whirlpool bath, a walk-in closet, and a private bathroom. The rooms have ski windows overlooking the village church steeples and Okemo mountain 1 mile away.

Deedy's credo is "warm and generous hospitality." One of her simplest items is on a table in the upstairs hallway: a "butler's basket," full of travelers needs. These are free for the taking and include just about everything. Even a seasoned traveler like myself has dipped into the basket because of leaving something at home. There are about twenty things, ranging from emery boards to antacids.

HOW TO GET THERE: Take exit 6 north from I–91 and follow Route 103 west to Ludlow and the inn.

# The Wildflower Inn

## Lyndonville, Vermont 05851

**INNKEEPERS:** Mary and Jim O'Reilly

**ADDRESS/TELEPHONE:** Darling Hill Road; (802) 626–8310 or (800) 627–8310

**WEB SITE:** www.pbub.com/vermont/wldflwr.htm

**ROOMS:** 12, plus 10 suites; 10 with private bath, 10 with kitchenette, 1 specially equipped for handicapped. No smoking inn.

**RATES:** $95 to $220, double occupancy, EPB.

**OPEN:** All year except April, the last week in October, and the first three weeks in November.

**FACILITIES AND ACTIVITIES:** Dinner. Gift shop, meeting room, heated pool, children's pool, sauna, spa, ice-skating pond, cross-country skiing, petting barn and farm animals, summer children's theater, art gallery.

Here's an inn that makes children feel more than welcome. It has a special children's playroom that comes complete with dress-up clothes and toys for all ages. There are also bumper pool and air hockey, television, and nightly games and a movie.

The inn is situated on its own 500 acres on a ridge overlooking the valley of Vermont's Northeast Kingdom. What a beautiful view it has! You're sure to enjoy roaming over the inn's property, discovering the pond, drinking in the fabulous view, petting the kittens, or walking up the hill to see the Burkland Mansion. Families will enjoy summer performances of the Vermont Children's Theater, which has taken up residence in one of the inn's barns. And in the winter, of course, cross-country skiing and ice skating are right here.

The main inn has four bedrooms with shared baths. The dining rooms are located here. One overlooks the glorious valley. Help yourself at the appetizer buffet while having a cocktail, and then dig into the main entrees, which change daily. Besides a daily special and fresh fish of the day, there are rib-eye steak, chateaubriand for two (a wonderful treat), and more. Black Forest cake and raspberry cheesecake caught my eye for dessert, but there are many more choices.

The carriage house has suites with kitchenettes and lots of beds and is wonderful for families. An old schoolhouse is a bit removed from the inn. It's the honeymoon cottage. More suites are located near the pool—and what a pool it is! It is heated and has a spectacular view. There is also a children's pool out here. The all-purpose room (also with a view) is nice for conferences or meetings. After a day of work or play, relax in the delightful sauna and spa.

**HOW TO GET THERE:** Take exit 23 off I–91 in Lyndonville. Go north through town on Route 5 to Route 114. Follow Route 114 for ½ mile. Darling Hill Road is a left turn immediately after the second bridge you cross. The inn is in 2 miles.

# The Inn at Manchester
Manchester, Vermont 05254

**INNKEEPERS:** Harriet and Stan Rosenberg and daughter Amy

**ADDRESS/TELEPHONE:** Route 7A; (802) 362–1793 or (800) 273–1793

**E-MAIL:** iman@vtweb.com

**WEB** www.vtweb.com

**ROOMS:** 14, plus 4 suites; all with private bath; 2 suites with fireplace and air conditioning.

**RATES:** $95 to $130, double occupancy, EPB.

**OPEN:** All year.

**FACILITIES AND ACTIVITIES:** Beer and wine license. Swimming pool. Full country breakfast and afternoon tea. Nearby: skiing, golf, tennis, theater, shopping outlets.

**RECOMMENDED COUNTRY INNS® TRAVELERS' CLUB BENEFIT:** Stay two nights, get third night free, Monday–Thursday, subject to availability.

*L*ush greenery in the bay window of the living room is the sight that greets you when you walk in the front door of this inn. The many fireplaces surrounded by restful sitting areas, the numerous good antiques, and the dining room with Tiffany lamps add up to a warm country inn atmosphere. The antique Champion oak stove is the focal point in the gameroom, which is an ideal spot to unwind after a day on the ski slopes. Here you can watch television or play games or cards at a card table. A good library is also in here.

The guest rooms are spotless and so very nice. Sheets, comforters, dust ruffles, and towels are color coordinated, and the beds are perfect for a good night's sleep. The carriage house is luscious. Each room has its own private bath and is individually decorated with coordinating sheets, comforters, towels, and antiques. There are Tiffany-style lamps, queen-sized beds, cast-iron and brass beds, and a beauty in cherry. Attractive artwork hangs throughout. All very nice indeed. The inn is not well suited to children under eight.

The food is homemade, even the breads. The homemade granola and apple pancakes with local maple syrup can start anyone's day right. Meals are served family-style. The menu changes daily and beer and wine are available.

The inn is conveniently located in the heart of just about everything, with skiing, downhill and cross-country, only minutes away. Summer brings great antiquing, summer theater, specialty craft shops, and boutiques. Golf and tennis are within walking distance of the front door, and the swimming pool is in a lovely meadow between the carriage house and the creek.

**HOW TO GET THERE:** The inn is approximately 22 miles north of Bennington, Vermont, on Route 7A. It is on the left.

# The Inn at Ormsby Hill
## Manchester Center, Vermont 05255

**INNKEEPERS:** Chris and Ted Sprague

**ADDRESS/TELEPHONE:** Historic Route 7A (mailing address: 1842 Main Street); (802) 362–1163 or (800) 670–2841; fax (802) 362–5176

**ROOMS:** 10; all with private bath, air conditioning, double whirlpool tub, fireplace, phones, and robes.

**RATES:** $160 to $290, double occupancy, EPB.

**OPEN:** All year.

**FACILITIES AND ACTIVITIES:** Friday-night supper, Saturday dinner by reservation only, BYOB. Hammock, porch. Nearby: golf, bicycling, antiquing, fishing, tennis, hiking, downhill and cross-country skiing.

**RECOMMENDED COUNTRY INNS® TRAVELERS' CLUB BENEFIT:** Stay three or more nights in one of the fireplace and Jacuzzi rooms and receive a $50 gift certificate for dinner at a local restaurant, which may be redeemed Sunday–Thursday, excluding foliage season and holiday weeks.

*I*t's nice to have good innkeepers back in business. Chris and Ted had a beauty in Maine, but this inn far surpasses that one. When you enter the inn, the first room on the left is a beautifully furnished formal living room. Go on into the gathering room, which has a huge fireplace, games, and books. Continue into the conservatory–dining room. It's a wow. When the inn is full, three tables are in use. There's a really different-looking fireplace in here. The mantel came from either Europe or Newport. It's a beauty. The glass windows at the end of the room remind me of a ship, and Chris has nice plants all around.

The view of the mountains is awesome. There's an apple checkerboard at the ready.

The inn was built around 1760 and added onto in the 1800s. The new wing was constructed in 1996. You cannot tell where the old and new meet. Innkeepers are clever people. The rooms are just beautiful. Almost all have two-person whirlpool baths and fireplaces, either gas or wood. The beds are kings and queens and so comfortable. There are four-posters and canopies. Everything is restful, and the colors are muted. The towels are big and fluffy. The inn reminds me of a gracious manor house in the English countryside and it has a full sprinkler system and alarms.

The tower room is the latest addition, and it's a dream. There are some steps, so be prepared (but it's worth every step). Up seven steps from the second floor to a queen-sized canopy bed, a gas fireplace, and lots of windows. Up a few more to an unbelievable bathroom with a Jacuzzi for two as well as a two-person shower/steam shower and more windows. Wow.

Breakfast is the main meal here, but Chris serves supper on Friday nights and a four-course dinner on Saturdays. I was lucky enough to be here then, and we had risotto with asparagus, porcini, and basil for the first course. This was followed by a garden salad with champagne vinaigrette and cream biscuits. The next course was peppered fresh tuna on top of garlic spinach with a shallot sauce. Dessert was a bittersweet chocolate soufflé with white chocolate and rum sauce. This is just a sample of Chris's spectacular food.

At breakfast time Chris makes breakfast desserts. Honest. I had one. Try the espresso coffee cake, cantaloupe with honey sauce, individual baked pancakes, and much more.

**HOW TO GET THERE:** From Route 30 go north to Historic Route 7A in Manchester. Turn left. Go south about 3 miles to the inn.

# The Reluctant Panther 📱
## Manchester Village, Vermont 05254

**INNKEEPERS:** Maye and Robert Bachofen

**ADDRESS/TELEPHONE:** West Road and Route 7A (mailing address: P.O. Box 678); (802) 362–2568 or (800) 822–2331; fax (802) 362–2586

**E-MAIL:** panther@sover.net

**WEB SITE:** www.reluctantpanther.com

**ROOMS:** 12, plus 5 suites; all with private bath, TV, air conditioning, and phone; 10 with fireplace, 5 with Jacuzzi, 1 specially equipped for handicapped. No smoking inn.

**RATES:** $185 to $375, double occupancy, MAP. Inquire about packages and EPB rates.

**OPEN:** All year.

**FACILITIES AND ACTIVITIES:** Dinner on weekends and holidays only from November through May, daily during rest of the year. Bar, lounge, florist. Nearby: golf, tennis, hiking, skiing, American Museum of Fly Fishing, health club.

**BUSINESS TRAVEL:** Phones in all rooms, desks in some; conference room; fax and audiovisual equipment available; midweek corporate rates.

*T*he inn is mauve on the outside, and a good bit of lavender and wine colors are inside. These are colors I love, and, believe me, the inn is hard to miss with its yellow shutters. There are marble sidewalks and beautifully manicured gardens and lawns.

Accommodations here are grand. The rooms are beautifully decorated, and all have a private bath. The suites have a whirlpool tub. All of the beds, no matter the size, are comfortable. I saw a wonderful king-sized brass bed. The goose-down quilts are heaven. Some of the rooms and all of the suites have a fireplace. There is nothing more restful than a crackling fire in your own fireplace. One suite in the Mary Porter House even has a fireplace in the bathroom. Wherever you stay, you'll find a split of Robert Mondavi wine in your room for you to enjoy.

Robert is a Swiss-trained hotelier and former food and beverage director for the Plaza Hotel in New York. He was born and educated in Switzerland, and he is the chef of the inn's restaurant. His menu is a fine blend of European and American specialties. The greenhouse extension of the  dining room is a spectacular setting for Robert's creations. His dinners begin with appetizers such as carpacchio of beef with fresh horseradish and olive oil, or cream of leeks and potato soup. Of course there are more. Some of the tempting entrees are Swiss veal—thinly sliced veal with mushrooms and white wine. Grilled flank steak marinated in dark beer and honey also

# The Jelly Mill . . . & Friends

On Historic Route 7A, you can visit the restored four-story dairy barn called the Jelly Mill. This barn, the brick home next door, and the surrounding acreage were once home to Loveland Munson, former Chief Justice of the Vermont Supreme Court. The barn now houses a wonderful country store that had its beginnings in an old cider jelly mill and later moved here. The proprietors still sell cider jelly plus eighty-eight other flavors of jellies, jams, and preserves. Along with these goodies you'll find jelly beans, chocolates, and Vermont maple sugar products and cheeses. Also here are "the Friends"—other businesses that sell country furnishings and accessories, jewelry, Christmas collectibles, handblown glass, pottery, handcrafted teddy bears, toys, and doll furniture, and much more. The Buttery Restaurant serves breakfast and lunch daily from 10:00 A.M. to 3:00 P.M. The rest of the Jelly Mill is open from 10:00 A.M. to 6:00 P.M. daily, except for New Year's Day, Easter, Thanksgiving, and Christmas Day.

sounds grand, as does roasted rack of lamb with minted béarnaise, Long Island duckling with raspberry-rhubarb sauce and sun-dried tomato. The wine list is extensive and very good. The dining room is nonsmoking, but smoking is permitted in the lounge.

The tavern is cozy, with a few bar stools, chairs, fireplace, and the sort of good company that is found only in a country inn.

Guests at The Reluctant Panther have spa privileges at the nearby spa and health club.

The new handicapped suite is a real winner; others, of course, may reserve it.

HOW TO GET THERE: As you approach Manchester Village from the south on Route 7A, keep an eye on the left. Soon The Reluctant Panther will pop into view.

# The Village Country Inn 💟

## Manchester Village, Vermont 05254

**INNKEEPERS:** Jay and Anne Degen

**ADDRESS/TELEPHONE:** Route 7A (mailing address: P.O. Box 408, Manchester); (802) 362–1792 or (800) 370–0300; fax (802) 362–7238

**E-MAIL:** vci@vermontel.com

**WEB SITE:** www.villagecountryinn.com

**ROOMS:** 12 standard rooms, plus 21 luxury rooms and suites; all with private bath, phone, and air conditioning; some with TV; 4 with fireplaces. No smoking inn.

**RATES:** $160 to $300, per room, double occupancy, MAP. Special packages available.

**OPEN:** All year.

**FACILITIES AND ACTIVITIES:** Bar-lounge, boutique, swimming pool, tennis, ice skating. Nearby: golf, skiing, shopping.

Manchester's favorite front porch beckons you as you arrive at The Village Country Inn, located in the heart of town. The porch is 100 feet long, with wicker furniture and rockers covered with rose chintz and full of pink flowers all summer long. It's the icing on this beautiful inn.

This is a French country inn, done in shades of mauve, celery, and ecru and stunning inside and out. Anne was a professional interior decorator, and the inn reflects her expertise. Mauve is a color I adore. The boutique is The French Rabbit, with well-dressed rabbits to greet you. Anne has wonderful taste, and the boutique is full of very nice things.

Tavern in the Green, the bar and lounge, has an upright piano and nice people who play and sing. One night when I stayed here, a playwright was in this room with a marvelous selection of music and songs. What an unexpected treat! A door from here leads out to the swimming pool and gardens. During the winter the large patio is flooded for ice skating. The inn has a large collection of skates for guests to use, and twinkling lights are hung in the trees all around the patio. In the summertime breakfast and dinner may be served out here.

There is a large fieldstone fireplace dating back to 1889 in the living room, with comfortable couches and chairs around it. Tables are provided for all sorts of games.

The rooms are magnificent, and each one is different. They are done in ice cream colors. Lots of canopied beds, lace, plush carpets, down pillows, and

nice things on dressers and tables give the rooms an elegant atmosphere. Good towels are such an important feature to inn guests and, needless to say, they are here.

There's a new suite called Chantel's Boudoir, and I was in it. Done in soft greens, the king-sized bed is a beauty. There's also a fireplace, television, phone, chaise lounge, and couch. I could live in here.

Victoria's Room has a queen-sized bed with a lovely spread, a gas fireplace, a chaise lounge, air conditioning, a television, phone, and a two-person soaking tub in a lovely large bathroom. It all overlooks the pool area.

Dining is a joy in the lovely dining room. The bishop-sleeve lace curtains and trellis alcoves create a cozy and romantic atmosphere for the glorious food. Chilled tomato bisque with dill is excellent. Salads aren't run-of-the-mill, and entrees are creative. Grilled loin of lamb with rosemary and juniper sauce, and medallions of veal with wild mushrooms, shallots, and Madeira in a natural veal sauce are just two of the selections. Vermont lamb chops with black currant cassis and almonds are a house favorite. I chose crème brûlée for dessert. It was grand. Freshly made bread pudding with apples and hazelnuts captivated my dinner companion. Very good indeed. Breakfast is a full one, with many choices.

Affairs of the heart are wonderful up here. Rekindle the romance by having an "Enchanted Evening," an affair for the "too busy" and "too stressed." As the inn literature notes, this "intimate dinner affair is perfect for those of you who: go out to dinner a lot, cook at home a lot, need a break, are looking for a good time and romance." Also offered is the "Blooming Affair," a romantic champagne picnic lunch in the lovely gazebo and formal gardens. These affairs are offered spring, summer, and winter. Christmas, as you can imagine, is very special up here.

**HOW TO GET THERE:** Coming north on historic Route 7A, you will find the inn on your left in Manchester Village.

# Wilburton Inn ♥
## Manchester Village, Vermont 05254

**INNKEEPERS:** Stanley Holton; Georgette and Albert Levis, owners

**ADDRESS/TELEPHONE:** River Road (mailing address: P.O. Box 468); (802) 362–2500 or (800) 648–4944

**WEB SITE:** www.wilburton.com

**ROOMS:** 11 in main house, 24 in other 5 houses; all with private bath.

**RATES:** $105 to $215, double occupancy, EPB (includes full breakfast mid-May through October and holidays). MAP rates available.

**OPEN:** All year.

**FACILITIES AND ACTIVITIES:** Breakfast, dinner. Tennis, heated pool, sculpture garden. Nearby: skiing, shopping, art gallery, theater, music festivals, swimming, canoeing, trout fishing, golf.

This inn was built in 1902 for a friend of Robert Todd Lincoln. In 1906 James Wilbur purchased the estate and lived here until his death in 1929. Later, during World War II, it was a boarding school for daughters of European diplomats. In 1946 the estate became a very elegant inn, and in 1987 Georgette and Albert became the new owners. The inn is set on a twenty-acre knoll that rises above the lush Battenkill River Valley.

When you enter the inn, you are in a large living room with couches and chairs, a huge table for serving tea, and a wonderful fireplace with a wood-burning stove. A library and a porch where breakfast is served are also on the ground floor, along with the dining rooms.

The food here is glorious. For starters I was able to try the vegetarian ravioli with a tomato-sage cream sauce. On another night the gravlax was ambrosia, as were the rack of lamb and the salmon, sweet potato crusted with raspberry gastrique. Very different. Salads are excellent, and the desserts—well, you'd better come up here and see for yourself. Breakfast? Usually I could turn it down, but not when it's this grand.  Fresh blueberry muffins and, of course, much, much more. The menus change twice yearly, and specials abound. The pink-and-white napery add to the pretty ambience.

Accommodations in the main inn are luxurious. Most beds are queen- or king-sized, with lovely bedspreads. Wonderful large windows provide a view of the surrounding mountains. Five other houses on the estate are just as well appointed and so nice for families, wedding parties, or corporate meetings.

After a day of whatever you do, return to the inn for tea or cocktails in the living room by the fireplace. This is a grand inn, watched over by Chauncy, the inn's beautiful English setter.

HOW TO GET THERE: From the blinking light in Manchester, go 1½ miles south on Route 7A to River Road. Go left for 1 mile—the driveway is on the left.

# Red Clover Inn
## Mendon, Vermont 05701

INNKEEPERS: Sue and Harris Zukerman

ADDRESS/TELEPHONE: Woodward Road (mailing address: P.O. Box 7450); (802) 775-2290 or (800) 752-0571

E-MAIL: redclovr@vermontel.com

WEB SITE: www.redcloverinn.com

ROOMS: 14 in inn and carriage house; all with private bath, 6 with fireplace and 5 with whirlpool tub. TV in some rooms. No smoking inn.

RATES: $150 to $375, double occupancy, MAP. Packages available.

OPEN: All year except mid-April to mid-May.

FACILITIES AND ACTIVITIES: Dinner every night except Sunday. Pub. Nearby: skiing at Killington and Pico, shopping, lakes, hiking, golf.

RECOMMENDED COUNTRY INNS® TRAVELERS' CLUB BENEFIT: 10 percent discount, Monday–Thursday.

*B*uilt as a summer estate for General John Woodward of Washington, D.C., the inn is nicely tucked off the main road, about 5 miles east of Rutland. All you hear are the sounds of nature.

The inn is very comfortable. The living room has cozy chairs and couches. This is also the library. Curl up in front of the fire with a good book or a friend. Adjacent to the living room is the pub, which will provide you with your favorite drink. The guest rooms are nicely appointed and restful—just what you expect in a good inn.

The dining rooms are lovely, and the food is just glorious. The chef has a good background, and his menu changes daily. There are fine soups and appetizers like broccoli and gorgonzola cream soup. Roasted tomato, garlic, and garden basil soup is a real winner. Medallions of beef, fettucine, vegetarian pasta, sautéed duck breast, pork tenderloin, and venison are sometimes served as the entrees. Save room, everyone; the desserts are all homemade.

Sue's license plate says Sue's Zoo. Well, there are Hoadie, a very friendly English bulldog, and Gruffy, the horse who belongs to the Zukermans' daughter. There's a saying about Gruffy: "have carrot, will nuzzle." You will also find a sheep and a cat named Dink. Quite a zoo.

The area offers a lot to do. Killington and Pico are nearby for skiing, or you can go hiking, golfing, swimming or fishing in nearby lakes, and shopping. Do go and have a great time. They have won the *Wine Spectator*'s award of excellence since 1995, and they have a grand wine cellar.

**HOW TO GET THERE:** Take Route 4 east from Rutland. The inn is on the right, down narrow Woodward Road.

# Middlebury Inn
## Middlebury, Vermont 05753

**INNKEEPERS:** Frank and Jane Emanuel

**ADDRESS/TELEPHONE:** Route 7; (802) 388–4961 or (800) 842–4666; fax (802) 388–4563

**E-MAIL:** midinnvt@sover.net

**ROOMS:** 73, including 6 suites; all with private bath, air conditioning, cable TV, and phone; 3 specially equipped for handicapped.

**RATES:** $95 to $170, rooms; $134 to $270, suites; double occupancy, EP. Package rates available. EPB available.

**OPEN:** All year.

**FACILITIES AND ACTIVITIES:** Breakfast, lunch, afternoon tea, dinner, bar. Wheelchair access to dining rooms and all public areas. Parking, elevator, gift shop. Nearby: skiing, swimming, golf, fishing, boating, museums.

**RECOMMENDED COUNTRY INNS® TRAVELERS' CLUB BENEFIT:** 10 percent discount, Monday–Thursday, subject to availability.

here has been an inn standing at this same location since 1788. There have been some changes, due to fire and the inroads of time, but the current brick building, known as the Addison House, was constructed in 1827. One hundred years later, when the Middlebury Hotel Company took over, extensive repairs were made, and in 1977 Frank and Jane Emanuel became the innkeepers. Their efforts to restore the inn to its former elegance have been aided by a grant from the Vermont Historic Preservation Division.

The inn has an excellent central location in the delightful town where Middlebury College is situated. There are many historic buildings, museums, and shops to visit in the town, and all around is an abundance of outdoor activities.

The Addison House has a delightful veranda and a really large lobby. The dining room is beautiful, and the food that is served here is delicious. The elegant candlelit buffets shouldn't be missed, from the served appetizer and sherbet courses to the finishing touch of a fingerbowl. Summer dining on the porch is a special delight. The Morgan Room Tavern and Terrace offers excellent liquid refreshment, including the inn's own Candied Apple. Upstairs, the wide halls wander and dip, up one step and down three, wide enough for those ladies of long ago to have maneuvered their hoopskirts with grace.

Additional rooms are in adjacent buildings or wings off the original building. The Jonathan Carver Wing was constructed in 1897, and the Thomas Hagar House, which was built in 1816, is now attached to the Addison House. The Porter Mansion, built in 1825, has five handsome guest rooms, several fireplaces of rare black marble, and a lovely curving staircase in the front parlor. More contemporary-style rooms are found in the Governor Weeks House and the Emma Willard House. The East Wing has been completely and beautifully refurbished.

Whatever type of room you need, you'll find a wide variety of good choices here.

I could stay forever, mooning over the jigsaw puzzle in the lobby or eating their nightly popovers.

**HOW TO GET THERE:** Go up Route 7, and you will run right into Middlebury. The inn is in the middle of town, overlooking the town green.

# Swift House Inn
## Middlebury, Vermont 05753

**INNKEEPER:** Karla Nelson Loura

**ADDRESS/TELEPHONE:** 25 Stewart Lane; (802) 388–2766;
fax (802) 388–9927

**ROOMS:** 21; all with private bath, air conditioning, and phone, some
with cable TV, working fireplace, or wheelchair accessibility. One room
specially equipped for handicapped.

**RATES:** $90 to $185, double occupancy, continental breakfast.

**OPEN:** All year.

**FACILITIES AND ACTIVITIES:** Full breakfast, dinner. Wheelchair access
to dining room. Sauna, steam room. Nearby: downhill and cross-
country skiing, hiking, fishing, golf.

he Swift House Inn consists of three grand buildings. There is the
carriage house, where I stayed in a glorious room with its own
patio, cable television, and fireplace. It is so nice to find terrycloth
robes and hair dryers in your own bathroom. The steam room and sauna are
in the carriage house. The gatehouse is down the hill, and the main house
has lovely rooms, individually decorated with handmade quilts and four-
poster beds. The room with facilities for a handicapped guest has a gas fireplace, a king-sized bed, and a
sleep sofa. An old elevator
up to this room is home to a
stuffed parrot.

The living rooms have
fireplaces and very comfortable chairs and couches.
Many guests like to spend
some time unwinding here
before going in to dinner.

The dining rooms have Queen Anne and Chippendale chairs. On the
extensive menu, you might find curried lamb soup with couscous; Norwegian smoked salmon wrapped around asparagus mousse; Wylie Hill pheasant with hazelnuts, herbs, and white wine; or steamed mussels, scallops, and
tiger shrimp in garlic, white wine, and herbs. The list goes on. Everything is
cooked to order. There are excellent wines by the glass. For dessert try the
crème brûlée or or the dark chocolate terrine with a tart raspberry sauce. Oh,

it's so hard to make choices! Wonderful coffees, even one called Fuzzy Navel, are served.

The complimentary continental breakfast is grand, but you can also order other wonderful things to eat—French bread, French toast, griddle cakes, eggs, and create-your-own omelets from a huge selection. There really is much more—what a way to start the day!

The grounds, quite glorious with their lovely flowers, are nice to wander on after your marvelous dinner. This inn is on the must-go-and-visit list. AAA must agree—it awarded the inn and restaurant four diamonds.

HOW TO GET THERE: Take Route 7 to Middlebury. The inn is 2 blocks north of the center of town on the corner of Route 7 and Stewart Lane.

# Zack's on the Rocks ♥
## Montgomery Center, Vermont 05471

INNKEEPERS: "Zack" and Gussie Zachadnyk

ADDRESS/TELEPHONE: Route 58; (802) 326-4500

ROOMS: 1 housekeeping cottage for two.

RATES: $100 per night, double occupancy, EP.

OPEN: All year except Mondays and Christmas Day.

FACILITIES AND ACTIVITIES: Dinner by reservation only, bar. Wheelchair access to the dining room.

*A*fter you finally find Zack's, you really will not believe what you see. His cottage home and restaurant are literally hanging on the rocks over an incredible valley.

This is my smallest inn. A cottage that sleeps two has a living room, a dining ell, a kitchen, two fireplaces, a bedroom, and a wow of a bathroom with a sunken tub. Even if you cannot stay here, stay in town and come up here to eat Zack's food. It is fantastic, and so are he and Gussie, his wife.

Zack's is so unique that it is almost impossible to describe. When you approach the door of his restaurant, you will find it is locked. Ring the sleigh bells, and the door will be opened by Zack. He will be in a wondrous costume, and the performance will begin. I will tell you no more except about the food. The menu is printed on a brown paper bag, which is in beautiful contrast to his restaurant and Gussie's bar. Zack does all of the cooking. He is the most inventive chef and innkeeper I have had the pleasure to meet. The dining room has to be seen to be believed.

And Gussie's bar is something special. It has an organ with a full grand piano top built over it. This is my first organ bar. The room has a stone fireplace and is done pub-style but with flair. The bar has five stools, but to go

## Jay Country Store

Just north of Montgomery Village on Route 242 in Jay is the Jay Country Store (802–988–4040), the perfect place to go for a taste of the real Vermont. "Sustenance for both body and spirit" is what they say you'll find here—and they are right. It's just fabulous, a destination in itself, filled to the brim with everything Vermont—handmade quilts, hand-forged lamps, gallery-quality primitives, trunks, and boxes, cookbooks by Vermont authors, wonderful hand-painted pottery, lead-free ceramics, and tons more. Two levels of art galleries include lots of American folk art, including the largest selection anywhere of limited edition lithographs by Will Moses, great-grandson of Grandma Moses. Also here are limited edition prints by a famed New York naturalist and lithographer—come spend the afternoon and see for yourself.

Don't be afraid to come in hungry. The store also has a terrific deli counter and lunch room where you can feast on an old-fashioned country-style sandwich, a steaming bowl of homemade chili or soup, crispy pickles, and Green Mountain coffee. Fine wines, Vermont cheeses, honey, maple syrup, and a full line of groceries and baked goods are also here. The Christmas World shop includes decorations and ornaments from around the world as well as some handcrafted by local artisans. I've probably left out a whole other list of the things they carry—come to discover whatever I left out. They are open from 8:30 A.M. to 7:00 P.M. (and until 9:00 P.M on Friday) every day of the year except Christmas and Thanksgiving. Say hello to owners Peggy and Art Moran.

with it is the best-stocked back bar in Vermont. To top it all, the inn plays music from the forties. What a pleasant sound!

Pyewacket is the name of both of the inn cats.

Zack's cottage is called Fore-the-Rocks. The private home is called Off-the-Rocks, and the inn is called On-the-Rocks. Gussie's bar is After-the-Rocks. Lots of rocks up here. Some of them are even purple.

Reservations here are an absolute must.

HOW TO GET THERE: Going north from Stowe on Route 100, turn left on Route 118 at Eden. When you reach Montgomery Center, turn right on Route 58. The inn is up the hill on the left, after the road becomes dirt.

# Black Lantern Inn
## Montgomery Village, Vermont 05470

INNKEEPERS: Rita and Allan Kalsmith

ADDRESS/TELEPHONE: Route 118; (802) 326-4507 or (800) 255-8661; fax (802) 326-4077

ROOMS: 10, plus 6 suites; all with private bath, fireplace, whirlpool tub, and TV.

RATES: $85 to $145, per person, double occupancy, EPB. MAP is available.

OPEN: All year.

FACILITIES AND ACTIVITIES: Taproom, bar, cross-country skiing. Nearby: downhill skiing, fishing, swimming, golf, tennis, bicycle rentals. Breakfast and dinner.

RECOMMENDED COUNTRY INNS® TRAVELERS' CLUB BENEFIT: 10 percent discount, subject to availability.

When you get to Montgomery Village, you are nearly in Canada, perhaps 6 or 7 miles from the border. This is a quiet Vermont village, and the Black Lantern has been nicely restored by its hardworking owners. Whether you come in the snow for a skiing vacation or on a green summer day, there is a warm welcome at this friendly inn. It is also surprising to encounter a rather sophisticated menu in this out-of-the-way corner of the world—French onion soup, stuffed mushrooms, and entrees like lamb Marguerite, Drunken Bird, veal cavalier, salmon steak, and much more.

You can ski at Jay Peak, where there are 50 miles of trails for every kind of skier, outright novice to expert. Not too far away, over the border, there are four Canadian mountains, and ski-week tickets are available. Cross-country skiing starts at the inn door and is undoubtedly the best way to see beautiful Vermont in the winter.

Summer brings the joy of outdoor life. Fishing, swimming, golf, tennis, and hiking are all very near. You've heard about those country auctions, haven't you? Or would you rather spend  the day browsing through antiques shops? Whatever you choose to do, there will be a superbly quiet night to catch up on your sleep. The inn's guest accommodations are very comfortable, and the three-room suite is a joy. It has a fireplace and a whirlpool tub. This is heaven. The Burdett House next door has more suites, all of which have a fireplace, a whirlpool tub, and a television with VCR. Some of these suites have a balcony. There is also a nice and bright lounge area.

The bar was the front desk in a hotel in Ohio—now that's recycled furniture.

The double-peaked roof on the old, 1803 farmhouse covers a typical north-country inn. Small, friendly, just a little bit different, and well enjoyed by Nellie, the inn's springer spaniel.

HOW TO GET THERE: Go north from Stowe on Route 100 and turn left on Route 118 at Eden. This will take you into Montgomery Center. Continue down the main street and out of town, and before too long you will reach Montgomery Village and the inn. From I–89 in Burlington turn right at St. Albans onto Route 105, toward Enosburg Falls. Pick up Route 118 at East Berkshire and follow it to Montgomery Village and the inn.

# The Four Columns Inn
## Newfane, Vermont 05345

**INNKEEPERS:** Gorty and Pam Baldwin

**ADDRESS/TELEPHONE:** West Street (mailing address: P.O. Box 278); (802) 365–7713

**ROOMS:** 10, plus 5 suites; all with private bath and air conditioning, 7 with gas fireplace. No smoking inn.

**RATES:** $110 to $195, double occupancy, EPB. MAP $210 to $295, double occupancy.

**OPEN:** All year.

**FACILITIES AND ACTIVITIES:** Restaurant closed Tuesdays. Wheelchair access to dining room and bar. Bar, swimming pool. Nearby: hiking, ice skating, skiing.

The inn is located on the most photographed town common in Vermont. The area is just beautiful, and so is the inn. New innkeepers Gorty and Pam are truly marvelous, with a friendly staff and a nice dog named Jack.

The rooms are full of antiques. One lovely room has a brass bed. Another room has a canopy bed with a lace top, and four-poster beds are in others. Fresh flowers and plants in your room are a wonderful touch. Big towels and good pillows and mattresses; all these things make up a fine inn. The third-floor suite has a lovely porch with wicker furniture facing the common. A nice place to sit and watch the world go by.

The inn has an attractive living room with a fireplace where you can gather to visit with other guests, read, watch television, or just relax. The dining room with a fireplace has pale green and pink napery. A beautiful armoire is used to display the superb wines served here.

The inn was given three well-deserved stars in the Mobil Travel Guide for its food and rooms and a four-diamond rating from AAA for its restaurant.

Chef Gregory was a protégé of the former owner, who was a fine chef himself, and he stayed on with Gorty. He is inventive and loves to use local fare. He buys Vermont-raised milk-fed veal and does his own butchering. I've had the veal here, and it is heavenly. One of the chef's appetizers is quail marinated in olive oil, hot peppers, and lemon, then grilled and served with creamy polenta and mushrooms. There's a soup of leek and onion with herb biscuits, another made of wild mushrooms. Oh my! One dinner offering is shrimp, littlenecks, and calamari cooked in tomato sauce, jalapeño, and tequila. Another is boneless breast of chicken with ginger, fermented black beans, vermouth, and cream. And the rest of the menu is glorious—the desserts are outstanding. Breakfasts may include fresh fruit with a dipping sauce, flaky croissants, granola, and more.

The lounge has a pewter bar, which is very unusual, lots of plants, and more country charm than you can shake a stick at. Do I like it here? Just wish I lived closer!

Outside is a lovely swimming pool. And down at the stream is a hammock waiting for you. The trout pond is stocked. Try your luck or let the staff catch you one. Can't get them much fresher than this.

**HOW TO GET THERE:** The inn is 220 miles from New York and 100 miles from Boston. Take exit 2 from I–91 at Brattleboro to Route 30 north. The inn is in Newfane, 100 yards off Route 30, on your left.

# Old Newfane Inn
Newfane, Vermont 05345

**INNKEEPERS:** Eric and Gundy Weindl

**ADDRESS/TELEPHONE:** Court Street; (802) 365–4427 or (800) 784–4427 (Vermont only)

**ROOMS:** 10; 8 with private bath.

**RATES:** Rooms, $105 to $115; suites, $135 to $155; double occupancy, continental breakfast. No credit cards.

**OPEN:** All year except April to mid-May, late October to mid-December, and Mondays.

**FACILITIES AND ACTIVITIES:** Dinner, bar. Parking. Nearby: skiing, swimming, hiking.

*T*he inn is well named, for old it is—1787, to be exact. It has been carefully kept, however, and the weary traveler will find great comfort and fabulous food.

Almost all the rooms have twin beds. The rooms are large and tastefully furnished. Gundy is a very good decorator. There is an informal bar and lounge, and the dining room has tables with pink cloths over white ones. Very effective. There is a huge brick wall with a fireplace in the dining room that gives a wonderful feeling of warmth and good cheer. The floors here are polished to a turn and beyond. And not just run-of-the-mill glassware for the inn. The drinks I had before lunch were served in crystal.

Eric is a fine chef. His soups are a bit different and very good. I have tried both the cold strawberry and the creamed watercress. Loved them both. By the way, I hate calf's liver, but Eric asked me to try his. What magic he performed I do not know, but I ate every bite. Veal is king here. Eric butchers his own, so he gets the exact cuts he wants. Of course, the menu also has seafood, lamb, fowl, pheasant, venison, and fine steaks. The dessert menu reads like poetry, from the flaming suzette and jubilee to a fabulous omelet surprise. There are also some cream pies that demand that you do not even think of calories.

**HOW TO GET THERE**: Take exit 2 from I–91 in Brattleboro, and follow Route 30 north. The inn is on the corner of Court Street and Route 30, on the left in Newfane.

# North Hero House
## North Hero, Vermont 05474

**INNKEEPER**: Derek Roberts

**ADDRESS/TELEPHONE**: Route 2 (mailing address: P.O. Box 106); (802) 372–4732 or (888) LAKENH; fax (802) 372–3218

**E-MAIL**: NHHLAKE@aol.com

**WEB SITE:** www.northherohouse.com

**ROOMS:** 23 in 4 buildings; all with private bath, most with screened porch overlooking the lake.

**RATES:** $68 to $140, double occupancy, continental breakfast.

**OPEN:** May 1 to October 16.

**FACILITIES AND ACTIVITIES:** Dinner, full license. TV in living room, sauna, games, swimming, boating, tennis, shuffleboard, fishing.

*G*etting here is a treat for the eyes. North Hero is the county seat of Grand Isle, one of the Champlain Islands. This is one huge lake. It's so scenic and offers so much to do. And as you look across Lake Champlain, you see Mount Mansfield.

Most of the rooms, located in four buildings, have screened porches overlooking the lake. There are spacious lakeside rooms in Homestead, which is done in barn siding; Southwind, made out of pine; and Cove House, in brick. North Hero House was founded in 1891.

There is outdoor dining on the porch overlooking the lake. Inside are a regular dining room and a very bright greenhouse–dining room behind it.

Dinner is a real treat. There are eight different appetizers. One rings my bell; it's bruschetta, which is grilled New York Italian bread topped with creamy garlic and Parmesan cheese. Entrees include steak, chicken, and veal, all done in many interesting ways, as well as seafood—salmon in four ways, scallops, and shrimp. For vegetarians the fettucine Alfredo and primavera and tortellini are good choices, and the main course salads are delicious. Do save room for dessert.

In the morning, breakfast offerings are fresh fruit, coffee, tea, cold cereal, and freshly baked muffins (blueberry, cinnamon apple, and carrot are some of the favorites).

There are boat rentals—paddleboats, canoe, Sunfish, sailboats—or come in your own boat and take advantage of the free docking for guests. Looking for another sort of adventure? Fishing is good for bass, walleye, and Northern pike. Need to relax? The sandy beach and lawn chairs are inviting. The sauna is the perfect ending for any day.

Champ is a cousin of Scotland's famous Nessie and lives in the lake. Come up and see if you can spot her.

**HOW TO GET THERE:** Take exit 17 from I–89 onto Route 2 west about 17 miles to North Hero. The inn is in the center of the village.

# The Norwich Inn
## Norwich, Vermont 05055

**INNKEEPERS:** Sally and Tim Wilson

**ADDRESS/TELEPHONE:** Main Street; (802) 649–1143; fax (802) 649–2909

**ROOMS:** 25, including 1 2-bedroom suite; all with private bath, cable TV, and phone.

**RATES:** Winter $69 to $129, double occupancy, EP; Summer $69 to $109, double occupancy, EP.

**OPEN:** All year.

**FACILITIES AND ACTIVITIES:** Breakfast, lunch, dinner, Sunday brunch, bar; dining room closed Mondays. Nearby: swimming, canoeing, golf, skiing, tennis, biking, hiking.

Right on the sign for the inn it says SINCE 1797, and it is truly said, because travelers up the beautiful Connecticut River Valley have been finding a warm welcome at this grand old house ever since. It is just a mile away from Dartmouth College, and alumni, skiers, tourists, and commercial travelers find a special homelike atmosphere here that is dignified but a lot of fun.

The friendly bar and lounge area is named "The Jasper Murdock Ale House" after the inn's first owner. All the draft beers are brewed on the premises, just as they were in Colonial "public houses" before the advent of commercial breweries. Some of them are Whistling Pig Red Ale, Jasper Murdock's Old Ale, Pompanoosuc Wheat Beer, and Fuggle & Barley Corn, and there are more. Go and have fun.

The food is glorious. The Sunday champagne brunch offers you a glass of bubbly or a mimosa, along with eggs Benedict, a crepe or quiche of the day, or chicken duffina (sautéed with artichoke hearts in Madeira and cream). Dinner is always good here. Blackened carpaccio is an appetizer done with thinly sliced sirloin, capers, and garlic rounds. For entrees there are poached North Atlantic salmon, crisp roasted boneless duckling with raspberry glaze, and escallops of veal with julienne prosciutto, among others. The desserts are wonderful. The wine list is one of the most extensive I have seen.

Breakfasts are ample, with fruit, cereals, toast, muffins, eggs any way, crepes, French toast, pancakes, and a deep-dish quiche of the day. There is a very full lunch menu; if you can't find something to eat, then you must not be very hungry.

The rooms have very good beds and mattresses. There are canopied beds and some iron and brass beds. All rooms are beautiful, and each one has its own telephone. Guest pets are welcome in the carriage house rooms.

Make sure you ask for a copy of the history of the inn—it's fascinating.

**HOW TO GET THERE:** Take exit 13 from I–91. Go west a bit less than 1 mile to the center of town. The inn is on your left.

## Montshire Museum of Science

A beautiful woodland setting of 100 acres along the Connecticut River is the site of the Montshire Museum of Science (802–649–2200) on Montshire Road in Norwich. Two floors of exhibit space include dozens of interactive displays about nature, space, and technology. Fresh- and saltwater aquariums, live animal exhibits, a gift shop of science and nature-related books and toys, and an outdoor network of walking trails and picnic areas await visitors of all ages. The museum is open year-round daily from 10:00 A.M. to 5:00 P.M.

# The Four Chimneys
## Old Bennington, Vermont 05201

**INNKEEPERS:** Ron and Judy Schefkind

**ADDRESS/TELEPHONE:** 21 West Road; (802) 447–3500 or
(800) 649–3503; fax (802) 447–3692

**WEB SITE:** www.vermontel.com/chimneys/inn

**ROOMS:** 11; all with private bath, Jacuzzi, air conditioning, phone, and
TV; 9 with fireplace; 1 specially equipped for handicapped.

**RATES:** $75 to $125, single; $100 to $175, double; continental breakfast.

**OPEN:** All year.

**FACILITIES AND ACTIVITIES:** Lunch, dinner, bar and lounge. Full
license. Wheelchair access to dining room. Nearby: facilities at Mount
Anthony Country Club.

When you come into the inn, straight ahead is the bar and lounge.
The lounge is so comfortable, with a fireplace and light-colored
couches and chairs. If you turn right down the hall, you'll find the
dining room, and the food is grand. Lunch is served, and the mustard soup
is glorious. A salmon burger on a croissant, a chicken-pot pie, or a steak
sandwich—all are so good. For dinner, appetizers might include Burgundy-
style snails in garlic but-
ter or crisp taro root
Napoleon with crab-
meat, spiced tomato,
avocado, and shrimp.
Main courses could be
seared tuna, lamb rack,
beef medallions, roasted
chicken, or lots more
really good choices.
Desserts? Oh boy—one
is crème caramel. In summer the porch overlooking the gardens is ambrosia.

There are eleven guest rooms, and they are beauties. They have queen- or
king-sized beds, quilts, and color-coordinated sheets and towels. Cut-glass
lamps in the bedrooms are pretty and give good light for reading. On the
third floor the bathroom has a huge Jacuzzi for two, with seats. The icehouse
has a wonderful suite; so does the carriage house.

The inn and restaurant together are a wonderful setting for weddings or family reunions.

Ron and Judy have traveled extensively throughout their corporate careers. Ron has a diverse background in the hospitality industry, having worked with leading restaurant and hotel chains throughout the world. Nice to have them here.

**HOW TO GET THERE:** From Boston take I–90 to Lee. Go up Route 7 to the center of Bennington, and then take Route 9 west to the inn. From Lee take Route 20, which becomes Route 7.

# Johnny Seesaw's
## Peru, Vermont 05152

**INNKEEPERS:** Gary and Nancy Okun

**ADDRESS/TELEPHONE:** Route 11; (802) 824–5533 or (800) 424–CSAW (2731)

**E-MAIL:** gary@jseesaws.com

**ROOMS:** 30; all with private bath, some with fireplace.

**RATES:** In summer, $35 to $55, per person, EPB; in winter, $45 to $75, per person, EPB. Pets welcome.

**OPEN:** All year except end of skiing to Memorial Day and end of foliage until Thanksgiving.

**FACILITIES AND ACTIVITIES:** Dinner, liquor license. Wheelchair access to dining room. TV, game room, swimming, tennis. Nearby: skiing, hunting, golf, horseback riding, fishing, hiking, biking.

*Skiing Magazine* says this inn has the best Yankee cuisine in New England. The food is good, tasty country food prepared with imagination, featuring home-baked bread and homemade soup. Val is the talented chef who turns out all this fine fare.

The inn has a unique character, mostly because of the guests who keep coming back. It is set 2,000 feet up, on Bromley Mountain. The 65-by-25-foot pool, marble-rimmed, is a great summer gathering place, and the tennis court is always ready. There are six nearby golf courses, and riding horses can be hired in Peru.

For the many skiers who come to Vermont, Bromley's five chairlifts and GLM Ski School are right next door. Stratton Mountain, the Viking Ski Touring Center, and Wild Wings X-C are but a few minutes away.

For fishers and hunters, or those who wish to take up the sport, the Orvis Fly-Fishing and Wing Shooting schools in nearby Manchester have classes. The classes are held twice weekly, in three-day sessions through October, and participants can stay at the inn. The nearby towns boast many attractive and interesting shops.

The circular fireplace in the lounge really attracts me at the end of a long day, to say nothing of the cushioned platform along one side of the library. Stoker, the inn dog, will keep you company here.

There is a lot of history in this inn. The back of the extensive menu details the legend of the inn and is well worth reading. On the menu are such appetizers as crab cakes, tortellini alfredo, and good soups. Entrees are veal, meat, fish, fowl, and vegetarian.

HOW TO GET THERE: The inn is 220 miles from New York, 150 from Boston. From Route 7 take Route 11 right at Manchester Depot. The inn is 6 miles east, on Vermont Route 11. From I–91, follow exit 6 to Route 103 to Chester. The inn is 20 miles west, on Vermont Route 11.

# Wiley Inn
Peru, Vermont 05152

INNKEEPERS: Judy and Jerry Goodman

ADDRESS/TELEPHONE: Route 11 (mailing address: P.O. Box 37); (802) 824–6600 or (888) 843–6600; fax (802) 824–4195

WEB SITE: www.wileyinn.com

ROOMS: 16; all with private bath, 2 with Jacuzzis and fireplace.

RATES: $130 to $150, winter; $75 to $95, rest of year; double occupancy, EPB.

**OPEN:** All year except two weeks in May.

**FACILITIES AND ACTIVITIES:** Breakfast buffet, picnic lunch available, dinner. Swimming pool. Large Jacuzzi outside. Gift shop. Nearby: hiking, skiing, riding, fishing.

The Wiley Inn has been greeting guests for more than half a century. The main house was built in 1835 and was turned into an inn in 1943. Over the years it has been a farmhouse, stagecoach stop, and tearoom. It has changed a lot since it was built, having had at least ten additions, which is typical of Vermont's continuous architecture.

Jerry and Judy are friendly and pleasant innkeepers who do a good job of making guests feel right at home. The lower living room has a fireplace, a bar, a huge couch, and tons of things to do, such as a player piano with a lot of rolls, a television and VCR with a library of films (including a lot of Disney films for the kids), and games.

The library has an old-fashioned phone booth from a Philadelphia drugstore. The phone still works. There are a lot of books in here. Would you like to surf the Net? Well, there's a cyber cafe in here, and next to it is a small bar and a fireplace.

You will always find something to do at the inn. The swimming pool is heated and has a new deck; there's an outdoor children's play set for climbing, sliding, and swinging; and the Long

and Appalachian trails are nearby. So are horseback riding, fishing, and the alpine slide at Bromley. During fall the foliage is king, and in winter there are Bromley and Stratton mountains for you downhill skiers. Cross-country ski touring centers are within minutes. Go and enjoy.

The Ginger Tree restaurant, which they call New England's most original restaurant, has a nice fireplace. I enjoyed the hot and sour soup—always one of my favorites—but there are also egg drop and wonton soups. For appetizers there are Northern-style dumplings and homemade vegetable egg rolls. Garlic roast pork, Phoenix Dragon Chicken, and Chicken in the Lu are just a few of the main dishes. Wednesday night is a Chinese buffet; the chef does wonders with these. The desserts are different, and the inn has a full liquor license.

# Pittsfield Inn
## Pittsfield, Vermont 05762

INNKEEPER: Tom Yennerell

ADDRESS/TELEPHONE: P.O. Box 685; (802) 746-8943

ROOMS: 9, all with private bath.

RATES: $55 to $75 per person, double occupancy, MAP; $30 to $50 per person, double occupancy, B&B.

OPEN: All year except between Easter and Memorial Day.

FACILITIES AND ACTIVITIES: Breakfast and dinner, 7 days when open. Beer and wine license.

Nice to have Tom back as innkeeper of his inn. When you arrive the living room is to your right and just beyond is the bar, a television, wood stove, and good bar stools. To the left is the dining room, named Sweet Peas. The menu changes weekly. Some good ideas of what they have are great beginnings like Vermont chevre and fresh herb crepes, fresh garden herbs wrapped in a delicate crepe served with a tomato-basil medley—yum yum—peanut soup, onion soup, and shrimp in beer batter. Entrees may be salmon with puff pastry, chicken a la Sweet Pea or Marsala, filet mignon, or rib-eye steak. Homemade desserts wow—after a day of hiking what a treat to come back to.

Escape routes are guided and self-guided outdoor adventures in the Green Mountains of Vermont. They offer biking, hiking, snowshoeing, and back-country skiing. Something for every season. The activities are customized to meet your desires and abilities. It would be just beautiful to ski in snow that no one else has ever seen.

The Tweed and White Rivers are close by and full of trout and salmon, so come on, you fishermen.

The inn has been here since 1835. A lot of history is around New England. Come and enjoy. The bar itself is antique; it's old marble.

**HOW TO GET THERE:** The inn is 20 miles northeast of Rutland. Take 4 east and Route 100 north to the village of Pittsfield. The inn is on the green.

# The Castle
## Proctorsville, Vermont 05153

**INNKEEPERS:** Erica and Dick Hart

**ADDRESS/TELEPHONE:** (802) 226–7222 or (800) 697–7222; fax (802) 226–7853

**WEB SITE:** www.thecastle-vt.com

**ROOMS:** 10, all with private bath, 4 with Jacuzzis; CD players in all; 6 with fireplaces.

**RATES:** $100 to $225, double occupancy, EPB.

**OPEN:** All year except mid-April to mid-May.

**FACILITIES AND ACTIVITIES:** Breakfast, dinner, five nights in season, full license.

For over thirty years, this English manor country house known as The Castle has been an inn. It is ninety years old. When you enter, you are in the great hall, and to the left is the library. Lots of books and windows and a huge fireplace with Arts and Crafts–movement tiles that came from The Moravian Pottery and Tile Works in Doylestown, Pennsylvania. Off to the right is a very unusual dining room. It's oval in shape, and the wood is gorgeous. Rich oak and mahogany woodwork and highly detailed cast plaster ceilings. This whole inn is fabulous. The staircase up to the second floor is nice. When you

get to the top, you will see a red love seat in the hall and Oriental rugs all over. The rooms are very romantic. There are blue, red, and green rooms. A television room is also on the second floor. There are more guest rooms on the third floor, and the views are awesome.

The food is glorious. The chef is very inventive. Some appetizers are carrot ginger soup, French onion soup, mushroom strudels, and escargot. Entrees may be trout, salmon, rack of lamb, game birds, duck, beef tenderloin, veal dishes, and the chef's daily vegetarian entree. Do save room for dessert.

HOW TO GET THERE: Take I–91 to exit 6. Go north on 103 after Chester. The Castle is located on the right after crossing Route 131.

# The Golden Stage Inn
## Proctorsville, Vermont 05055

INNKEEPERS: Paul Darnauer and Micki Smith-Darnauer

ADDRESS/TELEPHONE: Depot Street, off Route 131; (802) 226-7744 or (800) 253-8226

E-MAIL: gldstgin@ludl.tds.net

WEB SITE: www.virtualvermont.com/countryinn

ROOMS: 8; 6 with private bath; 1 suite.

RATES: $149 to $218, double occupancy, MAP.

OPEN: All year.

FACILITIES AND ACTIVITIES: Beer and wine license. Swimming pool, bike tours. Nearby: hiking, skiing, alpine slide, gondola rides, antiquing, golf, biking.

The Golden Stage Inn still is known locally as the Skinner place, for Otis, the actor, and his daughter Cornelia Otis Skinner, the author. The house was built more than 200 years ago, shortly after Vermont's founding. It was once a stagecoach stop and is reputed to have been a stop on the Underground Railroad.

When you drive in, you immediately notice the rockers on the porch and the abundance of flowers that surround the inn. It's very pretty in the summertime. Sit and rock on the porch and enjoy the breathtaking views of the Black River Valley and Okemo Mountain.

One of the rooms has its own little porch. There are lovely quilts, some antiques, and lots of books. The living room, with its cozy fireplace, is very comfortable after a day of doing your own thing. There are all sorts of games and puzzles, too, but maybe all you want to do is sit and knit or read or play with the inn dogs.

The food is delicious. Tomato wine soup is my favorite appetizer. Veal and mushrooms with a wine sauce and pork tenderloin in an orange-ginger sauce are just two of the good entrees. A chocolate walnut torte makes any chocolate lover swoon, and the fallen chocolate soufflé is a big hit, too. Croissants on Sunday morning are a heavenly way to start the day. The inn also has a huge vegetable and herb garden, so necessary to the good cooking here.

Four acres of rolling lawns, beautiful gardens, and trees are just what you need for a picnic, a long walk, or simply being alone. Surrounding this haven of loveliness are thousands of acres of forests to hike in and four mountains noted for their good skiing. They are Okemo Mountain, Mount Ascutney, Bromley (fun in summer, too, with its exciting alpine slide down the mountain), and Killington Peak, which has year-round gondola rides, the longest in the United States. Killington often has one of the longest ski seasons in the East.

Biking from inn to inn is another way to see this wonderful country. While you bike to the next inn, a support van transfers your luggage. This is my idea of neat.

The whole first floor is handicapped accessible. A nice touch for deaf guests are rooms specially equipped for the deaf; they have Strobe lights for the fire alarm. In the office is a phone for the deaf. The Otis room has a photo of Otis Skinner as Romeo—this room has a double hide-away bead, a regular bed, and books.

Tootsie, a Maltese terrier, is the inn dog. Elton John and June Bug are miniature donkeys, and three sheep also live here.

The inn has a cookie jar that is never empty. Nice.

**HOW TO GET THERE:** From I–91 take exit 6 to Route 103, then take a right off Route 103 at the Proctorsville sign. Inn is the first driveway immediately on the right.

# Okemo Lantern Lodge
## Proctorsville, Vermont 05153

**INNKEEPERS:** Pete and Dody Button

**ADDRESS/TELEPHONE:** P.O. Box 247; (802) 226-7770 or (800) 732-7077

**ROOMS:** 10; all with private bath.

**RATES:** $160 per couple, MAP; $80 per person, MAP.

**OPEN:** All year except April and November.

**FACILITIES AND ACTIVITIES:** Beer and wine license. Swimming pool. Nearby: golf, tennis, bicycling, skiing, skating, hiking, antiquing.

The inn was built in the early 1800s. It is a lovely Victorian with natural butternut woodwork and original stained-glass windows. The living room is all comfort, with armchairs, couches, a crackling fire to warm your toes, and a sunny window.

Bedrooms are cheerful, clean, and neat. Furnishings include a bit of wicker, antiques, and canopy beds. Would you like a champagne breakfast in bed? Just ask.

Heavenly aromas are always coming from the kitchen, whether they are from the freshly baked bread, freshly perked coffee, or bacon sizzling on the grill. And I hear Dody is getting rave reviews for her butterflied leg of lamb cooked to perfection on the grill.

Dinner begins by the fire with Vermont cheddar cheese and a relish tray. Then there's a compote of fresh melon with sherbet, followed by salad with a different entree each evening. Tenderloin of beef, chicken cacciatore, and homemade soups are good choices here. The menu changes seasonally. All the desserts are made here and are so good. Light fruit desserts are featured, and a lot of raspberries are used. Try the fresh raspberry pie with real whipped cream. Yum.

There are lovely cut flowers inside the inn from the flowers that grow all over the beautiful property. You just know that a lot of care goes into this inn.

There is so much to do in this area all year. Spring is the time to watch the maple sugaring or just go fishing in one of the well-stocked lakes or streams. In summer golf, tennis, hiking, and bicycling are close at hand. Fall is foliage and cider. Box lunches are available if you wish. Winter brings skiing and skating, or you could curl up with a good book by the fire.

HOW TO GET THERE: Take I–91 to exit 6 in Bellows Falls. Go north on Route 103 to its junction with Route 131 and turn right. The inn is ¼ mile on the left.

# Parker House
## Quechee, Vermont 05059

INNKEEPERS: Walt and Barbara Forrester and sons Jay and Nick

ADDRESS/TELEPHONE: 16 Main Street; (802) 295–6077

E-MAIL: parker-house-inn@valley.net

WEB SITE: www.pbpub.com/quechee/parkerhouse.htm

ROOMS: 7; all with private bath, some with air conditioning.

RATES: $100 to $125, double occupancy, EPB. Package plans available.

OPEN: All year.

FACILITIES AND ACTIVITIES: Dinner every night but Tuesday. Weekends only in winter and spring. Ask about Italian night (summer and fall only)—it's grand. Lounge, full license. Inquire about cooking classes. Nearby: full privileges at Quechee Club, fly-fishing, canoeing.

RECOMMENDED COUNTRY INNS® TRAVELERS' CLUB BENEFIT: 25 percent discount, Monday–Thursday, excluding September, October, and holidays, subject to availibility.

Parker House Inn, a registered National Historic Site, was built in 1857 by Vermont State Senator Joseph C. Parker for his family. The Ottauquechee River flows along the rear of the property, and 2 miles away is the Quechee Gorge. It's an amazing sight down into the gorge 165 feet below.

All the rooms, which are furnished in a Victorian style, have names. My friend Audrey and I had Emily. At the top of the steps is another beauty, Rebecca; down the hall are Joseph and Walter, which look over the river. The third floor has more rooms. There is also a cozy sitting room with a small television and games.

Up in one room is a desk that you have to see—an early Victorian Murphy-style bed that, when put together, looks like a desk. It's from the late 1800s.

The dining rooms are lovely. The tables are nicely spaced, and the food prepared by Walt and Bar-bara is glorious. He is a recent graduate of the Culinary Institute of America, and Barbara is a natural chef. The grilled portobello mushrooms, served on spinach salad with warm Vermont goat cheese, were superb. I think I could also  have eaten this for breakfast. Walt and Barbara offer a sampler—a tasting of three selected appetizers—which is a nice idea.

The menu changes quite often. When I was visiting, some of the entrees were roast rack of lamb, beef tenderloin, breast of chicken, and Vermont rabbit. And the desserts were heavenly, but you'll have to come see for yourself.

On the porch, which is shaded by an awning, are tables and chairs. Sit out here and watch the river. There's also a brick side patio. This is a very nice inn, with wonderful innkeepers.

Guests of the inn can enjoy full club privileges at the Quechee Club. It has two 18-hole golf courses, skiing, tennis, swimming, and a fitness center. There are golf and tennis packages and also a sports widow package for those who want to indulge in a massage, facial, pedicure, and manicure. And, of course, there's the wonderful river for fly-fishing or canoeing. There's a nice bar with a view of the river. Here you'll find two game boards; one is Life's Little Instructions—very funny.

HOW TO GET THERE: Take exit 1 off I–89 north. Turn left on Route 4 for 4 miles, crossing the Quechee Gorge. Turn right at the flashing traffic light. Cross the covered bridge and turn left. The inn is on the left.

# The Quechee Inn at Marshland Farm
## Quechee, Vermont 05059

**INNKEEPERS:** David Madison; Roger Perry, owner

**ADDRESS/TELEPHONE:** Club House Road; (802) 295–3133 or (800) 235–3133; fax (802) 295–6587

**E-MAIL:** quecheeinn@pinnacle-inns.com

**WEB SITE:** www.pinnacle-inns.com/quecheeinn

**ROOMS:** 24; all with private bath and TV.

**RATES:** $140 to $260, double occupancy, MAP. Package rates available.

**OPEN:** All year.

**FACILITIES AND ACTIVITIES:** Lounge, full license. Wheelchair access to dining room. Cross-country ski learning center, fly-fishing school, bicycles and canoes to rent, fishing, hiking. Nearby: downhill skiing, golf, tennis, squash, swimming, boating.

The first time that I saw and heard Quechee Gorge, I was standing on the bridge that spans it. Now I know another way to see this remarkable quirk of nature. The inn is but a half-mile from it, and the innkeeper will show you how to see it from an unusual angle.

The inn was a private home from 1793 until 1976. Beautifully converted to an inn, it reflects the care it's given. Some of the rooms have the largest four-poster, king-sized beds I have ever seen, and others have comfortable doubles. Seven more guest rooms, in the wing off the original building, have

windows overlooking the meadow and lake. All rooms are equipped with color cable television, and the whole inn is air-conditioned.

There are lovely stencils in the dining room and a beautiful awning over the porch. Adjoining the dining room is a small library and conference room wired for audiovisual equipment. It's a real treat to be able to have a business meeting at a place like this. The living room has an abundance of comfortable chairs and couches, a piano, color television, books, and a fireplace. One feels at home here any season of the year.

Breakfast is a sumptuous buffet. Everything is delicious. Dinner is equally good. Among their appetizers they include grilled shrimp wrapped in pancetta—and a different chef's pâté of the evening. Just a few of the entrees are brook trout rubbed with oven-dried tomatoes, fresh herbs, and olive oil; duckling seared, roasted, sliced, and served over a shiitake mushroom sauce with a counterpoint of fresh strawberries; and babyback pork ribs slowly braised with maple syrup, grilled, and served with fresh maple-apple puree.

## *Arts and Crafts in Quechee*

Downer's Mill in Quechee is now the site of Simon Pearce's beautiful glassworks, operated in part through the harnessing of the Ottauquechee River's hydropower. In the center of Quechee overlooking the waterfall of the dam and the covered bridge, you will find the Mill and its glassworks. Visitors can watch the glass-blowing process and view the hydroelectric turbine that fuels Simon's glass furnace. You might also see a potter throwing a piece of pottery on the wheel. You can admire or shop for the finished products; both first-quality pieces and seconds are sold in the lovely retail shop. Along with the glassware are Simon Pearce pottery, plus quilts, sweaters, baskets, linens, jewelry, and other Vermont-made handcrafts. The Simon Pearce Restaurant at the Mill serves lunch and dinner daily. For information on the glassworks and shop, call (802) 295-2711. For restaurant information or reservations, call (802) 295-1470.

Right at the Quechee Inn at Marshland Farm is the Quechee Inn Gallery. Visit during your stay for a look at paintings, prints, etchings, lithographs, and other work by fine artists from Vermont and elsewhere. Changing exhibitions of featured artists are hung frequently throughout the year.

Old-fashioned New England dining with homemade breads, sticky buns, and regional specials such as trout and venison make a visit here a must.

The inn guests have full club privileges at the nearby private Quechee Club. The two championship golf courses are breathtakingly scenic and are great tests of golf. You can also play tennis and squash here. Guest fees are charged for most of these activities.

HOW TO GET THERE: From I–91 take I–89 north to exit 1. Go west on Route 4 for 1²⁄₁₀ miles, then right on Club House Road for 1 mile to the inn.

# Three Stallion Inn 💟
## Randolph, Vermont 05060

INNKEEPERS: Al and Betty Geibel

ADDRESS/TELEPHONE: Lower Stock Farm Road; (802) 728–5575 or (800) 424–5575; fax (802) 728–4036

WEB SITE: www.vtweb.com/3stallion

ROOMS: 17; 13 with private bath.

RATES: $70 to $98, double occupancy, $110 in fall, EP. Packages available.

OPEN: All year.

FACILITIES AND ACTIVITIES: Breakfast, lunch, dinner. Two all-weather tennis courts. Nearby: cross-country and downhill skiing, golf, swimming and fishing in White River, Chandler Music Hall.

*T*he full name of this inn is Three Stallion Inn at the Green Mountain Stock Farm. This valley is the original birthplace of the Morgan horse. As a guest here, you can board your horse and enjoy using the extensive trail system.

Adjacent to the inn is the Green Mountain Ski Touring Center, with 50 kilometers of cross-country trails over varied terrain—good for beginners and experts alike. Along the White River the Montague Golf Club adjoins the inn's property. It is one of the oldest in the state. Downhill skiing is at Sugarbush, Mad River, Killington, Woodstock, Pico, and Stowe.

In the town you can rent mountain bikes, boots, in-line skates, and more. The Chandler Music Hall is here, featuring chamber music, jazz, and popular concerts. The town also has a movie theater, bowling alley, and ice-skating rink.

Back at the inn are two all-weather tennis courts. Swimming and fishing in the White River are a lot of fun; take a picnic lunch from the inn and your day is complete. At the end of the day, relax in the whirlpool or sauna. What an inn!

The spacious guest rooms and suites have the most modern amenities and lovely antiques. They are tastefully decorated, and the quilts match the wallpapers.

Morgan's Pub is striking and has its own menu, with soups, pastas, Mexican dishes, grill items, pizzas, and more. There is a nice children's menu.

The main dining room has glorious food. At lunch there are grand salads, quiches, crepes of the day, stir-fry, chili, sandwiches, and burgers. An appetizer I liked at dinner was crabcakes with an herbed mayonnaise. There is a specials board for lunch and dinner.

I think you can tell I like it here.

**HOW TO GET THERE:** Take exit 4 off I-89. Go 1⁸⁄₁₀ miles toward Randolph. Turn left on Lower Stock Farm Road and go ⁷⁄₁₀ mile to the inn.

# The Inn at Saxtons River
## Saxtons River, Vermont 05154

**INNKEEPERS:** Jeremy Burrell and Steven Griffiths; Ilene and Sandy Freiman, owners

**ADDRESS/TELEPHONE:** 27 Main Street; (802) 869–2110; fax (802) 869–3033

**WEB SITE:** www.inatsr.com

**ROOMS:** 16; all with private bath, 2 with porch.

**RATES:** $98 to $108, double occupancy, EPB.

OPEN: All year.

FACILITIES AND ACTIVITIES: Dinner, Sunday brunch. Pub. Nearby: downhill and cross-country skiing, horse-drawn sleigh rides, country fairs.

This wonderful Victorian inn started life in 1903 as a hotel and then became an inn several years later. It's a rare gem. When you see it, you'll see what I mean.

The guest rooms are well decorated, and two have private porches, so you can sit and listen to the quiet. There's a Victorian pub, and the porches have rockers. What a comfortable way to spend a summer evening. Winter is glorious. There's not a lot of dirty snow, just the pure white stuff. Take a sleigh ride or just enjoy the warmth of the inn and the fireplace.

When you enter the inn, you see the parlor on the left. It has a baby grand piano, fireplace, and good couches and chairs. On the right is the pub. Ahead is the dining room. I like Toby jugs, and there is a nice collection over the fireplace.

The menus are enticing. One really excellent appetizer is the baked cheese; it's a blend of three cheeses, sundried tomatoes, tarragon, and Dijon mustard, all wrapped in puff pastry. Go on to delicious soups, salads, and entrees like roast Vermont turkey, sautéed pork medallions, boneless roast duck, and pasta of the day. Espresso and cappuccino and lovely desserts cap off the meal.

The brochure says a lot: Service is the key word, and their definition of service is the same that has been practiced in small English hotels and inns for more than a century. It is "above and beyond."

HOW TO GET THERE: Take I–91 to exit 5. Proceed on Route 5 north to Route 121 to Saxtons River and the inn.

# Rowell's Inn
## Simonsville, Vermont 05143

**INNKEEPERS:** Lee and Beth Davis

**ADDRESS/TELEPHONE:** Route 11 (mailing address: RR 1, Box 267D, Chester, VT 05143); (802) 875–3658; fax (802) 875–3680

**ROOMS:** 5; all with private bath.

**RATES:** $160 to $175, double occupancy, MAP.

**OPEN:** All year except April and May to Memorial Day and first two weeks of November.

**FACILITIES AND ACTIVITIES:** Beer and wine license. Nearby: skiing, fishing, hiking, summer theater, and more.

*B*uilt in 1820 as a stagecoach stop, this inn has served many purposes over the years. It was a post office and general store, and then in 1900 F. A. Rowell came along and purchased it, and it became Rowell's Inn. He put in the elegant tin ceilings, cherry and maple planked dining-room floors, central heating, and indoor plumbing. The brochure says that during the mid-1900s the inn was a preferred luncheon stop on the "Ideal Tour" between Manchester, Vermont, and the White Mountains for a hearty fare of trout and chicken. Today the inn is on the National Register of Historic Places.

In Rowell's Tavern you will find an old checkers table, a shoeshine chair, an icebox, an upright piano, and a wood-burning stove. Now where else but a country inn would you find a room such as this?

One entree is offered each night at the five-course dinner. Some examples are beef tenderloin, the inn's own version of New England boiled dinner, veal marsala, and chicken. Pan-fried trout is a house specialty. This course is preceded by appetizers like mushroom strudel, hot cream soups, and salads such as fresh greens with oranges and grapes and a delicious homemade dressing. Dessert may be apple pie or chocolate mousse or another dreamy thing. All this good eating is served in a nice dining room or a sunporch decorated with plants. Breakfast is a good, full one.

Two of the lovely rooms have working fireplaces. Some brass beds, quilts, and hooked rugs add to the tasteful decor of the rooms.

Close at hand you'll find hiking, golf, tennis, biking, trail riding, and fishing in trout streams. The area provides summer theater, great shopping, and antiquing. All this plus—as you'd expect in a good Vermont country inn—alpine and cross-country skiing.

**HOW TO GET THERE:** The inn is on Route 11, 7 miles west of Chester.

# The Londonderry Inn
## South Londonderry, Vermont 05155

**INNKEEPERS:** Jim and Jean Cavanagh

**ADDRESS/TELEPHONE:** Box 301-20; (802) 824–5226

**E-MAIL:** londinn@sover.net

**ROOMS:** 25; 20 with private bath.

**RATES:** $39 to $105, double occupancy, EPB. No credit cards.

**OPEN:** All year.

**FACILITIES AND ACTIVITIES:** Dinner served weekends and holidays only, bar. Restaurant closed late October to mid-December and April to mid-June. Pool tables, Ping-Pong, swimming. Nearby: skiing, horseback riding, hiking.

The inn sits high on a hill overlooking the village of South Londonderry. It is central to two big ski areas—Bromley and Stratton. In summer there is a large swimming pool to relax in. Nearby they have horseback riding, hiking, and bicycle trails. At any time of the year, there is pool to be played on the inn's two vintage pool tables. In addition, there are many comfortable places to relax, read a book, do needlepoint, or just enjoy a blazing fire on the hearth.

The inn dates back to 1826, when it was built as a farmhouse. The rooms have twin, double, or king-sized beds with down comforters and down pillows and offer large, thirsty towels. Jean also puts fresh flowers in the rooms. These little touches are far too often overlooked by innkeepers.

The inn has a nice lounge and a service bar off the living room, so you can be comfortable by the fire before dinner, with your favorite cocktail in hand. The menu changes nightly but always includes four or five appetizers, at least one homemade soup, four to eight entrees served with fresh vegetables, and great desserts.

The dessert names are really creative—FBI Cake, Orient Express Torte, and Hungarian Rhapsody.

Astro is the inn dog. Say hello for me.

**HOW TO GET THERE:** Take exit 2 from I–91 at Brattleboro, and follow Route 30 north to Rawsonville. Then take Route 100 to South Londonderry. The inn is on your left.

# The Inn at South Newfane
South Newfane, Vermont 05351

**INNKEEPERS:** Neville and Dawn Cullen

**ADDRESS/TELEPHONE:** 369 Dover Road; (802) 348–7179; fax (802) 348–9325

**E-MAIL:** cullin@sover.net

**WEB SITE:** www.innatsouthnewfane.com

**ROOMS:** 6, all with private bath.

**RATES:** $80 to $95, single, EPB; $89 to $120, double, EPB. Map is available.

**OPEN:** All year except two or three weeks in November.

**FACILITIES AND ACTIVITIES:** Breakfast, dinner (July through October, six days, closed Wednesday; during rest of year, Thursday through Sunday), lunch (July 4 through October, Thursday through Sunday). Full liquor license, swimming and skating pond, lawn games, skiing, snowshoeing, hiking, biking, antiquing, horseback riding, and much more nearby.

**RECOMMENDED COUNTRY INNS® TRAVELERS' CLUB BENEFIT:** Stay two nights, get the third night free, Monday–Thursday, November–June; 15 percent discount for a stay of three or more nights, Monday–Thursday, July–October.

*T*his is an inviting inn. The living room has an old original Estery pump organ. There's a fireplace in here, comfortable couch and chairs, lots of games and chess.

The morning room is where breakfast is served to house guests and outside guests. Here are some ideas of what you might have: fresh orange juice, muffins, scones, pancakes, cereals, hot or cold eggs, omelets, coffees, and tea—all very nice. In the warmer months the French doors open onto a lovely porch for dining and looking. There are rockers out here, and the porch looks out on the grounds and pond. Dawn has a pet trout in the pond that she feeds. We sat out here and watched robins and their little ones in training—it sure was fun.

Lunch is served from July 4 through October and is splendid. Soups and shrimp cocktail, maybe the inn's turkey club sandwich or braised beef and wild mushrooms over noodles, fresh fruit plate, or Caesar salad.

Neville the chef, who apprenticed in Europe, sure is good at what he does. He uses local and regional produce. I had Maine lobster bisque, and it's good. So is the spinach and Vermont goat cheese tart, salads, fettuccine Alfredo, grilled teriyaki, tofu, and more. In the dining room each table has different colored napkins, picking up colors in the set plates. It looks like a rainbow. Fresh flowers are also on the tables.

Accommodations are lovely. The room I was in had a king-sized bed and lovely rose-colored wing-type chairs, and it was very comfortable. There are three queens, two kings, and one set of twins. Ceiling fans are in all. A grand place for a wedding.

HOW TO GET THERE: The inn is located 11 miles northwest of Brattleboro. From I–91 take Brattleboro exit 2, turn left at end of ramp, following signs for Route 5 north/Route 30 into the center of Brattleboro. Turn left at the traffic light and bear left at the split of Route 5 and Route 30. Follow Route 30 north for 9 miles. You will see our sign for the inn at South Newfane on your right. Take next left toward Williamsville/South Newfane, etc. and continue for 2 miles, turning left at end of cement bridge, through Williamsville, over the covered bridge, and proceed for about 1 mile to the inn at South Newfane. (It's on the left.)

# Kedron Valley Inn
## South Woodstock, Vermont 05071

**INNKEEPERS:** Max and Merrily Comins

**ADDRESS/TELEPHONE:** P.O. Box 145; (802) 457-1473 or
(800) 836-1193; fax (802) 457-4469

**E-MAIL:** kedroninn@aol.com

**WEB SITE:** www.information.com/vt/kedron

**ROOMS:** 23 and 3 suites, in 3 buildings; all with private bath; many
with fireplace or Franklin stove and TV; 2 with Jacuzzi.

**RATES:** $155 to $316, double occupancy, MAP; $99 to $260, double
occupancy, EPB. Substantial discounts midweek.

**OPEN:** All year except April and a few days before Thanksgiving.

**FACILITIES AND ACTIVITIES:** Bar, lounge, meeting facilities, private
beach on pond, ice skating. Nearby: golf, horseback riding, tennis,
skiing. Dinner five nights (not on Tuesday or Wednesday).

**RECOMMENDED COUNTRY INNS® TRAVELERS' CLUB BENEFIT:** 10 percent discount, Monday–Thursday, excluding foliage season and Christ-
mas/New Year's weeks, subject to availibility.

he inn's quilt collection alone is worth the trip here. There are
more than fifty of them, some of which came from Merrily's family. Two of them were made by her great-grandmother more than
a hundred years ago. I was
fascinated to find on display stories and pictures of
the women who made these
beautiful quilts.

There's wonderful his-
tory throughout the inn.
Two of the inn's buildings
date from the 1820s. A
secret attic passageway is
rumored to have been used
by runaway slaves during the Civil War. Another room has a walk-in safe with
an iron door. The main building was once a post office, dance hall, tavern,

and country store. More recently the inn has been used in the Christmas Budweiser commercial with the Clydesdale horses pulling a sleigh.

Nine of the rooms have a fireplace, and six have a wood stove. I slept in a very comfortable queen-sized canopy bed. There are twins and doubles in the log house. All the rooms have a television. One of the largest rooms has a three-sided fireplace and lounge chairs on its private porch. Three other rooms have a private deck or veranda, and one room has a Jacuzzi. This is real comfort, folks. There are also new suites, and they're beauties. In Room 12 do ask to see the wood drawer.

There is musical entertainment on weekends, on holidays, and during fall foliage season. Max sings. He really has a very good voice. The bar and lounge area is a fun spot.

Dining at Kedron Valley is wonderful. The menu changes quite often, and the chef is inventive. My spies tell me great stories about his food, and, of course, I've checked up on them and they're right. I thought the stuffed cape bay scallops were very different and good. The cool mixed-fruit soup is very tasty. I had chicken breast studded with fresh roasted pistachios in a beurre blanc sauce. Another entree that looked tempting was the salmon stuffed with an herbed seafood mousse, wrapped in puff pastry, baked, and served with a different sauce each night. Desserts are grand. This is truly excellent food. The air-conditioned dining patio is flanked by bulb and perennial gardens.

There's a new tavern menu for lighter appetites featuring such treats as pizza baked on their pizza stone, grilled shrimp and mixed green salad, and more. There's also a nice children's menu.

The inn dog is a yellow Lab–golden retriever mix. The inn allows well-behaved pets to stay here.

**HOW TO GET THERE:** Take Route 4 to Woodstock. Turn south on Route 106 and go 5 miles to South Woodstock and the inn.

# The Hartness House
Springfield, Vermont 05156

INNKEEPER: Edward Blair

ADDRESS/TELEPHONE: 30 Orchard Street; (802) 885–2115 or
(800) 732–4789; fax (802) 885–2207

WEB SITE: www.vermontstore.com/hartness.html

ROOMS: 39, including 1 suite; all with private bath, air conditioning,
and TV.

RATES: $79 to $100, double occupancy; $130, suite; EP. Package
rates available.

OPEN: All year.

FACILITIES AND ACTIVITIES: Breakfast, lunch on weekdays, dinner. No
smoking in main house. Lounge and bar, swimming pool, tennis.
Nearby: cross-country and downhill skiing.

RECOMMENDED COUNTRY INNS® TRAVELERS' CLUB BENEFIT: Stay
two nights, get third night free, subject to availability.

*T*he main house was built in 1903, and the rooms are all different
in size and decor. There are period wallpapers, some antiques,
and twins, doubles, and queens—even some canopies. The
Charles Lindbergh Room is in a corner. It's really lovely and has a wonderful window seat.

For relaxation try the swimming pool and nature trails. For exercise a
lighted clay tennis court and
skiing are nearby.

The dining room is lovely,
and the chandeliers are especially so. The color scheme is
mauve, deep rose, and white.
Luncheon selections are varied. The baked four-onion
soup is glorious. There are
salads, burgers, and sandwiches. The Black Forest is

roast beef and Swiss cheese with horseradish sauce, served on pumpernickel.
The chef's suggestions are varied; one is tortellini Alfredo.

The dinner menu lists about six different appetizers and soups. Some of
the entrees are approved by a registered dietician. The regular entrees and

chef's suggestions are super. The Seafood Weave is unique—fresh Norwegian salmon and mahimahi strips woven together and poached with a shrimp beurre blanc. Do save room for desserts.

The telescope lounge overlooks the pool, and the porch is a small, private dining room. There is no smoking in the main house.

Although James Hartness was something of a recluse and needed absolute quiet, he married a lovely butterfly of a lady. Do visit the house they created together.

HOW TO GET THERE: From the police booth in downtown Springfield, go up Summer Hill, starting at the light. Keep going up the hill as it curves around the left until it levels off (a cemetery is on the right) at the five-street intersection. Bear left on Orchard Street. The inn is 300 yards ahead of you.

## The Hartness House Observatory

Unique among all the inns in this book, the Hartness House is the only one with a historic observatory. James Hartness was an aviator, the builder of Vermont's first airport, an inventor who patented more than 120 different machines, and the governor of the state from 1920 to 1922. As if that were not enough, he was also an astronomer. When he completed his stone-and-shingle mansion, he added an observatory and a 600-power Turret Equatorial Telescope. Built in 1910, it was one of the first tracking telescopes in the nation. Guests can tour the 240-foot underground tunnel that links the observatory to the main house, and they can also see the Stellafane Museum where Hartness created his inventions. When the weather permits, you can scan the starry skies through the telescope. Tours are given daily at 6:00 P.M.

# Edson Hill Manor
## Stowe, Vermont 05672

INNKEEPERS: Eric and Jane Lande

ADDRESS/TELEPHONE: 1500 Edson Hill Road; (802) 253–7371, (802) 253–9797, or (800) 621–0284

ROOMS: 9, all with private bath, in the manor; 16, all with private bath and fireplace, in the carriage houses. Smoking in carriage houses only. Handicapped bathroom in 1 carriage house.

RATES: $110 to $170 per room, EPB; $150 to $210 per room, MAP. Package rates available.

OPEN: All year.

FACILITIES AND ACTIVITIES: Dinner, fully licensed bar, après-ski lounge. Wheelchair access to dining room. Pool, fishing, horseback riding, cross-country skiing with rentals and instruction, ice skating Nearby: ice skating and golf at Stowe Country Club.

Here you are, halfway between Stowe and Mount Mansfield, 1,500 feet above the hubble-bubble of that lively village of Stowe, which is growing every year. Here is truly luxurious living, in a house that was built in 1939 for a family that loved to ski and ride.

The swimming pool here is beautiful. It won an award from Paddock Pools of California. The stocked trout pond is a must for anglers, and you can use the inn's boat. How nice to go catch a fish and have it for your breakfast! When the snow comes, the stables turn into a cross-country ski center, so there you are, practically taking off from the inn door.

This attractive house has been run as an inn since 1953, and there are still homelike touches. The old delft tiles around many of the fireplaces are so appealing. The pine-paneled living room has an aura of quiet elegance that reflects the feeling of gracious living all too often missing from our busy lives. Look closely at the living-room curtains. Somebody shopped hard for that material.

Downstairs are a bar and lounge. A skier's lunch is served here. The dining room is splendid, and the food is grand. The menu changes quite often, but to give you an idea, here are some of the summertime offerings: chilled melon soup with honey and lime; summer beefsteak tomato with grilled eggplant; warm fresh mozzarella crostini with balsamic vinegar; grilled Vermont rabbit; barbecued shrimp; swordfish, salmon, steak . . . .

One wintertime favorite is the homemade butternut squash ravioli. They also serve sweetbreads, calf's liver, and pork tenderloin; this is really good food. Choose a wine from their wonderful wine cellar, or complete your meal with one of their great hot beverages.

The inn has very nice guest accommodations. The rooms in the carriage house have beamed ceilings, brick fireplaces, and private baths.

This is a beautiful inn, and the view from here is spectacular.

A note of particular interest to all you moviegoers is that Edson Hill Manor was the winter filming location for Alan Alda's *The Four Seasons*.

HOW TO GET THERE: Take Route 108 north from Stowe 4⁹⁄₁₀ miles, turn right on Edson Hill Road, and follow the signs uphill to the manor.

# Foxfire Inn
## Stowe, Vermont 05672

INNKEEPERS: Bob and Kate Neilson

ADDRESS/TELEPHONE: 1606 Pucker Street (Route 100); (802) 253–4887

ROOMS: 5; all with private bath.

RATES: $55 to $85, double occupancy, EPB.

OPEN: All year.

FACILITIES AND ACTIVITIES: Dinner, bar, full license. Wheelchair access to dining room. Parking. Nearby: downhill and cross-country skiing, fishing, skating, hiking.

RECOMMENDED COUNTRY INNS® TRAVELERS' CLUB BENEFIT: 10 percent discount.

The Neilsons want to welcome old and new friends, and they are myriad, to their inn. The house is more than 150 years old and has been restored to easy comfort by these enthusiastic innkeepers. And there is so much to do here, from the finest skiing in the East to great lounging in this comfortable inn.

The innkeepers have created a garden room that is a great spot for breakfast and dinner. It is all white lattice, with loads of hanging plants. This is a gazebo to end them all.

The best Italian kitchen in New England may seem a bit misplaced so far north in Vermont, but here it is. Taste, and you will agree. And do try things like baked broccoli, which is a combination of tomato sauce, ricotta cheese, and broccoli. There are seven different and delicious veal dishes. Boneless breast of chicken is prepared five ways, and the eggplant parmigiana has a special place in my heart. The shrimp marinara I can still taste. On my  last stay here, I had superb veal parmigiana and excellent clams casino. I also had a wonderful red wine to complement the dinner. As the front of the menu says, here you discover "The Italian Art of Eating."

And when you can push yourself away from the table, you have Stowe at your door, with antiques, shops, skiing, skating, walking, hiking, fishing, and more.

Pass me another tortoni, please. I am settled in for the season.

**HOW TO GET THERE:** Take I–89 to Route 100 north into Stowe. The inn is on the right, 1½ miles north of town.

# Green Mountain Inn
## Stowe, Vermont 05672

**INNKEEPER:** Patti Clark

**ADDRESS/TELEPHONE:** Main Street (mailing address: P.O. Box 60); (802) 253–7301 or (800) 253–7302; fax (802) 253–5096

**E-MAIL:** grnmtinn@aol.com

**WEB SITE:** www.greenmountaininn.com

**ROOMS:** 73, including 13 suites; all with private bath, air conditioning, TV, phone, clock radio, Jacuzzi, fireplace, and VCR.

**RATES:** $79 to $129, single; $89 to $150, double occupancy; $99 to $150, suites; EP. Higher rates in fall and during Christmas week.

**OPEN:** All year.

**FACILITIES AND ACTIVITIES:** Breakfast, lunch, dinner. Lounge; gift shop; Health Club with sauna, whirlpool, massage, exercise machines, heated swimming pool. Nearby: skiing.

*T*his lovely inn turned 150 years old in 1983, and to celebrate the event properly, it was completely restored. There are period wall-papers, paints, and stencils; smoke alarms and sprinkler systems; and a handcrafted reproduction furniture line, named after the inn by the manufacturer.

The Health Club is fantastic. What a place! It has everything you could want in it. Massage, sauna, whirlpool—such luxury. Inquire about the inn's complete health package, which includes diet. If the Health Club isn't for you, there's a heated outdoor swimming pool with a sun terrace, a glorious spot on a summer day.

The Whip is the lounge area, which provides a casual setting for the food that is served all day. A beautiful, huge fireplace is along one wall, and the beer tap is the most unusual I've seen. It is colorful ceramic and serves three different beers.

The dining room is charming. At lunch the chicken salad plate was hand-somely served and delicious. Dinner was even better. Everyone who works here makes you feel right at home.

After you've had an active day on the ski slopes, the public rooms are a great place to relax. The library has a chess set at the ready. The connecting parlor with a roaring fire in the fireplace has the daily newspapers, including the *New York Times*.

The guest rooms have twin beds or canopy-covered queen-sized beds, with comfortable mattresses. All are well appointed, with lots of towels and extra pillows. There are a number of nonsmoking rooms. Some suites have a Jacuzzi, and one has a fireplace. This inn really has everything.

**HOW TO GET THERE:** Take I–89 to Route 100 north into Stowe. The inn is at the intersection of Routes 100 and 108.

# Ten Acres Lodge
## Stowe, Vermont 05672

INNKEEPERS: Jane and Eric Lande

ADDRESS/TELEPHONE: 14 Barrows Road; (802) 253–7638 or
(800) 327–7357 (outside Vermont)

ROOMS: 16, plus 2 guest cottages; all with private bath and phone;
1 room specially equipped for handicapped. Pets welcome in cottages.

RATES: $110 to $140, double occupancy, EPB. $150 to $180, double
occupancy, MAP. Guest cottages higher.

OPEN: All year.

FACILITIES AND ACTIVITIES: Dinner every night in-season, Friday
through Sunday off-season. Bar, swimming pool, hot tub, tennis court,
cross-country skiing. Nearby: downhill skiing.

*T*he living rooms at Ten Acres Lodge are the most inviting and comfortable these bones have enjoyed in many a mile. You'll find soft couches and chairs, large fireplaces, bookcases full of good reading, and windows that look out on sheer beauty year-round. In summer dairy cows graze in the rolling farm fields across the road; in winter cross-country ski trails crisscross the hillside. Around the inn are maples more than a century old that provide lazy New England shade.

The dining rooms are beautifully appointed, from the poppy-colored wallpapers to the napery. The food
is thoughtfully prepared. The
menu changes every night.
There are starters like fresh
artichokes and scallops with
saffron mayonnaise or garlic
sausage with roasted red peppers. And this I love: fried brie
with apples. The menu has a
variety of fish, veal, steak, and

lamb entrees, all skillfully cooked by the chef. AAA has awarded the inn a four-diamond rating.

The very comfortable guest rooms are carpeted and pine-paneled or wallpapered with pine trim. The beds are queens and doubles, covered with lovely homemade spreads. The newest rooms have a beautiful black-and-brass king-sized bed, a nice couch, and air conditioning. Another room has a canopy bed and a lovely armoire painted white with birds and flowers. Hill House has eight deluxe rooms with cable television, telephone, fireplace, and deck or patio. It is really nice. The guest cottages have their own kitchens, working fireplaces, and terraces that look out at all the wonderful scenery that surrounds Stowe.

The inn has a neat bar and a gameroom all set for a game of backgammon, chess, or checkers. Outside, you are in the ski capital of the East. The mountains are just beautiful. Go and enjoy.

**HOW TO GET THERE:** From Route 100 north in Stowe, turn left at the three-way stop onto Route 108. Proceed approximately 3 miles, then bear left onto Luce Hill Road. Ten Acres is located in approximately ½ mile, on the left.

# Tucker Hill Lodge
## Waitsfield, Vermont 05673

**INNKEEPERS:** Susan and Giorgio Noaro

**ADDRESS/TELEPHONE:** RFD 1, Box 147; (802) 496–3983 or (800) 543–7841 (outside Vermont); fax (802) 496–3203

**WEB SITE:** www.tuckerhill.com

**ROOMS:** 20, plus 2 suites; 16 with private bath, 4 with wheelchair access. Also an 1824 farmhouse with fireplace, phones, and TV, for a family or two or three couples.

**RATES:** Rooms and suites, $130 to $200, per person, double occupancy, MAP; $70 to $130, double occupancy, midweek, EPB. Farmhouse, $180 to $200, double occupancy, MAP.

**OPEN:** All year, except April and November.

**FACILITIES AND ACTIVITIES:** Dinner nightly except October 16 to December 15. Cafe open when the inn is open. Wheelchair access to dining room. Trail lunches all year. Bar. Swimming pool, tennis, hiking. Nearby: fishing, golf, ski touring centers, also cross-country.

**RECOMMENDED COUNTRY INNS® TRAVELERS' CLUB BENEFIT:** 10 percent discount, Monday–Thursday, excluding holidays.

*Y*ou will find Tucker Hill Lodge nestled on a wooded ridge overlooking the road that winds up to the Mad River Glen Ski area. This is Route 17, and it is one of the most spectacular roads I have found in many a country mile.

Flowers are the first thing you see as you arrive at the inn. They are everywhere and are glorious.

Rooms here are not fancy, but they are clean and comfortable. You will find antiques and fresh flowers and, on the beds, handmade quilts. The living room is pine-paneled with a fieldstone fireplace.

Food is the name of the game here. The inn won the coveted 1985 Vermont Restaurateur of the Year award and is one of a few that has been given four diamonds by AAA. The innkeepers grow their own herbs and vegetables, smoke their own meats, and make their own jams and jellies and vinegars.

Giorgio's Cafe is rather new, and boy, is it neat! They built a stone oven for pizza. It has an eight-ton fieldstone base on a 4-foot-thick foundation. In it the wood fire maintains a temperature of more than 700 degrees, which gives their pizza its crispy, smoky-flavored crust. The chef uses an original pizza crust recipe from Italy. There are fourteen different toppings for the basic pizza.

There is also saltimbocca, which means "jump in the mouth." It is pan-roasted western beef with fontina cheese and prosciutto. For dessert I loved the Fonduta al Cioccolato, which is melted chocolate served with fresh fruit. Another is zabaglione, an old favorite. They also serve a couple of hot drinks that are real winners.

There is a lot doing up here. In cool weather a neat lounge is a fun spot, decorated with antique farm and kitchen tools. There are four ski touring centers within a ten-minute drive from the inn. In addition, there is a Robert Trent Jones golf course nearby, plus swimming, tennis, fishing, and more. Or you can just relax in this lovely inn.

**HOW TO GET THERE:** Turn west off Route 100 onto Route 17 in Waitsfield in the Mad River Valley. Go 1½ miles west; the sign for the lodge will be on your left.

# Thatcher Brook Inn
## Waterbury, Vermont 05676

**INNKEEPERS:** Deborah and Mark Gagnon; Lisa and John Fischer, managers

**ADDRESS/TELEPHONE:** Route 100 North (mailing address: P.O. Box 490); (802) 244–5911 or (800) 292–5911

**ROOMS:** 24; all with private bath, phone, clock radio; 6 with whirlpool tub, 1 specially equipped for handicapped, and 3 with wheelchair access.

**RATES:** $75 to $210, double occupancy, EPB.

**OPEN:** All year.

**FACILITIES AND ACTIVITIES:** Dinner, bar, and lounge. Wheelchair access to dining room. Nearby: canoeing, biking, hiking, cross-country skiing, golf, tennis.

**RECOMMENDED COUNTRY INNS® TRAVELERS' CLUB BENEFIT:** 25 percent discount, Sunday–Monday, two night minimum, not valid during peak periods.

Thatcher Brook, named after Colonel Partridge Thatcher, was quite a powerful stream in the late 1800s. It had two sets of beautiful waterfalls, and during the nineteenth century two mills were constructed at these falls. In 1894 Stedman Wheeler purchased the upper sawmill and a small house. He became so prosperous in his business that he decided to construct a larger house on land directly across from the mill. Today that house is Thatcher Brook Inn.

It is obvious from the fine attention to detail and workmanship in the inn that old Stedman spared no expense. The house took two years to construct. Several types of lumber were used in the inn, including oak, bird's-eye maple, spruce, cherry, and birch. The hand-carved fireplace and stairway are original to the house, as are the pocket doors between the two front dining rooms and the window seat in the lobby. Especially attractive is the gazebo-type front porch.

The rooms are colorful, neat, and clean. One has a canopied bed. The shower curtains are remarkably lovely. The decorating has been done well. A sitting area, well equipped with books and games, is up by the rooms. Another building has been added to the inn. It alone is worth a trip.

There are six dining rooms and a lovely deck with umbrellas. The tables are lovely, with restful pink cloths and darker, complementary napkins. Dinner is memorable. One favorite appetizer is Mushrooms a la Thatcher (I won't explain them; come see for yourself). Another is baked brie, and the dipping sauces change quite often. A great soup is country red potato and cheddar au gratin. These are followed by entrees like roast stuffed pork tenderloin, grilled lemon and rosemary duck breasts, seafood in parchment, and vegetarian pasta. The possibilities are truly wonderful. With all this good food, you can imagine that the desserts are delicious.

The Newsroom Bar & Grill opens at 5:00 nightly and serves its own menu. It has beef and black bean chili, Vermont hamburger, barbecued pork sandwich, and more.

Be sure to wander across the street to look at the two sets of beautiful waterfalls.

**HOW TO GET THERE:** The inn is ¼ mile north of exit 10 off I–89, on Route 100, the road to Stowe.

# The Inn at Weathersfield 💟
Weathersfield, Vermont 05151

**INNKEEPERS:** Mary and Terry Carter

**ADDRESS/TELEPHONE:** Route 106, Box 165; (802) 263–9217 or (800) 477–4828; fax (802) 263–9219

**ROOMS:** 9, plus 3 suites; all with private bath; 8 with fireplace.

**RATES:** $185 to $250, double occupancy, MAP plus afternoon tea.

**OPEN:** All year.

**FACILITIES AND ACTIVITIES:** Dining room closed Monday and Tuesday April 1 to 15. Tavern, recreation room with aerobics equipment, tennis, sauna; pool table, TV and VCR with movies, large library, gift shop. Outside amphitheater, gardens and recreation area suitable for weddings or small conference groups; horse box stalls for rent, horse-drawn sleigh and carriage rides.

*T*his beautiful old inn was built circa 1795 and has a wonderful history. Prior to the Civil War, it was an important stop on the Underground Railroad, sheltering slaves en route to Canada. The inn is set well back from the road on twenty-one acres of property. Your rest is assured.

Everything that has been done to improve this lovely inn has been undertaken with class and lots of care. In the reconstructed barn attached to the inn are five beamed-ceiling guest rooms with sensational old bathtubs. These are real honest-to-goodness Victorian bathrooms. There are twelve fireplaces in the inn, and each of these rooms has one. Two of the suites have a bedroom and sitting room—the innkeepers say that these are ideal for honeymooners; the other sleeps four and is good for families. All the rooms are beautiful with fresh flowers, fresh fruit, canopy beds, and feather pillows.

Over the years, the inn has built an extensive and well-balanced wine cellar. The tavern is modeled after eighteenth-century Massachusetts taverns. The nonsmoking greenhouse–dining room is a handsome complement to the other rooms. Stencils copied from those used in the early 1800s decorate many of the rooms.

Excellent food is served here. They have four-star and four-diamond ratings. Game consommé with chanterelle and leek and roasted quail with Tokay grapes and chêvre might begin your meal. Six or more entrees like rack of Vermont lamb or their own farm-raised pheasant with roasted corn, red peppers, and spring onion are offered each night. The menu changes daily, taking advantage of what is in season. They grow their own herbs in a special space in the garden. Be sure to save room for desserts, as they are glorious. The culinary staff are an extraordinary team. A wassail cup is served from a cauldron in the keeping-room fireplace. Afternoon tea, served daily, is special.

There's a horse named Erica.

**HOW TO GET THERE:** Take I–91 North to exit 7 (Springfield, Vermont). Take Route 11 to Springfield, and then take Route 106 in town to the inn on your left, set well back from the road.

# Deerhill Inn 💗
## West Dover, Vermont 05356

**INNKEEPERS:** Linda and Michael Anelli

**ADDRESS/TELEPHONE:** Valley View Road (mailing address: Box 136); (802) 464–3100 or (800) 993–3379; fax (802) 464–5474

**E-MAIL:** deerhill@sover.net

**WEB SITE:** www.sover.net/~dvalnews/deerhill.html

**ROOMS:** 13, plus 2 suites; all with private bath; many with fireplace, 6 with decks, 3 with balconies.

**RATES:** $150 to $220, double occupancy, MAP; $100 to $150, double occupancy, EPB.

**OPEN:** All year.

**FACILITIES AND ACTIVITIES:** Bar, full license. Wheelchair access to dining room. Swimming pool. Nearby: golf, fishing, cross-country and downhill skiing, tennis court, beaches, theater, and music hall.

**RECOMMENDED COUNTRY INNS® TRAVELERS' CLUB BENEFIT:** Call for details on all packages available to RCI members: "Wine, Dine, and Stay," golf, skiing, fishing.

*T*he setting for the Deerhill Inn is perfect. Surrounded by lovely maple and fruit trees, it is perched on a hill with views of the countryside's beautiful mountains and lush meadows. Everything is nice and quiet up here.

The inn dogs, Chuck and Tiff, may greet you when you arrive. The downstairs parlor has a beautiful copper-topped table, couches, and good chairs. There's a fireplace in here, too. As you wander on, you arrive in the dining rooms with their wonderful views and a magnificent mural done by a local artist. There is artwork for sale on the other walls. The plants are delightful.

For appetizers you may find grilled skewered shrimp with hot mustard sauce, smoked Atlantic salmon, the day's fresh pasta, and soup. Entrees may include fresh fish of the day, veal medallions hunter-style, pork loin, steak, or the day's meat pie. Save room for the chocolate Grand Marnier cake, or perhaps you'd like a lemon parfait. Oh my!

Upstairs is a great library, good couches, that view again, a fireplace, and television. The accommodations are lush. There are quilts on most beds, and flannel sheets in winter. Two rooms have decks. One room has a canopy bed, Oriental furniture, and a lovely Oriental fan on the wall.

The Anellis won the Room of the Year award from Waverly fabrics; I saw

the room, and it's a real beauty, as they all are.

If ever I had wanted to own an inn, this would have been the one.

There's much to do in the area. For skiing there are Mount Snow and Haystack, Stratton, and Bromley, as well as cross-country places. In the summertime cast for trout on the Battenkill River, go play a game of golf, or use the inn's pool. It's beautiful up here.

A flash for all anglers: The inn is a short drive to Lake Whitingham, the second largest lake in Vermont, and just 20 miles from the Connecticut River and New Hampshire lakes, so come on up! This gives you very productive fishing in the Northeast. Want more? Well, Jim Sweeney will pick you up at the door and away you go.

For something different at the end of summer, there's the wicked wild mountain bike race.

HOW TO GET THERE: Take Route 9 to Wilmington; turn north onto Route 100 at the traffic light and continue to West Dover village. Pass the church and post office; at the antiques store turn right onto Valley View Road. The inn is 300 yards up the road, on the right-hand side.

# Doveberry Inn
## West Dover, Vermont 05356

**INNKEEPERS:** Michael and Christine Fayette

**ADDRESS/TELEPHONE:** Box 1736, Route 100; (800) 722–3204 or (802) 464–5652; fax (802) 464–6229

**ROOMS:** 8, all with private bath; some with fireplaces, TV, and VCR.

**RATES:** $80 to $140 EPB, double occupancy, MAP rates available.

**OPEN:** All year except last two weeks of April and first two in May.

**FACILITIES AND ACTIVITIES:** Breakfast and dinner (no dinner on Tuesday night), sugar house nearby has swimming pool, sauna, basketball, exercise room. Nearby: cross-country trails (small fee).

This lovely inn is just 1¾ miles from Mount Snow on Route 100 in a lovely area with much to do. The Marlboro Music Festival is but a short drive away.

Accommodations are lovely. Some are small and very neat. Some are larger. It's really your choice. One has a sundeck; all are pretty and clean with televisions and VCRs. So you have lovely countryside and the modern world.

There's a Christmas village in the living room, along with a fireplace, a good couch, and a small bar. Next is the dining room. Two or three different table runners vary with the season and are very pretty. Christine does the desserts, and Michael is the head chef. The menu changes seasonally. Some appetizers on my last visit were grilled shrimp served on a bed of cucumber noodles, vegetable risotto topped with fresh reggiano Parmesan, and calamari sautéed with baby leeks, black olives, and roasted red peppers. There are very fresh good salads. Entrees may be sautéed halibut or soft-shelled crabs, lobster ravioli, pork chops, chicken breast, steak or veal chops. Do save room for glorious homemade desserts. There's a wine rack between the two dining rooms.

Nicholas is the young son, and I'm so glad I got to meet him. What a future he has!

**HOW TO GET THERE:** Exit 2 from I–91 in Brattleboro, then take Route 9 west to Wilmington and Route 100 north about 7½ miles to West Dover. The inn is on the right.

# The Inn at Sawmill Farm ♥
## West Dover, Vermont 05356

**INNKEEPERS:** Rodney, Ione, and Brill Williams and Bobbie Dee Molitor

**ADDRESS/TELEPHONE:** Cross Town Road (mailing address: P.O. Box 367); (802) 464–8131

**ROOMS:** 10, plus 10 in cottages; all with private bath, some with fireplace.

**RATES:** $320 to $360, double occupancy, MAP; cottage rooms, $370 to $400, MAP. During Christmas week, foliage season, Thanksgiving, and New Year's Eve, $10 higher.

**OPEN:** All year.

**FACILITIES AND ACTIVITIES:** Bar, lounge, swimming pool, tennis court, trout and two bass fishing ponds.

The Williamses have transformed an old Vermont barn into the gayest, warmest, most attractive inn that I have seen in a long time. Ione is a professional decorator and Rod is a noted architect, which makes for a wonderful marriage of talents for just a perfect inn. The Williamses' son, Brill, runs the kitchen, and he does a superb job of it.

The inn's copper collection is extensive. The oversized fireplace in the living room is surrounded with it, and there's a huge copper-topped coffee table that's a beauty. They also have a handsome brass telescope on a tripod for your viewing of Mount Snow. A most incredible bar of solid copper also lives here. This is in the Pot Belly Lounge.

Accommodations are very different, with some rooms done in Victorian motif, some in Chippendale, and all with the flavor of New England at its best. The cottage rooms have fireplaces. The accommodations upstairs in Spring House have a living room with fireplace, bedroom, and bath in the most glorious colors imaginable. I was in Farm House, and my room was done in the softest pastels, with a king-sized bed and a lovely dressing room and bath. They are all color coordinated, with thick towels and extra pillows. Little boxes of Godiva chocolates are in each room. A very nice touch. The inn's facilities are not well suited to children under ten.

Dinner is beyond belief. Brill is a fine chef. There are eight appetizers. Coquille of crabmeat imperial under glass was my choice. A friend of mine had thinly sliced raw sirloin of beef with shallot and mustard sauce. Of course, I tasted some of hers. Outstanding. The soups are inventive and good. One entree is medallions of pork tenderloin with cognac, cream, and walnuts. There are many others, like rack of lamb, roast duck, and grilled salmon. They are perfectly complemented by wines from Brill's impressive wine cellar. Desserts are all homemade. Breakfast is also special. Fresh orange juice and homemade tomato juice are just starters. The staff who serve all these goodies are very courteous.

The inn makes a specialty of special occasions. Do try to get up here for Christmas. It's something you will never forget.

**HOW TO GET THERE:** Take I-91 to exit 2 in Brattleboro. Take Route 9 west to Wilmington, and then follow Route 100 north 6 miles to West Dover.

# West Dover Inn
## West Dover, Vermont 05356

**INNKEEPERS:** Monique Phelan and Greg Granas

**ADDRESS/TELEPHONE:** Box 506, Route 100; (802) 464–5207;
fax (802) 464–2173

**E-MAIL:** wdvrinn@sover.net

**WEB SITE:** www.westdoverinn.com

**ROOMS:** 8, plus 4 suites, all with private baths and TV; suites have
Jacuzzis and fireplaces.

**RATES:** $80 to $200, double occupancy, EPB.

**OPEN:** All year except mid-April through Memorial Day weekend and
first and second weeks in November.

**FACILITIES AND ACTIVITIES:** Dinner (fall and winter, Thursday
through Monday; summer, Thursday through Saturday); cocktail
lounge. Nearby: Mountain Golf, swimming, hiking, skiing (all types).

*I*t's a lovely old inn, an inn since 1846. It became the site of the town
offices and had many changes. When you come in the front door, to
the left is the office and on the right is a nice living room with a fireplace, good couches, books, a television, and a VCR. Nice and comfortable
accommodations are very clean and neat. There are queen-sized beds and a
few doubles. For a family, a pair of twins and a double are nice. The suites are
a joy; all have a fireplace and
Jacuzzi tub. There are bears on
the bed, unique and handmade.

There is much to do here in
the area, whatever season you
would like to come. The inn is
just a short hop to every type of
outdoor activity, and the inn
itself is a nice place to be.

Breakfast is served in a
cherry breakfast room, and, as
they say, anything you can put
syrup on they have, along with fruit and eggs. The dining room is very pleasant—nice napery and good food. There are appetizers like bruschetta with an
antipasto of marinated tomatoes, roasted onion, olives, and capers or pan-
seared scallop and lobster cakes served with a spicy tomato remoulade sauce.

Entrees could be grilled salmon filet, honey Hoisin glazed duck, steak, pork, chicken, pasta, plus chef's specials. Save room for dessert. The lounge is nice; a bar with six comfortable stools is also full service and watched over by two inn dogs, Hungarian Vizslas named Sam and Zoe. I had a friend in Essex, Connecticut, who had one named Buda—what a character he was.

**HOW TO GET THERE:** From Brattleboro, take exit 2 off I–91 north to Route 9 west. Go 20 miles to Wilmington. Turn right at the traffic light onto Route 100 north. Proceed 6 miles to the inn. From Bennington, take Route 9 east 21 miles to Wilmington. Turn left at the traffic light onto Route 100 north. Proceed 6 miles to the inn.

# Willough Vale Inn
## Westmore, Vermont 05680

**INNKEEPER:** Tom Small

**ADDRESS/TELEPHONE:** Route 5A; (802) 525–4123 or (800) 594–9102

**E-MAIL:** info@ willoughvale.com

**WEB SITE:** www.willoughvale.com

**ROOMS:** 8, plus 4 cottages; all with private bath; 1 specially equipped for handicapped. Fireplaces in cottages.

**RATES:** $79 to $125, double occupancy; $99 to $179, cottages; continental breakfast. Higher in fall.

**OPEN:** All year.

**FACILITIES AND ACTIVITIES:** Lunch, summer and fall; box lunches all year. Dinner, bar, and lounge. Wheelchair access to dining room and restrooms. Fishing, swimming, and boating at the lake. Nearby: snowshoeing, snowmobile trails, hiking. Snowmobile trail from back door.

his is a scenic paradise with one of the most beautiful lakes I've seen in many a country mile. Do you like to fish? There are lake trout, landlocked salmon, perch, and rainbow trout just waiting for your line. In the main dining room is a large lighted display case of fishing rods, indicative of the fine fishing in the lake.

A porch with a gazebo at one end overlooks the lake. Under it are beautiful flowers. Lupine and wildflowers are all over the place.

The inn is full of antique and Vermont-handcrafted furniture. The guest rooms are all furnished differently. There are twin and double beds, and one room has a four-poster bed. There's even a Jacuzzi for two in a lovely bathroom. Clock radios are in all the rooms. I liked the nice parlor and library. It's a quiet spot for cards, writing, reading, or just relaxing after an active day.

The taproom has an elegant bar and tables. It offers a special menu during all the hours it's open. Steamed mussels, taproom nachos, today's soup, and grand salads. The Green Mountain Club is awesome—a mountain of turkey breast, baked ham, bacon, tomato, lettuce, Vermont cheddar, and mayonnaise, plus fries and a pickle. The burgers are also excellent. There is a lot more.

Dinner can be enjoyed along with the lake view. The menu features steak and delicious pork and chicken, also roast turkey with all the trimmings and

seconds are available. The seafood is glorious. Crabcakes, sea bass, sea scallops, and, of course, salmon. There is a nice vegetarian pasta dish. Freshly baked desserts and good teas and coffee bring your meal to a grand conclusion.

There are climbing trails on Mount Hor and Mount Pisgah and skiing at nearby Burke Mountain. Snowmobiling across the frozen lake is invigorating. Or go visit the nearby llama farm. A canoe ride on a moonlit night would be wonderful.

The fully equipped cottages have a fireplace, screened porch, deck, and private dock. There are two-bedroom cabins and one with one bedroom. Pets are welcome here.

HOW TO GET THERE: From the south leave I–91 at Lyndonville (exit 23) and proceed north on Routes 5 and 5A. From Canada get off I–91 at Barton and follow Route 16 to Route 5A.

# Windham Hill Inn
## West Townshend, Vermont 05359

**INNKEEPERS:** Pat and Grigs Markham

**ADDRESS/TELEPHONE:** RR 1, Box 44; (802) 874–4080 or
(800) 944–4080; fax (802) 874–4702

**E-MAIL:** meetings@windhamhill.com

**WEB SITE:** www.windhamhill.com/meeting.html

**ROOMS:** 21; all with private bath, phones, and air conditioning; some
with fireplace or porch; 1 equipped for the handicapped; some with
Jacuzzi or soaking tub.

**RATES:** $190 to $315, single; $245 to $370, double; MAP. Special
weekend packages available. B&B available.

**OPEN:** All year except one week in November.

**FACILITIES AND ACTIVITIES:** Full liquor license. Wheelchair access
to all public rooms. Conference facilities. Pool, tennis, hiking, cross-
country skiing, ice skating. Nearby: downhill skiing.

*I*f you are a dreamer as I am, and you dream of a perfect country inn,
this is as close as you will come. At Windham Hill you are sitting on
top of the world, and it is beautiful up here. The West River valley
stretches as far as the eye can see. The 160-acre site was a working dairy farm
when the house was built about 1825, and in 1962 it was converted to an inn.

When you arrive at the inn, on the right is one of the living rooms with a
fireplace. Keep on walking into the next room, where there are a nice bar and

three bar stools. Take another right into a room with a porch and a fantastic view. Here's where you'll find a piano, books, chess, and games.

Straight ahead are the lovely dining rooms. The Frog Pond dining room has a view of Frog Pond, of course, and the great beyond. It has a fireplace, private tables, and the "Big Table," which is a nice way to meet other inn guests.

The menu for the five-course dinner changes nightly. When I was visiting, there were crabcakes, sautéed sea scallops with a tomato-corn relish, sun-dried tomato ravioli with a pesto beurre blanc, good soups, and salads. For entrees I had my choice of grilled veal medallions, fillet of salmon, and grilled medallions of beef tenderloin. The desserts were very tempting—fresh peach almond tart, chocolate mousse cake, spiced rhubarb, raspberry cobbler, and fresh seasonal fruit. All this, plus you have your pick of wines from a wonderful wine cellar.

The accommodations are awesome. All have views that are enough to keep you in bed all day. Beds are queens and kings, and some rooms have a fireplace or porch. The White Barn has glorious rooms—always has, but now there are three more. I was in Meadowlook with a million-dollar view. Full of comfort, Marion Goodfellow has its own cupola and North Loft. The Markhams have really added to this wonderful inn. The new conference room is 1,000 square feet of sheer beauty. Birch and cherry floors, a fieldstone fireplace, Oriental rugs, and all of the business equipment necesary for anything. Up here you're so close to heaven.

There's a heated pool and tennis courts, and all with a view. Ten kilometers of groomed cross-country trails are also here at the inn, as are lessons and rental equipment. Hiking on the inn's trails is breathtaking. Downhill skiing is close by, or you can ice skate on the inn's pond. So much to do here, why go anywhere else?

What in the world are you waiting for? At least come and say hello to Bart the Bear in the lounge area and the real live goldens, Taylor and Monty, the inn dogs.

HOW TO GET THERE: The inn is located just off the road to Windham, approximately 1½ miles from Route 30.

# Fogged Inn ♥
## Williamstown, Vermont 05679

**INNKEEPER:** Ronald Saldi

**ADDRESS/TELEPHONE:** Clark Road (mailing address: P.O. Box 1540); (802) 433–6627; fax (802) 433–5501

**ROOMS:** 18; all with private bath, TV, VCR, phones, and air conditioning. Pets welcome.

**RATES:** $59 to $135, double occupancy, EPB. MAP rates available.

**OPEN:** All year except April.

**FACILITIES AND ACTIVITIES:** Dinner, weekends only. Full license. Twelve-stall barn. Nearby: cross-country skiing.

**RECOMMENDED COUNTRY INNS® TRAVELERS' CLUB BENEFIT:** 15 percent discount, April and November, excluding Thanksgiving season, subject to availability.

Fogged Inn is perched on a knoll overlooking the Williamstown Valley. The views are spectacular whichever direction you look in. It sits on 46 acres, surrounded by lovely meadows and nice white picket fences. The property had been known as Autumn Crest Farm for well over a century. It was a dairy farm for most of those years, and then a horse farm before being completely restored as a country inn. Horses are still here, and so are the deer and wild turkeys. This would be a beautiful place for a wedding or conference.

There is a wraparound porch where, in good weather, you can sit and contemplate whatever your heart desires. The large common room has a great fireplace, and tucked into one corner is a cute bar. There is a sideboard in the living room with little houses that are always lighted. A nice

touch. There's also a small gift shop. The rooms and suites are very comfortable. The decor is elegant country.

Dinner is by candlelight, and the food, well, let me name for you a few of their offerings. Lobster dumplings in spicy garlic sauce with mushrooms;

baked shrimp in Dijon mustard-Gouda sauce; and good soups (I enjoyed the conch chowder). There are entrees like mixed grill—one quail, one-half chicken, and one-quarter duck served with marsala sauce. You could also select the New York sirloin or the full rack of lamb. The salads are very nice.

All the desserts are made right here. Berry pie of the week is served a la mode. Cheesecake is served hot. Homemade key lime pie comes with raspberry coulis. An almond cup is filled with white chocolate mousse and raspberry coulis. I had a chardonnay from South Africa with my dinner. It was very good. They also have eighteen different beers and wonderful hot drinks.

This is a really nice country inn. Do give it a try.

**HOW TO GET THERE:** The inn is just two minutes from I-89; exit 5 on Route 64 east.

# The Hermitage
## Wilmington, Vermont 05363

**INNKEEPERS:** Jim and Lois McGovern

**ADDRESS/TELEPHONE:** Coldbrook Road; (802) 464–3759; fax (802) 464–2688

**E-MAIL:** hermitage@sover.net

**WEB SITE:** www.hermitageinn.com

**ROOMS:** 15; all with private bath, wheelchair accessibility, phone, TV, VCR, and fireplace.

**RATES:** $112.50 to $125, per person, double occupancy, MAP.

**OPEN:** All year.

**FACILITIES AND ACTIVITIES:** Brunch every Sunday. Wheelchair access to dining room. Restaurant is air-conditioned. Sauna, wine cellar, game bird farm, trout pond, tennis, hiking, cross-country skiing from the door. Swimming at Brook Bound.

**RECOMMENDED COUNTRY INNS® TRAVELERS' CLUB BENEFIT:** 10 percent discount (rooms and meals only), Monday–Thursday, not valid with other offers.

*H*igh on a windy hill facing Haystack Mountain, you will find a unique and heartwarming country inn, The Hermitage. The owner is a man for all seasons who knows what he is doing. He also has a certain charm. Maybe it is the quick smile or a fleeting twinkle as he says, "No piped-in music in my inn." You might, though, find a classical guitarist some night or someone at the piano in the lounge.

Come in the very early spring and you will find maple sugaring going full blast. There are four sugarhouses on the property, and Jim McGovern makes about 700 gallons of maple syrup a year. In summer the big kettles are kept simmering making homemade jams and jellies.

Sporting clays, a shotgun game imported from England, simulates the flight patterns of game birds in their natural settings. The clay "birds" are thrown from ten different fields, so there are grand challenges. Also here is a 500-acre hunting preserve.

Along with this talent for making the most of nature's bounty, Jim is an oenophile (wine lover) and has a wine cellar with a stock of 30,000 bottles. You are never at a loss for the perfect wine to enjoy with this inn's first-rate food.

Dining at The Hermitage is truly gourmet and includes homegrown game and fresh vegetables. The dining rooms are lovely. The Delacroix Room was named for Michael Delacroix, whose paintings are featured throughout the inn. (Michael has recently done the Hermitage—a beautiful winter snow painting, available here, of course.) In here is a fireplace to warm you while you enjoy some of Jim's wines.

Jim raises as many as sixty different species of game birds. Most of them, such as pheasant, partridge, duck, quail, turkey, and goose, are raised for gourmet dining. Jim also has show birds, brilliantly colored species of ducks and peacocks and a pair of black swans. Sindy, the inn dog, may come by to say hello, but he is likely to be distracted by a passing gaggle of geese that will fly off in a flurry of wings. Jim also has a large collection of decoys of every description on display and for sale.

The comfortable rooms, all with their own working fireplace, are furnished with antiques and, 'oh, those brass beds! In the carriage house you will even find a sauna.

Brook Bound, down the hill from The Hermitage, is also owned by the McGoverns. It has fourteen rooms with ten private baths. Dinner is at The Hermitage.

**HOW TO GET THERE:** Take Route 9 to Wilmington; follow Route 100 north 2 miles to Coldbrook Road on the left. The Hermitage is 3 miles down Coldbrook Road.

# Red Shutters Inn
## Wilmington, Vermont 05363

**INNKEEPERS:** Tad and Renée Lyon

**ADDRESS/TELEPHONE:** Route 9 West; (802) 464–3768 or (800) 845–7548; fax (802) 464–5123

**ROOMS:** 7 rooms, 2 suites, all with private bath; some with fireplace and TV.

**RATES:** $100 to $225, double occupancy, EPB.

**OPEN:** All year except Easter to May 15.

**FACILITIES AND ACTIVITIES:** Full license, breakfast, dinner every night except Monday. Nearby: shopping, skiing.

Nestled among many well-established maples, pin oaks, and evergreens on a lovely hillside is the Red Shutters Inn, located on the edge of Wilmington. There are five acres around the inn, which dates back to 1894. It is a handsome Colonial structure.

The carriage house, also built in 1894, was recently renovated. It has three rooms and a suite that has a skylight, a fireplace, and a magnificent brass bed. Of course, there's plenty of charm and comfort no matter where you are. There are ceiling fans in all of the rooms. The suite in the main house has a private deck overlooking the hillside.

There's a wood stove in the living room and pub—a

nice place to relax with a cocker called Taffy and another named Sadie. They are beauties.

The dining room is air conditioned for your comfort. And the food is yum yum. Choose from appetizers like a smoked seafood plate, baked brie with fresh fruit, and very good soups, and try entrees like lamb racks, pork tenderloin, venison with green peppercorn sauce and pickled red cabbage, chicken, and veal. The desserts and coffees are ambrosia. There's a nice fireplace in here and a dining porch with wicker furniture. A nice place to sit and read or just listen to the stream that goes by—very comforting. You are just steps away from the town, but you are in a country setting.

**HOW TO GET THERE:** Inn is located on Route 9 just west of the intersection of Route 100.

# The White House 💚
## Wilmington, Vermont 05363

**INNKEEPER:** Robert Grinold

**ADDRESS/TELEPHONE:** Route 9; (802) 464–2135 or (800) 541–2135; fax (802) 464–5222

**E-MAIL:** whitehse@sover.net

**WEB SITE:** www.whitehouseinn.com

**ROOMS:** 16 in main house and 7 in guest house; all with private bath; 9 with fireplace.

**RATES:** $108 to $178, double occupancy, EPB. MAP available.

**OPEN:** All year.

**FACILITIES AND ACTIVITIES:** Sunday brunch, skier's lunch in winter, dinner served all year except Easter to Memorial Day. Wheelchair access to dining rooms and common room and two guest rooms on first floor. Bar, lounge; swimming pool inside and out, health spa with sauna, steam room, whirlpool; cross-country skiing. Nearby: downhill skiing and sledding on the inn's own hill.

**RECOMMENDED COUNTRY INNS® TRAVELERS' CLUB BENEFIT:** 10 percent discount for two consecutive nights or 15 percent for three or more nights, Monday–Thursday.

*Y*ou would expect an inn named The White House to be elegant and, believe me, this one is. Built in 1914, the mansion has much to offer.

The gallery on the main floor has an extremely unusual wallpaper that was printed in Paris in 1912. There are high ceilings throughout the inn, and the living room is large, with a fireplace and beautifully covered (blue, of course) couches and chairs. The Casablanca bar has wicker chairs, couches, pretty flowered pillows, and Bob's collection of angels all around. So nice to come back to after a day on the ski trails.

There are two dining rooms, both of which are very elegant, and a small private dining room. The food served in this three-star inn is superb, but would you expect anything else in The White House? Here's just a sampling of what they offer. There are nine appetizers, including baked brie, carpaccio of beef, and interesting soups. Entrees are numerous and varied. One is bone-

less stuffed duck. Of course, all the desserts are homemade. I get hungry just writing about Bob's inn.

The grounds are sumptuous, with a lovely rose garden and fountain, and below this is a beautiful 60-foot swimming pool. There's another small fountain outside the lounge, and from this delightful room you watch spectacular sunsets over the Green Mountains.

The guest rooms here are all sizes. The new wing that faces west has four rooms with, as Bob says, two-passenger whirlpool tubs.

It seems appropriate that the inn dogs, both golden retrievers, are named Eleanor and Roosevelt.

The health spa is what you need after a day of fun: sauna, whirlpool, and showers. There's also an inside pool to relax in. Ah, what an inn!

Intrigue: Why did the original owner of the house put in a secret staircase? You will have to ask where it is.

**HOW TO GET THERE:** From I–91 take Route 9 to Wilmington. The inn is on your right, just before you reach the town.

# The Inn at Windsor
Windsor, Vermont 05089

**INNKEEPERS:** Larry Bowser and Holly Taylor

**ADDRESS/TELEPHONE:** 106 Main Street; (802) 674–5670

**ROOMS:** 2, 1 suite, all with private bath and fireplaces.

**RATES:** $95 to $125, double occupancy, EPB.

**OPEN:** All year.

**FACILITIES AND ACTIVITIES:** Breakfast only meal served. BYOB.

he inn is perched on a hill overlooking Main Street and shaded by tall trees. There's a driveway up the hill, next to a cemetery; you park at the top and proceed through the gate into a terraced garden. The door is here, and you may find shoes and slippers here because no one wears shoes inside—the innkeepers provide clean slippers for you.

There is so much history connected to this house it would take pages to tell it all, so come on up and ask because it's really a lovely story.

The bedrooms and suite are very pretty and comfortable. The suite has a TV and VCR, a library, a king-sized bed, and the original Indian shutters. Bathrobes are provided along with natural Vermont soaps. The living room looks out at a 250-year-old sugar maple.

The barn was built in 1791 by Green, an apothecary. It stayed in the Green family until 1963 when it was sold to the Knights of Columbus. During restoration they discovered hand-hewn beans, hand-planed planks on the walls, spruce flooring, and even pencil inscriptions on the bedroom walls made by Green's daughter Ann Elizabeth in 1847.

Breakfast may be orange Julius, fruit salad with yogurt and nuts, apple walnut French batter pancakes, hot glazed pears with cool yogurt topping, or baked herbed eggs. Before breakfast, coffee, tea, or juice may be brought to your room to wake you up.

**HOW TO GET THERE:** From I–91 take Exit 9; go down Main Street in Windsor to #106; it's on the right.

# Juniper Hill Inn 💙
## Windsor, Vermont 05089

**INNKEEPERS:** Rob and Susanne Pearl

**ADDRESS/TELEPHONE:** RR 1, Box 79; (802) 674–5273 or
(800) 359–2541; fax (802) 674–2041

**WEB SITE:** www.juniperhillinn.com

**ROOMS:** 16; all with private bath, 11 with fireplace. No smoking inn.

**RATES:** $95 to $175, double occupancy, EPB. MAP rates available.

**OPEN:** All year except April.

**FACILITIES AND ACTIVITIES:** Dinner by advance reservation six days a
week; open to the public by advance reservation Wednesday through
Sunday. No smoking in dining room. Full license, swimming pool.
Nearby: downhill and cross-country skiing.

**RECOMMENDED COUNTRY INNS® TRAVELERS' CLUB BENEFIT:** 10 percent discount, excluding September 15–October 30, holiday weekends,
and Christmas week, subject to availability.

The upper valley of Vermont is lovely and full of history. Windsor is
the birthplace of Vermont, and the longest covered bridge in
America is here. The inn is a 1902 Colonial Revival mansion that is
listed on the National Register of Historic Places. It was once known as a summer White House because former presidents Rutherford Hayes, Benjamin
Harris, and Theodore Roosevelt were frequent guests of the original owners.

Large white columns lead into a 30-by-40-foot oak-paneled entry hall.
You'll think it's big
enough to be a ball-
room, and it once was.
Hunting trophies used
to be displayed here.
Today it is one of the
parlors and called the
Great Room. There are
two smaller parlors for
reading or quiet con-
versation.

There is a beautiful grand staircase centered under a large Palladian window in a very private library wing. There are two guest rooms at the top of

the stairs. One has a canopied bed, the other has a porch, and both are charming.

Some of the other rooms have marble sinks, and one has a summer porch. Beds include a sleigh bed, brass beds, and four posters. They all afford a good night's sleep.

# Windsor Attractions

Billed as the birthplace of this nation's modern system of industrial production, Windsor offers visitors attractions related to this history as well as to arts and crafts still made as simply as in centuries past. For an entertaining and eye-opening look at the concept of interchangeable parts and mass production, visit Windsor's American Precision Museum (802-674-5781) at 196 Main Street (Route 5 North). Open Memorial Day through Labor Day, it houses the National Machine Tool Collection, a notable gun collection, and a scale model collection of actual working models of various manufacturing processes. See the products of Thomas Edison and Henry Ford; learn about the famed Sharps, Enfield, and Springfield rifles; peruse the outstanding collection of photographs, drawings, catalogs, and other documents related to the history of industry in the United States.

Windsor is also the place to enjoy fine handcrafts. Simon Pearce has another retail outlet of his hand-blown glassware, also on Main Street; call (802) 674-6280 for hours and information. The Vermont State Craft Center (802-674-6729) at Windsor House at 54 Main Street, not far from the Precision Museum, has a vast inventory of handmade furniture, quilts, pottery, wood crafts, weavings, baskets, sculpture, and Vermont-made foods by more than 250 Vermont artisans. It is open Monday through Saturday from 10:00 A.M. to 5:00 P.M., Sundays from 11:00 A.M. to 4:00 P.M. Just outside of town on Hunt Road, visit the beautiful gardens at Cider Hill (802-674-5293). Browse the footpaths through gardens and greenhouses, and visit the gallery for lithographs and prints. Plants and garden accessories are also for sale here. Cider Hill Gardens is open daily from May through July and on Friday through Sunday from August through October.

The whole inn, including the rooms, has been repainted. The innkeepers' goal is to keep the guest rooms among the finest in New England.

Please note the great table in the Great Room. Its top weighs more than 1,000 pounds. It is the original dining table of the house; now it holds a swan, books, and a lamp.

Ask about the special package plans they offer. There are pedal and paddle trips and canoeing trips on the Connecticut River. Bicycles are available for rental.

Some of the goodies from the chef are Vermont cheddar chicken, grilled trout, halibut, and steaks. There's no smoking in here; Tucker and Jane, the inn dogs, don't care for smoke.

**HOW TO GET THERE:** From I–91 going south take exit 9. Go about 3 miles on Route 5 south, then take a right onto Juniper Hill Road. Go ½ mile to the end of Juniper Hill and take a right. At the first junction turn left and go ½ mile up the hill to the driveway on the right.

# The Jackson House Inn
## Woodstock, Vermont 05091

**INNKEEPERS:** Juan and Gloria Florin

**ADDRESS/TELEPHONE:** (802) 457–2065 or (800) 448–1890; fax (802) 457–9290

**E-MAIL:** innkeepers@jacksonhouse.com

**WEB SITE:** www.jacksonhouse.com

**ROOMS:** 9, plus 6 one-room suites; all with private baths, Casablanca fans, and air conditioning; phones in the suites.

**RATES:** $170 to $260, double occupancy, EPB.

**OPEN:** All year.

**FACILITIES AND ACTIVITIES:** Full breakfast and dinner. Nearby: glass blowing, art galleries, biking, hiking, horseback riding, canoeing, swimming, golf, tennis, theater, skiing, sleigh rides, and more.

*W*hat a beauty this is! The long porch with both rockers and chairs and beautiful hanging plants is the first thing you see. And this that follows was said so well from the brochure.

The Jackson House was built with devotion in 1890 by Wales Johnson, a local sawmill owner. His aim was to erect the finest example of late Victorian architecture possible. Floors of cherry and maple complement fine furniture, walls, and moldings of the finest workmanship. The many exterior eaves and twin chimneys are a statement of pure classical design and dignity of workmanship. The building is listed on the National Register of Historic Places.

In 1940 the house was bought by the Jackson family and opened as the Seven Maples Tourist Home. In 1983 it was sold to the third owners in 100 years. They renovated the house, and in 1996 the Florins bought it. They have continued the tradition of excellence and personalized service.

The dining room is elegant, with white napery and a double fireplace. There's a chef's tasting menu—that's a grand idea—a spring vegetable menu, and a prix fixe menu. One appetizer that took my eye was wild ramp soup.

Entrees include veal tenderloin, free range chicken, lobster, beef, and fish. Desserts—well, as you can imagine, save room. Before the evening meal, complimentary wine or champagne and hors d'oeuvres are served. Breakfast the next morning is ample; almond-crusted French toast is just one idea.

A spa in the basement holds up to six people. A treadmill, stationary bicycle, and stair climber are also here for the guests' use. Those who prefer to relax may rest on the wicker furniture and enjoy a huge TV and VCR. Movies are provided. A juice bar is also here.

Handicapped access is to the first floor. Accommodations are grand. Four guest rooms are on the first floor; the rest are on the second and third floors. Two of the suites are on the third floor and are beauties. They open to a deck overlooking the landscaped gardens. One room has a Jacuzzi, and a few more have thermal massage tubs.

HOW TO GET THERE: Go through Woodstock and from the Green in town 1⁶/₁₀ miles on the right is the inn, on old Route 4.

# The Lincoln Inn
Woodstock, Vermont 05091

**INNKEEPERS:** Kurt and Lori Hildbrand

**ADDRESS/TELEPHONE:** Route 4; (802) 457–3312; fax (802) 457–5908

**E-MAIL:** Lincon2@aol.com

**ROOMS:** 6; all with private bath.

**RATES:** $99, double occupancy, MAP available. Higher rates in foliage season.

**OPEN:** All year except after Easter to May 1 and November 1 to Thanksgiving.

**FACILITIES AND ACTIVITIES:** Dinner Tuesday through Sunday. Sunday brunch. Bar, lounge, TV room, games, VCR for movies. Nearby: golf, fishing, cross-country and downhill skiing.

he Lincoln Covered Bridge is the only remaining wooden bridge of its kind and design left in America. In 1844 T. Willis Pratt invented and patented the bridge plans. In 1869 storm waters pushed the bridge from Dewey's Mill in Woodstock Village to an island downstream. In 1877 Charles Lincoln (cousin of Abraham) had the bridge moved to its current location by floating it on "jack" skates. It was renovated in 1947. It spans the Ottauguechee River and is at one end of the inn's property.

The inn, a 200-year-old farmhouse, sits on about six acres of rolling lawn alongside the river. It is a nice spot to go fishing or wading, so you fishermen should bring your pole and catch some fish.

There is an old stone fireplace for cookouts and a picnic table, so do come and relax. The swing in the old maple tree beckons me. In the wintertime it's snowmobiles and skiing that will keep you busy.

The nice living room offers a television and VCR with a library full of good movies. This is a great place to unwind on a snowy winter night. Accommodations are cozy. The beds are new and comfortable.

The dining room offers a full country breakfast and, in the evening, fireside dining. The chef-owner Kurt is a native of Switzerland—he has trained extensively in fine hotels. One of his appetizers is shrimp ravioli with leek puree, plus there are good soups and salads. Entrees include breast of chicken with tomatoes, basil, and a confit of garlic; loin of lamb; veal medallions; steak; and good seafood such as shrimp in phyllo with an orange-ginger-lime sauce or broiled lobster tail. Desserts—well, there's chocolate truffle cake with vanilla sauce and raspberries. There are more, but why go on after that one?

For a very special event, arrange to have your dinner in the gazebo on the knoll overlooking the river. What a way to go!

There is so much to do in this area. What are you waiting for? Come and enjoy.

**HOW TO GET THERE:** From I–91 take exit 9 and follow Route 12 north to Route 4. Take Route 4 to the inn; it is 3 miles west of the village green in Woodstock.

# The Village Inn
## Woodstock, Vermont 05091

**INNKEEPERS:** Kevin and Anita Clark

**ADDRESS/TELEPHONE:** 41 Pleasant Street; (802) 457–1255 or (800) 722–4571

**WEB SITE:** www.villageinnofwoodstock.com

**ROOMS:** 8, all with private bath and air conditioning; 1 with fireplace.

**RATES:** $110 to $190, double occupancy, EPB.

**OPEN:** All year.

**FACILITIES AND ACTIVITIES:** Dinner five nights, bar, lounge. Nearby: golf, tennis, skiing, swimming, boating, shopping.

Woodstock is a beautiful area. The Village Inn is within walking distance of the lovely village green. Once this was a forty-acre estate on the Ottauquechee River. The Victorian mansion and carriage house, built in 1899, are all that remain of the estate.

Lots of charm and comfort are found in the bar. The very pretty ceilings are of pressed tin, and there is a beautiful stained-glass window. The room also has a nineteenth-century oak bar. Upstairs is a large common room with a porch, television, and games. And—this is a good thing to know—the inn has a fire-alarm system.

Rooms are gracious, comfortable, and furnished nicely. Some have marble sinks in them. One has a king-sized bed and a working fireplace.

I loved the romantic dining room, complete with a working fireplace, the original tin ceilings, and natural oak woodwork. A chef-owned inn is always a plus. The menus are enticing. Among the appetizers I saw grilled minipizzas and fettucine Anita. I chose the stuffed baked potato skins, which were very good. Roast Vermont turkey is an entree that is too often forgotten on menus. Roast lamb, roast prime ribs of beef, fresh seafood catch of the day . . . and the menu goes on. Desserts, well, all I'll say is that they're homemade and delicious. The wine list is extensive and includes good wines at low prices.

Covered bridges, elegant shops, skiing, sleigh rides, golf, or tennis anyone? Go swimming or boating in one of the many lakes. Come on up and enjoy yourself. This whole area and this lovely refurbished inn get my applause.

**HOW TO GET THERE:** From I-91 take I-89 north to exit 1. Turn left into Woodstock. The inn is on the left.

# The Woodstock Inn
Woodstock, Vermont 05091

**INNKEEPER:** Tom List

**ADDRESS/TELEPHONE:** Fourteen the Green; (802) 457–1100 or
(800) 448–7900; international 0101–802–457–1100; fax (802) 457–6699

**E-MAIL:** woodstock.resort@connriver.net

**WEB SITE:** www.woodstockinn.com

**ROOMS:** 140 rooms, 4 suites, 1 house, all with private bath, color TV,
phones; 23 with fireplaces; some with VCR (tapes for rent at the front
desk).

**RATES:** $159 to $510, double occupancy, EP. Special package rates starting at $109 and MAP are available. No surcharges, no limits.

**OPEN:** All year.

**FACILITIES AND ACTIVITIES:** Breakfast, lunch, dinner. Richardson Tavern, full license, country club, golf, tennis, health and fitness center,
pool, classes, tennis, ski touring center. Nearby: horseback riding, hunting and fishing, bicycling.

**BUSINESS TRAVEL:** New York 260 miles, Hartford 166 miles, Boston
148 miles, Providence 180 miles, Montreal, Canada, 206 miles, Albany
138 miles, Burlington 89 miles.

What a beautiful inn! I cannot help but wonder why it's taken me
twenty-five years to put it in our guide. The grounds and flowers are lovely, and when you walk into the inn, it's glorious. The
old Woodstock Inn opened in 1892 and the new inn opened November 23,
1969. There are nooks to sit in and wonderful comfort. Accommodations?
There are a lot—144 rooms, four suites, and one house. Twenty-three rooms
have fireplaces; all are air conditioned, have color televisions, are beautifully
furnished, and so restful. The inn provides air mattresses for kids and they
love them—like camping, you know, for a kid.

The dining rooms are elegant, and so is the food. They have been awarded
four diamonds and four stars. Besides the ample menus the inn's culinary
staff gladly accepts special requests, and they pride themselves on featuring
Vermont products on the menus.

You might begin with baked onion soup or Michelle's soup of the day—they are always yummy. Fresh seasonal and exotic fruit, marinated chicken salad, and Caesar salad with grilled chicken or shrimp are some of the other appetizers. Among the grand sandwiches are hot shaved country ham on marbled rye or char-grilled sirloin burgers. There's also baked scrod and pizzas— wow! And freshly baked desserts.

The main dining room menu offers about six choices of first courses. The house-made tri-color lobster ravioli was wonderful. Of the delicious soups, well, a duet of tomato and wild mushroom bisque was oh so good. The main course menu has suggested wines with each entree. Roast rack of lamb got me, but there were some other wonderful choices of beef, pork, chicken, duck, and, of course, fish. The desserts are sinful.

Can't stop now because it's on to Sunday brunch and it's a beauty. The way the food is displayed boggles my mind. A display of domestic, imported, and Vermont cheeses with assorted crackers was awesome. Tri-colored pasta and vegetable salad, country pâtés, baked herb-encrusted chicken breast, lamb chop on lentil

mushrooms, and couscous with sun-dried tomato madeira sauce is just a sample. There is much more. The Woodstock Inn's pastry display—well, it's just spectacular.

For a hike, ski tour, trail ride, or the trip home, hearty box lunches are ideal. The names alone are great. The Hiker, the Long Haul, the Daydreamer, the Light Haul, and Wildflowers Picnic Basket for Two. I won't tell you what they are. Come on up and try some.

There is a shuttle bus to the inn's sports center and country club. No need to use your car.

Woodstock is one of the most beautiful villages in New England, and the unspoiled grandeur of Vermont is everywhere.

HOW TO GET THERE: From Boston, take I–93 north to I–89 north to Route 4 west. From Connecticut, eastern New York, or New Jersey, take I–95 or the Merritt Parkway to I–91 North, to I–89 north, to Route 4 west. Then travel

10 miles to the Village Green (traffic rotary). Keep the Village Green on your left, and the Inn will come up on your right. From western New York and other points west, take I-87 to Route 9 North to Route 149 east to Route 4 east. Travel 12 miles to Whitehall and bear right on Route 4 east near the Silver Diner, then travel 35–40 miles into Rutland. At the end of the four-lane road, turn left on Route 4 east/Route 7 north, travel about 3 miles, and take Route 4 east after the Grand Union on your right. Follow Route 4 31 miles to Woodstock. As you begin to circle the Village Green, the Inn will be on your right.

# Billings Farm and Museum

Established in 1871 by Frederick Billings, Billings Farm is still a working dairy. Come here to see its fine Jersey cows and learn about the concepts of responsible agriculture and land stewardship that distinguished this farm. Reforestation and selective breeding were among the practices of scientific farm management that led to the success of this dairy. Visit the fields, the barns, the 1890 farmhouse, the heirloom garden, and the farm museum. A museum shop and a dairy bar are also here. Be sure to watch the wonderful short film documenting farm life, the passage of the seasons, and the history of farming and logging in Vermont. Come to enjoy such seasonal activities as wagon rides and sleigh rides during November and December. The Farm and Museum (802–457–2355) are open daily from May 1 through October 31, plus weekends in November and December and daily from December 26 through 31. Admission is charged. This place is grand for the whole family.

# Select List of
# Other Vermont Inns

## The Willow B&B
Historic 7A
Arlington, VT 05250
(802) 375-9773

*3 rooms, 1 with private bath, in 1840 farmhouse.*

## Alexandra B&B
Historic Route 7A
Bennington, VT 05201
(802) 442-5619
(888) 207-9386
Fax: (802) 442-5592
Web site: www.alexandrainn.com

*6 rooms, all with private bath, in 1859 Victorian house.*

## Willard Street Inn
349 South Willard Street
Burlington, VT 05401
(802) 651-8710 or (800) 577-8712

*15 rooms, 12 with private bath; B&B in brick Victorian mansion.*

## Hugging Bear Inn and Shoppe
244 Main Street
Chester, VT 05143
(802) 875-2412 or (800) 325-0519

*6 rooms, all with private bath; B&B in Victorian house.*

## The Sumner Mansion

4 Station Road
Hartland, VT 05048
(802) 436-3386 or (888) 529-8796
E-mail: sumnerm@vermontel.com
Web site: www.sumnermansion.com

*5 rooms in mansion, all with private bath; 2 rooms in carriage house, 1 with private bath. Mansion on National Historic Preservation List.*

## 1811 House

Route 7A
Manchester Village, VT 05254
(802) 362-1811 or (800) 432-1811

*14 rooms (3 in cottage), all with private bath; full breakfast; B&B in 1770 home.*

## Basin Harbor Club

on Lake Champlain
Vergennes, VT 05491
(802) 475-2311 or (800) 622-4000

*130 rooms, all with private bath; two restaurants; private airstrip, eighteen-hole golf course, tennis courts, and pool.*

## West Hill House Bed and Breakfast Inn

1496 West Hill Road
RR1, Box 292
Warren, VT 05674
(802) 496-7162 or (800) 898-1427
E-mail: westhill@madriver.com
Web site: www.westhillhouse.com

*7 rooms, all with private bath; 5 with fireplace, 2 with Jacuzzi, 1 with steam shower; B&B in 1850s farmhouse; sometimes serves dinner on Saturday nights.*

# Indexes

## Alphabetical Index to Inns

# Romantic Inns

# Inns Serving Lunch

# Inns Serving Sunday Brunch

# Inns with Accommodations for Families

# Lakeside Inns

# Inns on or near Saltwater
## (* denotes on beach)

# Inns with a Swimming Pool

# Inns with Golf Course or Tennis Court

## Connecticut

## Maine

## Massachusetts

## New Hampshire

## Rhode Island

## Vermont

# Inns with Cross-country Skiing on Property

# Inns with Rooms Specially Equipped for Handicapped

# Inns for Business Travelers

# Inns Offering Traveler's Club Benefits

# *About the Author*

The "inn creeper" is the nickname ELIZABETH SQUIER has earned in her twenty-five years of researching this guide to the country inns of New England. And a deserved name it is, for she tours well over 200 inns every year, from top to bottom, inside and out, before recommending the best ones to you.

A recognized author on fine food and lodging, Elizabeth is a gourmet cook and has written travel and food columns for many periodicals. Like you, she recognizes readily the special ingredients that make a good inn exceptional.

For many years, Elizabeth called Essex, Connecticut, home. She now resides in Florida and has a rather long commute!